International Business and Tourism

Whether it's bungee jumping in Queenstown or visiting the Guinness factory in Dublin, where we travel – and what we do when we get there – has changed significantly in the past 20 years. This innovative textbook explores what is possibly the most unrecognised of international service industries, placing tourism in the context of contemporary globalisation and trade in services. It provides new perspectives on tourism as a form of international business, and the implications for firms, the state and individuals.

Split into four separate sections, with introductions outlining the key themes in each, the book examines such important topics as:

- the role of governance and regulation in tourism services
- the effects of increased global mobility on tourism entrepreneurship
- how tourism businesses are becoming internationalised
- why other business sectors are increasingly interested in tourism

Case studies are used throughout to highlight important issues, from developments in the aviation industry to the rise of working holidays. This book gets to the core of a crucial service industry, and is essential reading for any researcher or student of tourism or international business.

Tim Coles is University Business Research Fellow and Senior Lecturer in Management in the School of Business and Economics at the University of Exeter, UK, where he is also the co-director of the Centre for Tourism Studies.

C. Michael Hall is Professor of Marketing in the Department of Management, University of Canterbury, New Zealand; Visiting Professor, Faculty of Organisation and Management, Sheffield Hallam University, UK; and a Docent at the Department of Geography, University of Oulu, Finland. He is also co-editor of the journal *Current Issues in Tourism*.

Routledge International Series in Tourism, Business and Management

Edited by Tim Coles and C. Michael Hall

Taylor & Francis Group
LONDON AND NEW YORK

Routledge International Series in Tourism, Business and Management is an important series that explores the key contemporary issues in the business and management of tourism. The series is organised around two strands: core themes in the business and management of tourism; and comparative international perspectives. Authored by some of the world's leading authorities on tourism, each book in the series aims to give readers comprehensive, in-depth and accessible texts that combine essential theory and best practice. Topics to be covered include international business and tourism, HRM in tourism, tourism entrepreneurship, tourism and service quality, strategy in tourism and marketing tourism.

This is the first book in the series.

International Business and Tourism

Global issues, contemporary interactions

Edited by Tim Coles and C. Michael Hall

Routledge
Taylor & Francis Group

LONDON AND NEW YORK

First published 2008
by Routledge
2 Park Square, Milton Park, Abingdon, Oxon OX14 4RN

Simultaneously published in the USA and Canada
by Routledge
270 Madison Ave, New York, NY 10016

Routledge is an imprint of the Taylor & Francis Group, an informa business

Typeset in Times by Keyword Group Ltd
Printed and bound by TJ International Ltd, Padstow, Cornwall

British Library Cataloguing in Publication Data
A catalogue record for this book is available from the British Library

Library of Congress Cataloging in Publication Data
    International business and tourism : global issues, contemporary
    interactions / edited by Tim Coles and C. Michael Hall.
        p. cm. – (Routledge international series in tourism, business &
        management)
    1. Tourism. 2. International trade. I. Coles, Tim. II. Hall, Colin Michael,
    1961–
    G155.A1I4985 2007
    338.4'791–dc22   2007033807

ISBN10: 0–415–42430–5 (hbk)
ISBN10: 0–415–42431–3 (pbk)
ISBN10: 0–203–93103–3 (ebk)

ISBN13: 978–0–415–42430–1 (hbk)
ISBN13: 978–0–415–42431–8 (pbk)
ISBN13: 978–0–203–93103–5 (ebk)

Contents

Figures

Tables

Contributors

Sue Beeton is Associate Professor in Tourism in the Faculty of Law and Management at La Trobe University, Melbourne, Australia. She has been studying film tourism since 1998 and has been co-convenor of the biennial International Tourism and Media (ITAM) conferences in Australia.

Katrin Blumberg was, at the time of writing, a PhD student in the School of Business at the University of Otago, New Zealand. Her studies of networks in adventure tourism draw directly upon her business experience in adventure tourism in Switzerland and New Zealand.

Tim Coles is University Business Research Fellow and Senior Lecturer in Management in the School of Business and Economics at the University of Exeter, UK, where he is the co-director of the Centre for Tourism Studies. His research interests cover tourism and human mobilities, knowledge management and project ecologies of tourism and the interface between tourism, business and management studies.

Tara Duncan is Lecturer in the School of Business at the University of Otago, New Zealand. She has held teaching positions at Durham University and University College London and was also the International Travel Catering Association Research Officer in the School of Management at the University of Surrey. With a background in human geography, her research interests focus on the 'working tourist' and current debates in mobility, temporary migration and transnationalism.

David Timothy Duval is Senior Lecturer and Director of International Business in the School of Business, University of Otago, New Zealand. His research interests, for the most part, centre upon aviation management and he has written on issues of aeropolitics, alliances and international air service agreements.

Stefan Gössling is Associate Professor in the Department of Service Management, Lund University, and Research Coordinator of the Centre for Sustainable and Geo-tourism, Western Norway Research Institute. He studied Geography and Biology at Münster University, Germany. His PhD in Human Ecology (Lund University, Sweden) was on human–environmental relations with tourism. His research interests include sustainable tourism, mobility studies, and interdisciplinary perspectives on tourist–nature interactions.

C. Michael Hall is Professor of Marketing in the Department of Management, University of Canterbury, New Zealand and Docent, Department of Geography, University of Oulu, Finland. He also holds a Visiting Professorship at Sheffield Hallam University, UK. Co-editor of *Current Issues in Tourism*, he has wide-ranging research, teaching and publishing interests in tourism and human mobility, regional development, servicescapes, gastronomy and environmental history.

Tom Hinch is Professor in the Faculty of Physical Education and Recreation in the University of Alberta in Edmonton. His primary research programme focuses on the confluence of sport and tourism with a particular interest in the nature of sport tourism places. He has also made substantial contributions to the literature on tourism and indigenous peoples.

Johan Hultman is Senior Lecturer and Associate Professor in the Department of Service Management, Lund University, Campus Helsingborg, and is involved with tourism and service studies in research and teaching. Johan holds a PhD in Cultural Geography.

Daniel Mason is Associate Professor in the Faculty of Physical Education and Recreation and Adjunct Professor in the School of Business at the University of Alberta. His research takes an interdisciplinary approach and focuses on the business of sport and the relationships between its stakeholders, including all levels of government, sports teams and leagues, and the communities that host teams.

Richard Mitchell is Senior Lecturer in the School of Business at the University of Otago where he has been researching wine, food and tourism since 1998 in New Zealand, Australia and the Mediterranean. He focuses primarily on two areas of wine and food tourism: consumer behaviour and regional development. In 2007 he will visit the Chair in Champagne Management (France) for further research on the intellectual property of place.

Jan Mosedale is Lecturer in the School of Business at the University of Otago, New Zealand. His PhD research at the University of Exeter on the corporate geographies of transnational corporations was supported by a studentship from the Economic and Social Research Council (ESRC).

Greg Ramshaw is a doctoral student in the Faculty of Physical Education and Recreation at the University of Alberta in Edmonton, Canada. His primary research interests are sport tourism and heritage tourism, and his doctoral research project specifically examines the construction of sport heritage tourist attractions. His work has been published in *Current Issues in Tourism* and the *Journal of Sport Tourism*.

Nicolai Scherle is Senior Lecturer in the Department of Cultural Geography at the Catholic University of Eichstätt-Ingolstadt, Germany. His monograph on the presentation of cultural aspects in German-language travel guides was awarded a research prize by the International Tourism Fair (ITB) in Berlin in 2000.

Adam Weaver is Lecturer in Tourism Management in the Victoria Management School at the Victoria University of Wellington in New Zealand. His recent research has examined relationships between the credit card and tourism industries and the ways in which data surveillance, commerce and tourism are intertwined. Adam's work has appeared in *Annals of Tourism Research*, the *International Journal of Tourism Research* and *Tourism Geographies*.

Acknowledgements

This book is the first volume in a new series, the Routledge International Series in Tourism, Business and Management. At Taylor & Francis, we would like to thank Andrew Mould, Jacqueline Curthoys, Francesca Heslop, Terry Clague and Simon Whitmore as Routledge Commissioning Editors for their valuable advice not only in developing this book, but also in nurturing and positioning the new series. As the book has been connected with other issues, we would like to thank our contributors for their patience, diligence and professionalism over the past couple of years. Several of our friends, colleagues and students have offered interesting insights and advice along the way and we'd like to recognise the input of Andrew Church, David Duval, Rebekka Goodman, Nicolai Scherle and Gareth Shaw. We owe a deep debt of gratitude to Vanessa and Jody for their love, support and patience, and the priceless reminders that there is more to life than writing books. Michael Hall would like to thank Petrina Dodd (formerly University of Otago) for her kind assistance in the research contributing to Chapter 2 as well as Nicola van Tiel and Nicolette le Cren for comments with respect to services. Johan Hultman would like to acknowledge the financial support of Sparbanksstiftelsen Skåne for the work presented in Chapter 4. Jan Mosedale acknowledges the support of the Economic and Social Research Council (ESRC) for a doctoral studentship (PTA-030-2002-00677) during which much of the research contained in this chapter was conducted. Tim Coles would like to thank Dr Oliver Weigel (formerly Director of Stadtentwicklung, Leipzig city council), Dr Bianca Meinecke (Audi AG), Dr Nicolai Scherle (Catholic University of Eichstätt-Ingolstadt) and Steve Jakes (University of Exeter) for their kind assistance and advice in the research contributing to Chapter 13. The assistance of the British Academy in the form of a small research grant (SG33303), during which some of the initial research was undertaken, is also recognised. Figures 4.1, 13.1, 13.2, 13.3, 14.1 and 14.3 are reproduced courtesy of Tim Coles. Figure 1.1 is reproduced courtesy of Tim Coles and Michael Hall. Figures 1.3, 1.4, 2.1, 2.3 and Table 2.3 are reproduced courtesy of Michael Hall. Figure 14.2 is reproduced courtesy of Sue Beeton.

Introduction: tourism and international business – tourism as international business

C. Michael Hall and Tim Coles

Learning objectives

After considering this chapter, you will be able to:

- recognise key features of the relationship between tourism and international business;
- understand the different categories of international trade in tourism services;
- identify elements of the business environment for international tourism businesses.

Key terms

- international tourism;
- international business;
- services;
- cross-border supply;
- consumption abroad;
- commercial presence;
- presence of natural persons.

INTRODUCTION: ANOTHER RECORD YEAR FOR WORLD TOURISM

If one follows the line taken by many governments, institutions and public officials then tourism is a major international industry. The United Nations World Tourism Organization (UNWTO 2007a) reported under the heading 'Another record year for world tourism' that there were 842 million international tourism arrivals in 2006 (an increase of 36 million or 4.5 per cent on the previous year) and that the world is well on the way to reaching

Table 1.1 *International tourism arrivals and forecasts, 1950–2020*

Year	World	Africa	Americas	Asia & Pacific	Europe	Middle East
1950	25.3	0.5	7.5	0.2	16.8	0.2
1960	69.3	0.8	16.7	0.9	50.4	0.6
1965	112.9	1.4	23.2	2.1	83.7	2.4
1970	165.8	2.4	42.3	6.2	113.0	1.9
1975	222.3	4.7	50.0	10.2	153.9	3.5
1980	278.1	7.2	62.3	23.0	178.5	7.1
1985	320.1	9.7	65.1	32.9	204.3	8.1
1990	439.5	15.2	92.8	56.2	265.8	9.6
1995	540.6	20.4	109.0	82.4	315.0	13.7
2000	687.0	28.3	128.1	110.5	395.9	24.2
2005	806.8	37.3	133.5	155.4	441.5	39.0
Forecast						
2010	1006	47	190	195	527	36
2020	1561	77	282	397	717	69

Source: WTO (1997, 2006).

the UNWTO's 2020 vision forecast/target of 1.6 billion international arrivals in 2020 (Table 1.1). In addition, the tourism sector was touted as 'underscoring the links to economic progress' while 'as one of the most dynamic economic sectors, tourism has a key role to play among the instruments to fight against poverty, thus becoming a primary tool for sustainable development' (UNWTO 2007a: no pages).

The economic dimensions of tourism are also significant on an international basis. Indeed, they are of orders of magnitude that are difficult to imagine or comprehend for most people. According to the World Travel and Tourism Council (WTTC 2007) forecasts for the world travel and tourism industry in 2007:

- Travel and tourism demand is expected to generate US$7,060 billion of economic activity worldwide, growing to US$13,231 billion by 2017.
- Of total world exports, travel and tourism accounts for 12 per cent (US$1,847.8 billion) and is expected to grow at a rate of 4.6 per cent per annum in the immediate future.
- Travel and tourism is expected to contribute 3.6 per cent to gross domestic product (GDP) (US$1,851 billion), rising in nominal terms to US$3,121.7 billion (3.4 per cent of total GDP) by 2017. When including the direct and indirect impact of the industry, tourism is expected to account for 10.4 per cent of global GDP (equivalent to US$5,390 billion), rising to 10.7 per cent (US$9,781 billion) by 2017.
- Global travel and tourism economy employment is estimated to reach 231.2 million jobs, representing 8.3 per cent of total employment worldwide (1 in every 12 jobs). By 2017, this figure is expected to rise to 262.6 million jobs, accounting for 8.3 per cent of total employment.

Table 1.2 Benchmarking the global trade in travel and tourism against the GDP of 15 leading economies in the world

Ranking	Economy	GDP (US$ millions in 2005)
1	United States*	12,416,505
	Travel and tourism – direct and indirect	**5,390,000**
2	Japan*	4,533,965
3	Germany*	2,794,926
4	China	2,234,297
5	United Kingdom*	2,198,789
6	France*	2,126,630
	Travel and tourism – direct only	**1,851,000**
7	Italy*	1,762,519
8	Spain	1,124,640
9	Canada*	1,113,810
10	India	805,714
11	Brazil	796,055
12	Korea, Rep.	787,624
13	Mexico	768,438
14	Russian Federation*	763,720
15	Australia	732,499

Source: Adapted from World Bank (2007: 1) and WTTC (2007).
Note: *G8 member.

Taking just the third set of claims about GDP: Table 1.2 benchmarks the earnings generated by travel and tourism globally against the top 15 economies in terms of their total GDP in 2005 as calculated and published by the World Bank. The value of travel and tourism would appear to be greater than the total value of all final goods and services of three members of the G8 (Italy, Canada and Russia), or the group of the world's leading industrialised nations. If the direct and indirect impacts of travel and tourism are considered, then only the United States has larger GDP.

Of course, these are only broad comparisons and care must be taken especially with respect to indirect earnings. Nevertheless, even such a broad benchmarking emphasises two important points. Not only is it easy to see why states are keen to capitalise on the benefits of travel and tourism, but paradoxically, the sheer scale of travel and tourism earnings makes it all the more curious that tourism is marginalised in major global debates over the governance of society, economy, culture and environment. It is even more staggering, as we shall argue below, that tourism struggles for legitimacy in studies of international business. To be clear, all of this is not to start an account of international tourism yet again with the claim that tourism is the world's largest industry, as not only are the methodological and empirical accounts of tourism numbers and economic impact open to question, but so too is the very question of whether tourism can actually be treated as an industry. However, what it does do is highlight the undeniable fact that tourism is an international economic activity of considerable importance with associated implications for international business and international relations.

According to World Trade Organization (WTO) statistics, travel accounted for about 5.4 per cent of world exports of merchandise and commercial services in 2005, representing 28.4 per cent of world exports of commercial services (see Table 1.3). However, it is perhaps surprising to some readers, given the publicity surrounding international tourism growth, that while the absolute value of travel has been increasing, the relative value of travel as a contributor to world exports of commercial services has actually been declining since 1990 when it accounted for approximately 34 per cent of the total value (WTO 2006: 109). This pattern is demonstrated on a regional scale in Table 1.4. The reasons for such shift in the relative value of service exports primarily relates to the development of cheaper travel and communications that has allowed relatively more high value services to be

Table 1.3 World exports of merchandise and commercial services, 2000–2005

| Product group | Value 2005 ($bn) | Share 2000 (%) | Share 2005 (%) | Annual percentage change | | | | |
				2000–5 (%)	2002 (%)	2003 (%)	2004 (%)	2005 (%)
Merchandise	10,159	100.0	100.0	10	5	17	22	13
Agricultural products	852	8.8	8.4	9	6	16	15	8
Fuels and mining products	1,748	13.7	17.2	15	−1	24	33	36
Manufactures	7,312	74.9	72.0	9	5	16	21	10
Commercial services	2,415	100.0	100.0	10	7	14	20	10
Transportation	570	23.3	23.6	10	5	13	24	12
Travel	685	32.1	28.4	7	5	10	18	8
Other commercial services	1,160	44.6	48.1	12	10	18	18	11

Source: WTO (2006).

Notes:

WTO Definitions: *Transportation* covers all transportation services that are performed by residents of one economy for those of another and that involve the carriage of passengers, the movement of goods (freight), rentals (charters) of carriers with crew, and related supporting and auxiliary services (United Nations *et al.* 2002: 36); *travel* covers primarily the goods and services acquired from an economy by travellers during visits of less than one year to that economy. The goods and services are purchased by, or on behalf of, the traveller or provided, without a quid pro quo (that is, are provided as a gift), for the traveller to use or give away (United Nations *et al.* 2002: 38–9; a *traveller* is an individual staying for less than one year in an economy of which he or she is not a resident for any purpose other than (1) being stationed on a military base or being an employee (including diplomats and other embassy and consulate personnel) of an agency of his or her government; (2) being an accompanying dependant of an individual mentioned under (1), or (3) undertaking a productive activity directly for an entity that is a resident of that economy (United Nations *et al.*2002: 39).

Table 1.4 *Share of travel services in total trade of commercial services by selected region, 2005*

Region	Exports 2000 (%)	Exports 2005 (%)	Imports 2000 (%)	Imports 2005 (%)
North America	35.7	30.2	33.0	27.2
South and Central America	53.3	47.2	30.8	24.0
Europe	30.4	26.8	31.0	28.5
European Union (15 in 2000, 25 in 2005)	30.3	25.7	30.8	28.1
Africa	48.9	49.7	20.4	19.7
Asia	26.9	25.4	27.4	25.1

Source: Abridged from WTO (2001: 159, 2006: 184).

traded in financial services than in travel and tourism services (WTO 1998). Transportation services are usually regarded as the least dynamic category of services while within 'other commercial services' sub-categories such as financial services (including banking and insurance services), construction services, communication services and computer and information services have all demonstrated rates of export growth higher than that of travel.

Even though the relative proportion of tourism's contribution to international trade in services has declined, tourism remains an extremely significant contributor to the global economy, although its economic contribution, as with the flow of travellers, is uneven. Table 1.5 illustrates the top 15 exporters and importers of travel services on a national basis. The top 15 exporters account for approximately 62 per cent of travel exports while the top 15 importers account for approximately 68 per cent of all travel imports. A number of countries such as the United Kingdom, United States, Japan and Germany demonstrate significant imbalances between exports and imports of travel services (Table 1.6). The US, Spain and Italy have a significant positive balance of exports over imports which is reflected not only in their role as tourism destinations but just as importantly to the extent that nationals of those countries travel and spend internationally. In contrast, the UK, Germany and Japan are all significant international tourism destinations in their own right, however outbound travel and expenditure still significantly outnumbers inbound travel. The UNWTO (WTO 2006a, 2006b) ranked the UK sixth in the world in 2005 in terms of international arrivals and Germany eighth, while they were ranked fifth and seventh respectively in terms of international tourism receipts. Yet the international trading significance of travel services goes well beyond the developed world, with tourism being reported as the primary source of foreign exchange earnings in 46 of the 49 poorest nations that the United Nations (UN) describes as the least developed countries (Hall 2007).

Given the significance of tourism in the global economy in its own right and as an enabler of business mobility and connectivity (Malecki 2004), as well as the importance of international tourism for numerous national and regional economies, it may be expected that tourism has been a significant object of scholarship for the field of international business studies. However, this has most certainly not been the case with tourism rarely being a focal point of articles in the major international business journals or even in international

Table 1.5 Top 15 exporters and importers of travel services

	Value 2005 ($ bn)	World share 1990 (%)[1]	World share 2000 (%)	World share 2005 (%)	Percentage change 2000–5	Percentage change 2003	Percentage change 2004	Percentage change 2005
Exporters								
United States	102.0	19.0	20.5	14.9	1	−2	13	8
Spain	47.7	7.0	6.2	7.0	10	24	14	6
France	42.2	7.6	6.5	6.2	6	13	11	4
Italy	35.7	6.2	5.7	5.2	5	16	13	1
United Kingdom	30.3	5.9	4.5	4.4	7	10	24	7
China	29.3	0.7	3.4	4.3	13	−15	48	14
Germany	29.2	5.4	3.9	4.3	9	20	19	6
Turkey	18.2	1.2	1.6	2.7	19	56	20	14
Austria	15.6	5.1	2.1	2.3	9	24	11	2
Australia	14.9	1.6	1.9	2.2	11	21	21	9
Canada	13.6	2.4	2.3	2.0	5	−1	21	6
Greece	13.6	–	1.9	2.0	8	9	18	7
Japan [2]	12.4	2.1	1.8	1.8	8	1	27	10
Mexico	11.8	–	1.7	1.7	76	15	9	
Switzerland	11.3	–	1.6	1.6	8	16	13	9
Top 15	430.0	70.4	65.6	62.5	6	10	17	7
Importers								
United States	73.6	14.6	15.1	11.4	2	−1	14	6
Germany	73.0	13.0	11.9	11.3	7	23	9	3
United Kingdom	59.5	7.0	8.6	9.2	9	15	18	5
Japan	37.6	9.6	7.2	5.8	3	9	32	−2
France	31.2	4.7	4.0	4.8	12	20	22	9
Italy	22.7	4.0	3.5	3.5	8	22	−1	11
China	21.8	0.2	3.0	3.4	11	−1	26	14
Canada	18.3	4.2	2.8	2.9	8	14	19	15
Russian Federation	17.8	–	2.0	2.8	15	14	22	13
Netherlands	16.1	2.8	2.8	2.5	6	12	12	−2
Korea, Republic of	15.3	–	1.6	2.4	17	−3	22	24
Spain	15.0	–	1.3	2.3	20	24	34	24
Belgium	14.8	2.1	–	2.3	–	20	14	6
Hong Kong, China	13.3	–	2.8	2.1	1	−8	16	0
Australia	11.5	–	1.4	1.8	13	20	41	12
Top 15	440.0	73.5	72.0	68.6	–	11	17	7

Source: WTO(2001: 160, 2006: 184).

Notes:

1. 1990 world share percentages derived from WTO (2001), world share percentages for 2000 use WTO (2006) figures where possible as these are the most recent revised figures.

2. Secretariat estimates for exports prior to 2003 are based on the new methodology applied by the Bank of Japan.

Table 1.6 *Export/import relationship in select countries*

Country	Export value ($ bn)	Import value 2005 ($ bn)	Net gain or loss ($ bn)	Ratio export:import
United States	102.0	73.6	28.4	1:0.72
Spain	47.7	15.0	32.7	1:0.31
France	42.2	31.2	11	1:0.74
Italy	35.7	22.7	23	1:0.64
United Kingdom	30.3	59.5	−29.2	1:1.96
China	29.3	21.8	7.5	1:0.74
Germany	29.2	73.0	−43.8	1:2.50
Australia	14.9	11.5	3.4	1:0.77
Canada	13.6	18.3	−4.7	1:1.35
Japan	12.4	37.6	−25.2	1:3.03

Source: Derived from WTO (2006).

business texts (Hall 2003a). For example, on the resources page of the Academy of International Business as of mid-2007 no tourism journals are listed in the journal resources section and no tourism research associations in the professional organisations section (http://aib.msu.edu/resources/). Similarly, as a body of knowledge tourism studies, which is sometimes accused of adopting theoretical developments and insights from other business and social science disciplines rather than developing its own (Tribe 1997, 2000; Franklin and Crang 2001), has not drawn on the significant body of international business literature in all but the most limited extent. Despite apparently obvious connections there has been relatively little academic dialogue between the two study areas.

This book therefore aims to connect cutting-edge research and critical thinking in tourism and international business in order to develop greater understanding and conceptualisation of tourism as a form of international business as well as to mutually inform the two academic fields. This first chapter seeks to outline some of the empirical and philosophical connections between the fields as well as providing several frameworks with which to understand tourism in international business terms.

CONCEPTUALISING TOURISM AND INTERNATIONAL BUSINESS

'International business' as a term is conceptualised and discussed in two common ways. The first centres on the practice of international business in a more general and abstract manner. It relates to the performance of 'doing business' internationally; that is, people and organisations interacting with one another in order to transact exchanges of capital, labour and knowledge. This requires contact, social relations and the politics of intermediation. In the case of tourism, this political process and interaction results in outcomes, perhaps in terms of tourist spending, investment in tourist attractions and facilities, and/or setting the regulatory frameworks and operating environments in which tourism will flourish and tourism-related businesses will function. This first approach is similar to the way in which any service is traded internationally. Thus, one of the best means by which this can be understood is via the four modes of international supply of services under the General Agreement on Trade in Services (GATS) (UN *et al.* 2002) (see Figure 1.1).

Cross-border supply: from the territory of one into the territory of another (generally referred to as mode 1 under GATS). This mode is similar to the traditional notion of trade in goods where both the consumer and the supplier remain in their respective territory when the product is delivered, such as freight transport services or e-ticketing for travel and tourism services. Supply takes place when the consumer remains in his or her home territory while the service crosses national borders; that is, the supplier is located in a different country with the delivery of the service achieved, for example, by various forms of information and communications technology (ICT) as well as traditional mail.

Consumption abroad: a consumer moves outside his or her home territory and consumes services in another country (mode 2). International tourism provides the classic example of consumption abroad although, as well as leisure consumption, it may also include medical-related travel of non-residents and education and language courses (usually under GATS statistical advice this would be classified as being under 12 months in duration, however countries have a range of classification schemes for such consumption).

Commercial presence: the service is provided by a service supplier of a country through commercial presence in the territory of another at the various stages of production and delivery, as well as after delivery (mode 3). Significantly for tourism, under GATS 'supply of a service' includes production, distribution, marketing, promotion, sale and delivery. Examples include transport ticketing available via a foreign-owned company or accommodation in a foreign-owned hotel.

Presence of natural persons: occurs when an individual has moved into the territory of the consumer to provide a service, whether on his or her own behalf or on behalf of his or her employer (mode 4) and covers both self-employed persons as well as employees. A natural person is a human perceptible through the senses and subject to physical laws in contrast to an artificial or juridical person, such as a corporation or an organisation that the law treats for some purposes as if it were a person distinct from its owner or members. This category covers only non-permanent employment in the country of the consumer. However, to complicate matters there is no agreed definition of 'non-permanent' employment under GATS or other international agreements, although under each country's GATS commitments, the temporary status generally covers a period of two to five years, with it being different for different categories of natural persons. Mode 4 is becoming increasingly important for international tourism in both an empirical sense, with respect to the growth in seasonal international workforce or short-term labour migration, and in a conceptual sense, with the growth of the concept of working holidays.

The second broad conceptualisation focuses on the bodies involved in international business, typically those firms undertaking it. Indeed, arguably the firm has become the dominant unit of analysis in studies of international business. In this instance 'international business' is used as a synonym for firms where the singular is used practically as a collective noun for several businesses. Here the emphasis is on the international business as a body, an

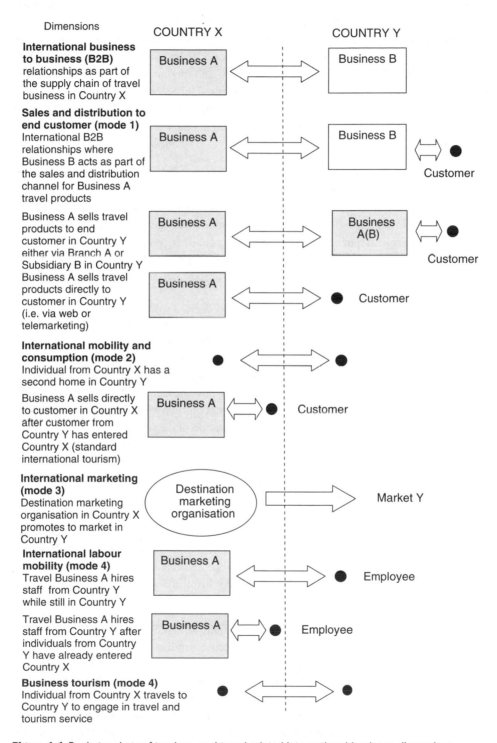

Figure 1.1 *Basic typology of tourism- and travel-related international business dimensions*

organisation or an institution. In this sense, studies of international business are understood to include accounts of the management, marketing, organisation, operation, governance and regulation of particular commercial entities. 'International business' might understandably generate stereotypical connotations of transnational corporations (TNCs) by virtue of their size, presences, competencies and requirements to operate in markets in more than one state. While TNCs are a key element of the book, small- and medium-sized tourism enterprises (SMTEs) are also considered, particularly as mode 2 of international trade in terms of consumption abroad means that even some of the smallest, even micro-tourism firms are engaged in international business (Jones and Haven 2005). Furthermore, it is increasingly common to find SMTEs operating across borders via e-business.

In tourism the organisational dimension is often extended beyond the private sector to incorporate the activities of government agencies that are engaged in tourism promotion and marketing to international markets as well as, in some jurisdictions, owning tourism infrastructure. In addition, the development of public–private partnerships has been an extremely widespread phenomenon in western countries, particularly with respect to urban redevelopment for tourism, leisure and retail purposes (Hall 2008). Some of these partnerships between state and non-state actors are spread across geographical scales, including the international (Hall 2005).

Both broad conceptualisations of international business are used in this book. The primary focus though is international businesses with cross-border operations that engage in tourism as a means of fulfilling their business objectives. The book examines how tourism (widely defined) benefits from the internationalisation of business in terms of such dimensions as profitability, pricing, service delivery, product development and knowledge transfer. 'Doing business' in the tourism sector shares many common characteristics with trade in other services, but crucially there are key differences too in the way that tourism businesses operate and how tourism products are produced and consumed; hence the book aims to deepen understanding in international business studies of a core sector and its cross-border dynamics. Tourism firms are not the exclusive focus of this book. Tourism may be the core concern of the business (e.g. airlines, cruise lines, hotel chains, tour operators) or alternatively it may be a secondary activity designed to ensure that other primary commercial interests are realised (e.g. vintners, car manufacturers, food and drink producers, and film production companies). Further important dimensions stressed in this book are the different scales of governance from the local to the international in which international tourism is regulated, as well as the embeddedness of firms in destinations and their business environment (Figure 1.2).

Figure 1.2 illustrates the way in which there are multiple layers of environmental analysis depending on whether the initial focus is a specific product, firm, destination or even industry. The industry environment is the core of the firm's business environment and it is formed by competitors, suppliers and other stakeholders, such as, but not restricted to, government agencies, non-government organisations, interest groups and consumers. Customers are regarded as a subset of the potential pool of consumers as a firm's actions can influence the size of any potential market for its product separate from an existing customer base (see Chapter 13). The firm and its immediate industry environment is in

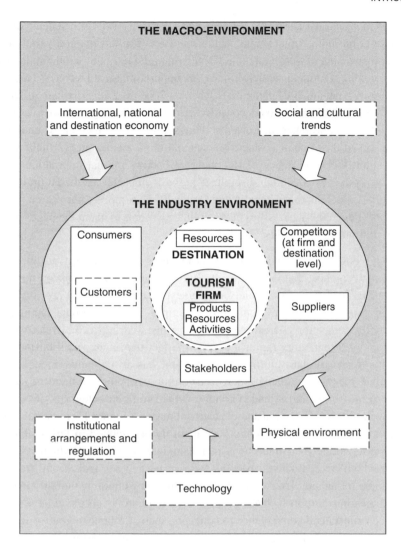

Figure 1.2 *The international business environment of tourism*

turn influenced by a number of macro-environmental factors. These factors – such as changes in international regulatory regimes, new transport technologies and economic and demographic trends – are critical determinants of future threats and opportunities in so far as how they affect a firm via their impacts on costs, product demand and its relative competitive position. The various chapters in this book address both the macro-environments and industry environments of firms and destinations with the conclusion outlining some macro-environmental issues that will affect international tourism in the immediate future.

To the above dimensions of tourism and international business we bring another conceptu-alisation with respect to the theoretical and philosophical underpinnings of the two areas. In a guest editorial for the *Journal of International Business* (the in-house journal of the

Academy of International Business) Buckley and Lessard (2005: 595) stated that 'the key to international business is that it approaches empirical phenomena at a variety of levels of analysis, using a variety of theoretical frameworks'. Exactly the same comment can be applied to the field of tourism studies. Indeed, for both international business (e.g. Buckley 2002; Buckley and Ghauri 2004; Peng 2004; Shenkar 2004) and for tourism (e.g. Tribe 2000; Coles *et al.* 2005, 2006; Hall 2005) considerable intellectual angst exists over the scope of the disciplines (or whether they are disciplines at all), their theoretical underpinnings and their places at the table of business studies and the social sciences. Buckley's (2002) comments about the trade deficit of international business – that international business borrows more concepts from other disciplines in the social sciences than it produces – has direct parallels in tourism (e.g. Franklin and Crang 2001). Similarly, the search for the next 'big question' (Peng 2004) and issues of disciplinarity seems to haunt the pages of many of the leading journals in both fields.

In many ways both tourism and international business are suffering from the effects of space–time convergence; that is, as a result of globalisation many firms are now in effect international. Even if they focus solely on domestic customers, they are likely to have international suppliers; they are competing to employ in international labour markets; they are usually competing against international firms; and they are increasingly subject to internationalised regulatory regimes despite the fact that many small businesses often do not always realise it. This blurring of space–time has also affected understandings of tourism. Not only is travel marked by increased voluntary mobility but there are now regular international commuting and extended holidays which combine categories of business and leisure, as well as travel for health and educational reasons. Figure 1.3 indicates the way in which some of the categories of temporary mobility are defined in terms of space and time while also noting that mobility is increasingly fluid, a point which is utilised in Figure 1.4, which conceptualises mobility with respect to distance decay from a point of origin (home for an individual or a city or settlement if examining mobility in aggregate terms). Changes in transport technology as well as regulations on travel have meant that there has been substantial convergence in concepts, such as labour migration and tourism, that were previously regarded as distinct categories. Similarly, the speed at which people can now travel in a given time has meant the development of international short-break holidays whereas a generation previously these would have almost certainly been domestic holidays for all but the most wealthy or for those living in border regions.

However, rather than reducing their significance the social, political and economic processes of globalisation and increased international mobility of people, capital, and firms means that tourism and international business are actually more academically relevant than ever. The historical foci of both fields suggest that they are better intellectually equipped than many disciplines to deal with the issues and vagaries of cross-border economic and social relations particularly given the multi-dimensional nature of the problems of internationalisation and globalisation. Nevertheless, the issue of building bridges between international business and tourism remains. In great part the reason for the lack of connectivity lies in the fact that the fields have historically tended to occupy different knowledge spaces (Figure 1.5).

International business has tended to give primacy to the firm and particularly to transnational commercial entities. In contrast tourism has given primacy to the local and the destination

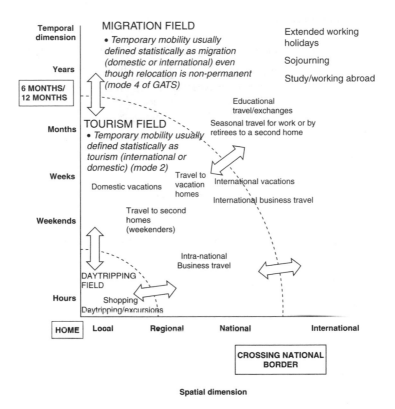

Figure 1.3 *Classifications of temporary mobility in space and time*
Source: After Hall (2003b).

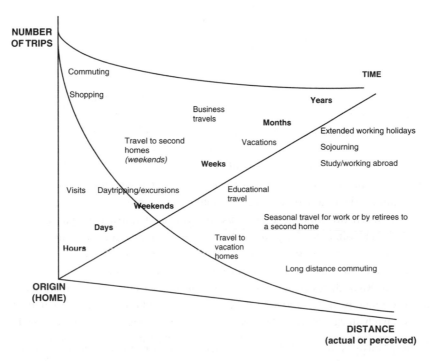

Figure 1.4 *Extent of temporary mobility in space and time*
Source: Hall (2003b).

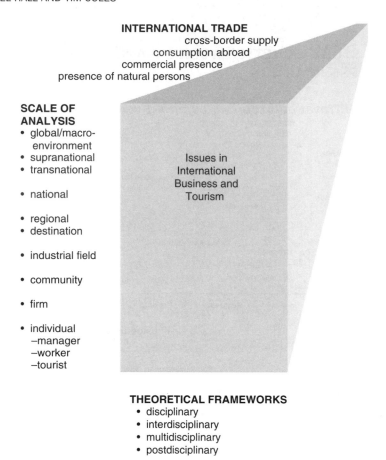

INTERNATIONAL TRADE
cross-border supply
consumption abroad
commercial presence
presence of natural persons

**SCALE OF
ANALYSIS**
• global/macro-
  environment
• supranational
• transnational

• national

• regional
• destination

• industrial field

• community

• firm

• individual
  –manager
  –worker
  –tourist

Issues in
International
Business and
Tourism

THEORETICAL FRAMEWORKS
• disciplinary
• interdisciplinary
• multidisciplinary
• postdisciplinary

Figure 1.5 The knowledge field of international business and tourism

as well as the category of 'the tourist', with the nature of the tourism firm, and SMTEs in particular, only being given significant attention since the late 1990s. Flows of individuals, the mode 2 of international trade in services has been given very little examination in international business whereas it is the mainstay of tourism. The presence of natural persons in another country (mode 4) is a potentially significant area of overlap, with recent studies on expatriate behaviour, career development (Inkson and Myers 2003; Boon 2006) and labour migration (Hall and Williams 2002) finding connection with studies of temporary mobility in which the roles of tourist and worker are regarded as extremely fluid for some individuals when working internationally as well as informing later personal and consumption behaviours over the lifecourse of individuals (Hall 2005) (see chapters in Part I). In addition, other areas in which common interests are developing relate to the internationalisation of firms, and the international governance and regulation of firms, capital and labour. Finally, although the international competitiveness of firms, regions and nations has been of significance in the wider international business and economic literature since the early 1990s, the relative competitiveness of destinations has now begun to attract interest in tourism.

CASE-STUDY VIGNETTE – TOURISM AND INTERNATIONAL BUSINESS IN ACTION

National travel and tourism competitiveness

Destination competitiveness has become an increasingly important area of research in tourism (e.g. Dwyer and Kim 2003; Ritchie and Crouch 2003; Dimanche 2005; Enright and Newton 2005; Mangion *et al.* 2005), encouraged in great part by the activities of the UNWTO, which has a specific programme on improving competitiveness under their Quality Support and Trade Committee. In 2007 the World Economic Forum (WEF) launched a travel and tourism competitiveness index (TTCI) that covered 124 countries around the world. The WEF provides a number of competitiveness studies that are 'aimed at contributing to a better understanding of why some countries grow prosperous, while others are left behind' (WEF 2007: xiii). According to the WEF (2007: xiii) the TTCI 'aims to measure the factors and policies that make it attractive to develop the [travel and tourism] sector in different countries'. The WEF TTCI was produced in collaboration with Booz Allen Hamilton, the International Air Transport Association (IATA), the UNWTO and the WTTC, with feedback also provided by 'a number of key companies that are industry partners in the effort' (2007: xiii): Bombardier, Carlson, Emirates Group, Qatar Airways, Royal Jordanian Airlines Silversea Cruises, Swiss International Airlines and Visa International. Data were obtained from publicly available sources (i.e. IATA, ICAO (International Civil Aviation Organization), UNWTO, WTTC, UNESCO (United Nations Education, Science and Cultural Organization)) and the results of a survey 'carried out among CEOs and top business leaders in all economies covered by our research – these are the people making the investment decisions in their respective economies' (WEF 2007: xiv).

According to UNWTO Assistant Secretary-General Geoffrey Lipman,

> The index provides a useful strategic tool for measuring those aspects that promote the development of the Travel & Tourism sector in different countries. The specific rankings reflect the overall competitiveness activity of the WEF itself over three decades. UNWTO is concerned about all states improving competitiveness, which is a means to an end rather than an end in itself and must ultimately contribute to the kind of socioeconomic goals sought in the Millennium Declaration and defined in our Global Code of Ethics. As the Doha Round moves into its final stages, there may be an important opportunity to increase tourism benefits from this process, turning the attention to the contribution of Tourism Services to reduce poverty and increase sustainability, even ahead of other sectors.

> (UNWTO 2007b)
>
> *Continued*

Table 1.7 *The structure of the WEF TTCI*

Number	Pillar	Sub-index
1	Policy rules and regulations	
2	Environmental regulation	
3	Safety and security	Regulatory framework
4	Health and hygiene	
5	Prioritisation of travel and tourism	
6	Air transport infrastructure	
7	Ground transport infrastructure	
8	Tourism infrastructure	Business environment and infrastructure
9	ICT infrastructure	
10	Price competitiveness in the travel and tourism industry	
11	Human resources	Human, cultural and natural resources
12	National tourism perception	
13	Natural and cultural resources	

Source: Adapted from WEF (2007).

The UNWTO welcomed the WEF (2007) report 'as a valuable new research process. It is a timely reference for states participating in the final stages of the Doha Development Round to provide proactive support for developing countries to help increase their tourism competitiveness to reduce poverty and advance sustainability' (UNWTO 2007b). The WEF TTCI is based on 13 'pillars' of travel and tourism competitiveness (Table 1.7) which, in turn, have been organised into three sub-indexes: regulatory framework; business environment and infrastructure; and human, cultural and natural resources.

Table 1.8 shows the world's top tourism destinations for 2004 (as determined by WTO figures) and their relative ranking and scores for the WEF TTCI. According to Blanke and Chiesa (2007) the correlation between the log of international tourist arrivals per 1,000 population in 2005 and the score given in the WEF TTCI was 0.77 while the correlation between the log of international tourism receipts (US$) per 1,000 population in 2005 and the score given in the WEF TTCI was 0.84.

Such rankings and scores are given substantial emphasis by the media, government and industry even though the basis by which they are developed is empirically highly questionable (Bristow 2005; Minford 2006). However, despite the influence of the concept on tourism policies at the national and local state the concept has been subject to relatively little critique, nor has there been a substantive discussion of

Continued

Table 1.8 *Relationships between international tourism arrivals for countries by rank and WEF competitiveness rankings*

Rank (2004)	Country	International tourist arrivals (million)	WEF TTCI rank	WEF TTCI score	WEF regulatory framework rank	WEF environment and infrastructure rank	WEF Human, cultural and natural resources rank
1	France	75.1	12	5.23	13	5	28
2	Spain	52.4	15	5.18	25	7	19
3	USA	46.1	5	5.43	33	1	12
4	China	41.8	71	3.97	78	61	93
5	Italy	37.1	33	4.78	42	30	32
6	UK	27.8	10	5.28	21	5	10
7	Mexico	20.6	49	4.38	48	57	50
8	Turkey	16.8	52	4.31	53	63	48
9	Germany	20.1	3	5.48	6	3	6
10	Russian Federation	19.9	68	4.03	100	49	65
11	Austria	19.4	2	5.54	3	12	1
12	Canada	19.2	7	5.31	15	4	16
13	Malaysia	15.7	31	4.80	27	27	57
14	Ukraine	12.5	78	3.89	76	73	89
15	Poland	13.7	63	4.18	63	62	60
16	Hong Kong	13.7	6	5.33	4	14	14
17	Greece	14.0	24	4.99	20	32	15
18	Hungary	12.2	40	4.61	26	51	51
19	Thailand	10.1	43	4.58	41	35	59
20	Portugal	11.6	22	5.05	11	22	30

Source: Derived from WTO (2006) World's Top Tourism Destinations (absolute numbers), http://www.world-tourism.org/facts/menu.html; WEF (2007).

---

the philosophical and ideological underpinnings of such a concept. Instead, competition, whether it be as a tourism destination or in a wider sense of regional competitiveness, is usually portrayed as a 'given' and what places 'must' do (Hall 2008).

Although competitiveness is a significant policy goal there is still substantial confusion 'as to what the concept actually means and how it can be effectively operationalised ... policy acceptance of the existence of regional competitiveness and its measurement

Continued

appears to have run ahead of a number of fundamental theoretical and empirical questions' (Bristow 2005: 286). This is especially the case in tourism where there is already substantial evidence of the role of price competitiveness as a major determinant in tourism flows and where its parameters are clearly defined (Dwyer *et al*. 2000a, 2000b). According to Dimanche (2005: 6) the 'competitive tourism equation' is that in order to achieve the goal of competitive advantage 'a destination must provide overall attractiveness and quality experiences that are equal or better than those of the alternative destinations for specific markets'. However, the concepts of regional or destination competitiveness are categories that Markusen (1999: 870) described as 'fuzzy concepts': 'characterisations lacking conceptual clarity and difficult to operationalise. In some cases, no attempt is made to offer evidence at all. Elsewhere, evidence marshalled is highly selective. Methodology is little discussed'. For example, Minford (2006: 177) in discussing the various indices of competitiveness, including those produced by the WEF, observed: 'It would seem that these are attempts to measure how well an economy's industries are doing. This is not the same thing as whether an economy has good policies from the point of view of liberal economic principles'. Malecki (2002: 941) commented with respect to research on city competitiveness, 'all of the issues that have risen to the top of the research agenda over the past 30 years are relevant – indeed, essential ... having only some of these conditions in good order is not enough'. Similarly, in reference to the key issue of what are the determinants of place competitiveness Deas and Giordano (2001) argued there is a tendency to offer a 'checklist' approach to identifying the relevant determinants of competitiveness, even though inadequate empirical research has been conducted as to the relative significance of such factors. Such criticisms therefore highlight the need for caution in destination management and marketing organisations in utilising competitive indices as a strategic international business tool and raises significant issues over whether a concept initially developed at the level of the firm can be elevated to a regional and national destination scale and successfully encompass the complexities of place.

Questions

- How might indexes of competitiveness be used by destination tourism organisations in policy formulation and strategy?
- If the reasons for destination competitiveness are not yet fully understood, why are indices still produced?
- How do the WEF's tourism competitiveness rankings compare with other rankings such as numbers of international visitors, extent of corruption, level of human rights or level of democracy? Explain the relationships, if any, between these various rankings.

IDENTIFYING BUSINESS WITH TOURISM

As noted above tourism is often described as the world's largest – and in some cases, most important – 'industry' in the popular media, policy circles and the academic community. As several commentators have noted, there are serious conceptual difficulties in describing tourism as a coherent industry and as a singular packaged 'tourism product' (Hall 2005). For some, tourism is best described as a sectoral activity and several key (sub-) sectoral activity domains such as accommodation, hospitality and transport have been identified (Hall and Page 2006). While work on identifying work on supply and commodity chains in tourism is welcome (see Chapter 8), what makes the perpetuation of the 'largest global industry' cliché so depressing is that it has diverted research attention from addressing more pressing critical issues that would enhance our understanding of business and tourism.

The first of these concerns the essentially consumption-driven agenda of much tourism research which often focuses on individual agency rather the structures, contexts and frameworks that may shape the experiential; that is, the subject of the tourism production process – the tourist – and the outcome of the production process – the tourism experience as 'product' – have been favoured over supply-side discourses of the production process itself, the operators involved, their intra-firm operations and their organisational cultures and operating contexts. When compared with businesses in other sectors such as manufacturing, retailing and producer services, there has been a relative dearth of detailed attention on the individual enterprises that comprise tourism supply chains, the 'sub-sectors', even 'the industry'. Issues such as the internal operation and organisation of tourism businesses; position in the political economy of supply chains; corporate culture; inter- and intra-firm politics; and networked relationships with other institutions and organisations have not been afforded the same importance as the consumer and consumption.

A second, related observation is that, in general, where such issues have been tackled, SMTEs have been at the forefront of discourse. SMTEs may make up the numerical majority of tourism businesses; they may characterise the 'tourism sector'; and they may be more convenient research subjects because many operate in a single market, they are pretty straightforward to identify, and they are easier to penetrate than larger operations (Thomas 2004; Jones and Haven 2005). It is perhaps an interesting paradox that many of the major international, cross-border operations are larger and more visible entities for consumers and academics alike, however they are only infrequently addressed in tourism debate. We would argue that this is a crucial lacuna because they are agenda-setting, leading firms on the global stage. For instance, travel and tourism firms routinely feature in the FTSE 100 (e.g. British Airways, Carnival [cruises], InterContinental Hotels Group) and NASDAQ 100 (e.g. Expedia Inc., Ryanair Holdings plc., Wynn Resorts Limited) indexes of leading companies on the London and New York stock exchanges. These are among some of the most highly capitalised enterprises in the world. Despite the difficulties of researching these major companies, they should not be considered as mere exemplars of wider trends in (many a textbook on) international business studies, but rather they set the trends that other types of enterprises in the same and/or different sectors follow.

International tourism businesses exert considerable power and influence in the production and consumption of tourism experiences. For instance, as gatekeepers of tourism (Ioannides 1998), tour operators such as TUI, Thomas Cook and MyTravel sell thousands of holidays per year (see Chapter 8). Internal management decisions taken in large tour operators are crucial to understanding the consumption of mobility and the production of tourism space. Furthermore, corporate amalgamations and internationalisation strategies will have clear and differential consequences for the destinations. Corporate cultures, inter-organisational politics and the regulation of domestic and international trade also have the ability to induce radical changes in tourism flows and to trigger reorganisation in destinations and their businesses (Papatheodorou 2006). For instance, Ryanair, the Irish low-cost airline listed in the NASDAQ 100, has pursued an aggressive policy of expansion through the use of regional airports within Europe, several of which are state-owned. The European Commission investigated the case of Charleroi airport (near Brussels, Belgium) and the relationships between airline and airport, which was owned by the regional government of Wallonia (BBC 2004). The airline business model hinged on payments made by the region to the airline which underwrote the cut-price tickets. The Commission explored whether this represented inappropriate state aid or subsidy. Supporters of the airline argued that, in return, the airline delivered new opportunities for revenue growth and image making for regional administrators and enterprises (BBC 2004). Passengers move through airports making purchases; they also boost the regional economy by staying in local accommodation, using hospitality and retail services, and contribute to local and regional taxation revenues. Irrespective of the merits and legalities of the case, the result of this and other low-cost carriers' strategies of expansion has been to modify irreversibly the nature and patterns of European visitor flows and to open up new regions as destinations.

International tourism businesses of whatever size, by definition, have quite different and, as yet hitherto largely overlooked, operating parameters. This raises a significant set of questions which this book attempts to address. For instance,

- How do such tourism businesses operate internally and externally?
- What motivates their activities – profit, shareholders, boards of directors, public interest?
- How do they enter into strategic alliances or networks with their current and potential partners?
- How do decisions taken within organisations by key actors impact upon the delivery and consumption of tourism experiences?
- Are the products and experiences delivered to the willing acolytes of consumption the outcome of optimal management processes and the best practice of *homo economicus*?
- How does the political economy in the supply chain and the regulatory environment in which supply chains and suppliers operate influence production and consumption?
- What consequences do structural frameworks of regulation and changing international labour markets have on the internationalisation of operations?

To a degree, there have been the first important signs that some of these key questions have been raised (Purcell and Nicholas 2001), with the focus quite literally on businesses traditionally considered to have a direct involvement in travel and tourism. For instance, the economic fortunes of individual airlines, their entry and participation in strategic alliances, and the international transferable currency of their promotional activities such as frequent flyer programmes have come under the spotlight (Beaver 1996; Garnham 1996; Hanlon 1999; Gilbert *et al*. 2001; Leiper 2002; Weber 2002; Morley 2003). Tour operators and their packages have likewise been extensively discussed (Evans and Stabler 1995; Gratton and Richards 1997; Davies and Downward 1998, 2001; Aguilo *et al*. 2003). Airports as business spaces and international businesses in their own right have been explored by Graham (2001) and Hobson (2000). However, international businesses in other sectors are increasingly making great and creative use of tourism in pursuing their core business activities.

Lifestyle consumption and commodity culture as organisational paradigms at the turn of the twenty-first century offer international businesses important promotional and marketing opportunities through tourism. Volkswagen, Audi, Porsche, BMW and Mercedes-Benz all use tourism as a means of allowing their customers to experiences their brands to the full (see Chapter 13). Volkswagen has even opened its own theme park, *Autostadt*, at its Wolfsburg headquarters. In countries such as France, South Africa, New Zealand and Australia, international vintners have combined forces with destination marketers to use wine and wine tourism as means of building marketing relationships for local brands (see Chapter 11). Other well-known brands that use factory visits and company museums to build relationships with their customers include: Bushmills (whiskey), Cadbury (confectionary), Carlsberg (brewing), Harley-Davidson (motorcycles), Heineken (brewing) and Royal Worcester (porcelain) to include but a few (see also Mitchell and Orwig 2002). In perhaps the starkest example of its type, as 'Lord of the Rings Country', New Zealand has reaped the benefits of mutual synergies with motion picture productions (Jones and Smith 2005). However, it is routine these days for international film companies to seek to benefit from the economic advantages of shooting overseas in a high skills environment, while destination marketers benefit from the association with film scenes and branding of settings (see also Chapter 14).

CONCLUSION

Tourism and international business have become two important and distinctive objects of study for scholars in the subjects of business and management. In spite of this initial progress in understanding tourism businesses, the relationships between tourism and international business is in need of additional impetus. Advances made elsewhere in business and management, as well as the social sciences more broadly, on international business activity have not made their way into tourism-related discourse. What limited work that has been on tourism and international business has appeared almost exclusively in tourism journals and outlets. Mainstream international business and management journals are conspicuous for the absence of papers on tourism-related businesses (Hall 2003a). This may be an outcome of the nature of extant strands of discourse in international business as a publication arena. More concerningly it may be indicative of intellectual snobbery and a willingness to marginalise the importance of tourism businesses and consumption abroad as a category of international trade, compared to those in other 'classic' sectors such as manufacturing, financial services, transport and biotechnology and the consequently usual focus on cross-border supply and commercial presence. Yet, as noted above, not only do the fields have much to learn from each other but they also have a capacity to inform greater understanding of the globalisation of mobility. A similarly diffident relationship exists between tourism and recent advances in understanding the geography of firms spanning state boundaries. Contributions on the role of cultural and social relations in the firm and between mergers and acquisitions (M&A) partners, the scaling of regulatory environments and the political economy inside the firm have not been embraced by those seeking to understand how tourism connects with contemporary production and consumption.

We would contend that these represent important gaps in understanding that this book intends to go some way towards correcting. They are gaps that limit our appreciation of how the tourism sector functions and how tourism businesses operate. For those with a more generic interest in services, business and management, we would contend that their comprehension is constrained because there is a failure to consider the full nature of tourism as a variable in the operation of, for example, retail businesses at the micro-scale and international trade in services overall at the macro-level. This book seeks to overcome the present situation in which on the one hand, texts on international business frequently invoke case-studies of tourism businesses to portray apparently pivotal concepts and principles without an appreciation of the intricacies of how international tourism functions; on the other, there has been an imbalance in studies of tourism in favour of demand-side accounts of *tourist* behaviour at the relative expense of interest in supply-side readings of how tourism is produced and regulated. Any understanding of tourism is inadequate without appreciating the contributions that international business might bring yet at the same time international business is substantially incomplete in its coverage of international trade unless tourism is considered. Therefore, it is a hope that this book will help enrich the domains of teaching, learning and research in both fields.

Discussion questions

- What are four modes of international supply of services under GATS?
- What are the implications of the relationship between international business studies and tourism studies in understanding tourism as a form of international business?
- Why is the relative contribution of travel to international trade in services falling (according to the WTO) while international tourism numbers continue to increase?

REFERENCES

Aguiló, E., Alegre, J. and Sard, M. (2003) 'Examining the market structure of the German and UK tour operating industries through an analysis of package holiday prices', *Tourism Economics*, 9(3): 255–78.

BBC (2004) Ryanair slates Charleroi ruling. Online. Available from: http://news.bbc.co.uk/1/hi/business/ 3453285.stm (accessed: 19/06/07).

Beaver, A. (1996) 'Frequent flyer programmes: the beginning of the end?', *Tourism Economics*, 2(1): 43–60.

Blanke, J. and Chiesa, T. (2007) 'The travel & tourism competitiveness index: assessing key factors driving the sector's development', in World Economic Forum (ed.) *The Travel and Tourism Competitiveness Report 2007: Furthering the Process of Economic Development*. Geneva: World Economic Forum.

Boon, B. (2006) 'When leisure and work are allies: the case of skiers and tourist resort hotels', *Career Development International*, 11(7): 594–608.

Bristow, G. (2005) 'Everyone's a "winner": Problematising the discourse of regional competitiveness', *Journal of Economic Geography*, 5: 285–304.

Buckley, P.J. (2002) 'Is the international business research agenda running out of steam?', *Journal of International Business Studies*, 33(2): 365–73.

Buckley, P.J. and Ghauri, P.N. (2004) 'Globalisation, economic geography and the strategy of multinational enterprises', *Journal of International Business*, 35(2): 81–98.

Buckley, P.J. and Lessard, D.R. (2005) 'Regaining the edge for international business research', *Journal of International Business Studies*, 36: 595–9.

Coles, T., Hall, C.M. and Duval, D. (2005) 'Mobilising tourism: a post-disciplinary critique', *Tourism Recreation Research*, 30(2). 31–41.

—— (2006) 'Tourism and post-disciplinary inquiry', *Current Issues in Tourism*, 9(4/5): 293–319.

Davies, B. and Downward, P. (1998) 'Competition and contestability in the UK package tour industry', *Tourism Economics*, 4(3): 241–52.

Deas, I. and Giordano, B. (2001) 'Conceptualising and measuring urban competitiveness in major English cities: an exploratory approach', *Environment and Planning A*, 33: 1411–29.

Dimanche, F. (2005) 'Conceptual framework for city tourism competitiveness', in World Tourism Organization Forum (ed.) *New Paradigms for City Tourism Management*, Istanbul, Turkey, 1–3 June.

Dwyer, L. and Kim, C.W. (2003) 'Destination competitiveness: a model and indicators', *Current Issues in Tourism*, 6(5): 369–414.

Dwyer, L., Forsyth, P. and Rao, P. (2000a) 'The price competitiveness of travel and tourism: a comparison of 19 Destinations', *Tourism Management*, 21(1): 9–22.

—— (2000b) 'Sectoral analysis of destination price competitiveness: an international comparison', *Tourism Analysis*, 5: 1–12.

Enright, M. and Newton, J. (2005) 'Determinants of tourism destination competitiveness in Asia Pacific: comprehensiveness and universality', *Journal of Travel Research*, 43(4): 339–50.

Evans, N.G. and Stabler, M.J. (1995) 'A future for the package tour operator in the 21st century?', *Tourism Economics*, 1(3): 245–64.

Evans, N., Campbell, D. and Stonehouse, G. (2002) *Strategic Management for Travel and Tourism*. Oxford: Butterworth-Heinemann.

Franklin, A. and Crang, M. (2001) 'The trouble with tourism and travel theory', *Tourist Studies*, 1(1): 5–22.

Garnham, B. (1996) 'Alliances and liaisons in tourism. Concepts and implications', *Tourism Economics*, 2(1): 61–78.

Gilbert, D., Child, D. and Bennett, M. (2001) 'A qualitative study of the current practices of "no-frills" airlines operating in the UK', *Journal of Vacation Marketing*, 7(4): 302–15.

Graham, A. (2001) *Managing Airports: An International Perspective*. Oxford: Butterworth-Heinemann.

Gratton, C. and Richards, G. (1997) 'Structural change in the European package tour industry: UK/German comparisons', *Tourism Economics*, 3(3): 213–26.

Hall, C.M. (2003a) 'Tourism and international business', paper presented at Australia and New Zealand International Business Academy 2003 Conference, Dunedin, New Zealand, November 2003.

—— (2003b) 'Tourism and temporary mobility: circulation, diaspora, migration, nomadism, sojourning, travel, transport and home', paper presented at the International Academy for the Study of Tourism (IAST) Conference, Savonlinna, Finland, 30 June–5 July 2003.

—— (2005) *Tourism: Rethinking the Social Science of Mobility*. Harlow: Prentice Hall.

—— (2007) 'Pro-poor tourism: Do "tourism exchanges benefit primarily the countries of the South"?', *Current Issues in Tourism*, 10(2/3): 111–18.

—— (2008) *Tourism Planning*, 2nd edn. Harlow: Pearson Education.

Hall, C.M. and Page, S. (2006) *The Geography of Tourism and Recreation*, 3rd edn. London: Routledge.

Hall, C.M. and Williams, A.M. (eds) (2002) *Tourism and Migration*. Dordrecht: Kluwer.

Hanlon, P. (1999) *Global Airlines*, 2nd edn. Oxford: Butterworth-Heinemann.

Hobson, J.S.P. (2000) 'Tourist shopping in transit: the case of BAA plc', *Journal of Vacation Marketing*, 6(2): 170–83.

Ioannides, D. (1998) 'Tour operators: the gatekeepers of tourism', in D. Ioannides and K.G. Debbage (eds) *The Economic Geography of the Tourist Industry: A Supply-side Analysis*. London: Routledge.

Inkson, K. and Myers, B.A. (2003) 'The "big OE": self-directed travel and career development', *Career Development International*, 8(4): 170–81.

Jones, D. and Smith, K. (2005) 'Middle-earth meets New Zealand: authenticity and location in the making of the *Lord of the Rings*', *Journal of Management Studies*, 42(5): 923–45.

Jones, E. and Haven, C. (eds.) (2005) *Tourism SMEs, Service Quality and Destination Competitiveness: International Perspectives.* Wallingford: CABI.

Leiper, N. (2002) 'Why Ansett failed ....', *Current Issues in Tourism,* 5(2): 134–48.

Malecki, E. J. (2002) Hard and soft networks for urban competitiveness, *Urban Studies*, 39: 929–45.

—— (2004) 'Jockeying for position: what it means and why it matters to regional development policy when places compete', *Regional Studies*, 38(9): 1101–20.

Mangion, M.-L., Durbarry R. and Sinclair M.T. (2005) 'Tourism competitiveness: price and quality', *Tourism Economics*, 11(1): 45–68.

Markusen, A. (1999) 'Fuzzy concepts, scanty evidence, policy distance: the case for rigour and policy relevance in critical regional studies', *Regional Studies*, 33(9): 869–84.

Minford, P. (2006) 'Competitiveness in a globalised world: a commentary', *Journal of International Business Studies*, 37: 176–8.

Mitchell, M.A. and Orwig, R.A. (2002) 'Consumer experience tourism and brand bonding', *Journal of Product and Brand Management*, 11(1): 30–41.

Morley, C.L. (2003) 'Impacts of international airline alliances on tourism', *Tourism Economics*, 9(1): 31–52.

Papatheodorou, A. (ed.) (2006) *Corporate Rivalry and Market Power: Competition Issues in the Tourism Industry*. London: I.B. Tauris.

Peng, M.W. (2004) 'Identifying the big question in international business research', *Journal of International Business*, 35(2): 99–108.

Purcell, W. and Nicholas, S. (2001) 'Japanese tourism investment in Australia: entry choice, parent control and management practice', *Tourism Management*, 22(3): 245–57.

Ritchie, J.R.B. and Crouch, G. (2003) *The Competitive Destination: A Sustainable Tourism Perspective*. Wallingford: CABI Publishing.

Shenkar, O. (2004) 'One more time: international business in a global economy', *Journal of International Business*, 35(2): 161–71.

Thomas, R. (ed.) (2004) *Small Firms in Tourism: International Perspectives.* Oxford: Elsevier.

Tribe, J. (1997) 'The indiscipline of tourism', *Annals of Tourism Research*, 24(3): 638–57.

—— (2000) 'Indisciplined and unsubstantiated', *Annals of Tourism Research*, 27(3): 809–13.

United Nations, European Commission, International Monetary Fund, Organisation for Economic Co-operation and Development, United Nations Conference on Trade and Development, and World Trade Organization (2002) *Manual on Statistics of International Trade in Services* Department of Economic and Social Affairs Statistics Division, Series M No. 86. New York: United Nations.

UNWTO (1997) *Tourism 2020 Vision.* Madrid: UNWTO.

—— (2006a) *International Tourist Arrivals, Tourism Market Trends, 2006 Edition – Annex.* Madrid: UNWTO.

—— (2006b) *Tourism Highlights, 2006 Edition – Annex.* Madrid: UNWTO.

—— (2007a) 'Another record year for world tourism', news release, UNWTO Press and Communications Department, UNWTO, Madrid, 29 January.

—— (2007b) UNWTO welcomes tourism competitiveness report and, calls for level playing field for developing countries, urges action in the [D]oha development round. News release, Berlin/Madrid. Madrid: UNWTO Press and Communications Department. Online. Available from: http://www.unwto.org/newsroom/Releases/2007/march/itb_competi.htm (accessed: 19/06/07).

Weber, K. (2002) 'Consumer perceptions and behaviour: neglected dimensions in research on strategic airline alliances', *Journal of Travel and Tourism Marketing*, 13(4): 27–46.

WEF (2007) *The Travel and Tourism Competitiveness Report 2007: Furthering the Process of Economic Development.* Geneva: World Economic Forum.

World Bank (2007) World Development Indicators database, 23 April 2007. Washington, DC: World Bank. Online. Available from: http://siteresources.worldbank.org/DATASTATISTICS/Resources/GDP.pdf (accessed: 19/06/07).

WTO (1998) *Annual Report 1998.* Geneva: WTO.

—— (2001) *International Trade Statistics 2001.* Geneva: WTO.

—— (2006) *International Trade Statistics 2006.* Geneva: WTO.

WTTC (2007) *World Travel & Tourism Council, Progress and Priorities 2007/8.* London: WTTC.

PART I

Framing international business and tourism: governance and regulation

INTRODUCTION: STRUCTURE OF THE BOOK

This book is structured into four main parts comprising 14 further chapters in total. Each part reflects a core set of concerns in the relationship between tourism and international business. The book is structured to reflect the dominant paradigms within the field of international business, as we will discuss below. In brief, the first part of the book explores governance and regulation issues as a framework for situating the state and other actors involved in configuring international business and tourism. Early theoretical work on the need for international business stems from Adam Smith's *The Wealth of Nations* (1776) and the view that international trade is a function of absolute and, in later Ricardian (1817) analysis, comparative advantage (Mtigwe 2006). While state- or, more accurately, nation-based views of international business are not as popular as they once were (Buckley 2002; Buckley and Lessard 2005), this part demonstrates that the state (often in concert with other actors) plays a pivotal role in shaping international business and tourism.

The state's place as the dominant focus in the field of international business studies has arguably been taken by the firm and the second part of the book examines the complexities of the internationalisation of tourism businesses; that is, the chapters deal exclusively with businesses for which travel and tourism are core business interests. Critiques of the hegemonic position of the firm have emerged, with many commentators pointing to the increasing importance in conditions of rapid globalisation and intense time–space compression of cross-border flows of people, money, goods, products, information, ideas and intellectual property (Ohmae 1996; Axinn and Matthyssens 2002; Andersson 2004; Zahra 2005; Mtigwe 2006). The third part explores how international business beyond the firm contributes to a fuller understanding of how tourism production works in practice. Of course, 'tourism businesses' are not the only ones to make use of tourism in their operations. In the final part, we explore how businesses with their core interests in other sectors use tourism deliberately to further their commercial aims and objectives. While there are clear resonances with theoretical and conceptual constructs from international business studies introduced earlier in the book, the purpose of this section is to warn against artificial intellectual distinctions and the production of knowledge silos. It demonstrates that the use of tourism as a business strategy is not exclusively limited to tourism businesses, and hence scholars who are interested first and foremost in the cross-border activities of businesses in other economic sectors would be well advised to take a wider view of the role of human mobility in international commerce.

IN SEARCH OF THEORETICAL TRADITIONS OF INTERNATIONAL BUSINESS STUDIES

Both international business and tourism studies are offspring of the academic reaction to globalisation. Like the expansion of tourism studies in relation to the growth of international mobility, international business has expanded in relation not just to the increased internationalisation of trade but more particularly to the global development of the transnational firm (Hall 2005). As we noted in Chapter 1, international business is an adolescent field of study within the social sciences which, like tourism studies, has experienced growing pains and 'disciplinary' angst (Buckley 2002; Peng 2004; Shenkar 2004). For all its problems, international business studies has been a prodigious youngster. Since it started to grow rapidly in the aftermath of the second World War , it has generated a large volume of theoretical discussion. Of course, in a book of this type and an introduction of this nature, it is impossible to review this in any great depth (see Axinn and Matthyssens 2001; Mudambi and Navarra 2002; Buckley and Lessard 2005; Mtigwe 2006). However, it is important to point to the shifting dominant interests over time (Buckley and Lessard 2005). Mtigwe (2006: 7) neatly summarises these macro-developments and he identifies four meta-groups of international business theory that have developed broadly sequentially: Classical Theories; Early Market Imperfection Theories; Latter-day Market Imperfection Theories; and Internationalization Theories. There may be a temptation to argue that the most recent contributions reflect state-of-the-art thinking and hence offer the most powerful explanatory potentials currently available on the basis that each subsequent new body of theory reflects the need to address limitations in previous contributions. As Mtigwe (2006: 17–18) argues, this need not necessarily be the case in international business. Instead, he urges intellectual tolerance and argues that a synthesis of theoretical components contributes to the development of theory in international entrepreneurship. Andersson (2004) points to the contextual application of theory depending on the nature of the enterprise and the international market(s) in which it intends to operate.

Be this as it may, this brief overview is important here for two reasons. First, it reminds us that international business studies as we know it today has its intellectual roots in international trade and broader processes of economic globalisation. In particular international business posits why the state, and firms within the state, need to be outward-facing and how trade occurs on the international stage. The search for advantage and the mosaic of operating conditions and market imperfections around the world creates a range of commercial possibilities to exploit. However, the question arises as to how markets, firms and the international business environment more widely are regulated and governed in such a manner as to create or frustrate opportunities. Second, the state has a number of functions in addition to wealth creation, including security and welfare provision. The state is not just a container for economic, social, cultural, political and environmental attributes, and it is not solely a passive recipient of international market conditions; rather, states, as well as the supranational bodies of which they are members, play a number of key roles in the governance and regulation of economic – as well as social, cultural, political and environmental – practices. These activities represent important interventions in the operation of markets as well as the creation of new ones – such as the development of carbon trading schemes – and provide sources of relative advantages or disadvantages for firms, enterprises and ultimately, with particular respect to the tourism sector, destinations.

REGULATION AND GOVERNANCE AS PERSISTENT CORE THEMES

The chapters in this section suggest that, while international business theory may have charted new intellectual territories, the state and institutions (Mudambi and Navarra 2002) remain powerful sources of explanation in international business and tourism. This is in direct contrast to the Ultraglobalists who argue that the nation-state plays precious little role because, in Ohmae's (1996: 2) reading of the contemporary world, 'the four "I's" – industry, investment, individuals, information – flow relatively unimpeded across national borders, the building-block concepts appropriate to a 19th century, closed-country model of world'. Thus, rather than develop approaches to understanding international tourism rooted exclusively in International Trade Theory (see for example Zhang and Jensen 2007), the chapters here explore the role of the state and its relationship with actors at other scales in shaping the practices of tourism (and other forms of human mobility).

Hall examines the role of the (nation-)state in regulating international mobility, with special reference to the legal measures and instruments brought to bear. He explores how a series of unilateral measures, bilateral and multilateral agreements affect international tourism flows with respect to individuals (mode 2 – consumption abroad; mode 4 – presence of natural persons) and organisations (mode 1 – cross-border supply; mode 3 – commercial presence) (Figure 1.1). A rich tapestry of regulatory measures and governance structures comprising supranational bodies and inter-state collaborations and partnerships form important backdrops to how states order the mobilities of their citizens and those from outside.

Both Hall and Coles point to the power of the state in rendering people immobile as well as enhancing their mobility. With all the rhetoric surrounding globalisation with suggestions of 'fluid modernity' (Urry 2000), it is all too easy to assume that we inhabit a highly mobile world with very few obstacles to movement (Ohmae 1996). Travel may be a fundamental human right according to several supranational bodies but it is rarely enshrined in law by states. As Coles points out, while state-based models of citizenship are important in configuring mobility and international business (mode 2 – consumption abroad; mode 4 – presence of natural persons), other alternative, contemporary types of citizenship may function in much the same manner. These new citizenships may at first sight point to the apparently declining relevance of state-based models, but the situation is far more complex. In some instances the state plays a role in inducing new forms of consumer citizenship; in others, the position of the state is reinforced by sub-state actors (from the private sector) whose activities contribute to the emergence of these new social groups. What is clear, though, is that contemporary studies of tourism and international business cannot continue to overlook the significance of citizenship as a regulatory mechanism.

Finally, in this part, Hultman and Gössling examine the ontology of tourism and international business. Ontology is essentially the study of being and their chapter questions how we know or construct issues such as 'nature', 'environment', 'local', 'global', 'tourism'. This may appear to be an elaborate, for some even an unnecessary, approach to studying international business and tourism. Such a response – albeit sadly limited and dated in our view – may be entirely predictable judging by the functional nature of many textbooks on international business and the (logical) positivist sympathies of the many quantitatively-driven investigations published in international business journals. However, it is worth noting that there have been attempts to diversify the research approach. For example, in 2006 *Management International Review* (vol. 46, no. 4) had a special issue on qualitative research methods in international business. Through case-studies of several high-profile, nature-based attractions around the world, Hultman and Gössling explore neoliberalism as an emergent organisational ethos for economic activity which is popular among, and routinely espoused by, many states and supranational bodies. Neoliberalism is commonly associated with free markets, free trade and private entrepreneurship, and they argue that neoliberalism in tourism can lead to the appropriation of nature, its dislocation from its natural environments, and its production elsewhere. As a result the territories in which nature was once indigenous have their competitive advantages of place eroded. In fact, this is interpreted as a form of 'biocolonialism' in the sense that significant inequalities result from the commoditisation of formerly local/national nature by external sub-state corporations and organisations.

REFERENCES

Andersson, S. (2000) 'Internationalization in different industrial contexts', *Journal of Business Venturing*, 19: 851–75.

Axinn, C. and Matthyssens, P. (2001) 'Limits of internationalization theories in an unlimited world', *International Marketing Review*, 19(5): 436–49.

Buckley, P.J. (2002) 'Is the international business research agenda running out of steam?', *Journal of International Business Studies*, 33(2): 365–73.

Buckley, P.J. and Lessard, D.R. (2005) 'Regaining the edge for international business research', *Journal of International Business Studies*, 36: 595–9.

Hall, C.M. (2005) *Tourism: Rethinking the Social Science of Mobility*. Harlow: Prentice-Hall.

Mtigwe, B. (2006) 'Theoretical milestones in international business: the journey to international entrepreneurship theory', *Journal of International Entrepreneurship*, 4: 5–25.

Mudambi, R. and Navarra, P. (2002) 'Institutions and international business: a theoretical review', *International Business Review*, 11: 635–46.

Ohmae, K. (1996) *The End of the Nation State. How Capital, Corporations, Consumers, and Communication are Reshaping Global Markets*. New York: Free Press Paperbacks (Simon & Schuster Inc.).

Peng, M.W. (2004) 'Identifying the big question in international business research', *Journal of International Business Studies*, 35: 99–108.

Ricardo, D. (1817) *On the Principles of Political Economics and Taxation.* London: John Murray.

Shenkar, O. (2004) 'One more time: international business in a global economy', *Journal of International Business*, 35: 161–71.

Smith, A. [1776] (1904) *An Inquiry into the Nature and Causes of the Wealth of Nations*, 5th edn, ed. F. Cannan. London: Methuen and Co.

Urry, J. (2000) *Sociology Beyond Societies. Mobilities for the Twenty-first Century.* London: Routledge.

Zahra, S.A. (2005) 'A theory of international new ventures: a decade of research', *Journal of International Business Studies*, 36: 20–8

Zhang, J. and Jensen, C. (2007) 'Comparative advantage. Explaining tourism flows', *Annals of Tourism Research*, 34(1): 223–43.

2 Regulating the international trade in tourism services

C. Michael Hall

Learning objectives

After considering this chapter, you will be able to:

- understand the role of the nation-state in regulating international mobility;
- appreciate the legal context of rights to personal international mobility;
- understand the role of bilateral and multilateral frameworks in facilitating the liberalisation of international trade in services;
- explain the different focus of developed and developing countries with respect to liberalisation of trade in tourism services.

Key terms

- nation-state;
- rights to international movement;
- bilateralism;
- multilateralism;
- rights to mobility.

INTRODUCTION: REGULATING TOURISM

Although the notion of tourism is often associated in the popular imagination with concepts of leisure and freedom, the reality is that tourism is substantially regulated at various scales. Whether it be the movement of an individual across a national border, or the transnational activities of an organisation such as a business or a non-government aid organisation, international tourism services are subject to a range of regulatory governance. In examining obstacles to trade in international travel and tourism services, a number of issues can be identified (Hall 2008):

• Government attention to tourism is usually focused more on promotion of inbound tourism rather than on a more general approach that deals with reduction or removal of restrictions to voluntary human mobility on a multilateral basis.
• Governments have not usually assessed the impact of laws and regulations specifically on tourism and travel services as there are very few tourist- or tourism-specific laws.
• Government international trade, security and diplomatic policies often conflict with, and usually override, tourism policies. This is particularly the case with respect to security policies in developed countries in a post-9/11 environment.
• International organisations that focus on trade issues have historically addressed tourism primarily in piecemeal fashion and not with tourism as an integral unit. This is changing with respect to the Organisation for Economic Co-operation and Development (OECD) and the General Agreement of Trade in Services (GATS) although because of the diffuse nature of tourism in many policy fields substantial gaps still remain, particularly as new issues arise.
• There is only limited coordination among international organisations on tourism matters.

This chapter will examine the regulation of tourism services with respect to both individuals (mode 2 of GATS, consumption abroad; mode 4, presence of natural persons – see Figure 1.1) and organisations (mode 1, cross border supply; mode 3, commercial presence) in the light of multi-level governance of international business. As this chapter illustrates, the regulatory framework of tourism services goes substantially beyond GATS and incorporates a range of supranational, bilateral and national governance regimes within which the international business of tourism is embedded. The first section of the chapter examines the role of governance and regulation with respect to international trade in services before proceeding to discuss rights to individual international mobility as well as bilateral and multilateral frameworks for liberalising trade in tourism services.

GOVERNANCE AND REGULATION

One of the most significant debates in the regulation of international business concerns the changing nature of the nation-state. Although the nation-state has been the cornerstone of international relations over the past two hundred years there are some who argue that we are entering into a period of post-sovereign, multi-layered governance architecture (Wallace 1999; Karkkainen 2004). This has meant that state authority, power and legitimacy have ceased to be bounded on a strict territorial basis that is the basis for sovereign governance. Instead, in the condition of post-sovereignty, the governance of key cultural, economic and financial issues,

> will be handled more and more by the transfer of goal-specific authority from states to regional
> or multilateral organizations and to local or subnational polities. Hence, the governance of key
> issue areas will be maintained not by territorial state-bounded authorities, as in the past, but rather

by a network of flows of information, power and resources from the local to the regional and multilateral levels and the other way around.

(Morales-Moreno 2004)

As Chapter 1 indicates the supranational state (for instance, the European Union – EU), and sub-(nation-)state actors are increasingly important elements in international business and relations (see also Chapters 3 and 5). Similarly, the growth of public–private partnerships and the notion of stakeholder involvement in public sector policy and decision-making gives credence to the significance of governance – the capacity for steering and managing transnational relations and flows in a given policy arena – as a function of the state (see also Chapters 11, 12 and 14). However, although some may regard the state as 'hollow' (Milward and Provan 2000), by virtue of the increasing use of third parties (often non-profit organisations) to deliver social services and act in the name of the state, sovereignty is still largely in hands of nation-states that clearly remain pivotal actors in the international sphere, especially when some states do not fully ascribe to the notion of a multi-levelled polity. In the case of Europe, it may even be argued that the power of the state has been increased as a result of integration rather than eroded, since the tendency does appear to be for the supranational EU to take over from the state those functions that the state performs less well under globalisation, such as the regulation of financial markets and international trade (Milward *et al.* 1993; Majone 1996). Moreover, even where arguments are made with respect to the establishment of cosmopolitan citizenship (see Chapter 3), for example with respect to placing more emphasis on extending democracy and human rights to the international sphere, this is not incommensurate with respect to the territorially-limited rights of the citizen at the level of the nation-state (Chandler 2003).

The notion that the state is finished is therefore substantially premature (Dunn 1995). Of course, as Peters (1998) observes,

> the capacity of states to behave as a unitary actor is sometimes greatly overstated in the state literature, but it still appears easier to begin with that more centralized conception and find the exceptions than to begin with a null hypothesis of no order and find any pattern.

Thus, state authority should remain the starting point in any assessment of the regulation of international trade of tourism services as, with the exception of the capacity of citizens of the EU to engage in direct elections of members of the European Parliament, the fundamental political unit of regulation within supranational and international governance remains the nation-state and its capacity to exercise territorial sovereignty. Indeed, the right to control and restrict entry into state territory have 'historically been viewed as inherent in the very nature of sovereignty' (Collinson 1996: 77).

Obstacles to tourism may be classified as to whether they constitute a tariff or non-tariff barrier. Non-tariff barriers include restrictions on entry by nationality or other screening processes, cost of application for visa, travel allowance restrictions, restrictions on credit card use, limitations on duty-free allowances, and advance-import-deposit-like measures (e.g. compulsory deposits prior to travel). Tariff barriers include import-duty measures, airport departures or airport taxes, and subsidies (e.g. a consumer-subsidy measure such as an official preferential exchange rate for foreign tourists or price concessions). Although tourism tariff barriers may be lowered by specific bilateral agreements, tariffs have historically tended to be dealt with under broader multilateral negotiations on tariff reductions on trade in goods and services (as in the case of the World Trade Organization – WTO) or, more recently, negotiations within a specific trading bloc, such as the EU or the Association of South East Asian Nations (ASEAN) (Hall 2008).

ENABLING MOBILITY

Despite declarations from the United Nations World Tourism Organization (UNWTO) and the United Nations as to the right to tourism and the liberty of tourist movements (Table 2.1),

Table 2.1 Resolutions of UN Global Code of Ethics for Tourism relevant to international mobility of persons

Right to tourism (Article 7)

1 The prospect of direct and personal access to the discovery and enjoyment of the planet's resources constitutes a right equally open to all the world's inhabitants; the increasingly extensive participation in national and international tourism should be regarded as one of the best possible expressions of the sustained growth of free time, and obstacles should not be placed in its way.

2 The universal right to tourism must be regarded as the corollary of the right to rest and leisure, including reasonable limitation of working hours and periodic holidays with pay, guaranteed by Article 24 of the Universal Declaration of Human Rights and Article 7.d of the International Covenant on Economic, Social and Cultural Rights.

3 Social tourism, and in particular associative tourism, which facilitates widespread access to leisure, travel and holidays, should be developed with the support of the public authorities.

4 Family, youth, student and senior tourism and tourism for people with disabilities, should be encouraged and facilitated.

Liberty of tourist movements (Article 8)

1 Tourists and visitors should benefit, in compliance with international law and national legislation, from the liberty to move within their countries and from one state to another, in accordance with Article 13 of the Universal Declaration of Human Rights; they should have access to places of transit and stay and to tourism and cultural sites without being subject to excessive formalities or discrimination.

2 Tourists and visitors should have access to all available forms of communication, internal or external; they should benefit from prompt and easy access to local administrative, legal and health services; they should be free to contact the consular representatives of their countries of origin in compliance with the diplomatic conventions in force.

3 Tourists and visitors should benefit from the same rights as the citizens of the country visited concerning the confidentiality of the personal data and information concerning them, especially when these are stored electronically.

4 Administrative procedures relating to border crossings whether they fall within the competence of states or result from international agreements, such as visas or health and customs formalities,

Continued

Table 2.1 *Continued*

should be adapted, so far as possible, so as to facilitate to the maximum freedom of travel and widespread access to international tourism; agreements between groups of countries to harmonise and simplify these procedures should be encouraged; specific taxes and levies penalising the tourism industry and undermining its competitiveness should be gradually phased out or corrected.

5 So far as the economic situation of the countries from which they come permits, travellers should have access to allowances of convertible currencies needed for their travels.

Rights of the workers and entrepreneurs in the tourism industry (Article 9)

1 The fundamental rights of salaried and self-employed workers in the tourism industry and related activities, should be guaranteed under the supervision of the national and local administrations, both of their states of origin and of the host countries with particular care, given the specific constraints linked in particular to the seasonality of their activity, the global dimension of their industry and the flexibility often required of them by the nature of their work.

4 Exchanges of experience offered to executives and workers, whether salaried or not, from different countries, contributes to foster the development of the world tourism industry; these movements should be facilitated so far as possible in compliance with the applicable national laws and international conventions.

Source: Adapted from United Nations (2001).

Note: The Global Code of Ethics for Tourism was initially adopted by resolution A/RES/406(XIII) at the Thirteenth World Tourism Organization General Assembly (Santiago, Chile, 27 September–1 October 1999). It was then adopted as a resolution of the United Nations General Assembly, 21 December 2001.

nowhere in international law is there enshrined a right to enter foreign spaces. Even the advisory Universal Declaration of Human Rights only postulates a right of exit and entry to one's own country and freedom of mobility within a citizen's own country. Article 13 states,

(1) Everyone has the right to freedom of movement and residence within the borders of each state.

(2) Everyone has the right to leave any country, including his [*sic*] own, and to return to his country.

(United Nations 1948)

Although many nation-states have entered into bilateral and multilateral agreements that facilitate mobility between state parties, the prerogative to control entry remains with the nation-state. However, such a situation is undoubtedly creating policy tensions for national governments as the economic and political imperatives of globalisation, even given concerns over security in a post-9/11 environment, demand more permeable borders for flows of goods, services, capital and people.

The international mobility of tourists, including business travellers, or persons who are part of the tourism labour force is therefore restrained by the regulatory authority of the nation-state. There are a number of direct and indirect measures by which such mobility is enabled or restrained by both the generating and receiving nation-state as well as the actions of nation-states that act as transit regions (Figure 2.1). One of the most important direct measures by government on mobility is the provision of passports and travel documents. In order to enter foreign spaces, travellers need passports or other documentation, which only nation-states have the right to issue, together with a valid visa depending on which

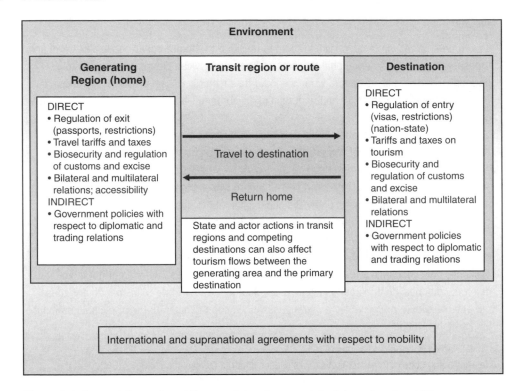

Figure 2.1 *Constraining and enabling regulatory framework for international mobility*

passport they hold and where they want to travel to (see also Chapter 3). Without such documentation an individual becomes stateless in an international regulatory system that is founded on the recognition of state authority (Hess 2006).

The extent to which access to travel documentation is a right depends on national legislation. However, even where rights exist such documentation is not provided for free and the financial cost of passport provision as well as the length of time required before it is issued may deter some potential travellers. Furthermore, recognition of passports by destination authorities also acts to influence travel decision-making as travel flows are embedded within a complex set of bilateral and multilateral arrangements with respect to recognition of various nation-states; visa provision to provide for entry; and even sanctions on those who come from or visit some states. For example, many nation-states require the issuance of visas so as to provide for entry, although these can sometimes be purchased at the border. In many cases visa-granting regulations require the temporary surrender of a passport to an embassy (or other authority) of the destination country, as well as other documentation relating to identity and purpose of visit and the payment of a fee.

The capacity of gaining access to foreign spaces is therefore highly unequal and hence is a function of

- imposition of visa restrictions;
- cost, access and availability of visas and passport;
- number of passports issued.

Table 2.2 *Estimates of passport possession for selected countries*

Country	Ratio of passports to the permanent resident population (%)
Australia	50
Canada	41
Ireland	100
New Zealand	78
United Kingdom	82
United States of America	22

Source: Hall (2006).

Table 2.2 provides an estimate of passport possession for several developed countries represented as a number of passports issued as a percentage of total population (Hall 2006). The high percentages of some countries also need to be understood in relation to passport holders living abroad who are entitled to a passport via their birthright or that of their parents. For example, the Irish Nationality and Citizenship Act of 1956 to 2004 provides that certain persons born outside of Ireland may claim Irish citizenship by descent. A person born abroad to a parent or grandparent who, although not born in Ireland, was otherwise an Irish citizen at the time of the person's birth, can become an Irish citizen by applying for foreign births registration. Nevertheless, the citizenship of a person born on the island of Ireland on or after 1 January, 2005 depends on the citizenship of the person's parents at the time of the person's birth or the residency history of one of the parents prior to the birth. As such, a high ratio of possession to permanent population may indicate a significant diasporic community (Coles and Timothy 2004; Hugo 2006).

The regulation of international mobility is further compounded by the nature of the visa that is issued (which provides certain rights with respect to activities and length of stay in a foreign jurisdiction) as well as other national policies with respect to security, migration, taxation and trade that may affect flows. For example, many jurisdictions impose a departure tax or other taxes on international visitors or nationals, often for revenue raising with respect to infrastructure, tourism promotion, combating climate change and/or adding to consolidated revenue, while others seek to reduce the extent of illegal immigration by having more rigorous and/or restrictive visa access for nationals of some countries (Thunø 2003).

The mobility of individuals is also dealt with under a series of bilateral and multilateral agreements between countries. For example, citizens of the UK, Ireland, Isle of Man, Jersey and Guernsey do not require passports to travel between them (referred to as the Common Travel Area) although they do require identity documents (Ryan 2001). Chinese group leisure tourists travel to numerous countries under a bilateral Approved Destination Status (ADS) arrangement (see case-study below). Significantly, many countries have bilateral agreements with respect to reciprocal visa regimes so that if Country X requires citizens of Country Y to have a visa to enter there, then Country Y may apply reciprocity and require a visa from citizens of Country X. Alternatively, if Country X allows Country Y's citizens to enter without a visa, Y may also allow X's citizens to enter without a visa. An example of the latter is the US Visa Waiver Program.

CASE-STUDY VIGNETTE – TOURISM AND INTERNATIONAL BUSINESS IN ACTION

Chinese ADS

The characters for tourism in Chinese ('Lu-You') translate as travel ('Lu') and sightseeing ('You'). Although travel for sightseeing was long frowned upon in communist China, post-1978 and the 'open-door' policy, international leisure tourism has become recognised as being a significant part of the economy and an important symbol of Chinese modern economic development. In 1981 Chinese citizens were only allowed to undertake group leisure trips to countries in southeast Asia (Hong Kong, Macau, Thailand and Singapore). In 1983 private travel with the purpose of visiting friends and relations (VFR) overseas was allowed. Since the early 1990s the Chinese government has enacted a number of policy changes in order to encourage outbound tourism (Zhang and Han 2004):

- The State Council enacted *Measures on Management of Outbound Tourism by Chinese Citizens*, which have improved the management system of outbound tourism, seek to protect the rights of outbound tourists and enterprises running outbound business. The measures stipulate the approved destination countries and regions; the qualifications, approval procedures and business process of travel agencies running outbound business; the responsibilities of tour leaders; the rights and obligations of tourists; and penalties for not meeting legal obligations.
- The application process for passports has been simplified.
- Foreign currency exchange management and control have been adjusted.

ADS is a bilateral programme developed by the People's Republic of China (PRC) to manage the international group leisure travel of its citizens to recipient destinations. Each destination country negotiates separately with the China National Tourism Administration and the Chinese government with respect to their specific ADS agreement. Introduced in 1995 the programme enables citizens of the PRC to use personal passports and apply for tourism visas to countries approved for visitation. For national destinations approved under ADS, mainland Chinese no longer have to contact embassies or consulates in order to obtain a visa. Instead visas for leisure group travel are provided by outbound travel agencies that have been authorised by the China National Tourism Administration. However, the visas are restricted by the itinerary, which must be fixed at the beginning of the trip. Travellers are also obliged to travel in a tour group (minimum of five people including a tour leader) and are not allowed to extend their stay or apply for other types of visas. The destination

Continued

tourist authority must provide a list of approved tour operators that can handle land arrangements for tour groups. Travel solely for pleasure is not allowed to non-ADS countries. If mainland Chinese wish to travel to non-ADS countries their trip must be for business, education or family (VFR) purposes in order to gain a departure visa.

As of January 2007 86 countries had ADS status. Australia and New Zealand were the first Western countries to receive ADS in 1999. The European Community (EC) signed an ADS accord in February 2004 with it coming into force in September 2004. Achievement of ADS is now recognised as crucial to the development of tourism and aviation relations with China and has become a significant economic tool in China's diplomatic arsenal, particularly with smaller economies (Windybank 2005; Shie 2007). The ADS is significant because as well as providing for tourist entry into the destination country, it also allows the destination country to open a tourist office in China and conduct marketing activities (King *et al.* 2006).

The significance of ADS can be illustrated by the Australian case. Between 1999 and the end of 2006 Australia hosted 264,000 Chinese tourists undertaking group leisure travel. As of 2007 China was Australia's fastest-growing inbound tourism market, and was forecast to grow at more than 12 per cent over the coming decade, resulting in over 900,000 Chinese visitors per year by 2015. As a result of a review of the ADS the Australian government reformed the programme

> ... to ensure Chinese tourists receive a quality Australian tourism experience. At this time, all existing ADS operators were required to re-apply for approval, with applications also invited from appropriately qualified Australian businesses wishing to enter the scheme. Applications were rigorously assessed, and approved operators are required to comply with a new ADS *Code of Business Standards and Ethics*.
>
> In August 2006, the Minister for Small Business and Tourism, the Hon Fran Bailey MP, signed a Memorandum of Understanding with Chairman Shao Qiwei of the China National Tourism Administration on the ADS scheme. This signals Australia and China's commitment to fostering the growth of sustainable and quality tourism.
>
> (DITR 2007)

The objectives of the ADS arrangements are to

- restore integrity, competition and fair trading to the operation of ADS inbound market, especially in relations between operators and shops, and operators and tourists; and
- empower Chinese inbound tourists with knowledge and choice to exercise effective consumer power in the inbound market (DITR 2006).

Continued

Key features of the ADS arrangements are (DITR 2006):

- applicants are assessed as to whether they are a 'fit and proper' person to be an ADS approved inbound tour operator;
- applicants must consent to being vetted for their 'good standing';
- applicants must also meet 'industry fitness' and immigration compliance tests;
- applicants are listed in the national press and comment from the public will be invited;
- under the strengthened ADS Code of Business Standards and Ethics:
  - operators have an express duty of care to tourists;
  - commission shopping is allowed, but it must be matched with free shopping in competitive retail areas, prior to commission shopping;
  - commissions must be declared and are subject to an audit trail;
  - there can be no improper influence on tour quality or value through commissions; and
  - tourists are to be alerted to commission shopping venues in their itineraries.

The ADS Code of Business Standards and Ethics is also backed by a compliance and monitoring regime that includes financial and random checks. Penalties for breaches of the Code may include suspension or revocation of an operator's ADS licence. The legal basis for specifying travel agents for the purposes of the ADS is found under the Commonwealth of Australia *Migration Regulations 1994*. As of February 2007 there were 57 travel agents in Australia and 79 travel agents in China recognised under the ADS.

Questions

- The regulation of outbound leisure travel from China is very different from that of developed countries. Explain these differences.
- The Australian ADS provides substantial focus on the ethics of approved operators. What might be the implications of considering the ethics of international trade in tourism services?
- Should human rights violations or lack of democracy in a country be a barrier on establishing links with respect to trade in tourism services?

Numerous multilateral arrangements enable cross-border mobility often through the creation of, in effect, a single domestic space for the purposes of human mobility for citizens of the state parties and/or international visitors. Some of these agreements are identified in Table 2.3. Interestingly, the desire to encourage tourism can be a direct influence on the development of multilateral mobility frameworks. For example, the 2010 FIFA World Cup in South Africa has been a driver for the establishment of the South African Development Community (SADC) Univisa. Similarly, during the hosting of the 2007 Cricket World Cup in the West Indies a CARICOM (Caribbean Community) visa was established for travel

Table 2.3 *Examples of multilateral mobility frameworks*

Multilateral grouping	Members	Mobility	Common visa
CA-4 (Central America)	El Salvador, Guatemala, Honduras, Nicaragua	Citizens of the four countries do not require a passport to travel between any of the four countries with a national ID card being sufficient	Central American Single Visa (Visa Única Centroamericana)
East African Community	Kenya, Tanzania, Uganda	An East African passport can be issued to members of each country for travel within the community. Visas are not required for nationals of the community who use their national passports	East African Single Tourist Visa
ECOWAS (Economic Community of West African States)	Benin, Burkina Faso, Cape Verde, The Gambia, Ghana, Guinea, Guinea Bissau, Ivory Coast, Mali, Niger, Nigeria, Senegal, Sierra Leone, Togo	Citizens of community members do not require a passport to travel between community countries with a national ID card being sufficient	No
EU – European Economic Area(EEA), Schengen Agreement	Most EU states and Iceland, Norway and Switzerland Ireland and the UK only participate in the cross-border policy cooperation measures	The 1985 Schengen Agreement among European states allows for the abolition of systematic border controls between participating countries; includes provisions on a common policy on the temporary entry of persons (including visas), the harmonisation of external border controls, and cross-border police cooperation	Schengen Visa – citizens of non-EU or non EEA countries who wish to visit Europe as tourists can obtain a common Schengen Visa

Continued

Table 2.3 *Continued*

Nordic Passport Union	Denmark, Faroe Islands, Finland, Greenland, Iceland, Norway, Sweden	Any citizen can travel between countries without having passports checked with an ID card being sufficient. Other citizens can also travel between the Nordic countries' borders without having their passport checked, but still have to carry a passport or another kind of approved travel identification papers	Yes, within the context of the Schengen Visa (except the Faroe Islands)
SADC (South African Development Community) (expected to be introduced in 2008)	Angola, Botswana, Democratic Republic of the Congo, Lesotho, Madagascar, Malawi, Mauritius, Mozambique, Namibia, South Africa, Swaziland, Tanzania, Zambia, Zimbabwe	Protocol on the Development of Tourism has the objective of enabling the international and regional entry of visitors	SADC Univisa – Originally intended just for main source markets, it is likely to apply to all long-haul markets by the time of the 2010 FIFA World Cup in South Africa

among the host countries (Antigua and Barbuda, Barbados, Grenada, Guyana, Jamaica, Saint Kitts and Nevis, Saint Lucia, Saint Vincent and the Grenadines, Trinidad and Tobago, and Dominica).

Arguably the most well-known form of multilateral mobility arrangement is the Schengen Agreement in Europe. The Agreement provides for a number of measures with respect to cross-border mobility and control. The Schengen Agreement is significant as it reinforces the connection between human mobility and the circulation and mobility of goods, services and capital as fundamental to European economic development and integration. By signing the Single European Act in 1986 the member states of the EC (the official name of the European Union) agreed to establish a single European market defined as '... an area without internal frontiers in which the free movement of goods, persons, services and capital is ensured ...' (EC 2002: Article 14, Item 2). The Agreement, which went far beyond the already existing freedom of movement of labour, means that all EU citizens have the right '... to move and reside freely within the territory of the Member States ...' (EC 2002: Article 18, Item 1) and is regarded as something of a model with respect to international mobility regimes (see also Chapter 3). Indeed, the relative non-liberalisation of human mobility at a global scale for the international movement of labour and, to a lesser extent, tourism often appears at odds with the attempts to liberalise other economic and social realms (Hatton 2007). However, mobility regimes are not negotiated in isolation and need to be seen as connected to wider discussions of trade in services at an international and supranational scale. Therefore, the next section will examine some of these broader frameworks of liberalising trade.

MULTILATERAL FRAMEWORKS FOR LIBERALISING TRADE IN TOURISM SERVICES

As noted in Chapter 1, arguably the most significant framework for the regulation of tourism services is GATS (Figure 2.2). Liberalising trade in services is designed to allow easier movement of companies, capital and people across boundaries and borders in order to encourage international trade. According to Arkell (2003: 18):

> The liberalisation of tourism is not so much to do with a few restrictive measures relating to tourist guides, but the development of hotels, restaurants, water and electricity supplies, and the liberalisation of a wide range of supporting services, from transport in many forms, to distribution and financial services.

A good example of what developed countries seek to have liberalised for tourism under GATS comes from a December 2000 communication to members of the Council for Trade in Services, in which the US presented its liberalisation agenda for three sub-sectors: hotels and lodging; duty-free services; and the meetings, incentives, conventions and exhibitions (MICE) industry. The US argued that WTO members should place 'no limitations' on market access and national treatment, even though 'some members, including the United States, already have done', and proposed that all members 'consider undertaking additional commitments relating to travellers and international conferences' (WTO 2000: paragraph 5). The 'obstacles' identified by the US with respect to the liberalisation of the tourism and travel sector are listed in Table 2.4. However, in contrast to the position of the US, the developing countries had a substantially different agenda, which can be illustrated by the proposals of Columbia with respect to tourism- and travel-related services (Table 2.5).

Substantial differences exist between developed and developing countries with respect to the international mobility of natural persons (mode 4). Although service liberalisation has tended to focus on issues of cross-border supply (mode 1) and commercial presence (mode 3), developing countries – such as India, Egypt and Thailand – have argued that their service sectors do not have the capital to establish commercial presence abroad but they could supply services via the movement of skilled and unskilled natural persons. Although GATS does not interfere with immigration decisions on economic, health or security grounds, it does provide a framework for negotiating the temporary entry of foreign personnel. However, many countries have declined to apply the GATS non-discrimination clauses because of their arrangements with selected state parties and therefore they restrict

USUAL UNIT OF ANALYSIS

FIRMS

MODE 1 CROSS-BORDER SUPPLY	MODE 3 COMMERCIAL PRESENCE
Service delivered within the territory of Country X, from the territory of Country Y	Service delivered within the territory of Country X, through the commercial presence of the supplier from Country Y
Importance: • professional services • computer services • reservation services • telecommunications • courier and postal services • consultancies	*Importance:* • telecommunications • hospitality services • finance and investment • marketing • environmental services
Measures affecting trade: • commercial presence requirements • residency requirements • citizenship requirements • authorisation and/or licensing requirements • limitations and restrictions on insurance	*Measures affecting trade: restrictions on* • type of legal entity • number of suppliers • participation of foreign capital • discriminatory taxation
MODE 2 CONSUMPTION ABROAD	**MODE 4 PRESENCE OF NATURAL PERSON**
Service delivered outside the territory of Country X, in the territory of Country Y, to a service consumer of Country X	Service delivered within the territory of Country X, with supplier from Country Y present as a natural person
Importance: • tourism consumption and travel	*Importance:* • management, marketing and other professional services • consultancies • construction services
Measures affecting trade: • commercial presence requirements • residency requirements • citizenship requirements • authorisation and/or licensing requirements • limitations and restrictions on insurance • discriminatory taxation	*Measures affecting trade:* • visa and work permit processing delays • quotas and/or restricted entry for some professions • economic needs and market tests • licensing and/or certification requirements • spousal employment or entry conditions • residency and nationality requirements • training, educational and qualification requirements

PERSONS

Service supplier **not present** within the territory of the GATS member (Country X)

Service supplier **present** within the territory of the GATS member (Country X)

Figure 2.2 GATS modes of supply, their significance for tourism and measures affecting them

Table 2.4 *Obstacles to the liberalisation of the travel and tourism sector as identified by the US*

- Overly burdensome exit fees or taxes, or similar restrictions on the departure of outbound travellers.
- Unavailability of information for travellers on applicable duty-free allowances for returning residents on specified merchandise purchased abroad for personal or household uses.
- Limitations on the participation of foreign capital in terms of maximum percentage limit on foreign shareholding or the total value of individual or aggregate foreign investment.
- Measures that restrict or require specific types of corporate, partnership, or other business organisation structure.
- Limitations on the purchase or rental of real estate for this sector.
- Economic needs test on suppliers of hotel and lodging services.
- Suppliers of hotel and lodging services are not permitted to enter into and exit from joint ventures with local or non-local, private or government partners.
- Measures requiring the use of local partner to establish in the market.
- Where government approval is required, exceptionally long delays are encountered and, when approval is denied, no reasons are given for the denial and no information is given on what must be done to obtain approval in the future.
- Lack of national treatment for financing arrangements for construction and operation of hotels and lodging places.
- Denial of access to and use of public services on reasonable and non-discriminatory terms and conditions.
- Denial of access to government programmes available to domestic service providers.
- Tax treatment that discriminates against foreign service providers.
- Discrimination against foreign service suppliers with respect to choice of business organisations available to domestic suppliers.
- Discrimination against foreign partners in a joint venture.
- Discrimination against franchises as opposed to other forms of business organisation.
- Discrimination against foreign franchises.
- Lack of readily available information on zoning and lack of an opportunity for service suppliers to meet with local officials and community representatives to discuss location of facilities.
- Lack of transparency of domestic laws and regulations and fairness of administration.
- Denial of full consumer access to electronic means for making hotel reservations.
- Denial of freedom for service providers to select sources of supply of services.
- Denial of freedom for service providers to offer incentives, rewards and other promotional programmes.
- Minimum requirements for local hiring that are disproportionately high, causing uneconomic operations.
- Lack of means to facilitate temporary entry and exit of specialised, skilled personnel (including managers).
- Restrictions or excessive fees/taxes on international currency transactions.

Continued

Table 2.4 *Continued*

- Lack of means to facilitate temporary entry and exit of event organisers and specialised, skilled personnel (including managers) needed to conduct international conferences and conventions efficiently.
- Restrictions or excessive fees/taxes on licensing or royalty payments.
- Lack of means to facilitate temporary entry and exit of conference and convention participants from various countries.
- Information on provisions for temporary entry and exit of equipment, supplies and other materials are not made readily available to organisers of prospective international conferences and conventions.

Source: Adapted from WTO (2001: paragraph 6).

Table 2.5 *Proposals with respect to the liberalisation of the travel and tourism sector as identified by Columbia*

- Full commitments should be adopted under the consumption abroad and commercial presence modes of supply, which would promote two-way tourism.
- Restrictions involving an economic needs test to gain market access to tourism-related activities should be eliminated.
- Given that the provision of such services depends on the cross-border movement of persons, members should endeavour to ensure that their migration authorities facilitate such movement.
- Market access conditions under the presence of natural persons mode of supply should be improved in order to facilitate the temporary entry of natural persons supplying services in this sector.
- The competent authorities should take account of professional qualifications related to tourism services acquired in the territory of another member, on the basis of equivalency of education and using qualification recognition methods.
- Anti-competitive behaviour by dominant operators can result in imbalances in the framework of liberalised trade in services.
- The existing classification of trade in tourism and travel-related services should be revised to include all services characteristic of this sector.

Source: WTO (2001: paragraphs 4–10).

access of natural persons from certain countries who might otherwise be able to provide services (WTO 1996).

Despite the role of tourism in all of the different modes of trade in services, particularly its overt role in mode 2, the place of tourism in GATS negotiations is therefore at times almost as problematic as the pace at which agreements are reached within the WTO (Hall 2008). For example, with respect to the UNWTO's proposed annex on tourism to GATS, the EC (i.e. the EU, sometimes referred to as European Communities) was the only WTO member to formally submit a reaction to the proposed Annex. Although the EC stated its support for 'the main intentions' of the proposal, it did not explicitly endorse the establishment of a new Tourism Annex to the GATS. Instead, the EC proposed that the list of sectors proposed to be included in the Annex were too broad. Furthermore, it noted that air transport services were currently excluded from the GATS negotiations (at present GATS only applies to: (1) aircraft repair and maintenance services, (2) the selling and marketing of air transport services, and (3) computer reservations system (CRS) services. All traffic rights and directly related aviation transport activities are excluded), and that some of the issues raised by the sponsors could be better addressed in the WTO's Working Party on Domestic Regulation (WPDR) (Dunlop 2003).

The GATS Article on Domestic Regulation (Article VI) has been described as the 'cornerstone of the GATS structure. Disciplines on domestic measures that affect trade in services form the *raison d'être* of the GATS' (Arkell 2003: 10). Under GATS a 'measure' is defined as any measure by a member, whether in the form of a law, regulation, rule, procedure, decision, administrative action, or any other form (Article XXVIII (a)). The Article therefore focuses attention on the sovereign right of nation-states to regulate against restricting trade in services as little as possible.

Interestingly, in terms of issues of sustainable tourism, Dunlop (2003: 10) also noted that the EC, along with the United States, suggested that sustainable development needed to be considered within the proposed UNWTO Annex, with the EC stressing 'the importance of access to high-quality environmental services – a key offensive negotiating interest for the EC (and US) in the GATS negotiations' which would have significant impacts in a wide range of countries with respect to tourism trade with the EU. In addition, the EC sought to use any Annex to eliminate restrictions on foreign direct investment in tourism. Nevertheless, it is apparent that there is a wide gulf between the developed and the developing countries with respect to sector liberalisation, with developing countries seeking more gradual liberalisation strategies in particular out of concern over the extent to which international destinations in their countries may be subject to the dominant market position of international airlines and tour operators (PATA 2004) as well as their inability to gain concessions with respect to the movement of natural persons (mode 4). Indeed, many developing countries are arguing that no agreement is better than a bad one and that therefore 'many developing countries are turning to regional and bilateral free trade agreements, which they believe allow them to liberalise trade and services in a more progressive manner without unnecessary external pressure and in a way more suited to local conditions' (PATA 2004: 4).

An example of a multilateral move towards the liberalisation of tourism services at the supranational level is that of Asia-Pacific Economic Cooperation (APEC). The Seoul Declaration on an APEC Tourism Charter that was announced at the first APEC meeting of tourism ministers in 2000 in South Korea established four policy goals:

1 remove impediments to tourism business and investment;
2 increase mobility of visitors and demand for tourism goods and services in the APEC region;
3 sustainably manage tourism outcomes and impacts; and
4 enhance recognition and understanding of tourism as a vehicle for economic and social development.

(Paraphrased from APEC 2000)

The first two goals are particularly significant with respect to the liberalisation of trade. The removal of impediments should be achieved by

- promoting and facilitating the mobility of skills, training and labour;
- promoting and facilitating productive investment in tourism and associated sectors;
- removing regulatory impediments to tourism business and investment; and
- encouraging liberalization of services trade related to tourism under the GATS.

(APEC 2000: paragraph 16, a–d)

Simultaneously, increasing mobility and demand would be undertaken by

- facilitating seamless travel for visitors;
- enhancing visitor experiences;
- promoting inter- and intra-regional marketing opportunities and cooperation;
- facilitating and promoting e-commerce for tourism business;
- enhancing safety and security of visitors; and
- fostering a non-discriminatory approach to the provision of visitor facilities and services.

(APEC 2000: paragraph 17, a–f)

Although progress in the Asia-Pacific region with respect to these goals has been slow, some progress has been made. For example, APEC has created an APEC Business Travel Card (ABTC) which is designed to facilitate short-term entry through pre-clearance measures. As of the beginning of 2007, 17 APEC member economies participated in the scheme: Australia, Brunei Darussalam, Chile, China, Hong Kong (China SAR (special autonomous region)), Indonesia, Japan, Korea, Malaysia, New Zealand, Papua New Guinea, Peru, the Philippines, Singapore, Chinese Taipei, Thailand and Viet Nam. Of course, such measures also raise questions as to why they privilege only a small proportion of the travelling population, an issue discussed further in Chapter 3.

However, another key issue, often missed in discussion of international tourism policy (Hall 2007), is that it is extremely difficult to separate the tourism services policy arena from other policy areas related to such issues as migration or international trade in general (Figure 2.3). Indeed, tourism policy per se only represents a very small proportion of the overall number of policy fields that affect tourism and for which decisions are made often with little consideration of the impacts on trade in tourism services. Arguably, such a situation provides another reason for the adoption of a broader international business perspective with respect to international tourism development rather than identifying explanations of tourism change solely with the decisions of tourism organisations.

This is not to deny the significance of such tourism-specific bodies, such as the UNWTO, but to highlight that their overall influence on trade discussions is actually quite limited although their position usually does serve to reinforce broader moves for liberalisation. For example, the UNWTO (2003: 1) argues that it is seeking 'liberalisation with a human face' while seeking 'full inclusion of tourism in commercial growth in developing and

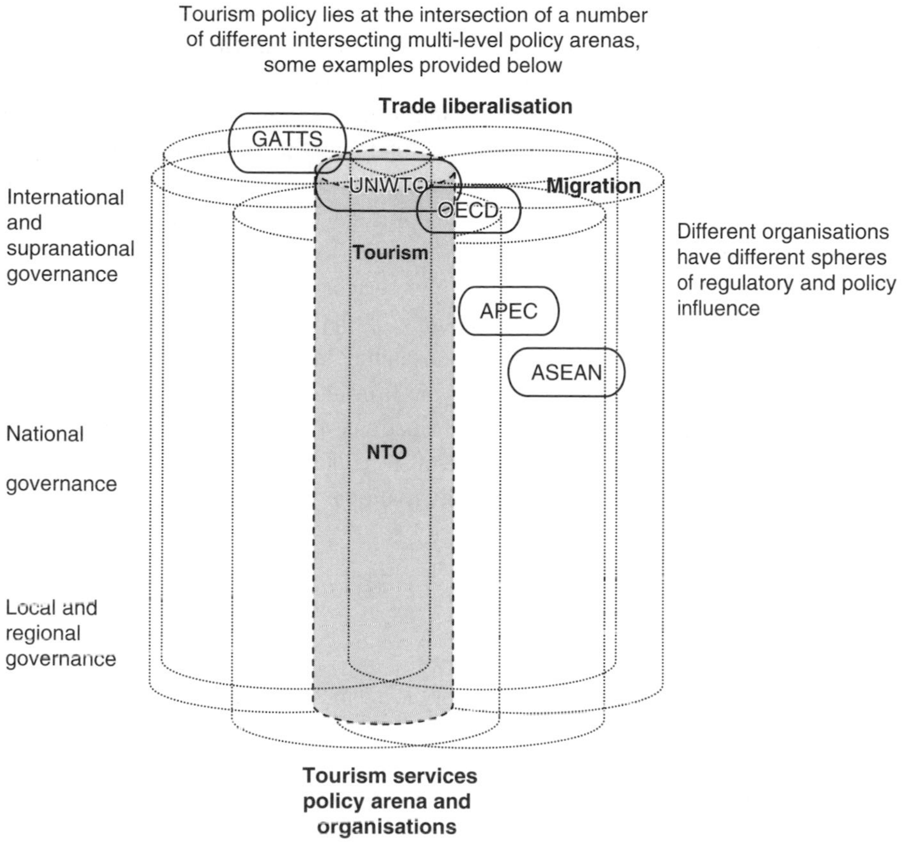

Tourism policy lies at the intersection of a number
of different intersecting multi-level policy arenas,
some examples provided below

Figure 2.3 *Multilayered tourism governance*

developed markets'. Indeed, critical areas for future tourism research are the organisational and political relationships between the various international tourism bodies such as the UNWTO, World Travel and Tourism Council (WTTC) and Pacific Asia Travel Association (PATA), which are poorly understood, as well as the relationships of these bodies to others in the network of organisations working towards the liberalisation of trade in services – such as the OECD and the World Economic Forum – and the supranational bodies associated with regional trading blocs, such as ASEAN (Hall 2008).

CONCLUSION

This chapter has provided an overview of some of the issues with respect to the regulation of tourism-related international mobility. A key point is that there is no right under international law to 'be a tourist' and visit a foreign country. Such an observation is extremely significant given the lack of attention in tourism studies to the regulation of individual mobility and the constraints that this imposes on international tourism and therefore trade in tourism services. Such issues of citizenship and mobility are further taken up in the following chapter.

Although there are no global *de jure* rights to mobility in international law, a range of bilateral and multilateral frameworks serve to enable individuals to participate in international travel and companies to engage in the international business of tourism and travel services. At a global scale most significant of these is the GATS, but several other supranational agreements are important for trade and mobility. The chapter has also highlighted that there are substantial differences in focus between the developed and developing countries on the best way to proceed to the liberalisation of trade in tourism and travel services. Developed countries seek greater access for investment while the developing countries desire access for their service workers and they have further concerns over the impacts on their destinations of the market power of transnational and foreign firms. Such issues will have substantial implications for the structure of international trade in tourism at the level of the firm and the mobility of individuals as well as significant effects on the viability of destinations. Yet, as this chapter has also noted, the understanding of such issues in political terms lies not so much in the realms of tourism policy but in a broader appreciation of the international business dimensions of trade in services.

Discussion questions

- Is there such a thing as a right to engage in international tourism?
- What are the main differences between the focus of the developed and developing countries with respect to liberalisation of tourism under GATS?
- What are the relative advantages of bilateral and multilateral agreements for countries seeking to pursue the liberalisation of tourism and travel services?

REFERENCES

APEC (2000) first APEC Tourism Ministerial Meeting, the First APEC Meeting of Ministers Responsible for Tourism 7 July 2000, Seoul, Korea, Seoul Declaration on an APEC Tourism Charter, A Ministerial Statement of Purposes and Intent.

Arkell, J. (2003) 'Background paper on GATS issues'. Paper presented at Commonwealth Business Council, *Symposium on Trade Policy Challenges in East Asia: The New Regionalism and the WTO*, Singapore 20 February, Landon: Commonwealth Business council.

Chandler, D. (2003) 'New rights for old? Cosmopolitan citizenship and the critique of state sovereignty', *Political Studies*, 51(2): 332–49.

Coles, T.E. and Timothy, D.J. (2004) '"My field is the world": conceptualising diaspora, travel and tourism,' in T.E. Coles and D.J. Timothy (eds) *Tourism, Diasporas and Space*. London: Routledge.

Collinson, S. (1996) 'Visa requirements, carrier sanctions, safe third countries and readmission – the development of an asylum buffer zone in Europe', *Transactions of the Institute of British Geographers*, 21(1): 76–90.

DITR (Department of Industry, Tourism and Research) (2006) *A Strengthened China ADS Scheme – Key Facts*. Canberra: DITR.

—— (2007) *China Approved Destination Status (ADS) Scheme*. Online. Available from: http://www.nml.csiro. au/content/itrinternet/cmscontent.cfm?objectid=8406AE50-65BF-4956-BA90AC2C508A80DC&search ID=279099 (accessed: 20/06/07).

Dunlop, A. (2003) *Tourism Services Negotiation Issues: Implications for Cariform Countries*. Barbados: Caribbean Regional Negotiating Machinery.

Dunn, J. (ed.) (1995) *Contemporary Crisis of the Nation-state*. Oxford: Blackwell.

EC (2002) Consolidated version of the treaty establishing the European Community. *Official Journal of the European Communities*, 24 December 2002, C325: 33–184. Online. Available from: http://europa.eu.int/eur-lex/en/treaties/dat/EC_consol.pdf (accessed: 01/04/07).

Hall. C.M. (2006) 'Human mobility: barriers, constraints and "open borders"', paper presented at Tourism and Travel Research Association, Dublin, June 2006.

—— (2007) 'Tourism, governance and the (mis-)location of power', in A. Church and T.E. Coles (eds) *Tourism, Power and Space*. London: Routledge.

—— (2008) *Tourism Planning*, 2nd edn. Harlow: Prentice Hall.

Hatton, T.J. (2007) 'Should we have a WTO for international migration?', *Economic Policy*, 22(50): 339–83.

Hess, J.M. (2006) 'Statelessness and the state: Tibetans, citizenship, and national activism in a transnational world', *International Migration*, 44(1): 79–103.

Hugo, G. (2006) 'An Australian diaspora?', *International Migration*, 44(1): 105–33.

Karkkainen, B.C. (2004) 'Post-sovereign environmental governance', *Global Environmental Politics*, 4(1): 72–96.

King, B., Dwyer, L. and Prideaux, B. (2006) 'An evaluation of unethical business practices in Australia's China inbound tourism market', *International Journal of Tourism Research*, 8(2): 127–42.

Majone, G. (1996) *Regulating Europe*. London: Routledge.

Milward, A.S., Sorensen, V. and Ranieri, R. (1993) *The Frontier of National Sovereignty*. London: Routledge.

Milward, H.B. and Provan, K.G. (2000) 'Governing the hollow state', *Journal of Public Administration Research and Theory*, 10(1): 359–80.

Morales-Moreno, I. (2004) 'Postsovereign governance in a globalizing and fragmenting world: the case of Mexico', *Review of Policy Research* 21(1): 107–17.

PATA (2004), 'WTO tourism negotiations: steady does it' *PATA Issues and Trends*, December.

Peters, B.G. (1998) *Globalization, Institutions and Governance*. Jean Monnet Chair Paper RSC No. 98/51. Florence: European University Institute.

Ryan, B. (2001) 'The Common Travel Area between Britain and Ireland', *Modern Law Review*, 64(6): 855–74.

Shie, T.S. (2007) 'Rising Chinese influence in the South Pacific: Beijing's "island fever"', *Asian Survey*, 47(2): 307–26.

Thunø, M. (2003) 'Channels of entry and preferred destinations: the circumvention of Denmark by Chinese immigrants', *International Migration*, 41(3): 99–133.

United Nations (1948) *Universal Declaration of Human Rights, Adopted and Proclaimed by General Assembly Resolution 217 A (III) of 10 December 1948*. New York: United Nations. Online. Available from: http://daccessdds.un.org/doc/RESOLUTION/GEN/NR0/043/88/IMG/NR004388.pdf?OpenElement.

—— (2001) *Global Code of Ethics for Tourism*, A/RES/56/212. New York: United Nations.

UNWTO (2003) 'Liberalization with a human face: poverty elimination, fair trade & sustainable tourism', *WTO News*, 1st quarter(1): 1.

Wallace, W. (1999) 'Europe after the Cold War: interstate order or post-sovereign regional system?', *Review of International Studies*, 25: 201–23.

Windybank, S. (2005) 'The China syndrome', *Policy*, 21(2): 28–33.

WTO(1996) Press brief: movement of natural persons. Online. Available from: http://www.wto.org/English/thewto_e/minist_e/min96_e/natpers.htm (accessed: 01/04/07).

—— (2000) *Communication from the United States: Tourism and Hotels*. Council for Trade in Services, Special Session, 18 December 2000 (00-5572) WTO S/CSS/W/31.

—— (2001) *Communication from Columbia: Tourism and Travel-related Services*. Council for Trade in Services, Special Session, 27 November 2001 (01-6056), WTO S/CSS/W/122.

Zhang, W. and Han, Y. (2004) 'An analysis on China's international tourism development and regional cooperation', *Conference Proceedings, The Sixth Asian Development Research Forum General Meeting*, The Siam City Hotel, Bangkok, Thailand, 7–8 June 2004.

Citizenship and the state: hidden features in the internationalisation of tourism

3

Tim Coles

Learning objectives

After considering this chapter, you will be able to:

- recognise many features of the complex relationship between tourism, citizenship and international business;
- understand citizenship as a central construct in contemporary international mobility;
- identify how the state and a range of other actors work to shape tourism mobilities.

Key terms

- citizenship;
- state;
- sub-state actors;
- medical tourism;
- tourism citizens.

INTRODUCTION: CITIZENSHIP AS A HIDDEN COMPONENT IN MOBILITY

August 2006 saw another round of chaos at British airports. Following tip-offs of alleged bomb plots to attack transatlantic airliners, the government introduced new restrictions on hand-luggage and other security measures with immediate effect. Thousands of travellers were rendered temporally immobile, as long cues formed, flights were missed, and holidays were ruined. As the crisis deepened, airline executives started to question the handling of the affair. At one point, Michael O'Leary, the chief executive of the low-cost carrier, Ryanair, threatened to sue the British government over an alleged loss of earnings (BBC 2006a).

The 2006 crisis highlights how many tourists largely take for granted their rights of travel and their responsibilities to other travellers, the airlines and national governments, and how the state often operates in concert with a number of other actors to choreograph their movements around the world. In an age of deregulated border controls, it is often tempting to stress their potentials for movement while overlooking immobility. As subject areas, international business and tourism are inherently interested in mobility, but by and large they fail to recognise the importance of citizenship as a catalyst for or retardant of temporary migratory flows. This is despite some recent discussion of the concept in studies of human mobility (Urry 2000; Coles and Timothy 2004; Molz 2005).

This chapter explores the relationship between tourism, citizenship and international business. Four interlinked arguments are presented here. The first and most important is simply that contemporary studies of international tourism and international business cannot continue to overlook the significance of citizenship as a social construct. Linked to this is the basic and perhaps somewhat obvious observation that citizenship is a vital feature in shaping an individual's mobility in relative terms. Third, contemporary citizenship is best thought of as a multi-layered concept. It is no longer possible to talk of a person's citizenship in a singular sense, but rather of 'citizenships' plural. More orthodox forms of state-based citizenship are being supplemented by new types of citizenship that reflect changing social conditions. Individuals increasingly belong to more than one group, and such multiple memberships are conveniently deployed in the traveller's best interests. Finally and perhaps most contentiously, there are new forms of citizenship directly related to tourism, and which in turn further facilitate travel experiences. These are mediated by a number of different actors. These include the state as a traditional focal point for citizenship studies as well as supranational bodies and sub-state actors such as businesses, local and regional governments. The first part of the chapter explores how citizenship has been conceptualised in the social sciences and how traditional politico-legal forms of citizenship based on the state as a construct orchestrate human mobility and tourism flows. In the second half of the chapter, the discussion progresses to examine the ways in which international businesses as sub-state actors interact with the state to deliver new forms of tourism-orientated citizenships as well as new and modified forms of visitor flows.

CITIZENSHIP: SOME CONCEPTUAL FOUNDATIONS

There have been a number of historical forms of citizenship from the Ancient Greeks and Romans through the Republican models in Revolutionary France and America to the present day (Heater 2004). Nevertheless, some of the most influential, enduring and now highly contested views of citizenship are Marshall's ([1950], 1992). He identified three forms of citizenship and their historical appearance. Civil citizenship emerged in the eighteenth century and established basic rights to individual freedom such as property ownership, personal liberty and justice; political citizenship was a product of the nineteenth century and resulted in the right to rights to participate in elections to institutions that exercise power; and social citizenship was seen as first an essentially twentieth-century phenomenon that involved rights to economic welfare, security, social heritage and a socially acceptable way of life. These forms of citizenship materialised sequentially and Marshall evidenced the third form of citizenship in the rise of the welfare state in Britain.

Marshall's views on citizenship reflected their appearance in the immediate aftermath of the Second World War, and they had their origins in the inter-war Modernist belief that in some way society could be understood and managed scientifically like an organisation. By the application of a series of laws and principles the behaviour of the population could in some way be engineered and regulated. Crucially, the state was the central institution around which social life was organised. First and foremost the state played several civic roles and it provided an array of amenities and services that would allow people to conduct their lives. The state provided justice, means of exchange, defence, health and welfare support. In exchange, individual subjects were expected to demonstrate their loyalty to, and subscribe to the principles of the state; in other words, rights were accompanied by responsibilities. The changing nature of citizenship even formed part of the framework for early travel. Social reform and legislation in the United Kingdom, such as the 1938 Holidays with Pay Act, ensured statutory paid-holiday entitlements for workers as a right. Nationalised (i.e. state-run) public transport systems conveyed newly empowered working-class tourists to growing resorts on the coast. At the international scale, passports and systems of entry and exit visa became necessary travel documents in the late nineteenth and early twentieth centuries.

Passports offered citizens the prospect of travelling abroad with a semblance of legal protection based on their citizenship, as the text on the inside page of the UK passport makes clear even today:

> Her Britannic Majesty's Secretary of State Requests and requires in the Name of Her Majesty all those whom it may concern to allow the bearer to pass freely without let or hindrance, and to afford the bearer such assistance and protection as may be necessary.

Interestingly, in most states citizens do not own their passports; rather, the passport remains the property of the state. This is despite the fact that over time the passport will increasingly contain a wealth of biometric data specific to the individual who is entrusted with its safekeeping usually to its expiry (i.e. return and/or renewal). The passport can be withdrawn at any time by the state, in particular where a citizen's rights to travel have been revoked. For instance, British soccer hooligans convicted in court (as an apparatus of the civic state) had their passports withdrawn before and during the 2006 FIFA World Cup to prevent them from travelling to Germany as 'sports tourists' (Harding and Culf 2006). Thus, citizenship can be used as much as an instrument to render people immobile as to encourage mobility (see Hall Chapter 2). In some European states, such as National Socialist Germany in the 1930s and 1940s (Semmens 2005), exit visas were used to prevent citizens from leaving. Even now British citizens need an exit visa to depart Russia (and states of the former Soviet Union) although this is usually granted at the same time as an entry visa.

Marshall's work retains some significance because it articulates several basic conceptual building blocks of citizenship (rights, duties, responsibilities, membership, participation, awareness), although its relevance is sometimes questionable in light of recent transformations of society, economy and polity. For Isin and Wood (1999: 4), modern citizenship is no longer exclusively tied to membership of a nation-state; that is, restricted to 'legal obligations and entitlements which individuals possess by virtue of their membership in a state'. Citizenship is a more complex form of identity which is distinctive because it is based on reciprocal social relations and common interests among a particular group. Pearson (2002) notes that in Marshall's view nation and state were mutually implicated, with ethnic or national identity taken for granted and differences in society overlooked. Today citizenship functions in a more complex array of spatial arrangements. For Murphy and Harty (2003), citizenship rights may exist at the sub-state level, in particular for national groups denied state representation. Schattle (2005) discusses the concept of 'global citizenship' and the emergence of a number of social groups brought together by an awareness of, and a collective interdependency with respect to, issues played out at a global scale (see also Urry 2000). Tambini (2001) argues that globalisation has challenged the traditional role and status of national citizenship. Instead, rights associated with social group membership can in fact exist across state boundaries; that is, citizenship beyond the state, or 'post-sovereign citizenship' because it is no longer institutions with sovereignty over a territory that exclusively ascribe rights and responsibilities.

According to Isin and Wood (1999: 4) one of the most problematic features of the Marshallian view is its dominant focus on the political and the legal. Instead, they point to the importance of citizenship as 'an articulating principle for the recognition of group rights ...' and in addition to polity-based views, this perspective opens the way for the conceptualisation of contemporary citizenship as 'the practices through which individuals and groups formulate and claim new rights or struggle to expand or maintain existing rights'. Thus, Isin and Wood (1999) identify an array of other alternative social groups in contemporary global society, not necessarily bound to a state or territory, which have common features of group membership, behaviour and reciprocal relations, including those participating in diasporic and aboriginal citizenship, sexual citizenship, cosmopolitan citizenship and cultural citizenship. Among the latter group and of particular interest here, they identify the existence groups of consumer citizens who are defined by their rights to consume goods and services. Of course, ethnicity and lifestyle widely conceived are just as valid as legal constructs in constituting citizenship, and it is possible to have multiple belongings to more than one citizenship group. Terms such as 'expanded citizenship' (van Steenbergen 1994: 6) or 'civic cosmopolitanism' encapsulate the notion that individuals participate in a number of citizenships simultaneously, and these identities may be either mutually inclusive or, alternatively, contradictory and difficult to reconcile with one another. The next section of this chapter considers the way in which multiple citizenships are deployed and have been resolved to result in distinctive temporary mobility flows associated with European Union (EU) enlargement.

DUALITY OF CITIZENSHIP AND EVOLVING MOBILITY FLOWS IN THE NEW EUROPE

On 1 May 2004, ten new member states – Cyprus, Czech Republic, Estonia, Hungary, Latvia, Lithuania, Malta, Poland, Slovakia and Slovenia – were admitted to the EU in the latest but largest of a series of expansion episodes. At a stroke the EU population expanded by 75 million people to 430 million in total. Within the EU, it is not only the individual member state that is responsible for bestowing rights on its citizens, but also the EU. That is, EU citizens share certain additional common rights of freedom of movement, justice, trade and defence with their fellow citizens in other countries by virtue of birth or domicile in the EU. In terms of tourism and mobility, the dual nature of EU citizenship has two important consequences. First, as Verstraete (2002) has pointed out, freedom of movement is seen as a fundamental right and hence travel is one of the more obvious ways in which many citizens experience the union and its benefits. Travel restrictions, such as those connected to the Schengen Zone, can have a similar but opposite effect. Thus, second, while citizenship can introduce new travel potentials, it can simultaneously frustrate movement and as a result induce new differential travel flows. In reasserting their own power, legitimacy and sovereignty over the EU as a supranational body, EU states have ultimate control over whether individuals have access to or must relinquish those rights. Dunkerley *et al.* (2002: 20) suggest that the so-called 'principal of subsidiarity' functions so that EU citizenship is intended to complement, not replace national citizenship. In so doing, it creates two groups of EU citizens through residence with respect to tourism and mobility: those who may benefit from freedom of movement and those who may not (because other states opt out of deregulation).

After enlargement, not only did citizens of the ten so-called accession states (AC10) enjoy citizenship rights in their own countries, but new rights were bestowed on them as EU citizens. As a result, EU leaders made general forecasts of the restructuring of visitor flows in the months following enlargement (Coles and Hall 2005). Cyprus and Malta were exceptions as established destinations. In principle, citizens of both old and new member states would find it easier to travel to previously restricted destinations in the former socialist states, while AC10 citizens were offered the prospect of travel westwards. For western Europeans, this was the final and conclusive evidence that the Iron Curtain had fallen once and for all. Within Britain, the travel media extolled the virtues of Tallinn, Vilnius, Riga and Prague which were earmarked as potential venues for excessive, hedonistic yet cheap 'stag' and 'hen' parties (Coles 2007). Bratislava, the capital of Slovakia, was portrayed as a low-cost alternative to nearby Vienna, while Slovenia was extolled for its similarity to nearby Austria and Italy but with its far more favourable prices. The economic conditions in the eastern states (as well as the Balkans), were perceived to offer British citizens new opportunities to buy second homes. Affordable and appropriate properties in traditional destinations such as Spain, Portugal and France were argued to have become scarce. Given their new rights of movement and abode in AC10 states, moves to harmonise market regulations, the cheapness and supply of potential homes, the new locations were seen as highly desirable for British (as well as other northern European) citizens. Moreover, they could access some of cheapest and most effective health care services and clinics in Europe (see Coles and Hall 2005; Coles 2007).

For citizens of old member states, rights were stressed over responsibilities, and rights delivered new opportunities for consumption; new modes of community living and participation as second-home owners; and financial empowerment because their properties would appreciate as the AC10 markets were forecast to grow in the coming years. For citizens of the new member states, the situation was quite the reverse. Responsibilities were stressed over rights and responsibilities were used as a means of blocking travel to the new member states. As argued elsewhere in detail (Coles 2007), only in summer 2003 did many member states start to consider the implications of enlargement for east–west visitor flows. The AC10 states were, and remain, considerably poorer than the old member states, and it was argued that this would lead to large-scale (temporary) migratory flows from countries such as Poland, the Czech Republic, Slovakia and the Baltic States. Workers would head west to find work, earn as much money as they needed personally and to remit back home, and then they would return home. This would constitute a form of business tourism, labour tourism or a form of longer 'working holiday' (see Chapter 10) that may last, on and off, for a year or two. Skilled workers and artisans, not just unskilled labourers, would chase the economic dream, with the result that the economies of the AC10 states may be further disadvantaged by a 'brain drain'.

Many old member states enacted legislation, as was their right under the Treaty of Accession (i.e. subsidiarity), to limit mobility until 2011; that is, restrictions were placed to limit free movement for AC10 citizens. Eventually, the United Kingdom government followed suit in spring 2004. It could not be sure how many people would come, how long they would stay, and what pressure they put on the welfare state and other services. Moreover, the UK was perceived to be especially popular with AC10 citizens because its economy was performing strongly and access to its welfare state was relatively open. In certain alarmist accounts, hordes of gypsies were reported to be sweeping west to take advantage of 'roads paved in gold'. Other estimates varied between 5,000 and 40,000 migrants for the year after enlargement (see Coles 2007). These were intended to add a degree of statistical legitimacy to the view that the UK would be popular with so-called 'benefit tourists':

> Benefit tourism is the English name given by Britain's prime minister Tony Blair to the perceived threat that after May 1, 2004, huge masses of citizens from the European Union's ten new membership countries would invade the previous fifteen member states only to benefit from their generous social welfare systems. This threat has been used as a motivation for some (initial, temporary) restrictions in the free movement of labour within the union.
>
> (Cited in Coles 2007)

As the then UK Home Secretary (Interior Minister), David Blunkett, put it, the government was determined not to allow AC10 citizens to exercise their new-found privileges without first considering the implications for British citizens: 'They cannot draw down on benefits without contributing themselves to the rights and entitlements which should go hand in hand with the responsibilities and duties' (in Mason *et al.* 2004: n.p.). Thus, in the case of new EU citizens, their citizenship and the simple likelihood that they would most probably travel after enlargement, was used in the UK as a justification to regulate their tourism mobilities. The supposition that they would then impact on the ability of UK citizens to enjoy the services they paid for as taxpayers, made the case for limitation all the more compelling for the opponents of European integration. As noted above, these discussions were not restricted to the UK. Other countries enacted similar restrictive legislative measures. In the case of the UK, the debate was arguably higher profile and more drawn out (Coles 2007). In terms of mapping out tourism flows, to calculate the precise effect of this imbalance in granting rights of movement is immensely problematic; although the discourses appear to suggest it was easier for old EU citizens to make temporary movements to the east, we have little in the way of precise data on what has actually happened since enlargement either across the continent or alternatively with respect to particular (macro-)destinations such as the UK. The *Financial Times* reported in 2005 that it is in fact difficult to evaluate whether the invasion of benefit tourists to the UK did in fact take place (George *et al.* 2005). What we can say with some certainty is that the UK government learned its lessons. In the case of the accession of Rumania and Bulgaria in 2007, it acted early to put in a strict quota system to limit the number of visitors of various types from these even poorer eastern European states (BBC 2006b).

NEW MOBILITIES OF TOURISM CITIZENSHIPS

Traditional, politico-legal views of citizenship centred on the state are clearly relevant features in determining visitor flows, as the recent case of EU enlargement demonstrates. However, this case is also important because it offers some empirical clues as to the role of new forms of post-modern citizenship specifically involving, or organised around, tourism and mobility.

British second-home owners could be also described as one subset of an increasingly significant type of consumer citizens, post-sovereign in nature (Hall and Müller 2004). In the new vocabulary, like 'round-the-world' travellers (Molz 2005, see also Chapter 10), they may even be identified as a group of 'tourism citizens', the commonality between whom is the expression of their particular rights to travel, the distinctive form of their travel and their obligations to others in civic society. In this particular instance, membership is defined by those who exercise their dual rights of movement; who take advantage of cheap, frequent, short-haul flights; and who are in the financial position to be able to run two domiciles. Their ability to switch homes at frequent intervals and their peripatetic existence between states and communities sets them apart from other social groups. For some weeks of the year they take advantage of their basic rights to amenities as United Kingdom citizens in the first instance. They exercise their rights to free movement in the EU and reciprocal arrangements of access to welfare and other services in states where their second homes are located. They are bound by responsibilities to recognise and uphold the regulations of two states and a supranational body.

Medical tourists as 'tourism citizens'

In the case of second-home owners, it is primarily state-to-state relations that facilitate the temporary sojourns. The concept of the state *per se* is not challenged because the state in both locations provides an adequate framework of resources and services to support life in both destinations. Nevertheless, it is possible to identify other groups of 'tourism citizens' distinguished by their travel preferences, consumer behaviours and their collective understandings of their rights.

Estimates suggest that medical tourism accounts for 19 million trips or about 2.5 per cent of all international tourism, with earnings of US$20 billion a year (TRAM 2006: 59).

In the past this travel may have been solely for surgery or treatment before returning home (Connell 2006; TRAM 2006). The latest trend has been for patients to access more sophisticated, integrative tourism products in which their treatments are followed (and in some cases preceded) by a period of recuperation in attractive destinations with high-quality accommodation, amenities and hospitality services. All the stereotypical features of a holiday are integrated in an experience primarily intended for remedying ailments. Sophisticated packages of several weeks or months have been developed by international hospitals, clinics and medical companies which in some cases are in diagonally integrated groups, or which in other cases enter into strategic alliances with preferred providers of accommodation, hospitality and transport services. As the marketing brochure for Phuket Heath and Travel Co. Ltd (PHT), a prominent market player, makes clear:

> Our philosophy is to select and determine the very best products and services in the travel and health industries for our clientele at all times ... . Appreciating that this niche market requires a dedicated and highly professional team in both the medical and travel industries, PHT is clearly positioned as a unique travel facilitator, which can combine activities for a memorable holiday with world-class medical care – all in the midst of the blue skies, white sandy beaches and pristine waters of the island of Phuket located in the South of Thailand.
>
> (PHT undated: 2)

Several motives have driven the strong recent growth of medical tourism. Price differentials between countries for similar procedures have allowed patients to shop around for the best treatment at the optimal price (see Table 3.1). Expensive private treatments, medical insurance that excludes the less well-off, and the lack of universal health care provision among their bundles of rights has prompted many US and Canadian citizens to become medical tourists (Adams 2005). Dissatisfied citizens become medical tourists in their desire to receive quicker treatments and because of their willingness to pay where the state is perceived to fail. Long waiting lists in certain countries for sometimes life-saving procedures have reportedly forced some to seek help overseas. Although British citizens have access to the National Health Service (NHS) – a universal and free at the point of delivery service – the standard of, and waiting time for, treatment has been perceived as inferior to other countries (Ramesh 2005). Others have travelled to receive treatments that are currently

Table 3.1 *The comparative cost of private health care treatments in selected international markets*

State	Type of medical intervention		
	Heart bypass	Hip replacement	Cataract operation
UK	£15,000	£9,000	£2,900
France	£13,000	£7,600	£1,000
US	£13,250	£15,900	£2,120
India	£4,300	£3,180	£660

Source: Adapted from Ramesh (2005).
Note: All prices in GB£ at 2005 prices.

outlawed or heavily regulated in their home states, perhaps because of religious doctrines or for medical reasons such as fears of a potential public health risk. For instance, 'xeno tourists' travel to obtain medical procedures involving the transplantation of living animal cells, tissues or organs into a human recipient (Cooke *et al.* 2005). In the Republic of Ireland – where abortions have been declared illegal except where the mother's life may be threatened – women travelling to have abortions in the UK or elsewhere in Europe have been labelled 'abortion tourists'. Finally, some parents and single women travel to external states specifically to give birth in the hope and expectation that that specific citizenship rights will be conferred on their newborns under *jus soli* ('birthright citizenship'). In recent times some states such as Ireland have legislated to curb 'birthright tourism' (BBC 2004), while in the United States, another preferred destination, a solution has been more difficult to find because of the constitutional position.

Irrespective of the type of medically motivated tourism, several sub-state actors simultaneously have taken advantage of the inability of a state to deliver adequate welfare services, and the willingness of citizens to exercise their rights as consumers to travel for medical interventions. Indeed, arguably there is a second level of exploitation by the sub-state actors. One of the main ethical discussions concerns what happens if anything goes wrong, and who is responsible – financially, morally and/or legally – for sorting it out? Sub-state actors attempt to dodge these difficult questions by extolling the success rates of their procedures in order to allay the concerns of potential customers (Ramesh 2005). However, no surgical procedure has a 100 per cent success rate. British citizens could refer themselves to the NHS which has a duty of care to treat them; however, because their new ailment was caused by treatment overseas (for which they paid independently and in which the NHS played no direct role), the question is whether it is right for the state to provide remedial treatments to address the complications resulting from private 'care'? After all, it is taxpayers who are ultimately picking up the bill, a substantial majority of which chose not to, or are unable to afford to, travel for treatment.

The relationship between state and sub-state actors is complex. Rather than challenge the status of the state, the activities of sub-state actors can reinforce the position of the state. In countries such as India and Thailand, the state appropriates medical tourism in its marketing and public relations as an indicator of the vibrancy of its tourism offer (Champagne 2006). In some cases, states facilitate the local growth of the medical tourism industry in order to import patients and export services. Not only is medical tourism potentially fruitful for the balance of payments, it also generates important forms of taxation revenue and multipliers (Adams 2005, TRAM 2006). For instance, Singapore is not alone in its great ambitions for the sector (see TRAM 2006). It intends to attract '1 million patients by 2012 which would generate US$1.8 billion in revenues, [and] create at least 13,000 jobs' (Connell 2006: 1099).

Loyalty scheme members as 'tourism citizens'

Other groups of tourism citizens have been established by sub-state actors. The growing ranks of frequent flyers and hotel loyalty card holders are testament to the popularity of assumed rights that include: priority check-in; access to lounges and dedicated amenities; waitlist and upgrade priority; special bonuses; exclusive special offers with strategic partners; dedicated and exclusive bookings services; and express, prioritised service lanes for members. These rights are bestowed on travellers who discharge their responsibilities to consume the brands to particular levels, and who subscribe to the values of the brand and behave appropriately, as it were, in the 'brandspaces' (e.g. hotels, aeroplanes, lounges). In the airline sector, each airline has its own loyalty card scheme and in the three largest global airline alliances – Oneworld, SkyTeam and Star Alliance (see Chapter 5) – that dominate the market, members of one airline are able to accrue benefits while using their partners' services. For instance, a gold-level Miles and More member from Lufthansa of Star Alliance can also earn miles (responsibility) and use the lounges and special airport facilities (rights) by flying with Thai Airways or Air New Zealand on a trip from Frankfurt am Main to Auckland via Bangkok. Membership of an airline loyalty scheme is not restricted and it is possible to be a member of each airline scheme, although it is more likely or sensible to be a member of one airline in each of the large alliances. Depending on the rewards offered and the price of the ticket for a particular route, travellers can make tactical decisions as to which airline to fly with in order to optimise their travel experiences and their status as consumer citizens. Several websites exist to advise travellers on the relative merits of particular loyalty schemes, how to maximise their benefits, and hence how to qualify for the best service in the quickest time with the minimum effort. Indeed, there are agreements between different consumer citizenship groups affecting different parts of the tourism experience. So, the Miles and More member from Frankfurt may also be a member of Priority Club of Six Continents; thus, any stay in, for example, a Holiday Inn or Intercontinental Hotel would earn the member points for Priority Club status, as well as award miles with Miles and More to be spent on perks and benefits. Similar corporate agreements exist between airlines and major car hire companies among other strategic partners (Table 3.2).

Table 3.2 Selected non-airline strategic partners from which Air New Zealand Airpoints Dollars can be earned

Business	Sector
Accor Hotels and Resorts	Hotels
The Hilton Family	Hotels
InterContinental Hotels Group	Hotels
Starwood Hotels and Resorts	Hotels
Avis Rent a Car	Vehicle Rental
Budget Car and Truck Rental	Vehicle Rental
Hertz	Vehicle Rental
All Blacks Mastercard	Other card rewards programme
ANZ Rewards – Australia	Other card rewards programme
Westpac (Australia and New Zealand)	Other card rewards programme
Diners Club Rewards (Australia and New Zealand)	Other card rewards programme

Source: Adapted from *Air New Zealand Magazine* (January 2007: 107).

CASE-STUDY VIGNETTE – TOURISM AND INTERNATIONAL BUSINESS IN ACTION

Have passport, will travel?

After a passport, a travel insurance policy is probably the second most important travel document. Travel insurance is perceived as security in the event of misfortune or emergency when travelling. Of course, given the number of caveats built into policies, protection is far from universal. It is only when they read the fine print that many travellers realise how their policies may determine their mobility patterns. There may be restrictions on the type of activities they may undertake (for instance, participating in skiing, diving or other adventurous activities) as well as how long they may spend overseas. 'Annual' travel insurance policies often provide cover for a specified maximum number of days away from home in a given calendar year or in particular trips. Travel insurance policies may effectively limit the choice of destinations and several policy documents in the UK contain similar exclusion clauses to Direct Line's (2007: 8):

> The policy does not cover travel to areas where the Foreign and Commonwealth Office has advised against 'all travel'. If you are not sure whether there is a travel warning for your destination, please check with the Foreign and Commonwealth Office.

At the time of writing, The Foreign and Commonwealth Office (FCO) website travel advisory section (see www.fco.org.uk; FCO 2007) advises British nationals citizens against *all travel* to Ivory Coast and Somalia. It also advises against *all travel* to *parts of*: Afghanistan, Albania, Azerbaijan, Burundi, Cameroon, Chad, Colombia, Congo (Democratic Republic), Eritrea, Ethiopia, Georgia, India, Indonesia, Iran, Iraq, Israel and the Occupied Palestinian Territories (OPTs), Lebanon, Mali, Nigeria, Pakistan, Philippines, Russian Federation, Sri Lanka, Sudan, [and] Uganda.

For many potential travellers such 'advice' is almost compulsory because a lack of cover imposes de facto restrictions on the nature and timing of their travel. In theory, such advice has the potential to affect visitor flows and the fortunes of destinations. In practice, it is difficult to assess the extent to which this is the case, not least because people may chose to reject the advice (and hence travel effectively uninsured).

So, why does the FCO not just impose restrictions? The use of the word 'advice' cushions the FCO from criticisms of authoritarian or 'nanny state' governance and the infringement of civil liberties by placing formal restrictions on where there are rights to travel. After all, many people do travel to countries on the FCO list without problem. For insurance companies, the benefits would appear to be in the empowerment of their clients with up-to-date information about their destinations without having to gather and disseminate

Continued

the intelligence themselves. Risks are reduced while the premiums paid by customers can be kept to a minimum.

Questions

▨   How may travel insurance policies affect changes in visitor flows and what methods and data sources could be used to detect these?

▨   Examine the wording of the exclusion clause: what difficulties can you identify in the implementation of this and other similar clauses?

▨   What are the commercial risks to the FCO (and similar agencies in other countries) of their imposing restrictions on the rights of travel to overseas destinations?

In order to deliver enhanced rights to their members, some airlines as sub-state actors conspire with the state. Levels of collaboration vary and in some cases sub-state actors' commercial operations are subtly, but importantly, affected by their reference to the state's standard advice on travel and destinations (see case-study vignette). In other instances, sub-state actors work more closely with the state to deliver consumer advantages in the form of new or accelerated forms of mobility. Emirates has introduced differential immigration controls based on ticket type. Business and first class are provided with fast-track lanes (compared to economy-class passengers), while Dubai residents clear customs and immigration even quicker through a system of electronic gates which they open by swiping with their electronic identity cards.

During the 2006 security crisis, reports appeared in the US questioning the probity of the so-called 'Registered Traveler' programme; that is, those who had submitted themselves voluntarily to additional security checks and who had been cleared by the state, could access high-speed lanes for security in addition to the priority lanes used by frequent flyers. The US government through its Transport Security Administration (TSA) had announced earlier in the year that it intended to forge ahead with the scheme. It had invited expressions of interest on how best to operate such a scheme commercially with the private sector (TSA 2006).

Critics argued that security was a responsibility of state and in this respect all passengers, irrespective of the class of their ticket should be subject to the same security measures (Reed 2006). So the argument went, as all (US) passengers were all equal in their obligations to the state, nobody should receive preferential treatment; hence, all individuals irrespective of the class of their ticket should have to join the back of security queues. In fact, the airport authorities own their properties (under different ownership models), and space in airline terminals is leased to the airlines. Although the TSA is legally required to undertake security checks of passengers, the real estate in front of a TSA checkpoint is effectively owned by the airlines (Reed 2006) and hence it is for the airlines, in conjunction with the port authorities, to set policy for passenger throughflows.

In the event, this new form of travel citizenship was piloted in Orlando (Florida) (Reed 2006). Through the private operator, Verified Identity Pass Inc. and its brand Clear® (Clear 2007), the 'Registered Traveler' scheme has grown since the first citizens were recruited in 2005. So-called 'Clear lanes' also operate in Cincinnati/Northern Kentucky, Indianapolis, New York JFK Terminals 4 and 7, and San José, with further lanes intended for Albany, Little Rock, Newark, New York JFK Terminal 1, and Toronto. A fee of US$99 (which includes the TSA vetting fee of $28) for one year's membership pays for the card after submitting basic biographic data (name, addresses, social security number), photograph, biometrics (iris scans and all fingerprints) and two pieces of government-issued identification ahead of a TSA security threat assessment (Clear 2007).

On this occasion, travel citizenship (membership of the 'Registered Traveler' programme) appears to run alongside basic state citizenship (and other forms of travel citizenship) to induce differential rates and practices of mobility. Moreover, rather than exploit a deficiency in the state's ability to deliver basic rights and services (as in the case of medical tourism), sub-state actors are argued to be working in close cooperation with the state to preserve and to reinforce its politico-legal integrity by reducing the threat of terrorism (TSA 2006). The logical progression of this debate is to suggest that in the future there could be multiple grades of state citizenship (based on the security risk individuals present) that afford differential right to travel and free movement through airports and security checks.

CONCLUSION: CITIZENSHIP AS THE MISSING LINK IN THE TOURISM AND INTERNATIONAL BUSINESS NEXUS

Citizenship is a major concept in the social sciences but regrettably it is one that has not penetrated far into studies of international business and tourism. Four strands of argumentation are presented here, the most important of which is that citizenship is vital to understanding how tourism as a form of human mobility functions. For so long, though, citizenship – or more correctly citizenships, for individuals have multiple belongings and no citizenship group covers an entire polity (Isin and Wood 1999: 20) – has been obscured as a possible explanation of tourism flows. Often a sign of the times, citizenship is a fluid, evolving concept. Traditional views of citizenship that portray the state as the basic building block retain their relevance but several new groups of citizens that reflect contemporary conditions in economy, society, culture and politics have emerged, each of which exhibits distinctive patterns of mobility. It is possible to identify groups we may term as 'tourism citizens' due to their common commitment to and participation in travel and tourism. These have emerged not least from the complex and ongoing relationships between the state and sub-state actors. Some of these in the form of international businesses (in the field of medical tourism) have taken advantage of the commercial opportunities to arise from the state's inability to provide adequate welfare services. Other transnational corporations have effectively created their own groups of corporate citizens who are characterised by the privileges they enjoy by membership of loyalty schemes. In some cases international businesses are conspiring with and reinforcing the position of the state. As the evidence here demonstrates, citizenship should not and cannot be taken for granted by scholars of tourism and international business. The next challenge is to develop effective empirical frameworks to be able to map out with greater precision the effects of citizenship on tourism and international business.

Discussion questions

- What are the problems of attempting to measure the impact of citizenship on determining international mobility flows?
- In which other way may states use citizenship to regulate mobility flows? Hint: look at the foreign service website of international governments.
- What other forms of contemporary citizenship involve or create distinctive tourism flows?

REFERENCES

Adams, M. (2005) Rising popularity of medical tourism reveals deterioration of U.S. healthcare system. Online. Last updated: 21/04/05. Available from: htttp://www.newstarget.com/007097.html (accessed: 16/06/06).

BBC (2004) Ireland votes to end birth right. Online. Updated: 13/06/04. Available from: http://news.bbc.co.uk/1/hi/world/europe/3801839.stm (accessed: 31/05/07).

—— (2006a) Ryanair to sue government for £3m. Online. Updated: 25/08/06. Available from: http://news.bbc.co.uk/1/hi/business/5285102.stm (accessed: 05/04/07).

—— (2006b) Reid outlines new EU work curbs. Online. Available from: http://news.bbc.co.uk/1/hi/uk_politics/6076410.stm (accessed: 02/11/06).

Champagne, W. (2006) Surgery with a view. Online. Last updated: 01/06/06. Available from: http://www.smh.com.au/articles/2006/05/31/1148956412656.html (accessed: 16/06/06).

Clear (2007) Clear. The fast pass for airport security. Online. Available from: http://www.flyclear.com/ (accessed: 07/06/07).

Coles, T.E. (2007) 'Telling tales of tourism: mobility, media and citizenship in the 2004 EU Enlargement', in P.M. Burns and M. Novelli (eds) Tourism and Mobilities. CABI: Wallingford.

Coles, T.E. and Hall, D.R. (2005) 'Tourism and EU enlargement. Plus ça change?', International Journal of Tourism Research, 7(2): 51–62.

Coles, T.E. and Timothy, D.J. (2004) '"My field is the world": conceptualising diaspora, travel and tourism', in T.E. Coles and D.J. Timothy (eds) Tourism, Diasporas and Space. London: Routledge.

Connell, J. (2006) 'Medical tourism: sea, sun, sand and ... surgery', Tourism Management, 27: 1093–100.

Cooke, D.T., Caffarelli, A.D. and Robbins, R.C. (2005) 'The road to clinical xenotransplantation: a worthwhile journey', Transplantation 78(8): 1108–9.

Direct Line (2007) Off on Your Travels. Your Annual Travel Policy. Online. Available from: http://www.directline.com/travel/AnnualTravelPolicy.pdf (accessed: 07/06/07).

Dunkerley, D., Hodgson, L., Konopacki, S., Spybey, T. and Thompson, A. (2002) Changing Europe. Identities, Nations and Citizens. London: Routledge.

FCO   (2007) Travel advice. Online. Available from: http://www.fco.gov.uk/servlet/Front?pagename=OpenMarket/ Xcelerate/ShowPage&c=Page&cid=1007029390572 (accessed: 07/06/07).

George, N., Mulligan, M., Parker, G. and Williamson, H. (2005) Invasion of benefit tourists from EU's east fails to materialise. *Financial Times*, 28/04/05. Online. Available from: www.ft.com (accessed: 01/10/06).

Hall, C.M. and Müller, D.K. (2004) *Tourism, Mobility and Second Homes. Between Elite Landscape and Common Ground*. Clevedon: Channel View.

Harding, L. and Culf, A. (2006) German police detain football hooligans. *Guardian*, 08/06/06. Online. Available from: http://football.guardian.co.uk/worldcup2006/story/0,,1792605,00.html (accessed: 05/04/07).

Heater, D. (2004) *A Brief History of Citizenship*. Edinburgh: Edinburgh University Press.

Isin, E.F. and Wood, P.K. (1999) *Citizenship and Identity*. London: Sage.

Marshall, T.H. and Bottomore, T. (1992) *Citizenship and Social Class*, updated edn. London: Pluto Press. (Originally T.H. Marshall, published under the same title in 1950, Cambridge: Cambridge University Press.)

Mason, T., Moncrieff, C. and Sheringham, S. (2004) 'EU migrants will have to register for jobs', *Press Association*, 23/02/04.

Molz, J. (2005) 'Getting a "flexible eye": round-the-world travel and scales of cosmopolitan citizenship', *Citizenship Studies* 9(5): 517–31.

Murphy, M. and Harty, S. (2003) 'Post-sovereign citizenship', *Citizenship Studies*, 7(2), 181–97.

Pearson, D. (2002) 'Theorizing citizenship in British settler societies', *Ethnic and Racial Studies*, 25(6), 989–1012.

PHT (undated, c.2005) *Phuket Health and Travel. Offering More than Sun, Sand and Sea*. Phuket: PHT Co., Ltd.

Ramesh, R. (2005) This UK patient avoided the NHS list and flew to India for a heart bypass. Is health tourism the future? *Guardian*, 01/02/05. Online. Available from: http://www.guardian.co.uk/medicine/story/ 0,11381,1402881,00.html (accessed: 16/06/06).

Reed, D. (2006) 'Elite security lines bug some not others', *USA Today*, 29/08/06: 5B.

Schattle, H. (2005) 'Communicating global citizenship: multiple discourses beyond the academy', *Citizenship Studies*, 9(2): 119–33.

Semmens, K. (2005) *Seeing Hitler's Germany. Tourism in the Third Reich*. Basingstoke: Palgrave Macmillan.

Tambini, D. (2001) 'Post-national citizenship', *Ethnic and Racial Studies*, 24(2), 195–217.

TRAM (Tourism Research and Marketing) (2006) *Medical Tourism: A Global Analysis*. London : ATLAS for Tourism Research and Marketing.

TSA (2006) TSA announces key elements of registered traveler program. Online. Last updated: 20/01/06. Available from: http://www.tsa.gov/press/releases/2006/press_release_0645.shtm (accessed: 31/05/07).

Urry, J. (2000) *Sociology beyond Societies. Mobilities for the Twenty-first Century*. London: Routledge.

van Steenbergen, B. (1994) 'The condition of citizenship: an introduction', in B. van Steenbergen (ed.) *The Condition of Citizenship*. London: Sage.

Verstraete, G. (2002) 'Heading for Europe. Tourism and the global Hinerary of an idea', Thamyris/Intersecting 9: 33–52.

4 Nature and the environment as trans-boundary business strategies

Johan Hultman and Stefan Gössling

Learning objectives

After considering this chapter, you will be able to:

- reflect on how nature is used to create economic and social value in international tourism ventures;
- discuss conditions for and consequences of the commodification of nature and environmental values;
- explain how nature and the environment can be understood as trans-boundary business strategies.

Key terms

- ontology;
- nature;
- environment;
- commodification;
- neoliberalisation;
- biocolonialism.

INTRODUCTION: LOCATING NATURE AND ENVIRONMENT IN TOURISM

In orthodox views of tourism, commentators stress that tourism experiences differ from everyday life: different places are experienced, different people(s) are gazed upon, tourists get to know different ways of doing things, and so on. To do tourism, then, in these circumstances is to encounter a series of changes from the ordinary but several things change in the course of the making and consumption of a tourism experience. For instance, everyday structures such as strict school and workplace time regimes or commuter timetables might be exchanged for structures and orderings that are potentially experienced as liberating and empowering, including journeys, tours and events (e.g. Franklin 2004). During such journeys, tours and events, everyday structures might be temporarily suspended or transformed into narratives where myth, history and the future are seductively conflated. Theme parks, for example, transcend borders between reality and fiction, with the result that the distant is conjured right in front of one's eyes and in effect the local becomes an exotic experience. In this way, tourism studies offer the possibility to reflect on the ontological status of categories and concepts whose meaning we often take for granted. Within philosophy, ontology is the study of being or of existence, and it involves the study of different conceptions and constructions of reality. For instance, what is 'nature', 'environment', 'local' or 'global'? How do these concepts relate to each other, to everyday life, to the economy or to the ways in which we understand ourselves in the world? This chapter will highlight and examine such an instance of ontological ambiguity; that is, how nature and the environment become disembedded from place-bound contexts and what consequences such a dislocation may have.

Based on a number of examples, this chapter discusses how nature and environment have become the focus of tourism interest as mobile commodities. We consider how they are created in cultural economies of nature where the locus of meaning is the corporeal tourist rather than geographical locations with specific characteristics. As commodities, nature and the environment are utilised in international business strategies to generate value and to create competitive advantages in global markets. In particular, we argue there has been an identifiable neoliberalisation of nature. The workings, outcomes and definition of neoliberalisation per se, and of the neoliberalisation of nature more specifically, are much debated issues (see Castree 2006). Neoliberalisation is a regime of value creation, or a 'theory of political economic practices' (Harvey 2005: 2), that emphasises the virtues of free markets, free trade and private entrepreneurship. It can be taken to mean that everything that is possible to deregulate and commercialise will be deregulated and commercialised. Here, neoliberalisation of nature refers to distinctive new forms of governance over nature and environmental values. The dislocation of nature from national territories and traditional boundaries is stressed in order to suggest how a deregulation of nature may unfold in international tourism contexts. It is possible to speak of new markets for nature, but as with all economic transactions this implies unequal access to and control over nature as a resource. The term 'biocolonialism' will be used to signify the inequalities that result from the commoditisation of formerly local/national nature by, for example, sub-state corporations and organisations. In more than one sense, the chapter is about the greening of the tourism industry and the incorporation of nature and environmental values into the tourism economy. It is not, however, an investigation into the extent of the environmental commitment of specific tourist ventures, or mechanisms of translation between green rhetoric and environmental action (see Newton 2005; Newton and Harte 1997 for management perspectives on these issues). The focus is on how nature and environment become value creators and not so much on how they are used to add value to other products or services.

TRANSCENDENT NATURE: CENTER PARCS

Center Parcs is probably one of the earliest attractions to have systematically blurred the specificity and importance of place in tourism based on selling nature experiences. Comprising some 20 villages in France, Netherlands, Belgium, Germany and the UK, Center Parcs is an example of staged vacation environments that seek to transcend the dichotomy between urban and natural environments, and outdoor and indoor experiences. Center Parcs are arranged as park-like landscapes, characterised by three main 'nature' elements – open lawns, patches of forests, and water bodies – into which urban elements, such as apartment houses and large centrally positioned facilities with pool landscapes and restaurants, are implanted. The landscape is of particular importance in the marketing strategy of Center Parcs, as the website makes obvious (Center Parcs 2006). Images are generally held in shades of green, depicting various landscape elements or people carrying out outdoor activities such as cycling, fishing or taking a walk. Urban environments are carefully integrated and presented, often as a subordinate theme, as exemplified by a picture of a couple drinking a glass of wine at the lakeside. No urban infrastructure is present in this photograph, but table, chairs and glasses indicate that 'the urban' – mirroring civilisation and its comforts – is never far away. Each of the Center Parc villages has its own pages on the website, with a multitude of 360° short films inviting to explore urban facilities (rooms, pools, restaurants and, most importantly, apartments) before arrival.

Although landscape elements dominate the marketing of Center Parcs, it is clear that not one particular landscape is of importance, but rather a plot of land with the potential to be turned into a cultural landscape matching the romantic gaze of eighteenth-century nature aesthetics meeting twenty-first-century expectations of urban comfort. Demands on location are existent in terms of proximity to a market, and a minimum distance to the next highway to avoid noise pollution. Center Parcs can thus be seen as an example of staged attractions addressing tourists with the wish to escape 'the city' in favour of 'nature' but with the guaranteed precondition of comfort and safety. Nature in these vacation entities is dominated by, and shaped for, the humans inhibiting it. These allow for alternate indoor/outdoor uses of the environment, as manifested by forest walks and relaxation in the pleasure pool areas. Center Parcs are thus socially constructed representations of 'ideal' nature that are only partially place-bound. These have now existed for more than 30 years, and can thus be seen as early examples of staged and commoditised representations of nature. Consequently, nature and environment are socially constructed by the commercial exchanges taking place at tourist attractions or, to put it another way, tourism shapes ontology. The ontology shaped by this specific encounter between tourists and nature/environment will be the starting point for the following discussion of how nature and the environment function as international business strategies.

THE UNIVERSE(UM) IN GOTHENBURG

Everything is connected – everyone matters! Explore the natural sciences and technology – everything from sharks and rainforest to high-tech and hands-on experiments! All in Gothenburg, right next to the Liseberg amusement park.

This is the welcome that greets the digital visitor to Sweden's National Science Discovery Centre, Universeum (Universeum 2006). The centre is situated – as is clearly pointed out to the potential visitor – next to Liseberg, the single most popular tourist attraction in Sweden with 3.4 million visitors in 2005, approximately 10 per cent of these international tourists (Liseberg, personal communication). Universeum is a place that combines the two fastest growing and most important segments of Swedish tourism, *activities* and *nature* (Swedish Tourist Authority 2005), and it received half a million visitors in 2005 of which approximately 15 per cent were international (Universeum, personal communication).

In its short welcome, Universeum contextualises and positions itself, the visitor, nature and the environment in several ways. First of all, it is an international tourist attraction. Universeum has translated itself into a digital representation accessible from any part of the world with Internet access. The function of this representation is to persuade at a distance; Universeum is a node in local, regional and national economies. One of its purposes is to displace consumption by attracting consumers from near and far and convince them to stay and consume. The strategic resources used to create attractiveness in this particular case are nature, the environment and technology. Consequently, Universeum is a place designed to promote knowledge gathering framed as a commercial exchange. In this sense, it is an explicit servicescape; that is, a place '… calculated to produce commercially significant actions … [that] may serve as the [focus] for the production of socially and personally significant meanings, intentions and purposes' (Arnould *et al.* 1998: 90; cf. Bitner 1992). Hence, Universeum not only mediates knowledge about nature and the environment to the consumer, but it also creates meaning through the interaction with the consumer.

The welcome to Universeum summons the visitor to experience. Having entered the building, the visitor is expected to immerse him/herself in nature by moving through (re)created habitats from distant parts of the world as well as through staged national biotopes. Bartram and Shobrook (2000) have considered the simulation of natures, and discussed the hyper-reality of such natures. They contend that it eventually becomes difficult to distinguish between 'original' and simulated nature. Sounds, sights, humidity and temperature create an exotic atmosphere here consistent with this position. Tactile encounters, for instance, with snakes, bugs, stingrays and leeches are encouraged and transformed into play through the performance of the staff. This, combined with the explicit spatial affiliation with Liseberg, situates Universeum in a geography of pleasure. The welcoming text associates the two attractions with each other and prescribes a chain of events, but the association with Liseberg also tells the visitor how nature and the environment should be understood. Thus, at first glance, Universeum is about having fun. Nature, and exotic nature in particular, is exciting and adventurous. The environment is a strange and wonderful thing. But how do you get to know it?

The Science Centre has a motto: 'everything is connected – everyone matters!' This is a statement embodying the present-day scientific wisdom of holism, expressed for example in the global environmental change discourse (IPCC 2001; Schellnhuber *et al.* 2006; in relation to tourism, see Gössling and Hall 2005). It stresses the fact that nature and the environment cannot be seen as local parcels fitted together in a neat mosaic. Rather, nature and the environment must be conceptualised as (a) network(s) where there are no truly isolated parts. Thus, categories of the local and the global are nullified right at the very beginning of the interaction with nature in Universeum. The motto globalises not only the environment as a totality, but also the visitor *in* nature. Furthermore, it empowers the visitor: *you* matter too! *Your* actions have a direct impact on the planet Earth! Universeum is also a place for doing things. More specifically, it is a place where visitors are urged to manipulate nature by experimentation. Universeum situates itself within a discourse promoting the scientisation of nature (cf. Macnaghten and Urry 1998; Urry 1999). Nature and the environment become objects in a scientifically-based ontology.

Universeum's logo consists of four icons: a leaf, a heart, a light bulb and an eye. It is easily interpreted as reflecting the three major themes of discovery in this Centre – nature, the body and technology – and the (principal) means to gain knowledge about them – sight. The understanding of nature follows from systematic investigation, where visualisation and sight are central practices. Consequently, Universeum is primarily a place for seeing. The sight-attraction stressed in the welcome is nature displaced from distant locations. Danger (sharks) and exoticism (rain forest) are the two narrative threads that are used to shape visitor expectations of nature – before the actual experience takes place.

It seems clear that Universeum, a site marketed to a potentially global body of consumers, is characterised by two paradoxical ontologies. In one, nature is positioned to amuse, as a tourist attraction within the experience economy. Exotic nature has here become a mobile subject, disembodied from local contexts and transformed into a servicescape where interaction with nature is framed by commercial exchanges. In the other ontology, nature shifts towards the scientific field of systems ecology. Nature is here understood as a system, seen and acted upon as a scientific object. Understanding is based on systematic investigation. This perspective objectifies nature and distances it from the knowing subject – it is not an environment that the tourist experiences sensually. Neither is nature a mobile subject. This ontology rather reinforces different geographical scales of nature where the local and the global become important structuring categories.

In short, Universeum seeks to integrate knowledge and spectacle into one 'sustainable' product. Even though Universeum has not made the full step of placing nature and the environment in a global experience economy discourse, it is clear that notions of place and distance are dissolved in the Science Centre.

THE EDEN PROJECT: REAL-TIME, MATERIAL NARRATIVES OF ENVIRONMENT, KNOWLEDGE AND HAPPINESS

Universeum hints at a process where the mobilisation of the environment as a strategic resource diminishes the meaning of essentialist, place-bound, natural characteristics and it liberates nature from constraints of time and space. This becomes even more evident looking at another international attraction, the suggestively named 'Eden Project':

> The Eden Project communicates its story in a 'Living Theatre of Plants and People' based in a large crater in which nestle two vast greenhouses (Biomes). These house plants, crops and landscapes from the humid tropics and warm temperate regions and act as a backdrop to the temperate landscape, which we call the Outdoor Biome. Eden uses exhibitions, art, storytelling, workshops, lectures and events to put messages across to both the public and formal education groups. The underlying concept presents to the widest possible public audience the need for environmental care through a celebration of what nature gives to us. Eden is demonstrating behaviour change on site, holding a mirror to our values and civilisation and encouraging respect for the things that sustain us.
>
> (Eden Project 2006)

The Eden Project, located in Cornwall in the United Kingdom is a material narrative of biocentric values expressed through displaced nature and environment (Figure 4.1). A whole range of performative and narrative techniques – exhibitions, art, storytelling, workshops, lectures and events – is used to annihilate modern conceptions of space – time in order to shape an ontology where the visitor and his/her everyday practices and actions are incorporated into nature (cf. FitzSimmons and Goodman 1998). In doing so, the Eden Project also indicates that tourism is best conceptualised as a general issue of production, consumption and mobility, which is embedded in everyday life, rather than a ritualistic/modernistic dichotomy in contrast to it. This project presents itself as 'an international visitor destination, an extraordinary education facility and a new Foundation for the future' (Eden Project 2006). Trans-boundary mobility – of nature, environment and

Figure 4.1 *Famous for their striking visual appearance from the outside, inside the biomes at the Eden Project nature is dislocated from its (Humid Tropics) origins*

consumers – is used to invoke a place where myth, history and the future come together as an extremely attractive proposition:

> If you believe there should be a place ... that celebrates life and puts champagne in the veins ... is all about education but doesn't feel like school ... to hold conversations that might just go somewhere ... where research isn't white coats in secret but shared exploration to help us all ... that is a sanctuary for all who think the future too precious to leave to the few – because it belongs to us all. Then welcome.
>
> (Eden Project 2006)

The locus of meaning creation is the individual visitor, materially and discursively placed in the middle of nature, which in turn is placed in the middle of, well, anywhere. The geographic location is not important for the meaning that is created, although this meaning encompasses all places. In a sense, this equals the deregulation of nature. This shift of locus from place to individual would seem to suggest that the function of nature as national signifier is weakening, or at the very least changing. Nature is a common vehicle for the promotion of nations as destinations, a practice that is sometimes correlated to a history of placing nature in a central position in nineteenth- and twentieth-century nation-building (see Gössling and Hultman 2006 for Scandinavian examples), but also often as an expression of the myths of mystery and pre-modernity that frame (primarily) long-distance travel to locations marketed and understood as exotic. National governments have historically played an important role in protecting place-bound nature from commercial forces. When nature and environment become mobile commodities, the governance of nature becomes a matter for other actors (cf. Hall 2005, 2006). In the case of Eden, sub-state actors (such as regional tourism, marketing and development agencies, county councils and local marketing agencies) as well as a supranational body (the European Union) are involved in the internationalisation of nature, having been mobilised by a particular entrepreneur (Tim Smit) and the commercial organisation he started.

Capital accumulation by sub-state stakeholders through the deregulation of formerly state-controlled resources suggests that nature and the environment are subjected to a process of neoliberalisation. For instance, this is the case with creativity and culture in several regional development contexts (see Gibson and Klocker 2005; Hultman 2007). What is particularly striking about this kind of neoliberalisation is the strong moral and ethical vision underpinning the process as manifested both in the Universeum and the Eden Project. But neoliberalisation usually entails an uneven distribution of wealth in both economic and environmental terms. Arguably, not all projects such as Universeum and Eden have ethical visions. Nevertheless, the examples show that trans-boundary business strategies could turn nature and the environment into mobile commodities, and thereby undermine the attraction of place-bound, essentialist nature. There is thus a potential danger that the mobilisation of nature as a tool for regional development in some places could in a real sense equal the displacement of nature from other, less human, financial capital intense regions. For example, ecotourism is a mode of travel that explicitly aims to conserve local natures by reinvesting tourist expenditures in local projects. But as ecotourism 'usually conjures up such images as jungle treks to far away places', what happens if 'natives of the UK no longer need to travel abroad to "ecotour" [since] some of the most exotic habitats are now available on their doorstep' (Chaffey 2001: 295)? The simulation or 'endless duplications' of nature, of which the Eden Project may be considered a prime exemplar (Bartram and Shobrook 2000: 371, drawing on arguments developed by Jean Baudrillard), would then have direct material and economic ramifications.

The commoditisation of nature as described above has a range of socio-cultural conse-quences. Clearly, all examples are based on a narrative of nature as something inherently good, hereby setting up nature as a normative model for thought and practice. Myth, history and the future come together in a spatialised ecological cosmology where the quest for pleasures and experiences guides the visitor and fills nature and the environment with meaning. It is, according to Bartram and Shobrook (2000), the achievement of ecoutopia – nature purified and perfected with the help of science and technology. Nature is used as a trans-boundary business strategy to promote a better future, which is fully in accordance with the United Nations World Tourism Organization (UNWTO) awareness campaign Tourism Enriches with its motto: 'Tourism enriches individuals, families, communities and all the world' (UNWTO 2006).

The Tourism Enriches campaign, with its aim to commoditise culture and nature on a truly global market where: 'tourism [is] a basic human right and a way of life' (UNWTO 2006), spells out what the neoliberalisation of nature is about. Even though neoliberalisation does not necessarily equal deregulation (Peck 2004: 395), Tourism Enriches sets nature free among a global collective of consumers and positions sub-state (individuals, families, communities) and a cooperative conceptualisation of supranational (all the world) actors as the beneficiaries of the commoditisation of nature. The emergence of nature as a mobile commodity is here obviously an entrepreneurial strategy liberating nature from national boundaries. This is mediated through the discourse of benefits in various spheres: tourism enriches culturally, it generates income and jobs economically, and it serves the purpose of preserving nature and the environment (UNWTO 2006).

'OH, I ALMOST FORGOT, WE WILL BE GROWING OUR OWN CORAL ...' – THE DIVE DOME

The narratives embedded in and expressed by Universeum, the Eden Project and Tourism Enriches all communicate the message that nature and the environment – if properly commoditised – can be used for a common good. An undefined human collective is more or less explicitly proposed as the ultimate beneficiary of these servicescapes and discourses. In the neoliberalisation of nature, the practices of sub-state stakeholders are, in all our examples, represented as having an altruistic rationale. This is also the case with the Dive Dome, a planned underwater playground outside London, although here altruism emerges more as an afterthought, a 'bolt-on' accessory to the commoditisation of nature in terms of sensual pleasures, luxury and adventure. But it is not, in the end, forgotten: when nature is used as a trans-boundary business strategy, exoticism and virtue are combined to create the product. And as with most tourism products, instructions for the interpretation of the commoditised experience are mediated before the actual experience takes place: You're dreaming of your last diving holiday to the Red Sea. Or perhaps the Maldives. Wish you were there today? Well, very soon you can be, without ever leaving the UK; (Jason 2004). When the Red Sea and the Maldives are displaced to Milton Keynes, the result '... is paradise', and paradise, not surprisingly, is made up of 'palm trees, tropical grasses, white powdery sand ... crystal clear warm seas, brimming with brightly coloured tropical fish' (Jason 2004). The Dive Dome, just as Universeum and the Eden Project, is tourist nature brought to the consumer instead of vice versa. Here, however, what greets the visitor is more an archetypal tourist brochure that has come to life in a bio-climatologically incongruous setting than a servicescape grounded in the scientisation of nature. Indeed, the Dive Dome *is* the realisation of a tourist brochure, a materialised tourist discourse of liminoid hedonism. Here 'dreams can become a reality', you can have 'a cocktail ... on the Caribbean beach while watching your buddies have fun', or enjoy 'bars, restaurants, a health spa, beauty treatment rooms and a space age fitness centre' (Jason 2004). Generic denominations such as rain forest, humid tropics or warm temperate regions have been exchanged for geographical names that – in this tourism context – act as brands: the Red Sea, the Maldives, the Caribbean. These are all international destinations with well-developed tourist infrastructures and marketing strategies. Within the Dive Dome project, nation-specific nature becomes a mobile commodity. A colonial principle embedded in nature as a trans-boundary business strategy becomes evident. Place-bound, essentialist nature can hardly be more displaced than this. You *can* visit the Maldives without having to undertake a long-distance journey. Not only nature and specific environments are subjected to a process of neoliberalisation but so too are geographical brands as well; nations and regions are unwittingly enrolled as critical selling points for a sub-state business development.

Through this strategy, the Dive Dome not only relies upon its own representations but also capitalises on marketing and branding campaigns carried out by tourism organisations in a number of other countries and regions. Dive Dome is a private venture in which the future visitor is encouraged to join as a founder member. Thus, any consumer can take active part in the colonial practice of trans-boundary mobilisation of nature. Founder members are offered a number of exclusive benefits, among these the privileged access to a real diving vessel operating in the real Red Sea until the time that the Dive Dome itself becomes reality. This would seem to ensure that the transition from 'specific' nature to displaced nature becomes a smooth process, and it also ensures that 'specific' nature is positioned as expendable. The experience of this branded nature will remain the same, down to the level of individual key organisms: 'Oh, I almost forgot, we will be growing our own coral at the Dome and this will be returned to the ocean at a date in the future' (Jason 2004). The re-creation of displaced and simultaneously endangered nature, safely shielded away from global environmental change – here, nature and the environment conceptualised as trans-boundary business strategies – can be interpreted as a response to negative environmental effects caused by tourism practices. Global environmental change will radically change the conditions for individual destinations (Gössling and Hall 2005), and nature and environment as mobile commodities add further complexity to the situation.

We have outlined a process of what might be termed biocolonialism within a neoliberal regime of capital accumulation. That is, so far, we have discussed examples where nature is displaced and recreated in settings that are biologically and climatologically incongruous. Another instance when nature and environment become trans-boundary categories, in a different way, is the emergence of the discursive claim that experiences of nature can take place anywhere, and hence the subsequent staging of nature experiences is independent of location. Here, the issue is not so much the physical recreation of nature. Rather, this strategy is about a specific way of discursively framing nature and the management of tourist bodies in nature.

THE PLACE-INDEPENDENT CONSTRUCTION OF NATURE: NATURE'S BEST

The Swedish Ecotourism Society operates the certification scheme Nature's Best, which is presented to the customer under the guiding principle of more fun for all involved: the tourist, the operator, local people and nature (Nature's Best 2006). The objective of the certification is to commoditise the best of Swedish nature in the form of tourism products that 'offer the traveller an unforgettable nature experience …. [from] operators who go the extra mile for … the environment' (Nature's Best 2006, author's translation). The Swedish Ecotourism Society accomplishes this by associating Swedish nature with the same connotations that commonly characterise distant, exotic nature. However, here the experience *as such* becomes the product, and this, in turn, means that the location loses value in favour of a more generalised locality: 'Ecotourism … is about experiencing nature [and this] works just as well in the Swedish mountains and archipelagos as in Nepal or in New Guinea' (Swedish Ecotourism Society 2006a, author's translation; see Hultman and Andersson Cederholm 2006). For this to work, the ordinary must be transformed into the exclusive and exotic. Just as with Center Parcs, Universeum, the Eden Project and the Dive Dome, this is a process of creating meaning, which ultimately builds on specific representations of nature. In the case of the Swedish Ecotourism Society, nature is coded as a 'cutting edge product' (Swedish Ecotourism Society 2006a, author's translation), and then defined as exotic-even-though-close-by. National artefacts, practices and environments, including, for instance, moose, dogs, charcoal-burning pits, traditional forestry, hay harvests, mushroom collection, reindeer herding, farming and bird watching are incorporated as the primary objects in this regime of value-adding where 'pristine nature [is given] economic value' (Swedish Ecotourism Society 2006a, author's translation). For this transformation to succeed, adherence to the protocol (i.e. the certification criteria) is critical. The protocol, however, is in no way place-specific. The Swedish Ecotourism Society currently seeks to actively implement the protocol globally – the North Pole, Alaska, Canada, Norway, Finland, Greece, Romania and Barents Sea are first in line (Swedish Ecotourism Society 2006b). This widespread implementation of the protocol would mean a standardisation of the practice of the ubiquitous construction of generic locality. The primacy of experience over geography, just as the biocolonialism practised by the Dive Dome, annihilates everyday categories of time and place. The protocol translates nature and the environment into free-floating commodities where national boundaries become meaningless. It is another instance of the neoliberalisation of nature where the financial beneficiaries of the protocol are primarily individual entrepreneurs, commoditising nature that was formerly free of charge:

> Nature tourism in Sweden is characterized by simple rental endeavours, and the Swedish Right of Public Access [free access to nature, even if it is privately owned, author's note] has for decades been the most important national selling point. Ecotourism is about refining today's supply, and Nature's Best wants to contribute to the development of this simple supply, where the visitor arranges things by him/herself, into attractive, commercial and bookable travel products.
>
> (Swedish Ecotourism Society 2006b, author's translation)

The neoliberalisation of nature in the context of (Swedish) ecotourism diminishes the influence of the national state over nature, transforming instead a formerly national selling point into a great number of regional development projects operated by sub-state actors. On the one hand, this is a process aimed at setting consumers in motion over large distances; that is, for instance, tourism as displaced consumption. The construction of nature within ecotourism thus differs, for example, from the biocolonialism practised by the Dive Dome where brand-nature is brought to the consumer. On the other hand, the certification protocol owned by the Swedish Ecotourism Society is a vehicle for the social construction of nature independently of place; thus, nature is turned into a mobile commodity in a manner similar to the examples presented above. Nature's Best hereby completes our analysis of how nature and environment are presently mobilised in circuits of value-adding where different kinds of mobilities intersect and interact. In the final paragraphs, we will briefly outline the complexities we find most intriguing in these developments.

DISCUSSION AND CONCLUSION: NATURE AND THE ENVIRONMENT AS INTERNATIONAL TOURISM BUSINESS STRATEGIES

Several examples of successful tourist attractions and product developments, both existing and in the planning process, have been presented in this chapter to show that, through international tourism, specific sites lose their importance as destinations, while 'nature' in its various guises is increasingly becoming a social construction designed as experiencescape. Consequently, nature and the environment are being staged and re-invented as commodities, losing intrinsic value in favour of instrumental (financial) value. Our relationships with nature are increasingly defined over commercial, staged encounters, with the price paid for arrangements of various kinds ultimately regulating issues of access to, and value of, nature and the environment. We interpret this as instances where nature and environment are incorporated in a neoliberal regime of capital accumulation. These formerly regulated ontological categories are in a number of tourism contexts dissociated from both national borders and governments. Instead, sub-state actors down to the level of individual entrepreneurs, and, through funding or subsidies, supra-state bodies such as the European Union, are turning nature and environment into trans-boundary mobile commodities. In several of the cases we have discussed, this is done within an altruistic and even biocentric discourse, whose storylines focus upon salvation and a truly common good.

This shows that nature as an international business strategy is a complex, often paradoxical issue.

We have highlighted one such paradox by pointing out how seemingly altruistic schemes and visions represent patterns of biocolonialism. Another is the situation where the practice of biocolonialism is implicitly or explicitly proposed as an answer to problems for tourism stakeholders arising from global environmental change. With the perspective we have adopted in this discussion – that tourist understandings of nature are mediated and created through commercial exchanges in incongruous settings – a complex picture emerges, which is summarised in Figure 4.2. Two idealised paths of engagement between tourists and nature are identified based on the different conceptions and constructions of nature and environment as reality in the global tourism industry. In the traditional one, tourists travel to experience place-bound nature. This physical flow of tourist bodies has the potential to alter destination environments fundamentally. Tourists engage with nature and environment as ecotourists. Here, tourist bodies are mobile in a way that seeks to conserve nature and the environment, however, generally ignoring the environmental consequences of global travel (see for instance Gössling *et al.* 2005). The second path suggests that nature becomes the mobile entity, staged independently of origin through a process of neoliberalisation; in effect, nature and environment become mobile commodities. This has the potential either to change place-bound nature through the practice of biocolonialism, or to re-invent/create nature in settings not threatened through, for instance, global environmental change. Either way, this second path indicates that nature and environment are becoming subjects for new management practices, they are incorporated in new discourses, and they are understood in new ways. There are several similarities between the two paths as well. For example, the consumption of nature as a communicative practice, nature as a knowledge project, and the attraction of the exotic are common denominators for past, present and future interactions between tourists and nature. What we see as fundamentally different, however, are the changing relationships that constitute the consumer-mediator-producer-product networks,

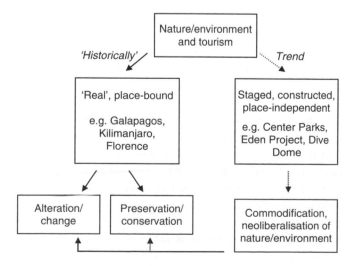

Figure 4.2 *Nature as business strategy within tourism*

and the various ways in which nature becomes placeless and mobile within commercial contexts.

Discussion questions

▨ What could be historical precedents to the use of nature and environment as trans-boundary business strategies?

▨ Can you identify any other examples of this shift from the natural environment as attraction to constructions of nature as tourist attractions?

▨ Have you had any personal experience of biocolonialism as a tourist? If so, discuss the means by which nature and environment became mobile commodities in your case.

▨ How does the shaping of ontology through constructions of nature in tourism affect perceptions of nature and environment in contemporary society?

REFERENCES

Arnould, E.J., Price, L.L. and Tierney, P. (1998) 'Communicative staging of the wilderness servicescape', *The Service Industries Journal*, 18: 90–115.

Bartram, R. and Shobrook, S. (2000) 'Endless/end-less natures: environmental futures at the Fin de Millennium', *Annals of the Association of American Geographers*, 90(2): 370–80.

Bitner, M.J. (1992) 'Servicescapes: the impact of physical surroundings on customers and employees', *Journal of Marketing*, 56(2): 57–72.

Castree, N. (2006) 'From neoliberalism to neoliberalisation: consolations, confusions, and necessary illusions', *Environment and Planning A*, 38: 1–6.

Center Parcs (2006) Various sites. Online. Available at: http://www.centerparcs.com (accessed: 24/04/06).

Chaffey, N. (2001) 'Domesday, here at last!', *TRENDS in Plant Science*, 6(7): 295.

Eden Project (2006) Various sites. Online. Available at http://www.edenproject.com (accessed: 15/03/06).

FitzSimmons, M. and Goodman, D. (1998) 'Incorporating nature: environmental narratives and the reproduction of food', in B. Braun and N. Castree (eds) *Remaking Reality. Nature at the Millennium*. London and New York: Routledge.

Franklin, A. (2004) 'Tourism as an ordering. Towards a new ontology of tourism', *Tourist Studies*, 4(3): 277–301.

Gibson, C. and Klocker, N. (2005) 'The cultural turn' in Australian regional economic development discourse: neoliberalising creativity', *Geographical Research*, 43(1): 93–102.

Gössling, S. and Hall, C.M. (eds) (2005) *Tourism and Global Environmental Change. Ecological, Social, Economic and Political Interrelationships*. London and New York: Routledge.

Gössling, S. and Hultman, J. (eds) (2006) *Ecotourism in Scandinavia: Lessons in Theory and Practice*. Wallingford: CABI Publishing.

Gössling, S., Peeters, P., Ceron, J.-P. et al. (2005) 'The eco-efficiency of tourism', *Ecological Economics*, 54(4): 417–34.

Hall, C.M. (2005) *Tourism. Rethinking the Social Science of Mobility*. Harlow: Pearson/Prentice Hall.

—— (2006) 'Policy, planning and governance in ecotourism', in S. Gössling and J. Hultman (eds) *Ecotourism in Scandinavia. Lessons in Theory and Practice*. Wallingford: CABI Publishing.

Harvey, D. (2005) *A Brief History of Neoliberalism*. Oxford: Oxford University Press.

Hultman, J. (2007) 'Through the protocol: culture, magic and GIS in the creation of regional attractiveness', *Tourism Geographies*, 9(3): 318–36.

Hultman, J. and Andersson Cederholm, E. (2006) 'The role of nature in Swedish ecotourism', in S. Gössling and J. Hultman (eds) *Ecotourism in Scandinavia. Lessons in Theory and Practice*. Wallingford: CABI Publishing.

IPCC (Intergovernmental Panel on Climate Change) (2001) *Climate Change 2001: The Scientific Basis*. Contribution of the working group I to the third assessment report of the IPCC. Cambridge: Cambridge University Press.

Jason, D. (2004) *Virtual tour of the Dive Dome*. Online. Available at: http://www.cpdev.co.uk/dome2/virtualtour/David Jason_DiveDome.pdf (accessed: 20/03/06).

Macnaghten, P. and Urry, J. (1998) *Contested Natures*. London: Sage.

Nature's Best (2006) Ett urval av de bästa naturresorna i Sverige. Online. Available at: http://www.naturensbasta.se (accessed: 29/03/06).

Newton, T. (2005) 'Practical idealism: an oxymoron?', *Journal of Management Studies*, 42(4): 869–84.

Newton, T. and Harte, G. (1997) 'Green business: technicist Kitsch?', *Journal of Management Studies*, 34(1). 75–98.

Peck, J. (2004) 'Geography and public policy: constructions of neoliberalism', *Progress in Human Geography*, 28(3): 392–405.

Schellnhuber, H.J., Cramer, W., Nakicenovic, N., Wigley, T. and Yohe, G. (eds) (2006) *Avoiding Dangerous Climate Change*. Cambridge: Cambridge University Press.

Swedish Ecotourism Society (2006a) The guide to a better travel experience – for all involved. Natures' Best. Approved Swedish Ecotourism. A quality labelling system for Swedish Ecotourism. Online. Available at: http://ekoturism.perlin.nu/illustrationer/fil_20050123225732.pdf (accessed: 30/03/06).

—— (2006b) Various sites. Available at: http://www.ekoturism.org (accessed: 30/03/06).

Swedish Tourist Authority (2005) *Tourist Destinations in Sweden. An Analysis of Attraction and Regional Development 1998–2003*. Stockholm: Swedish Tourist Authority.

Universeum (2006) Welcome to Universeum. Online. Available at: http://www.universeum.se (accessed: 14/03/06).

UNWTO (2006) *Tourism Enriches*. Online. Available at: http://www.world-tourism.org/newsroom/menue.htm (accessed: 24/03/06).

Urry, J. (1999) 'Sensing leisure spaces', in D. Crouch (ed.) *Leisure/tourism Geographies. Practices and Geographical Knowledge*. London and New York: Routledge.

The internationalisation
of tourism businesses

TOWARDS THE FIRM AS A CENTRAL CONSTRUCT IN INTERNATIONAL
BUSINESS AND TOURISM

One of the advantages of using International Trade Theory in tourism analysis is that it offers the opportunity to progress beyond demand-side perspectives that are both so dominant and yet so partial in their ability to explain tourism flows (Coles *et al.* 2006). Recently, from a supply-side perspective Zhang and Jensen (2007: 230) have explored the presence of comparative advantages in trade in (tourism) services between states. They concluded that there is 'strong support for the relevance of certain supply-side factors in explaining international tourism flows such as natural endowments, created assets associated with technology, infrastructure and international knowledge spillovers' (Zhang and Jensen 2007: 239). As helpful as such analyses may be in pointing to general sets of factors and conditions in attracting a tourist to a country, the country is equated with the destination and a causal chain is inferred between country conditions and tourism flows (a situation similar to the tourism competitiveness rankings of the World Economic Forum discussed in Chapter 1). Such views fail to recognise intra-state variations in attractiveness and hence differential flows, but more importantly they neatly side-step the agency of individual businesses in assembling attractive tourism products.

The limitations of International Trade Theory formed the basis for two seemingly parallel sets of ideas that Mtigwe (2006: 9) categorises as Early Market Imperfection Theories. These correspond with the changing nature of international political economy and the rise of the multinational enterprise after 1945 (see also the theoretical shifts identified in international business research and scholarship by Buckley (2002) and Buckley and Lessard (2005)). Briefly put, Foreign Direct Investment Theory considered such features as the role of exchange rate disparities, unsatisfied foreign demand, market failures and market intelligence as the drivers for international business. These were accompanied by Product Life Cycle Theory that interpreted the mobility of international firms as a function of the continuous search for and maintenance of cost advantages, in particular in the area of labour costs. Latter-day Market Imperfection Theories, according to Mtigwe (2006: 9–11) build on these earlier ideas. International Portfolio Theory interprets internationalisation as the attempt to maximise profits while minimising risks in the home market. Internationalization Theory effectively presents an extension of Product Life Cycle Theory with an emphasis on the most cost-efficient mode at all times (Mtigwe 2006: 10). Eclectic Theory pioneered by Dunning (1977, 1995, 2000) suggests that a firm will internationalise if it has three types of advantage (Mtigwe 2006: 12): ownership specific advantages (O), or assets that a firm possesses that foreign competitors do not; location-specific advantages (L), or more favourable operating conditions and hence transaction costs resulting from siting its operations abroad; and internalisation advantages (I), which refer to the benefits of its retaining ownership internally of particular techniques, processes, products, skills etc. rather than allowing external parties to use them. Indeed, the international hotel industry provided an early empirical testing ground for Eclectic Theory (Dunning and McQueen 1981). Last but by no means least in this fiat, according to Mtigwe (2006: 13), Resource Advantage Theory recognises that 'internationalisation is an adaptive response to environmental complexity and chaos through the marshalling of resources, skills, and routines, designed to achieve congruency with the environment and therefore secure a competitive advantage and superior financial performance.'

Market Imperfection Theories have informed two recent studies of international tourism businesses. Quer *et al.* (2007) examined the internationalisation of Spanish hotel firms from 2001 to 2003 with reference to Transaction Cost Economics as a dimension of Internationalisation Theory (Mtigwe 2006: 10–11). Kantarci (2007) investigated foreign (i.e. Turkish) investors' perceptions of investment conditions more generally, in the tourism sector and the sustainability of investments in four Central Asian states based on the Eclectic Paradigm of advantages in ownership, location and internationalisation. In quite separate ways, both studies offer interesting insights, but significantly they accept that the behaviour of firms in the tourism sector is rational, predictable and is eminently 'knowable'. They present post-hoc explanations in which expansion is interpreted to reflect decisions and choices made by firms based on the performance of certain conditions. Firm-centric views in which the firm's agency is paramount have their limiting assumptions. There are several policy instruments and tools that market regulators (predominantly the state) can use if not to frustrate international expansion, then to moderate the benefits accrued by external parties operating overseas and to minimise the adverse effects (locally for the state, destinations, firms and institutions) (Kusluvan and Karamustafa 2001).

Thus, while such contributions are able to advance our understanding of the general framing conditions for the internationalisation of tourism businesses, they provide only a partial view of why and how business decisions are made. Instead, as Mosedale (2007) indicates, based on a reading of firm-level studies in economic geography, organisational behaviours both between and within firms are often far from objective, logical and easily researched. Firms are, after all, social and cultural institutions in their own rights. Sub-optimal economic decisions can be made, non-market factors may intervene, and the internal and external politics of firms may impact on their commercial operations, all of which the quantitative approaches typical of international business studies are not equipped to deal with.

THE INTERNATIONALISATION OF TOURISM BUSINESSES

Although the firm has become such a dominant feature in international business studies, there has been practically no attention given to international tourism enterprises. What investigations there have been, have focused on hotel internationalisation and the way in which it differs from more common applications in manufacturing, as Quer *et al.* (2007) make clear. The chapters in this part examine three other major types of businesses commonly equated with the 'tourism industry'. While many of the ideas traditionally present in Market Imperfection Theories are implicit in the chapters, they portray the internationalisation of tourism businesses as complex, messy and sometimes plainly unpredictable from more formal, even mathematically driven modes of investigation. Duval examines the internationalisation of the aviation industry. It may seem almost oxymoronic to talk about the internationalisation of aviation because it is inherently involved with conveying persons (thereby enabling modes 2 and 4, Figure 1.1) and supply (modes 1 and 3) across borders to destinations (but as Chapter 1 noted, transportation is defined separately to travel for purposes of United Nations statistical definitions). However, airlines are continuously on the lookout for new and profitable routes, destinations and slot spaces at airports. As a result, airline networks have become more dense and their coverage wider. Duval's chapter indicates the importance of external aeropolitics as much as internal firm-based criteria on the ability for airlines to act internationally. While the airlines perceive the need to expand as a response to greater demand from the travelling public, a number of regulatory and governance issues conspire to mediate the delivery of routes, flights and hence ultimately passengers. Airlines may be 'gatekeepers of tourism' to use Ioannides' (1998) memorable characterisation, and they structure patterns of mobilities at a number of temporal and spatial scales. However, as Duval notes, their ability to act as gatekeepers is, in turn, a function of the outcomes of global aeropolitics. For example, as Chapter 2 noted air transport services are currently excluded from the General Agreement on Trade in Services (GATS) negotiations with GATS only applying to: (1) aircraft repair and maintenance services, (2) the selling and marketing of air transport services, and (3) computer reservations system (CRS) services. All traffic rights and directly related aviation transport activities are excluded.

Weaver and Duval examine the international and transnational characteristics of modern cruise tourism. The development of cruise tourism is set in the broader contexts of contemporary patterns of consumption and, more significantly, production. Through their operations, cruise lines embody many of the aspects of the international trade in (tourism) services: cruise holidays may be packaged and sold across international borders to consumers in other countries (modes 1 and 3); passengers are conveyed from destination to destination and offered the opportunity to disembark in order to purchase local goods, offers and experiences (mode 2); and as floating resorts in their own right, cruise liners make frequent use of natural persons from low-cost economies as their (temporary), flexible labour force (mode 4). Weaver and Duval examine the regulation of the cruise industry and there are some interesting comparisons to be made with the airline industry in terms of deterritorialised practices. Cruise lines have registered offices usually in the home country of the parent organisation and, according to international law, cruise liners have to sail under the flag of a sovereign state for issues of legal accountability. In many cases, boats fly so-called 'flags of convenience', registered as they are off-shore in order to take advantage of local governance regimes and conditions, lower taxes, lower labour costs and less unionised workforces among other factors; that is, they gain from the benefits of ownership, location and internalisation. One of the interesting issues raised by this chapter (and later revisited in Chapter 14) is the issue of corporate social responsibility (CSR). In particular, through their mobile operations there are issues of where cruise lines should be held accountable. Legal transgressions, such as pollution incidents, and their enduring legacies may occur in destinations far away from where the organisations have their headquarters and/or are held accountable in courts. Of course, for all parties concerned, the preferable position is that such events should not take place in the first instance, and Weaver and Duval explore CSR as a means of encouraging self-regulation in a sector that faces substantial regulatory and governance challenges because businesses are literally travelling through different transnational and national regulatory spaces over time.

Finally, in this section, Scherle and Coles remind us that we should question, especially in this day and age, what it means to be an international business. There may be an understandable temptation to concentrate on the transnational corporations with their headquarters in the core regions of the 'global north'. Not only are these enterprises highly capitalised and often widely spread throughout the world, but they also have wide reach in terms of destination coverage and marketing. However, it is increasingly common in conditions of greater time–space compression and enhanced communications to find small- and medium-sized tourism enterprises (SMTEs), even micro-enterprises and individual entrepreneurs, involved in cross-border relationships to produce or distribute tourism products. Scherle and Coles examine the interactions between German and Moroccan tour operators over the supply and delivery of tourism experiences to German consumers. The partners are connected in supply chains – or even commodity chains, as Mosedale (Chapter 8) may describe them – that stretch over international boundaries (mode 1), with holidays marketed (mode 3) and bought in Germany and consumed in Morocco (mode 2). This chapter adopts an approach that is well established in international business studies: namely, it examines intercultural communications, competences and exchanges (Hofstede 1980, 2004). Chain metaphors in distribution point to the interactions of businesses and individual actors within businesses but they fail to recognise that the individuals concerned may have quite different socio-demographic characteristics. Moreover, the actors concerned may come from quite different cultures and their cultural backgrounds may influence to one degree or another the way in they transact their business. Culture has been quantified and appeared as a variable in quantitative analyses of (tourism) internationalisation (Quer et al. 2007). Cross-cultural interactions have been examined on the demand-side using this conceptual framework (Reisinger and Turner 2003; Litvin et al. 2004). However, their chapter argues for a greater and more nuanced treatment of culture in supply-side studies of tourism production.

REFERENCES

Buckley, P.J. (2002) 'Is the international business research agenda running out of steam?', *Journal of International Business Studies*, 33(2): 365–73.

Buckley, P.J. and Lessard, D.R. (2005) 'Regaining the edge for international business research', *Journal of International Business Studies*, 36: 595–9.

Coles, T., Hall, C.M. and Duval, D. (2006) 'Tourism and post-disciplinary inquiry', *Current Issues in Tourism*, 9(4/5): 293–319.

Dunning, J.H. (1977) 'Trade, location of economic activity and the MNE: a search for an eclectic approach', in B. Ohlin, P.O. Hesselborn and P.M. Wijkmon (eds) *The International Allocation of Economic Activity*. London: Macmillan.

—— (1995) 'Reappraising the eclectic paradigm in the age of alliance capitalism', *Journal of International Business Studies*, 26(3): 461–91.

—— (2000) 'The eclectic paradigm as an envelope for economic and business theories of MNE activity', *International Business Review*, 9(2): 163–90.

Dunning, J.H. and McQueen, M. (1981) 'The Eclectic Theory of international production: a case-study of the international hotel industry', *Managerial and Decision Economics*, 2(4): 197–210.

Hofstede, G. (2004) *Cultures and Organizations: Software of the Mind*. New York: McGraw-Hill (revised edition, original published in 1980).

Kantarci, K. (2007) 'Perceptions of foreign investors on the tourism market in central Asia including Kyrgyzstan, Kazakhstan, Uzbekistan, Turkmenistan', *Tourism Management*, 28: 820–9.

Kusluvan, S. and Karamustafa, K. (2001) 'Multinational hotel development in developing countries: an exploratory analysis of critical policy issues', *International Journal of Tourism Research*, 3: 170–97.

Litvin, S.W., Crotts, J.C. and Hefner, F.L. (2004) 'Cross-cultural tourist behaviour: a replication and extension involving Hofstede's Uncertainty Avoidance Dimension', *International Journal of Tourism Research*, 6: 29–37.

Loannides, D. (1998) 'Tour operators: the gatekeepers of tourism', in D. Loannides and K.G. Debbage (eds) *The Economic Geography of the Tourist Industry: A supply-side Analysis*. London: Routledge.

Mosedale, J.T. (2007) Corporate geographies of transnational tourism corporations. Unpublished PhD thesis University of Exeter.

Mtigwe, B. (2006) 'Theoretical milestones in international business: the journey to international entrepreneurship theory', *Journal of International Entrepreneurship*, 4: 5–25.

Quer, D., Claver, E. and Andreu, R. (2007) 'Foreign market entry mode in the hotel industry: the impact of country- and firm-specific factors', *International Business Review*, 16: 362–76.

Reisinger, Y. and Turner, L.W. (2003) *Cross-cultural Behaviour in Tourism: Concepts and Analysis*. Oxford: Butterworth-Heinemann.

Zhang, J. and Jensen, C. (2007) 'Comparative advantage explaining tourism flows', *Annals of Tourism Research*, 34(1): 223–43.

Aeropolitics, global aviation networks and the regulation of international visitor flows

5

David Timothy Duval

Learning objectives

After considering this chapter, you will be able to:

- recognise the complexity of regulatory environments in which air services operate;
- provide examples of open skies agreements and their impact on air service operations;
- understand how air services are influenced by agreements governing access.

Key terms

- airlines;
- carriers;
- aeropolitics;
- freedoms of the air;
- tourism flows.

INTRODUCTION

The purpose of this chapter is to interrogate issues of regulation and political manoeuvring in light of transnational air service operations. The wider context presented is one of aeropolitics, which is broadly defined as the dynamic relationship between state and non-state interests in the regulation and operation of air services. Aeropolitics is a framework that situates decisions regarding air service access, particularly where national governments are generally tasked with regulating air services and the degree to which foreign carriers are able to service local gateways or hubs (Forsyth 2001). This is especially salient since many countries have one or more 'flag carriers', or those carriers in which local regulations regarding ownership and effective control (i.e. usually a certain proportion of ownership and control must be in the hands of citizens) have been satisfied such that they are certified as so-called 'national' carriers.

The chapter begins by outlining the basic structure of international regulations relating to air service accessibility, notably the format of bilateral agreements or 'Freedoms of the Air'. Regulatory options are discussed next, focusing on a continuum of liberalisation and protectionism. Different forms of each are discussed, using examples from New Zealand, the European Union (EU), North America and South Africa. Aeropolitics is then discussed with reference to airline alliances, particularly where equity and competition are concerned. The chapter concludes with an overall assessment of the function of aeropolitics in the wider context of operations and global mobilities.

REGULATORY ENVIRONMENTS

The regulatory environment in global aviation is manifested primarily through extensive air service agreements. These are sometimes referred to as bilateral or multilateral agreements depending on the number of parties involved. In principle, these address specific airline operations between two countries, in particular the extent to which access by a carrier (or carriers) designated by one state is granted to another state. Agreements may also include routing, frequency, capacity, fares, restrictions on ownership of airlines, and levels of effective control of airlines by nationals of the state concerned. More liberalised approaches to air service agreements may culminate in 'open skies agreements' or even single aviation markets (SAMs). In these cases, restrictions on routing, frequency, capacity and fares may be open (and thus restricted only on the basis of infrastructural support such as slot space at airports) (Debbage 2002, 2004); however, ownership and effective control of carriers themselves may still be restricted.

The presence of air service agreements ultimately dictates the spatial extent of an airline network, which in turn dictates the flow of tourist traffic. In smaller regional networks, such as Australia and New Zealand, negotiations over air access may follow existing and wider agreements of trade. When global network planning is involved, the bilateral air service agreement system becomes slightly more complex, and it may often require substantial negotiations on the part of two or more governments that have previously not been involved in any (or limited) trade negotiations.

Table 5.1 outlines the key elements of the Freedoms of the Air that dictate international air traffic. The first five Freedoms were established at a special conference in Chicago in 1944. There, the United States and 54 other countries established a common practice of regulating international air access. While this was particularly difficult given the number of countries involved, the end result was that individual states could decide whether or not to grant reciprocal rights to their air space. Gradually, four more Freedoms have been added

Table 5.1 *Freedoms of the air*

Term	Privilege
First Freedom	The right or privilege granted by one state to another state or states for a carrier to fly across its territory without landing; as such, an airline registered in Country A can fly to Country B by freely flying over Country C.
Second Freedom	The right granted by one state to another state or states for a carrier to land in its territory for non-traffic purposes (e.g. fuel or other technical/mechanic reasons); thus, an airline from Country A has the right to land in Country C en route to Country B, but it cannot pick up or drop off passengers in Country C.
Third Freedom	The right or privilege granted by one state to another state to put down, in the territory of the first state, traffic coming from the home state of the carrier; in other words, the right of an airline registered in Country A to carry passengers from Country A to Country B.
Fourth Freedom	The right or privilege granted by one state to another state to take on, in the territory of the first state, traffic destined for the home state of the carrier; that is, the right of an airline registered in Country A to bring back passengers from Country B (thus, the Third and Fourth Freedoms are normally tied together).
Fifth Freedom	The right or privilege granted by one state to another state to put down and to take on, in the territory of the first state, traffic coming from or destined to a third; this means the right of a carrier registered in Country A can fly to Country C, drop off and pick up passengers, and continue on to Country B. This will require an agreement between Country A and Country B as well as Country A and Country C. Holloway's (2003: 217) definition is as follows: 'a privilege allowing an airline to uplift traffic from one foreign state and transport it to another state along a route which originates or terminates in that airline's home state'.
Sixth Freedom	The combination of Third and Fourth Freedoms, 'resulting in the ability of an airline to uplift traffic from a foreign state and transport it to another foreign state via an intermediate stop – probably involving a change of plane and/or flight number – in its home Country (e.g. American carrying traffic from London to Lima over its Miami hub)' (Holloway 2003: 218). Doganis' (2001: 227) definition is as follows: 'The use by an airline of Country A of two sets of Third and Fourth Freedom rights to carry traffic between two other countries but using its base at A as a transit point.'
Seventh Freedom	The right or privilege granted by one state to another state, of transporting traffic between the territory of the granting state and any third state with no requirement to include on such operation any point in the territory of the recipient state, i.e. the service need not connect to or be an extension of any service to/from the home state of the carrier. This means that an airline registered in Country A has Seventh Freedom rights to carry traffic between Countries B and C without stopping in Country A. If traffic was required to stop in Country A, Fifth Freedom privileges would be enacted (or required).

Continued

Table 5.1 *Continued*

Eighth Freedom	The right or privilege of transporting traffic between two points in the territory of the granting state on a service which originates or terminates in the home Country of the foreign carrier or (in connection with the so-called Seventh Freedom of the Air) outside the territory of the granting state. 'Consecutive cabotage' is enacted when an airline registered in Country A can have service that originates in Country A, continues to a first port in Country C, picks up and drops off passengers, and continues to another point in Country C (Holloway 2003, who uses the example of a international flight landing first in Hawai/i and then on-flying to Los Angeles). 'Full cabotage' 'is the operation by an airline of services within a single foreign Country' (Holloway 2003: 218), and is referenced by some as the Ninth Freedom.
Ninth Freedom	The right or privilege of transporting cabotage traffic of the granting state on a service performed entirely within the territory of the granting state (also known as 'stand alone' cabotage). This Freedom is somewhat rare (as are the Seventh and Eighth Freedoms) outside of formal open skies agreements, but it means that an airline registered in Country A can operate entirely within, for example, Country C without initiating or terminating a service in Country A.

Source: Adapted and abridged from ICAO (2007), Doganis (2001) and Duval (2007).

(Doganis 2001; Holloway 2003) as the expansion and complexity of air service networks have increased in the past four to five decades.

The provision of Freedoms in air traffic can certainly influence the global business environment (in particular the shape of competition) and, by extension, accessibility and connectivity across air route networks. Two of the perhaps most contested and controversial Freedoms are the Fifth and Sixth Freedoms. Fifth Freedom agreements often trigger concerns regarding unfair advantages enjoyed by these Fifth Freedom carriers, especially with respect to the increased capacity on existing routes previously dominated by existing flag carriers. Fifth Freedom carriers often have the ability to price closer to marginal cost, which can be beneficial in a price-sensitive market. Indeed, responses to proposals for allowing Fifth Freedom access to international carriers often include introducing protectionist policies by governments (Duval 2005), as evidenced in the Australia–Singapore example discussed below.

In the past decade, Sixth Freedom carriers (operating on pairs of Third and Fourth Freedoms) have received significant media attention owing to their massive expansion of routes. Most of the largest Sixth Freedom carriers are based in Asia or the Middle East (e.g. Emirates, Qatar Airways, Singapore Airlines) and route passengers from major markets such as Europe, transfer them through their own hubs (e.g. Dubai, Singapore) before on-flying them to other destinations (e.g. United States, Australasia). The result is very profitable international route networks without the added burden of cumbersome domestic networks that other non-Sixth Freedom carriers (e.g. British Airways, Qantas) must service. In many respects, Sixth Freedom carriers have attracted significant criticism over the equity involved in allowing their access to lucrative markets such as Europe and Australia. For example, allowing Singapore Airlines access to London Heathrow after routing passengers originating in Australia through Singapore may be criticised by some as detrimental to British Airways' market share of the Australian market (even though British Airways itself benefits from Fifth Freedoms through Singapore for its Sydney–Singapore–London flights). This leads to consideration of the role of government in protecting existing flag carriers in certain markets from the aggressive expansion efforts of Sixth Freedom carriers. The balance between protectionism and liberalisation of air services, then, is a delicate one that trades protection of national flag carriers against increased accessibility leading to (potentially stronger) performance in the national economy.

LIBERALISM AND PROTECTIONISM IN AIR SERVICES

Air service agreements are based in politics in one sense, but often the overarching context of their negotiations is rooted in international trade (access for wider economic benefit) and foreign direct investment (ownership and control) to encourage competition and potential benefits to consumers. Governments are thus tasked with determining whether air access is worthy of protectionist policies that ultimately favour a national carrier in terms of airlift or a more liberalised approach. At present, the scale of liberalisation of air services around the world is extremely variable. Some countries, such as Australia, permit full domestic competition whilst restricting international access. Others have been more restrictive due to existing political orientations. China, for example, has traditionally been restrictive of competition but this may be changing as many are forecasting significant growth in the Chinese domestic and international market as a consequence of a growing middle-class segment (Telegraph 2006). How, then, should we seek to explain the existing variations in air access around the world?

A useful way of examining government approaches to the regulation of air services is a spectrum where one end represents full liberalisation and the other full protectionism of incumbent and/or national carriers. Where a particular government or country can be positioned on the spectrum depends on several factors, including market considerations and any historical precedents. Full liberalisation represents an environment in which a national government allows foreign interests to operate or own a majority shareholding in an airline or allows foreign airlines unfettered access to local markets. In some instances, foreign carriers may be allowed to operate on domestic routes. Full liberalisation is generally only inhibited by existing logistic or infrastructural limitations. A good example is the limitations in slot space (for aircraft movement) at major gateway airports which can be extremely limited and thus impede expansion by both foreign and national carriers.

Protectionism stems from a conscious policy where a national government may outright deny (or limit access to the point of reduced financial benefits) access by foreign carriers to domestic markets. Alternatively, they impose restrictions on foreign ownership and control such that carriers operating within a country must have majority ownership and control in the hands of nationals. Hanlon (1999: 33) suggests that such policies may be problematic:

> Governments traditionally regarded air transport as, in some sense, a public utility. Strictly speaking, it is not. Economists prefer to reserve the term 'public utility' to enterprises that have characteristics of natural monopolies. Natural monopolies exist where the advantages of size are so great that a service can only be provided at least cost if it is supplied by one, and only one firm.

Hanlon (1999) also suggests that airlines, unlike other service sector activities such as telecommunications, have relatively lower fixed-to-variable costs, and thus fall outside of the traditional sense of needing full protection from competition. Further complicating the matter is the fact that, despite massive deregulation in the global aviation environment, governments may act as majority shareholders in particular airlines.

CASE-STUDY VIGNETTE – TOURISM AND INTERNATIONAL BUSINESS IN ACTION

Singapore Airlines and Freedoms to fly to and from Australia

Protectionist policies towards international and domestics air services are still evident today such as the recent example of the decision in 2006 by the Australian Cabinet to (again) deny access by Singapore Airlines to the so-called 'Pacific Route' between Australia and the United States (particularly Sydney–Los Angeles), despite the existence of a Singapore–Australia Free Trade Agreement established in 2003. Singapore Airlines had, for some time, lobbied the Australian government for access to this route, but the Australian Cabinet needed to consider several issues before rendering a decision. First and foremost was the potential impact of the introduction of Singapore Airlines services on Qantas' (Australia's flag carrier) own operations on the route, which is known to be extremely profitable for the airline. Thereafter, the Cabinet needed to weigh up the benefits to Australia's tourism sector (and indeed general accessibility) as well as whether Qantas may benefit from any reciprocal agreements. The Cabinet decided against Singapore's application to allow Singapore Airlines to fly the route. The government was not convinced that allowing Singapore Airlines access would result in significant economic benefits to Australia. Moreover, Qantas' own network could not expand beyond the already-existing rights it has out of Changi International Airport in Singapore because the rights to the 'beyond countries' (primarily in Europe) are not available over and above the routes it already operates. Singapore had

Continued

previously granted Fifth Freedom rights to any Australian carrier through Singapore, but Singapore as a country cannot obviously grant rights to points beyond. The debate over access to the Pacific Route by Singapore Airlines was recently re-opened following the proposed sale of Qantas to Airline Partners Australia (comprised of local and overseas interests but led by Maquarie Bank in Australia). The Liberal Opposition in Australia has suggested that the route should be opened to competition should the sale be finalised (Kerr 2007). Singapore Airlines spokesperson Kate Pratley expressed similar sentiments: 'To suggest that Qantas, controlled by a multi-billion-dollar international consortium, should be protected by the Australian Government is beyond reason. The reality is that protection comes at a direct cost to the consumer' (The Australian 2006).

Questions

- How would the Australian Cabinet justify its decision to the Australian public given that increased competition may, according to Singapore Airlines, have been beneficial to them in terms of lowering mean fares?
- In light of the decision, would it be possible or feasible for Singapore simply to remove the Fifth Freedom rights of Australian carriers (predominantly Qantas) in protest at being denied access to the Pacific Route?
- If Singapore removed Fifth Freedom rights to Australian carriers, how would this contravene existing trade agreements? How would this be perceived by other countries that have existing bilateral and multilateral air service agreements with Singapore?

Not all countries have embraced the liberalisation of air services (see case-study vignette). In one example, South African Airways has been attempting to negotiate Fifth Freedom rights to pick up passengers in Accra (Ghana) bound for the United States. The Ghanaian government, however, has refused access to South African Airways. *Business Report* (a South African newspaper) has suggested that protectionist policies are to blame. Given that Ghana Airways ceased operations in 2003, the newspaper argued that Ghana is worried that South African Airways will capture a significant proportion of the Ghanaian market and thus prevent any future Ghanaian airlines from establishing a presence on the route (d'Angelo 2005).

Other examples of protectionist policies are focused on ensuring that national carriers continue to operate despite dire financial conditions. In September 2005, British Airways Chief Executive Rod Eddington suggested that the United States' protectionist policies of 'propping up' failing US-based airlines, particularly after 11 September 2001, is unwise. Eddington argued that 'they're operating in protected markets, they're hoovering up public funds and still they can't make a profit' (Forbes 2005).

OPEN SKIES AGREEMENTS

The more extreme end of the liberalisation–protectionist spectrum is represented by full liberalisation of air access. Many countries are moving toward a more liberal form of regulating international air services. In Europe, for example, regional bilateral agreements after 1985 have been mainly of the 'open market' type. These have allowed open-route access and they have been largely unrestrictive in terms of capacity control (Doganis 2001).

Beginning in the early 1990s, India also radically revised its policies towards competition and access by foreign airlines (Hooper 1997). The result was a significant expansion in the number of bilateral agreements between India and various other regional and more distant countries, although not all of these 'bilaterals' are currently being used by Indian carriers (Financial Express 2006a). With a population of over one billion, the introduction of competition has stimulated both domestic travel as well as inbound and outbound travel (Travel Daily News 2005). The result has been that India's aviation environment has become one of the strongest in terms of competition and it is currently leading Asian growth according to the Centre for Asia Pacific Aviation (Financial Express 2006b). Jet Airways, for example, was launched in 1993 and currently enjoys a sizeable share of India's domestic market. Air India, the flag carrier owned fully by the government of India, subsequently launched a low-cost spin-off, Air India Express, in April 2005 in order to compete with Jet Airways and, at the same time, not reduce the strength of the existing brand of Air India. Several other airlines have been launched, including Kingfisher Airlines, SpiceJet, Go Airlines and Paramount Aviation, all of which began operations in India in 2005. Two more (IndiGo and Indus Airways) commenced services in late 2006 (Manorama Online 2005).

Open skies agreements between two countries are a form of increased liberalisation. Several recent examples point to the aeropolitical underpinnings of these kinds of agreements and hence their importance in engineering patterns of international business and mobility. At present, cross-border air services traffic in the EU generally operates under a wide, free market area (the EU Single Air Market or more commonly known as the European Common Aviation Area, ECAA). The ECAA is designed to allow for the unencumbered movement of goods and people throughout the EU. Prior to this, regulatory activities were largely in the domain of international bilateral agreements (Dearden 1994; Graham 1998). Despite the presence of the ECAA, which governs intra-EU air services, individual states within the EU still ratify bilateral agreements with other governments. The European Court of Justice, however, penalised eight member states (UK, Denmark, Sweden, Finland, Belgium, Luxembourg, Austria and Germany) for concluding air service agreements with the United States that violate European Community (EC) law (Holdgaard 2003).

Related to the EU's open skies agreement are discussions in November 2005 between the United States and the EU that centred on a potential open skies agreement. The goal was to arrange new agreements that would replace many of existing and complicated bilateral agreements that the United States holds with many individual countries in Europe, many of which date back to the 1970s. Earlier, in November 2002 the European Court of Justice ruled that these multiple (and varied) agreements (which covered routes, capacity, frequency and even fares in some instances) violated EC law. Despite general support from within

Europe for the idea of open market access, many European states, particularly the United Kingdom, argued throughout 2005 and 2006 that the United States should be required to relax controls on its own domestic air services market and thus allow foreign ownership and rights for foreign airlines to operate domestically in the US. The United States was reluctant to do this which indicated a somewhat protectionist policy standpoint that favoured its own national carriers. A tentative agreement was reached (the first of several to come) in November 2005 that would have allowed European carriers to depart from countries other than their own for the United States (ostensibly, Fifth and Seventh Freedom rights). Some commentators, such as Firey (2003), argue that a full open skies agreement would likely benefit European carriers by way of mergers and alliances with American carriers rather than actually competing with them; however, it is not unreasonable to ponder the poor financial state of several United States carriers and thus whether the attractiveness of such mergers with European carriers may be limited for the latter? In April 2007, an agreement was reached between the EU and the United States for open skies that allowed airlines of either jurisdiction unfettered access without restriction. Further, the agreement allowed for investors from the United States to invest in a EC airline as long it retains majority ownership and effective control within the EC. European investors can own up to 49.9 per cent of a US carrier although foreign nationals may not individually hold more than 25 per cent voting stock. European carriers, however, did not receive permission to operate domestic flights (under what is referred to as a cabotage arrangement) within the United States.

Finally in this respect, in November 2005, the United States and Canada ratified an updated version of their existing open skies agreement. In the new version, airlines of each country will have complete Fifth Freedom access or beyond rights to other countries as along as, of course, landing rights are secured in those beyond countries. In other words, a United States carrier would be able, for example, to fly from Chicago to Toronto and then onward to Paris, as long as the existing agreements with France permit this kind of traffic. However, the benefits to passengers may not be immediate as there are already in place substantial transatlantic and Caribbean-bound services from both the United States and Canada.

Once again, as this case demonstrates, despite moves toward liberal air services, issues of competition and protectionism are still routinely debated and considered at national levels. Nevertheless, other kinds of agreements have been designed to abolish the function of geopolitical borders in the establishment of international air service agreements. For example, the SAM between Australia and New Zealand, while not technically a fully operational and sanctioned open skies agreement, was designed to allow New Zealand-based and Australian-based carriers to operate within and between the two countries without any regulatory barriers or restrictions.

COMPETITIVE AND LOGISTICAL ALLIANCES

Apart from government-sanctioned regulatory environments, firm-level alliances often catch the attention of regulatory bodies. In some respects, the formation of airline alliances may be interpreted as quick-fix solutions to otherwise out-of-reach markets (for aeropolitical reasons discussed above). The President and Chief Executive Officer of KLM, Leo van Wijk, once remarked: 'Alliances are ... a reasoned response to an antiquated regulatory system ... [They] permit indirect access to restricted markets' (Staniland 1998). All airline alliances are, in their own right, strategic in that they are designed to introduce operational efficiencies and markets to one or more existing carriers' networks. Often these networks span international boundaries and as such result in significant market penetration opportunities.

The most visible alliances are those which are global in their operational outlook. The best-known examples are Star Alliance, OneWorld and SkyTeam (Table 5.2). Star Alliance captures the largest global passenger share and enjoys the highest operating revenue (Table 5.3). Other alliances are less visible, but generate significant debate from the perspective of aeropolitics. Tretheway and Oum (1992) identify several types of alliances:

- *Route-by-route alliance*: generally involves coordination between two or more airlines on a specific route (i.e. reduction of 'wingtip' flights, where two flights from competing airlines leave from an origin bound for the same destination) or a combination of routes. One example could be the concept of interlining, which allow for the agreement by two carriers to accept tickets, baggage and even cargo from each other (Hannegan and Mulvey 1995). For example, Qantas interlines international flights across the Pacific with American Airlines flights within the United States.
- *Commercial alliance*: generally involves the 'coordination of flight schedule and ground handling, joint use of ground facilities, shared frequent flyer programs, code sharing, block seat sale, and joint advertising and promotion' (Oum and Park, 1997: 138). These types of alliances are more general than route-by-route alliances and can often allow for a journey across several carriers to be ticketed through one airline and running on one airline flight code (Hannegan and Mulvey 1995). One example is the code share agreement between Qantas and British Airways on flights from Australia to the United Kingdom (as a result of both being members of the OneWorld global alliance).

Table 5.2 *Major global alliances – key members*

Alliance	Star Alliance	OneWorld	SkyTeam
Carriers (as of September 2007)	Air Canada, Air New Zealand, ANA, Asiana Airlines, Austrian, bmi, LOT Polish Airlines, Lufthansa, Scandinavian Airlines, Singapore Airlines, South African Airways, Spanair, SWISS, TAP Portugal, Thai Airways International, United Airlines, US Airways	American Airlines, British Airways, Cathay Pacific, Finnair, Iberia, JAL (Japan Airlines), LAN, Malev, Qantas, Royal Jordanian Airlines	AeroMexico, Aeroflot, Air France, Alitalia, CSA Czech Airlines, Continental Airlines, Delta, KLM, Korean Air, Northwest Airlines

Source: Based on IATA (2004), Duval (2007) and company data.

Table 5.3 *Major global airline alliances – key statistics*

Alliance	Star Alliance	OneWorld	SkyTeam
Global passenger share (%)	17.6	13.2	16.0
Global operating revenue share (%)	25.2	18.4	19.1
Destinations served	883	671	751
Passenger numbers (millions)	386	290	352

Source: Airline Business, September 2007.
Note: All figures as at September 2007.

- *Alliance of equity*: one airline obtaining a share of holdings in another airline, thus ideally leading to operational efficiencies as well as the benefits as identified in commercial and route-by-route alliances. For example, in October 2006, the Chair and CEO of United Airlines suggested that equity acquisition in foreign airlines was one way to ensure international coverage in their networks, largely because of significant consolidation of carriers in Asia and Europe. This outlook is not limited to international acquisitions, however. The threat of airline mergers and acquisitions has been substantial in the United States since 11 September (2001), with examples including early discussions in December 2006 surrounding a merger between Continental and United, and US Airways bidding for control over Delta.

In many respects, aeropolitics can be observed in these agreements as well. Glisson *et al.* (1996: 29) point out that equity alliances can actually be problematic in that they need to acquire regulatory approval in many jurisdictions:

> These equity holdings are looked on by some as a method of cementing the relationship between two airlines for the long run. However, they can be difficult to obtain because of severe restrictions and equity positions held by home governments. Those who oppose equity arrangements do not see the need for the investments, and feel they are nothing more than a waste of management time and an inappropriate use of investors' money. To many, equity alliances are becoming a system of airlines in distress. Others see them as defence postures.

An excellent example of a (failed) equity and commercial alliance is the Air New Zealand–Qantas Strategic Alliance Agreement (SAA) (Duval 2007). Air New Zealand and Qantas (along with Air Pacific, as Air New Zealand held 1.9 per cent and the Fijian government, as majority shareholder, held 51 per cent) applied for authorisation from the New Zealand Commerce Commission (NZCC) in December 2002 to ratify an SAA between the two parties.

The SAA would have, in effect, resulted in a joint network across the Tasman Sea and throughout the Pacific. The proposed SAA included elements from all three of Tretheway and Oum's (1992) typology of airlines alliances, thus covering ground handling, marketing and equity. Under Section 67 of the New Zealand Commerce Act of 1986, and filed in conjunction with the proposed SAA, Qantas was seeking to purchase 22.5 per cent of shares in exchange for NZ$550 million. Importantly, the applications were based within several existing Australia–New Zealand policy and trade agreements, including: the New Zealand–Australia Closer Economic Relations Trade Agreement (established in 1983 in order to harmonise trade relations); the SAM as discussed above; and the Trans-Tasman Mutual Recognition Arrangement (TTMRA) (introduced in 1996 to allow unrestricted flows of goods and skilled personnel between the two countries).

The applicants (Air New Zealand and Qantas Airways Limited, 2002a, 2002b) argued the case on three main grounds (Duval 2005): first, cost savings by arguing that existing market pressure and competition under the SAM between Australia and New Zealand did not warrant the profitable operations of two full service airlines; second, for reasons of scheduling and direct services, particularly with respect to harmonising customer and market bases, because code-sharing on some trans-Tasman routes would result in more efficient operations overall; and finally, the effect on tourism was raised on the basis that both were heavily involved in the promotion and marketing of tourism for both countries. Thus it would not be in their own best interests to jeopardise this through price collusion if the SAA were approved.

As the official regulatory body in New Zealand charged with considering this (and other similar, non-aviation related mergers and alliances), the NZCC had to consider, from an aeropolitical perspective, the impact of the proposed SAA on domestic, trans-Tasman and trans-Pacific markets and operations, and the implications of having Qantas own almost 25 per cent of Air New Zealand. Several factors influenced the NZCC decision. In the factual, while Qantas would own nearly 25 per cent of New Zealand's flag carrier, at the same time some, if not all, of the arguments made in favour of the proposed agreement (e.g. efficiencies, cost savings) would be passed on to the consumer. In the 'counterfactual', it recognised that Air New Zealand would operate on its own at a time when the global aviation market was unstable and several international carriers around the world were either under bankruptcy protection or had become insolvent.

The SAA was ultimately rejected by the NZCC, although the decision was appealed by Air New Zealand (on behalf of the applicants) in July 2004 to the High Court at Auckland. A few months later in September 2004, the High Court endorsed the NZCC decision. It is interesting to note that the Australian Competition and Consumer Commission (ACCC), the Australian equivalent to the NZCC, also rejected the application on similar grounds, but the Australian Competition Tribunal, upon appeal, threw out the ACCC ruling and granted authorisation for the SAA to move forward. By this point, however, both airlines had moved on regardless (largely because they were still subject to the High Court ruling in New Zealand) and further options were being considered. One option was the pursuit of an 'air share agreement' which would effectively allow both carriers to sell seats on either's aircraft, although both airlines, in February 2007, opted to abandon this plan.

The Air New Zealand–Qantas SAA case highlights the complex regulatory environment within which airlines operate, and it encapsulates the balancing of commercial realities with public interest. On the one hand, as majority shareholder, the New Zealand government needed to consider the profitability of its flag carrier and, indeed, its future. On the other, however, it also needed to consider the implications for allowing its flag carrier to form an alliance, the results of which were entirely uncertain from the perspective of the impact on the travelling public. Air New Zealand, as an airline, was facing a rather uncertain future at the time of the SAA application, while Qantas enjoyed strong financial performance during the year the SAA application was lodged and furthermore in the following three to four years (based on revenue per passenger kilometre).

CONCLUSION

The scope of global regulation in the context of air service provision ultimately dictates the extent to which people (and goods) are mobile. While the argument could be made that air services appear to be excellent examples of the globalised nature of transport, international business and travel, the reality is that the manner in which services are organised and regulated would suggest that they are anything but global. Existing regulatory frameworks, as discussed in this chapter, highlight the fragmented and regionally focused aeropolitical policies that often blur the distinction between liberalist and protectionist efforts.

The shape of the global air services environment is not likely to change, largely because there is little incentive for global equity to be introduced with respect to international access when the financial and operational realities of the carriers are so different/varied. Despite the push toward more open skies in a variety of regions (e.g. the EU and North America), most national governments will likely continue to monitor and regulate access with an eye to ensuring maximum economic benefits and political capital. In other words, full deregulation or liberalisation will only transpire if there are economic and political incentives. Far from being examples of globalisation, air services in a global sense are rather dictated by political realities within regionalist trading blocs (although see Hettne 2005 for a re-evaluation of 'new' regionalism). Decisions by governments in relation to regulation obviously have an impact on operational decisions by air service operators; as such, they are very much involved in lobbying efforts internationally in order to ensure their own operational and financial survival. Thus, what may be said of the future of air services is likely to be the result of a tug-of-war between international air service operators keen on expansion and government oversight committees keen on ensuring their own national flag carriers either receive equitable access or are capable of competing with new players.

Discussion questions

- How would you describe the importance of air service agreements for the movement of manufactured goods and people around the world?
- What are the implications of the EU–US open skies agreement on traffic to and from congested airports?
- To what extent do air service agreements ultimately dictate global flows of tourists? Can it be argued that, beyond local marketing efforts, the success of destinations relies on the political and economic relationships formed between state governments?

REFERENCES

Air New Zealand and Qantas Airways Limited (2002a) Commerce Act 1986: Restrictive Trade Practice, Section 58: Notice Seeking Authorisation, 09/12/02. Public version accessed via New Zealand Commerce Commission website (since removed).

—— (2002b) Commerce Act 1986: Business Acquisition, Section 57: Notice Seeking Authorisation, 09/12/02. Public version accessed via New Zealand Commerce Commission website (since removed).

D'Angelo, A. (2005) Ghanaian protectionism thwarts SAA, 25/10/05. Business Report. Online. Available from: http://www.businessreport.co.za/index.php?fArticleId=2964617 (accessed: 09/11/05).

Dearden, S.J.H. (1994) 'Air transport regulation in the European Union', European Business Review, 94(5): 15-9.

Debbage, K. (2002) 'Airport Runway Slots: Limits to Growth', Annals of Tourism Research, 29(4): 933-51

—— (2004) 'Airlines, airports, and international aviation', in L. Pender and R. Sharpley (eds) The Management of Tourism. London: Sage Publications.

Doganis, R. (2001) The Airline Business in the 21st Century. London: Routledge.

Duval, D.T. (2005) 'Public/stakeholder perceptions of airline alliances: the New Zealand experience', Journal of Air Transport Management, 11(6): 355-462.

—— (2007) Tourism and Transport: Modes, Networks, Flows. Clevedon: Channel View.

Financial Express (2006a) 47 airline bilaterals remain unused. Updated: 16/04/06. Online. Available from: http://www.financialexpress.com/print.php?content_id=124003 (accessed: 17/04/06).

—— (2006b) India to fly high on international traffic. Online. Available from: http://www.financialexpress.com/print.php?content_id=139029 (accessed: 04/09/06).

Firey, T. (2003) Nothing to fear from open skies with European Union. CATO Institute. Online. Available from: http://www.cato.org/research/articles/firey-030924.html (accessed: 15/11/05).

Forbes (2005) BAs Eddington says US protectionism props up failing airlines – report. Updated: 22/09/05. Online. Available from: http://www.forbes.com/markets/feeds/afx/2005/09/22/afx2240404.html (accessed: 09/11/05).

Forsyth, P. (2001) 'Promoting trade in airline services', Journal of Air Transport Management, 7: 43-50.

Glisson, L.M., Cunningham, W.A., Harris, J.R. and Di Lorenzo-Aiss, J. (1996) 'Airline industry strategic alliances: marketing and policy implications', International Journal of Physical Distribution & Logistics Management, 26(3): 26-34.

Graham, B. (1998) 'Liberalization, regional economic development and the geography of demand for air transport in the European Union', Journal of Transport Geography, 6(2): 87-104.

Hanlon, P. (1999) Global Airlines, 2nd edn. Oxford: Butterworth-Heinemann.

Hannegan, T.F. and Mulvey, F.P. (1995) 'International airline alliances: an analysis of code-sharing's impact on airlines and consumers', Journal of Air Transport Management, 2(2): 131-7.

Hettne, B. (2005) 'Beyond the "new" regionalism', New Political Economy, 10(4): 543-71.

Holdgaard, R. (2003) 'The European Community's implied external competence after the open skies case', European Foreign Affairs Review, 8: 365-94.

Holloway, S. (2003) Straight and Level: Practical Airline Economics. Aldershot: Ashgate.

Hooper, P. (1997) 'Liberalisation of the airline industry in India', Journal of Air Transport Management, 3(3): 115-23.

IATA (International Air Transport Association) (2004) World Air Transport Statistics, 48th Edition (for 2003). Geneva/Montreal: IATA.

ICAO (International Civil Aviation Organisations) (2007) Freedoms of the air. Online. Available from: www.icao.int/icao/en/trivia/freedoms_air.htm (accessed: 27/05/07).

Kerr, R. (2007) Open route to LA if Qantas bid succeeds: Libs. Updated: 07/02/07. Online. Available from: http://theaustralian.news.com.au/story/0,20867,21177329-23349,00.html?from=public_rss (accessed: 07/02/07).

Manorama Online (2005) Aviation 2005: sky is not the limit. Updated: 27/12/05. Online. Available from: http://www.manoramaonline.com/servlet/ContentServer?pagename=manorama/MmArticle/CommonFull Story&cid=1135260645119&c=MmArticle&p=1002194839100&count=10&colid=1002258272843& channel=News (accessed: 27/12/05).

Oum, T.H. and Park, J.-H. (1997) 'Airline alliances: current status, policy issues, and future directions', *Journal of Air Transport Management*, 3(3): 133–44.

Staniland, M. (1998) 'The vanishing national airline?', *European Business Journal*, 10(2): 71–7.

Telegraph (UK) (2006) Chinese flight plan takes off. Online. Avilable from: www.telegraph.co.uk (accessed: 13/05/06).

The Australian (2006) Singapore hopes for US routes rethink. Updated: 15/12/06. Online. Available from: http://theaustralian.news.com.au/printpage/0,5942,20929539,00.html (accessed: 15/12/06).

Travel Daily News (2005) The skies open up over India. Online. Avilable from: http://www.traveldailynews.com/makeof.asp?central_id=894&permanent_id=33 (accessed: 09/11/05).

Tretheway, M.W. and Oum, T.H. (1992) *Airline Economics: Foundation for Strategy and Policy*. Vancouver: The Centre for Transportation Studies, University of British Columbia.

International and transnational aspects of the global cruise industry

Adam Weaver and David Timothy Duval

Learning objectives

After considering this chapter, you will be able to:

- understand the recent evolution and structure of the cruise industry;
- articulate the transnational scope of cruise businesses and regulation;
- appreciate the extent to which cruise lines have come under increased scrutiny from industry observers and social commentators.

Key terms

- cruise ships;
- cruise lines;
- corporate consolidation;
- corporate social responsibility.

INTRODUCTION

Tourism services are typically produced and consumed concurrently. Cruise ships, as sites where both production and consumption occur, do not have fixed locations. They are floating holiday enclaves – vehicular destinations – that travel between ports of call. That ships are mobile and routinely cross international boundaries has been an advantage to a cruise industry that has become increasingly transnational in terms of its orientation and business practices.

The purpose of this chapter is to examine the international and transnational characteristics of modern cruise tourism. First, we address the manner in which cruise tourism has become a mass-market travel product. The rise of mass-market cruise tourism is interwoven with the development and intensification of both mass production and mass consumption. Second, the chapter explores the significance of corporate consolidation, brand differentiation and emerging markets within the cruise industry. Larger cruise-ship companies as international businesses are using acquisitions to further their growth strategies, to diversify their operations, and to explore new opportunities in burgeoning markets and segments. Third, the globalization and transnationalization of cruise-ship firms are discussed, particularly in terms of the way in which their operations, such as employee recruitment, have become internationalized. Different components of a manufactured good may be produced in different countries, and we argue that the production of cruise vacations is not entirely dissimilar to the way in which particular manufacturing processes have become more geographically dispersed. Within the cruise industry, however, the internationalization of production can be seen within the circumscribed environment of a ship. Fourth, re-supply networks within the cruise industry, as examples of international business operations, are examined; large cruise lines must master the complexity of re-provisioning ships that are spread across the world. Finally, we situate the activities of cruise-ship companies within recent discussions of corporate social responsibility. Cruise tourism represents a clear example of the globalized nature of tourism enterprise development, management, and marketing, and we suggest that cruise operations are decidedly transnational in their composition and operations.

INTERNATIONAL BUSINESS, MASS CONSUMPTION AND THE CRUISE INDUSTRY

Travel by ship for the purpose of leisure used to be associated with a largely older and affluent clientele. Cruise vacations, however, have subsequently become more affordable and appealing to a broader market. The original *The Love Boat* television series, broadcast on US television between 1977 and 1986, catapulted cruise ships and cruise holidays to the forefront of consumer consciousness in North America. Cruising was marketed as a travel experience infused with sun, fun and romance (Dickinson and Vladimir 1997). Cruise lines adapted their product to suit the tastes and preferences of the rising number of first-time cruise tourists: the duration of cruises was shortened; cruise ships were built so that, in a number of ways, they bore a resemblance to holiday resorts and franchise hotels; and the fly–cruise concept was introduced. The fly–cruise was essentially a travel package that included the cruise vacation as a well as a flight to an airport close to the port of disembarkation (Dickinson and Vladimir 1997). By combining the flight with the cruise, travellers were offered added convenience.

The democratization of cruise travel was part of a much broader democratization of consumption and the rise of modern market economies (Cowling and Tomlinson 2005). Similar to other products and services – for example air travel and automobiles – cruise holidays have become more affordable to a larger proportion of the population within Western countries. Goods and services that were at one time affordable to only the most affluent members of society became easier for a broader spectrum of consumers to acquire.

A number of transformations during the post-Second World War era – for example, the rise of consumer credit, innovations in transport, increased social and geographical mobility, the emergence of mass advertising, and the growing appeal of goods and services as markers of social status and distinction – made mass consumption possible (Strasser 2002). Over time, people have come to travel further distances, wear more and different clothes, drive more sophisticated motor vehicles and, in general, enjoy rising standards of living that involve the consumption of the latest products and services. International business has played an important role in this process. Companies have devoted more attention to packaging and advertising so that products appear more attractive. Colourful brochures and pamphlets have made services, such as travel, more inviting. A consumer society has been fostered by more materialistic depictions and perceptions of the good life.

One must be careful not to articulate the story of the rise of consumer society as a tale of conspiracy. To argue that modern-day consumption in the Western world is shaped by well-crafted indoctrination schemes, created in the interests of international business is rather simplistic. While consumers are encouraged – even exhorted – to make purchases and consume in so many ways, they are not duped into consuming (Jackson 1999). The process that transforms people into consumers is a complex combination of changing ideas and values, technological advances, demographic trends, and many other aspects of culture and the economy that even the most influential marketers and advertisers cannot completely anticipate or control. Mass consumption takes place at an intersection between corporate strategy and consumer choice; companies seek to satisfy markets and create them.

The contemporary travel industry – and, more specifically, the cruise industry – would not exist in its current form if it were not for a large number of consumers who could afford leisure travel. Middle-income consumers were crucial to the rise of mass tourism. Travel companies, including cruise lines, promoted their products to middle-income consumers as 'carefree' holidays. Advertisements promised that travel could offer luxury, comfort, and freedom from day-to-day concerns. In recent decades, the growing demand for cruise tourism has been particularly pronounced. The United Nations World Tourism Organization (UNWTO 2003) reported that cruise tourism's popularity increased rapidly during 1990s (see Table 6.1), where demand for international cruise trips grew during the decade at a cumulative rate of 7.9 per cent (compared to 4.3 per cent for overall world demand for international travel). Indeed, Miller and Grazer (2002) note that the North American market alone has experienced an annual growth rate of over 8 per cent since 1980. According to the US-based Cruise Lines International Association (CLIA), cruise tourism could be worth some US$85 billion in 2007 (Douglas and Douglas 2004).

Wood (2004: 135) suggests that the mass-market cruise sector can be divided into three segments. First, ships within the 'budget' segment typically offer basic onboard amenities. The companies that own these ships have tended to adopt a 'no frills' approach to service provision that is popular with travellers who want value for their money. For example, easyCruise, launched in May 2005, will serve primarily younger European travellers seeking inexpensive holidays. The ships within the easyCruise fleet will mainly visit warm-weather ports in Europe and the Caribbean (LaHuta 2006). Shipboard furnishings and décor are very plain; onboard restaurants and cafés do not offer elaborate meals (Sherwood 2005). Second,

Table 6.1 *Worldwide demand for cruise tourism (millions)*

Year	North America	Europe	Rest of world	Total
1989	3.29	0.53	0.20	4.02
1993	4.48	0.88	0.25	5.61
1997	5.05	1.36	0.46	6.87
2000	6.88	1.95	0.78	9.61

Source: Adapted from UNWTO (2003), based on data from CLIA (US and Canada), Passenger Shipping Association (Europe), GP Wild Ltd International (rest of world).

Wood's (2004) 'contemporary' segment includes most major cruise lines (e.g. Carnival Cruise Lines, Royal Caribbean International, Princess Cruises, Disney Cruise Line). Ships within this segment are typically referred to as 'floating destinations' or 'floating resorts' (Teye and Leclerc 1998: 155) and generally feature a wide variety of amenities, activities and services on board. Finally, the 'premium' segment is largely targeted toward upscale markets (and older consumers). 'Premium' cruise vacations may feature specific destinations or ports of call that appeal to these markets. Ships that serve more affluent passengers include all-suite vessels operated by Regent Seven Seas Cruises, the Yachts of Seabourn, and Silversea Cruises. *Queen Mary 2*, a passenger ship that can accommodate over 2,600 passengers, also serves the 'premium' segment. The vessel's ambience evokes the prestige once associated with first-class, ocean-liner travel.

That the cruise industry has been able to attract larger numbers of consumers to its ships led to the evolution of cruising into an affordable and fashionable escape. The cruise industry has offered vacation packages that have competed directly with mass-market holiday resorts (Dickinson and Vladimir 1997). As cruising has become increasingly democratized, it has become big business and, at the same time, international business. Several of the larger cruise-ship companies have become global entities, owning as they do the most prominent, or 'flagship' brands. However, large operators have also acquired smaller cruise lines that may only serve narrower, more specialized market niches.

CORPORATE CONSOLIDATION, BRAND DIFFERENTIATION AND EMERGING MARKETS

A considerable amount of consolidation has occurred within the cruise industry since the 1980s. This consolidation process has resulted in the creation of two substantial corporate entities: Carnival Corporation and Royal Caribbean Cruises Ltd. Together these corporations account for over 80 per cent of total market share within the cruise industry (Marti 2005). The concentration of ownership is the result of recent large-scale acquisitions (Hannafin and Sarna 2006). Carnival Corporation, which owns Carnival Cruise Lines, acquired Holland America Line and Princess Cruises in 1989 and 2003, respectively. In 2000, Carnival Corporation became the sole owner of Costa Cruises, an Italian-themed cruise line. Royal Caribbean Cruises Ltd – the company that owns Royal Caribbean International – acquired Celebrity Cruises in 1997. Efforts made by

Royal Caribbean Cruises Ltd to merge with Princess in 2001 were thwarted by Carnival Corporation's successful takeover bid (Table 6.2).

One impetus behind these acquisitions is the desire on the part of larger corporations to diversify. For example, Carnival Corporation is a diverse collection of cruise-line brands (Table 6.3), each of which serves a different market. This consolidation process has occurred concurrently with the rise of ever more distinctive and sophisticated brand differentiation (Ioannides and Debbage 1998). Acquisitions made by Carnival Corporation have enabled it to obtain cruise lines that already have expertise and experience in serving particular markets. A broad product portfolio means that cruise-ship passengers may trade up segment-wise if they so desire, but still remain customers of the same corporate entity.

Corporate consolidation is certainly not an uncommon global phenomenon in many sectors. Mergers and acquisitions have occurred in the automobile industry, the entertainment industry, banking and finance, retailing, and telecommunications among others. Through acquisitions, corporations can obtain less tangible assets, namely companies with reputable brand names. It may also be more efficient and less expensive for a corporation to acquire an existing business than to start an entirely new product or service line. To date, the most dominant cruise-ship companies seem to have benefited from the acquisition of established cruise lines (Table 6.4). Carnival Corporation has even developed an umbrella brand – World's Leading Cruise Lines – that encompasses its diverse range of brands (Beirne 1999).

Despite consolidation within the global cruise industry, brand identities and ship names have often been preserved. When Carnival Corporation acquired Holland America Line, it maintained Holland America's distinctive identity and ships within the Holland America fleet were not renamed. Holland America, prior to the acquisition, only recruited its shipboard service workers from the Philippines and Indonesia. Carnival Corporation has maintained this practice (Hannafin and Sarna 2006). Initially, there were fears that Holland America would be 'Carnivalized' after the acquisition (Slater and Basch 1989). Carnival Cruise Lines describes its vessels as 'Fun Ships' and it caters to consumers who enjoy a more boisterous shipboard environment. Public areas on board Carnival's ships feature colourful décor and fantasy-themed ornamentation. Passengers are also invited to participate in high-spirited activities such as hairy-chest contests and game-show trivia contests. Holland America, however, by and large caters to an older, more upmarket clientele (Hannafin and Sarna 2006). The cover page of the cruise line's brochures features the phrase 'A Signature of Excellence', which signals to prospective passengers that Holland America appeals to those with more discerning tastes. It is nearly impossible to find reference to Carnival Corporation within promotional materials produced by Holland America; to make explicit reference to this relationship would simply not contribute to Holland America's efforts to portray itself as a company with a rich and storied maritime legacy.

The acquisition of different brands by a corporation may also be part of a strategy to serve different national markets. Certain brands may be well known to consumers in some countries, but are not necessarily recognized by consumers in other countries. For example, Carnival Corporation acquired AIDA Cruises when it took over Princess Cruises in 2003. AIDA Cruises serves the German market. The brand has been in existence since 1993 and there is every indication that Carnival Corporation plans to preserve the brand's current

Table 6.2 *Major cruise lines and their ships*

Cruise line	Size of fleet	Core markets	Main destinations	Corporate headquarters	Registry of ships
Carnival Cruise Lines	22 ships – 20 accommodate over 2,000 passengers	North America	Caribbean, Mediterranean, Alaska, Mexico, Hawaii	Miami, Florida	The Bahamas and Panama
Royal Caribbean International	20 ships – 6 accommodate over 3,000 passengers	North America, Asia, South America	Caribbean, Mediterranean, Alaska, Panama Canal, Mexico, Hawaii	Miami, Florida	The Bahamas and Norway
Princess Cruises	15 ships – 2 accommodate over 3,000 passengers	North America	Caribbean, Mediterranean, Alaska, Panama Canal, Australasia, Mexico	Santa Clarita, California	Bermuda, the United Kingdom, and Gibraltar
Celebrity Cruises	11 ships – 4 accommodate over 2,000 passengers	North America	Caribbean, Mediterranean, Alaska, Panama Canal, Mexico, Hawaii	Miami, Florida	The Bahamas and Ecuador
Costa Cruises	12 ships – 2 accommodate over 3,000 passengers	North America, Italy, South America	Caribbean, Mediterranean, Northern Europe, South America	Genoa, Italy	Italy
Holland America Line	14 ships – 1 accommodates over 2,000 passengers	North America	Caribbean, Alaska, Panama Canal, Mexico, South America, Australasia	Seattle, Washington	The Netherlands
Norwegian Cruise Line	14 ships – 7 accommodate over 2,000 passengers	North America	Caribbean, Alaska, Hawaii, Panama Canal, Mexico	Miami, Florida	The Bahamas, the United States, Panama
Star Cruises	7 ships – 2 accommodate over 1,500 passengers	Singapore, Malaysia, Hong Kong, Thailand	Malaysia, Thailand, Vietnam, China, India	Hong Kong	Panama
Disney Cruise Line	2 ships accommodate 1,754 passengers	North America	Caribbean	Lake Buena Vista, Florida	The Bahamas

Source: Adapted from Hannafin and Sarna (2006).

Table 6.3 Carnival Corporation: a collection of cruise-line brands

Cruise lines owned by Carnival Corporation	Short description of cruise line and its ships
Carnival Cruise Lines	• A mass- or middle-market cruise line that operates many large, resort-style ships • Brochures liken the cruise line's 'Fun Ships' to cities – places where many different types of dining and entertainment are on offer
Princess Cruises	• Still a mass-market cruise line even though it is considered to be more upmarket than Carnival Cruise Lines • The cruise line's brochures promise customers 'affordable luxury' and 'big ship choice with small ship feel'
Holland America Line	• The shipboard ambience evokes the cruise line's seafaring history and tradition • This ambience also reflects the company's Dutch ancestry – for example, the large number of Indonesian shipboard employees speaks to Holland's colonial past
Cunard	• Operates two of the world's most renowned passenger ships – *Queen Elizabeth 2* and *Queen Mary 2* • *Queen Mary 2* is one of the world's largest passenger vessels; it frequently makes transatlantic crossings between New York and Southampton
Costa Cruises	• The ships have an Italian-themed atmosphere on board • Shipboard cuisine, activities and entertainment are said to possess Italian 'flair'; the cruise line's brochures and Internet site feature the slogan 'Cruising Italian Style ... That's Amore'
Windstar Cruises	• Operates three upmarket ships that have sails as well as engines • Two ships can accommodate 148 passengers; one ship can accommodate 308 passengers
The Yachts of Seabourn	• Operates ultra-luxury, all-suite vessels • The cruise line's three ships each accommodate up to 208 passengers
AIDA Cruises	• Caters primarily to the German market • Many of its vessels visit European ports of call

Source: Adapted from Hannafin and Sarna (2006).

identity (Blenkey 2005). This sensitivity to the value and character of different brands and their ability to speak to particular markets is a component of a broader, overarching global strategy. Carnival Corporation's success depends upon a coordinated portfolio approach in which each brand caters to a specific customer segment. Placing newly acquired companies

Table 6.4 *Corporate consolidation within the cruise industry*

Name of corporation	Short description
Carnival Corporation	Carnival Corporation is the parent company of Carnival Cruise Lines. In addition to owning Carnival Cruise Lines, Carnival Corporation has acquired Princess Cruises (in 2003), Cunard (1998), the Yachts of Seabourn (1991), Holland America Line (1989) and Windstar Cruises (1989). Carnival Corporation purchased shares in Costa Cruises between 1997 and 2000 until it became sole owner
Royal Caribbean Cruises Ltd	Royal Caribbean Cruises Ltd, the company that owns Royal Caribbean International, acquired Celebrity Cruises in 1997
Star Cruises	Star Cruises, a Malaysian-owned cruise line, acquired Norwegian Cruise Line in 2000

Source: Adapted from Hannafin and Sarna (2006).

under a single master brand would not necessarily be a wise strategy if it suppresses distinctive brands.

The expansion of international firms has been well documented (Cooke 1988; Cowling and Tomlinson 2005). Cruise operations are no exception in this regard, and there is clearly potential for them to expand even more as new markets in Asia emerge and mature. Open market policies implemented by some governments have also resulted in the expansion of cruise activities in certain parts of the world. For example, the Indian cruise market has recently expanded to the point where the national government has opened up the sector to foreign direct investment (FDI) (Express Travel and Tourism 2005). This process could involve the loosening of regulations relating to the registration of foreign companies operating or accessing Indian markets, and thus mirrors movements witnessed in other transport sectors of the Indian economy, particularly aviation liberalisation (see Chapter 5). Carnival Corporation is already 'testing the waters' in China. In July 2006, Costa Cruises will begin offering a five-day cruise for Chinese travellers departing from Shanghai (Katz 2006). Star Cruises, a Malaysian-owned cruise line, has a number of large cruise ships visiting ports of call in Southeast Asia. At present, these ships primarily cater to travellers from Asia, but they also attract Australians, Britons and Americans (Gunderson 2005). Star Cruises would appear to be well positioned to serve growing markets across Asia, one of the fastest growing cruise regions in the world.

GLOBALIZATION, TRANSNATIONALISM AND DETERRITORIALIZATION

Globalization in the business world is often equated with the free movement of capital across international borders. The United Nations Conference on Trade and Development (UNCTD) in 2004 noted that the prospect for global FDI flows is likely to be strong for the period of 2004 to 2007 (UNCTD 2004). Due to the globalization of business activities and investment, companies are increasingly able to perform different parts of the production process in different places. Companies use strategies, such as moving investment to low-wage countries, or dividing production chains spatially, to minimize costs and optimize production overall. While a wide range of industries have become increasingly internationalized, cruise lines and their ships are arguably some of the most globalized entities in the world. For instance, Carnival Cruise Lines primarily serves North American passengers; its ships are European-built; they are registered in Panama and the Bahamas; and they routinely visit ports of call in the Caribbean, the Mediterranean, Alaska and Mexico. The shipboard employees are recruited from an array of more affluent countries (in North America and Western Europe) and poorer countries (in Eastern Europe, Central America and Southeast Asia).

Many distant places seem to converge when one examines cruise ships and the cruise industry. Indeed, Wood (2000, 2002, 2004) writes of the deterritorialized nature of the cruise industry worldwide. The industry's ships are 'highly mobile' and largely emancipated from the 'constraints of place' (Wood 2002: 420). This deterritorialized aspect of the industry manifests itself in several ways: first, labour and employment regulations are, for the most part, determined by a cruise ship's country of registry; second, major international cruise lines have offices and 'home ports' around the world; and finally, cruise lines try to use 'divide and rule' tactics when they negotiate with the different countries their ships visit. In regions such as the Caribbean, cruise lines ensure that the per-passenger 'head tax' they pay to countries remains low by threatening to avoid destinations that raise the tax (Klein 2002). Efforts by cruise lines to keep this tax relatively low have been more successful in some destinations (i.e. the Caribbean) than in others (i.e. Alaska).

With respect to employment and labour, shipboard employees may be recruited from as many as 40 countries (Wood 2000). A cruise ship is a culturally diverse workplace. Employees from all parts of the world, including Asian countries such as the Philippines and Indonesia, and Eastern European countries such as Poland and Romania, have to work together despite cultural differences and linguistic barriers. With access to a global labour market, cruise lines seek to reduce operating costs by employing crew members from countries where wage demands are lowest. The working environment for cruise-ship employees is far from ideal in terms of conditions, workload and welfare provision (Wood 2000; Klein 2002). Ships tend not to be democratically run, global villages. Instead, they tend to have rigid hierarchies. The captain, the officers, the cruise director and various activity and event coordinators are often from North America and Western Europe. These employees tend to be the best paid, have the most job security and reside within the best cabins available to crew members. Workers who perform more menial tasks – washing dishes, cleaning floors and fixtures, and collecting rubbish – are mostly from poorer countries. The contact these workers have with passengers is usually more strictly managed and controlled.

The workers on board a cruise ship are often deterritorialized with respect to the country where the vessel was built, the location of the cruise line's head office and the ship's flag of convenience. The European shipyards where many very large cruise ships are built, Kvaerner Masa and Fincantieri, are located in Finland and Italy, respectively. Some of the world's largest cruise ships are owned by cruise lines that are typically identified with the United States such as Carnival Cruise Lines and Royal Caribbean International. The corporate headquarters of both of these cruise lines are located in Miami, Florida. So-called 'flags of convenience' are typically associated with countries outside of North America. In fact, a cruise ship may not necessarily visit the country in which it is registered. International law stipulates that ocean-going vessels must be properly registered. The UN Convention on the Law of the Sea indicates that a ship operating on the high seas is required to sail under the flag of a sovereign state.

At the end of the nineteenth century and the beginning of the twentieth century, it was relatively easy to associate a passenger ship with a particular country. Transatlantic liners were symbols of national prestige as well as important modes of transportation (Dickinson and Vladimir 1997). They were promoted as technological marvels that were emblematic of a country's 'progress'. This clear-cut relationship between a ship and its country of origin started to disappear with the introduction of flags of convenience (Barton 1999). After the Second World War, ship owners began to move away from traditional maritime flags in an effort to evade high taxes and strong labour unions. Flag-of-convenience countries are neither able to, nor necessarily interested in, regulating the ships they register. Countries such as Panama offer their flag for the revenue it generates in terms of registry fees as a valuable source of hard currency. Panama essentially markets and sells its inability to regulate ship owners at a price that enables them to undercut most other countries (Barton 1999). Certain European countries – such as Norway and the Netherlands – have responded to the emergence of flags of convenience by establishing 'second registries' that offer ship owners many of the same benefits as flags of convenience (Wood 2004).

While the cruise industry possesses certain qualities that are not shared by others, it is apparent that globalization has enabled cruise lines to achieve many of the same objectives as firms in other economic sectors. The deregulation that has occurred through flags of convenience is not dissimilar to the deregulation many companies have sought through capital mobility. Companies in a variety of other industries participate in a 'race to the bottom' (Zhao and Amante 2005) by seeking jurisdictions where taxes are lower, labour is less organized and constraints imposed upon corporate decision-making by, for instance, air and water quality standards are minimized. The globalization of the world economy has probably exacerbated this by reducing the inconveniences and expenses associated with crossing national borders in pursuit of lower costs and weaker regulatory regimes. Cruise lines are similar to other types of companies in that they have become adept at seeking out and exploiting differences and disparities between countries (Wood 2000, 2004).

The ability that cruise lines have to fashion a business environment that is favourable to their own interests extends to dealings with ports of call, which are an important component of the cruise vacation. A cruise line may add or drop a port of call from a cruise ship's itinerary based on a number of variables. One important variable is the amount of money it costs the cruise line to visit a particular port as many ports require that cruise lines pay a head tax for each passenger who is brought to port (Klein 2002). Ports often compete in order to obtain cruise-ship visits because of the spend and tax revenues while passengers are disembarked (Douglas and Douglas 2004). Through the mobility of their ships, the similarity of features offered by several destinations and the apparent flexibility this introduces to their itineraries, cruise lines can encourage ports of call to undercut one another. Cruise lines, then, are able to play different ports of call off one another in order to negotiate arrangements that are advantageous to them. By such tactics, the cruise industry has successfully thwarted efforts by Caribbean countries to increase the head tax. Cruise lines have threatened to bypass countries that try to raise the tax. Voters in Alaska have recently endorsed a plan to levy a tax of US$50 per passenger (Perez 2006). However, Alaska is a destination that is more difficult for cruise lines to replace with substitutes. Other cruise destinations that possess Alaska's scenery, and which are so close to the US market, do not exist.

INTERNATIONAL BUSINESS, INTERDEPENDENCY AND LOGISTICS

While ports of call are an important component of cruise vacations, the ship also spends a considerable amount of time at sea. Part of the appeal of cruise travel is that the ship can becomes an 'away' place; it can separate itself from shore and ultimately becomes a destination in and of itself. However, cruise ships do not function in isolation from the wider world for very long. They depend upon their supply networks. These networks are essentially commercial relationships that underpin the operation of the ships.

Cruise lines have become very effective in maximizing the number of days their ships are at sea. Efforts are made to minimize the turnaround time between cruises (Dickinson and Vladimir 1997). After a ship comes into its home port, it is typically able to leave the same day with a new complement of passengers. The ship is re-provisioned and refuelled. Effective logistics ensures that the ship is operational most of the year, and therefore able to produce revenue for the cruise line. Similar to cruise lines, airlines depend on achieving high capacity utilization (Doganis 2002). Cruise ships may carry passengers up to 365 days a year. A short visit to a dry dock (perhaps 10 days) may only be necessary once every two years (Ely 2006). Minor repairs and routine maintenance work are usually undertaken while the ship is in operation.

Cruise lines can be very particular about the supplies they procure. For example, American beef is typically served to American passengers. Even when a ship is travelling an itinerary in the Mediterranean, the cruise line may fly American beef to the port where the ship is being re-provisioned (Dickinson and Vladimir 1997). This practice ensures that the American passengers on board receive beef that is familiar to them in terms of its taste and texture. In order to obtain supplies that are seen to meet specific standards for quality, cruise lines depend on transnational supply chains.

Carefully developed procedures and systems need to be in place in order to ensure the efficient management of a fleet of ships across the world's oceans. As a business grows, coordinating supply chains can become a more complex endeavour. It has been reported that one prominent cruise line did not take measures to modify the management of its supply chains as it added a number of new ships to its fleet (Cook and Hagey 2003). The company's rapid growth exceeded its ability to re-supply its ships efficiently. For example, this cruise line sometimes sent chocolate and a variety of other supplies as air freight so that they could be delivered to the ship in a timely fashion. Transporting these supplies by air was costly. The cruise line's strategy for expansion was not accompanied by a plan to refine its re-provisioning strategy. However, measures have subsequently been taken by the cruise line to re-work the way in which it handles procurement by adopting a more sophisticated inventory management system and gathering more detailed data about the consumption patterns of passengers (Cook and Hagey 2003).

The cruise industry's relationship with commercial airlines also speaks to the importance of logistics and interdependency within international business. Underpinning the operation of the entire cruise industry is the need to transport passengers – who may reside some distance from the port of disembarkation – to and from the cruise ship in a timely manner. These consumers are, in a sense, part of a supply chain. Passengers fly from many points of departure to airports close to the cruise-ship port. The widespread availability of air travel has enabled cruise lines to draw their customers from a broad catchment area. The back pages of some cruise-line brochures provide a list of ticket prices for flights from more than 100 North American cities to US ports of departure (Hannafin and Sarna 2006: 58). Many passengers fly in from countries outside of North America as well.

As noted earlier, an important factor that contributed to the expansion of the cruise industry was the fly–cruise concept (Dickinson and Vladimir 1997). Passengers can, for example, be transported by commercial airlines to the warm-weather base ports from which they can cruise directly. The fly–cruise concept represents a carefully coordinated network of linkages. For the cruise industry, these linkages are of vital importance; they demonstrate that coordination is increasingly important within an environment where interdependency and time-related pressures shape so many business-related activities.

INTERNATIONAL CRUISE TOURISM AND CORPORATE SOCIAL RESPONSIBILITY

Much like other publicly listed firms, cruise companies are largely responsible to their shareholders, which can often mean a resolute focus on bottom-line profitability. In recent years, however, concerns have been expressed about business practices within the cruise industry. Internet sites such as www.cruisejunkie.com, for example, record the fines levied against cruise lines for violations of maritime pollution laws (Table 6.5). The actions of multinational enterprises are more closely scrutinized than ever before because of the impacts they can have in places where regulation is almost absent (e.g. London and Hart 2004). Corporations are under greater pressure to earn profits in a socially and environmentally responsible manner (Collier and Wanderley 2005).

On a number of occasions, cruise lines have illegally disposed of waste at sea (Klein 2002, 2006). Furthermore, a number of journalists have written damning exposés about poor working conditions on board cruise ships (e.g. Frantz 1999; Weinberg and King 2003). Some cruise lines have responded to this negative publicity by redefining their ethical values and implementing new projects under the guise of 'corporate social

Table 6.5 *The cruise industry and environmental violations: some examples*

Cruise line	Nature of the offence
Carnival Cruise Lines	Five ships discharged oil at sea between 1998 and 2001. The cruise line paid US$18 million in fines and restitution
Royal Caribbean International	Several ships dumped oil-contaminated water at sea. The cruise line paid an US$18 million fine after pleading guilty to a number of breaches of the law in 1999
Norwegian Cruise Line	In 2002, the cruise line pleaded guilty to pollution-related offences involving the disposal of oil-contaminated water at sea. The cruise line paid a fine of US$1 million

Source: Compiled from Klein (2002, 2006).

responsibility'. For example, Royal Caribbean International introduced a programme called 'Save the Waves' that promotes the company's commitment to protecting marine environments. The merits of this programme were advertised in Royal Caribbean's brochures and on board the company's ships even as waste oil was being illegally dumped from a number of ships within Royal Caribbean's fleet (Wald 1998). Future research needs to explore the dynamics of the evolution of cruise lines' environmental policies. This research could investigate the extent to which corporate images of environmental or social responsibility are matched by tangible actions – or if they merely represent, as some commentators would have it, 'greenwashing' (Ramus and Montiel 2005).

The misdeeds of cruise lines should prompt industry observers (and concerned consumers) to consider the tremendous power that is exercised by certain corporations within the world of international business. At present, the cruise industry is regulated by a loose patchwork of different organizations (Klein 2002). For cruise ships that visit US ports, sanitary conditions and shipboard safety are monitored by the Centers for Disease Control (CDC) and the US Coast Guard, respectively. With respect to marine pollution, an international treaty – the International Convention for the Prevention of Pollution from Ships (MARPOL) – outlaws the disposal of plastic and oil at sea. The International Maritime Organization (IMO), an agency of the United Nations, developed MARPOL, but individual countries are responsible for its enforcement. Flags of convenience provide cruise lines such as Carnival Cruise Lines and Royal Caribbean International with the benefits of operating as US companies without having to pay US corporate taxes or abide by US labour laws. The regulation of the cruise industry is therefore fragmented; in many respects, cruise lines take advantage of the laissez-faire environment of international shipping. Cruise lines, for the most part, are largely only accountable to themselves. Is corporate governance, then, a suitable substitute for regulatory bodies that can ensure some degree of accountability? It is worrisome that forward-thinking and enlightened company-sponsored programmes could be withdrawn or scuttled at the company's own discretion (and not necessarily with the full consultation or agreement of the shareholders). To argue that these programmes simply serve the strategic interests of a corporation is perhaps overly cynical. Nevertheless, most cruise lines currently operate largely within a regulatory vacuum. The question thus remains: who can guarantee that cruise lines will continue to undertake their 'ethical' activities over the long term?

Klein (2002) has suggested that labour and environmental practices within the cruise industry will not change without pressure from consumers. At present, the absence of large-scale consumer activism may, in part, be attributable to the problem of invisible complexity (Bellah *et al.* 1996). This problem refers to the way in which essential activities that underpin consumption are rendered invisible to the consumer's eye. Cruise ships – and, for that matter, shopping malls, casinos and theme parks – have been described as 'cathedrals of consumption' (Miles and Miles 2004), but they are also workplaces (i.e. sites of production and human labour) and voracious consumers of resources. While these cathedrals of consumption use exotic associations in order to sell merchandise and commodified experiences, they also minimize and mask the labour of often poorly-paid workers who create so many 'affordable' goods and services. Also, cruise ships have an environmental impact that is typically out of sight; the consequences of consumption are hidden from view. Consumers typically take measures to acquaint themselves with the price of many goods and services, but they also need to make more of an effort to contemplate the social and environmental costs of the goods and services they buy.

This recommendation should not be seen as an attempt to blame only consumers for the problems created by mass consumption and affluence. Indeed, the emergence of a convenience-driven consumer society after the Second World War is intertwined with the rise of international business. Consumers have witnessed, and have participated in, a profound transformation, led by large companies that could distribute goods and services over greater distances. There have been many adverse implications to the rise of consumer culture, and corporations are as much at fault as consumers. Activist investors and shareholders – as well as conscientious consumers – may therefore become increasingly central in a global push for corporate-governance reform (see case-study vignette).

CASE-STUDY VIGNETTE – TOURISM AND INTERNATIONAL BUSINESS IN ACTION

The cruise industry and corporate social responsibility: dilemmas and conundrums

It is now understood that companies should pursue not only shareholder value but also broader contributions to the public good. The term 'corporate social responsibility' has entered the business lexicon. A global movement that encourages businesses to pay closer attention to their social and environmental impacts has gained momentum. In their effort to maximize profit, cruise lines have, at times, behaved irresponsibly.

Continued

The cruise industry may be a testament to what happens when commercial activity is almost entirely free of government regulation.

The low wages paid by cruise lines means that affordable prices can be offered to consumers. By developed world standards, working conditions on board cruise ships are poor. Is the issue of workplace exploitation straightforward, however? What types of benchmarks should be used to gauge exploitation? When viewed within the context of the international pool of unskilled labour, a cruise-ship workplace compares favourably to a factory sweatshop. The opportunity cruise-ship workers have to earn hundreds – even several thousands – of US$ each month is better than some of the alternatives available to them. What level of exploitation, then, should be deemed intolerable?

Visual images are a powerful means to convey messages. Photographs and television can generate awareness about a problem or issue. When cruise lines dump waste at sea, the consequences are not plainly visible. Environmental violations by cruise lines have often been insidiously systematic over a period of time, not one-off, catastrophic eco-disasters. The disposal of waste at sea does not have the same dramatic impact as a large, conspicuous oil tanker spill. Cruise ships also tend to dump waste in the middle of the sea. There are no shocking images of dying seabirds on the shore covered with oil. Mainstream photojournalists and television reporters have not been able to produce a defining image of cruise-industry irresponsibility that has managed to galvanize public outrage.

Reform usually does not happen without widespread public scrutiny. But what form will this scrutiny take? Citizen journalism, perhaps in the form of consumers armed with video cameras, poses a serious threat to cruise lines. Video images, more than words, have true punch. Portable video cameras are now widely owned and give thousands of tourists the power to record the actions of cruise lines in real time to devastating effect. Damning video footage that finds its way to YouTube may cause consumers around the world to see cruise vacations in quite a different light.

Questions

- How could cruise lines be encouraged to behave more responsibly? How might it be in the best interests of cruise lines to behave in a socially and environmentally responsible fashion?
- Is there a risk that consumers may soon experience – if they have not already – 'exploitation fatigue', a weariness about all of the connections journalists, filmmakers and social commentators make between the production of everyday goods and services and the exploitation of workers and the environment?
- Should cruise-ship workers from poor countries be grateful that they earn more money than many of their compatriots? Or should these workers have the same rights and benefits as service workers in affluent countries?

CONCLUSION

The cruise industry is one of many industries that has benefited from the emergence of a critical mass of consumers with discretionary income. When *The Love Boat* became a popular US television programme in the late 1970s, the cruise industry received a tremendous boost. The pleasure and romance of cruise travel was seeded into the North American imagination. Over time, the cruise industry has evolved. More and larger ships are being built; the rise of mass-market cruise tourism has been accompanied by the emergence of large, well-capitalized firms. Ownership within the cruise industry is becoming increasingly concentrated as brand segmentation becomes more sophisticated and more effectively exploited by the dominant corporations within the cruise industry.

As a result of globalization, companies have come to view the world as a place where differences and disparities between countries can be exploited. Cruise lines have developed an acute understanding of the crucial differences that exist between legal jurisdictions. Flags of convenience, in particular, have enabled cruise lines to avoid the regulatory reach of countries that possess a corpus of laws that would increase ship owners' compliance costs (and perhaps even threaten cruise travel's relative affordability). The cruise line therefore tries to create a situation for itself whereby its ships essentially operate under circumstances where there is an absence of regulation. As a result, cruise lines are able to function largely in accordance with their own corporate policies.

Cruise lines seek autonomy from organizations and regulatory bodies that could potentially circumscribe the way in which they conduct business. However, it would be difficult for cruise lines to achieve autonomy from the many businesses that re-provision their ships. Cruise ships are at the confluence of transnational 'flows' – flows of passengers, supplies and recruited employees. The need for coordination and integration has become an increasingly important consideration for international business. Outsourcing has increased the demand for planning, logistical synchronization and just-in-time provisioning. Cruise lines and the companies that re-supply their ships are interdependent; companies, such as cruise lines, that sell products and services to consumers rely on suppliers, and vice versa. Interdependent activities may be part of the same production process, and all of these activities are often necessary in order to create a product or service.

The interdependent nature of production and consumption is not always plainly visible to consumers. There is often an unattractive underside to the orchestration of consumption-related fantasies and enchantment. If circumstances are going to change, widespread awareness of – and engagement with – issues that many individuals would rather ignore may be necessary. Improving the material circumstance of poorly-paid service employees, and managing the unwanted by-products of mass consumption more effectively, will also certainly have a price, most noticeably perhaps an increase in price. International companies face an important and timely challenge: namely, to ameliorate the exploitation of labour and the environment that is so frequently part of the mass production/mass consumption nexus while, at the same time, trying to ensure that mass consumption remains affordable and accessible.

Discussion questions

▨ How does the regulation of cruise lines compare to the regulation of other sectors or activities within the tourism industry, and how has regulation changed down the years?

▨ How do you explain the apparent contradiction between the internationalization of the cruise industry and the 'mallification' of large cruise ships? The operation of a cruise ship links many distant countries but cruise ships are becoming 'mallified' – comfortable, insular and homogenous pre-designed spaces for consumers.

▨ What should be the cruise industry's responsibilities to society and the environment?

REFERENCES

Barton, J. (1999) '"Flags of convenience": geoeconomics and regulatory minimization', *Tijdschrift voor Economische en Sociale Geografie*, 90(2): 142–55.

Beirne, M. (1999) 'Carnival augments six lines' image', *Brandweek*, 12 April: 14.

Bellah, R., Madsen, R., Sullivan, W., Swidler, A. and Tipton, S. (1996) *Habits of the Heart: Individualism and Commitment in American Life*. Berkeley: University of California Press.

Blenkey, N. (2005) 'New ships, new thinking', *Marine Log*, 110(2): 23–6.

Collier, J. and Wanderley, L. (2005) 'Thinking for the future: global corporate responsibility in the twenty-first century', *Futures*, 37(2/3): 169–82.

Cook, M. and Hagey, R. (2003) 'Why companies flunk supply-chain 101: only 33 percent correctly measure supply-chain performance; few use the right incentives', *Journal of Business Strategy*, 24(4): 35–42.

Cooke, T.E. (1988) *International Mergers and Acquisitions*. Oxford: Blackwell.

Cowling, K. and Tomlinson, P.R. (2005) 'Globalisation and corporate power', *Contributions to Political Economy*, 24(1): 33–54.

Dickinson, R. and Vladimir, A. (1997) *Selling the Sea: An Inside Look at the Cruise Industry*. New York: John Wiley & Sons.

Doganis, R. (2002) *Flying off Course: The Economics of International Airlines*. London: Routledge.

Douglas, N. and Douglas, N. (2004) 'Cruise ship passenger spending patterns in Pacific island ports', *International Journal of Tourism Research*, 6(4): 251–61.

Ely, E. (2006) 'The pull of the seas and human mysteries', *Boston Globe*, 27/08/06: D9.

Express Travel and Tourism (2005) Cruise industry: future is bright. Updated: November 2005. Online. Available from: http://www.expresstravelandtourism.com/200511/lookout08.shtml (accessed: 15/04/06).

Frantz, D. (1999) 'For cruise ships' workers, much toil, little protection', *New York Times*, 24/12/1999: A1.

Gunderson, A. (2005) 'Cruise lines set their sights on Asia', *New York Times*, 02/10/05: 5.3.

Hannafin, M and Sarna, H. (2006) *Frommer's Cruises & Ports of Call 2007: From US and Canadian Home Ports to the Caribbean, Alaska, Hawaii & More*. Hoboken, NJ: Wiley Publishing, Inc.

Ioannides, D. and Debbage, K. (1998) 'Neo-Fordism and flexible specialization in the travel industry: dissecting the polyglot', in D. Ioannides and K. Debbage (eds) *The Economic Geography of the Tourist Industry: A Supply-side Analysis*, London: Routledge.

Jackson, P. (1999) 'Consumption and identity: the cultural politics of shopping', *European Planning Studies*, 7(1): 25–39.

Katz, R. (2006) 'Carnival plunges into cruise market', *China Daily*, 08/03/06: 11.

Klein, R. (2002) *Cruise Ship Blues: The Underside of the Cruise Industry*. Gabriola Island, BC: New Society Publishers.

—— (2006) 'Troubled seas: social activism and the cruise industry', in R.K. Dowling (ed.) *Cruise Ship Tourism*. Wallingford: CAB International.

LaHuta, D. (2006) 'Simplifying easyCruise', *Arthur Frommer's Budget Travel*, 9(1): 25.

London, T. and Hart, S.L. (2004) 'Reinventing strategies for emerging markets: beyond the transnational model', *Journal of International Business Studies*, 35(5): 350–70.

Marti, B. (2005) 'Cruise line logo recognition', *Journal of Travel & Tourism Marketing*, 18(1): 25–31.

Miles, S. and Miles, M. (2004) *Consuming Cites*. New York: Palgrave.

Miller, A.R. and Grazer, W.F. (2002) 'The North American cruise market and Australian tourism', *Journal of Vacation Marketing*, 8(3): 221–34.

Perez, E. (2006) 'Alaska may soon raise cruise taxes', *Wall Street Journal*, 24/08/06: D6.

Ramus, C. and Montiel, I. (2005) 'When are corporate environmental policies a form of greenwashing?', *Business and Society*, 44(4): 377–414.

Sherwood, S. (2005) 'The Riviera easyCruiseOne', *New York Times*, 28/08/05: 5.5.

Slater, S. and Basch, H. (1989) 'Carnival buys up Holland America', *Los Angeles Times*, 12/02/1989: 7.

Strasser, S. (2002) 'Making consumption conspicuous: transgressive topics go mainstream', *Technology and Culture*, 43(2): 755–70.

Teye, V. and Leclerc, D. (1998) 'Produce and service delivery satisfaction among North American cruise passengers', *Tourism Management*, 19(2): 153–60.

UNCTD (2004) Prospects for FDI flows, transnational corporation strategies and promotion policies: 2004–2007. Online. Available from: www.unctad.org/sections/dite_dir/docs/survey_FDI.pdf (accessed: 12/03/06).

UNWTO (2003) *Worldwide Cruise Ship Activity*. Madrid: UNWTO.

Wald, M. (1998) 'Big cruise line to plead guilty in oil dumping', *New York Times*, 03/06/1998: A19.

Weinberg, T. and King, J. (2003) 'Cruise ship workers find hardship, hope on the high seas', *South Florida Sun-Sentinel*, 01/06/02: 1A.

Wood, R.E. (2000) 'Caribbean cruise tourism: globalization at sea', *Annals of Tourism Research*, 27(2): 345–70.

—— (2002) 'Carribean [sic] of the east? Global interconnections and the Southeast Asian cruise industry', *Asian Journal of Social Science*, 30(2): 420–40.

—— (2004) 'Cruise ships: deterritorialized destinations', in L. Lumsdon and S.J. Page (eds) *Tourism and Transport: Issues and Agenda for the New Millennium*. Amsterdam: Elsevier.

Zhao, M. and Amante, M. (2005) 'Chinese and Filipino seafarers: a race to the top or the bottom?', *Modern Asian Studies*, 39(3): 535–57.

International business networks and intercultural communications in the production of tourism

7

Nicolai Scherle and Tim Coles

Learning objectives

After considering this chapter, you will be able to:

- describe the role of intercultural communications in tourism production;
- identify the characteristics of intercultural competence within tourism businesses;
- assess the degree to which culture features in business relations in tourism.

Key terms

- tourism production;
- intercultural communication;
- intercultural competence;
- transnational corporations (TNCs);
- small- and medium-sized tourism enterprises (SMTEs).

INTRODUCTION: TOURISM AS GLOBAL INTERFACING

The majority of tourist activity may be domestic in nature, but the internationalisation of tourism consumption and production continues apace. Tourists are looking further afield for their trips and these are increasingly mediated across international borders between businesses transnational in scope and operations (see Chapters 5, 6 and 8). Inevitably, this brings tourism entrepreneurs and employees from one culture into contact with those from other cultures and social groups. Intercultural exchanges are required in the packaging of tourism experiences, especially through commodity chains (see Chapter 8) and these distinctive social relationships have the potential to impact on the performance of the respective businesses as well as the visitors' experiences (see case-study vignette).

CASE-STUDY VIGNETTE – TOURISM AND INTERNATIONAL BUSINESS IN ACTION.

A major international diplomatic incident?

Picture the scene: it is about 08.15 in the breakfast room of a four-star hotel operated by a major transnational chain. Outside in central Brussels it is a sunny spring morning. A man of North African origin, who speaks seemingly perfect French, is sitting quietly and enjoying his breakfast over the newspaper. Immaculately attired in a Tommy Hilfiger shirt with his mobile phone holstered and at the ready, a Chinese man strides into the room energetically and joins him without announcing his presence. The two men engage in some chit-chat but they soon turn to the real issue: the breakfasts. Based in Germany, the Tunisian is a guide for an international tour operator. He is leading a group of Chinese visitors on a coach tour of European city highlights. His fellow diner is also a tour guide and erstwhile translator from a large Beijing travel agency.

The Chinese man comes straight to the point: apparently, as part of the booking made in China, 'American breakfasts' had been stipulated for the entire 14-day trip. Here 'continental breakfasts' had been served and duly sent back. The waiters were, he reported, blissfully ignorant that they had commited such a faux pas, and claimed they'd received no alternative instructions. To avert what he saw as a major loss of face for his agency, the Chinese tour guide paid a surcharge of €3 per head for his group, 'American breakfasts' were duly served, and a major diplomatic incident had apparently been averted.

About €200 in supplements provokes little response from the Tunisian. Increasingly agitated, his Chinese counterpart wants to arrange a refund.

> 'Why not immediately?' the Chinese guide demands.
> 'The office will not open till 09.00, and anyway don't worry, we can deal with it later. You won't lose out. I am sure of it.'
> 'Does your company want to blacken its reputation in Beijing? Don't forget, you're working hard in China.'
> 'No, No! I understand, but there's little we can do right now; let's drink a coffee and I can finish my breakfast.'
> 'What you think are little things like this cause me and the company great humiliation because our visitors feel deeply embarrassed to complain! Beijing will not be happy about this.'

Continued

This grabbed the Tunisian's attention and the hotel manager was duly called to explain himself....

Questions

- What cultural strategies do the two tour guides use in this conflict?
- What stereotypes are used by the two guides?
- Was culture a reason for the conflict or a help in resolving it?

The concept of 'doing business' across cultures has become a central feature in studies of international business. Conversely, there has been only limited interest in tourism studies on intercultural communication, with a greater emphasis on host–guest relations (Reisinger and Turner 2003; Jack and Phipps 2005) than business-to-business trans-actions (Scherle 2006). Encapsulated in the vignette is the importance of intercultural competence in international tourism production. Even in 2004, when this encounter took place, low-levels of intercultural skills were still evident. The Tunisian demonstrated rudimentary awareness of intercultural difference when 'face' was invoked. Apparently briefed in the basics of Chinese protocol, this signified to him it was time to resolve the matter before it escalated dangerously. The Chinese tour guide interpreted the offer of a 'friendly coffee' as a delaying tactic after which the matter might be forgotten 'among friends'. Gentle threats regarding the fledgling relationship with the Beijing agency in light of potential new demand in China, were used to unsettle the Tunisian.

Tourism enterprises are used in business studies as paragons of internationalisation, and routinely much larger organisations such as InterContinental, Sheraton, Hilton, TUI, and Thomas Cook tend to be invoked in case-studies and as exemplars (see Chapter 8). As significant as these may be, there are, in fact, now many more SMTEs that are collaborating with partners across borders to assemble tourism experiences for their customers and SMTEs are numerically dominant in the tourism sector. Here it is argued that all tourism businesses should acknowledge the importance of intercultural communication in their operations. We start by surveying the general concepts surrounding intercultural business communications and competence. We consider the lessons to be learned from the identification of cultural differences, their relationships with business organisation, and their potential to impact on the practices of 'doing business' between international tourism enterprises. Case-study evidence of intercultural contacts between German and Moroccan businesses is used to reveal how these abstract concepts are played out in everyday commerce. Germany has been identified as an important source market by the Moroccan government in its attempts to use tourism to drive economic growth. TNCs may have specific teams tasked with partner relations, versed in international etiquette, and trained through dedicated programmes, but through our examination of the interactions among SMTEs, we argue that there is an interesting paradox in operation: often intercultural communications between such organisations focus on quite banal and modest themes, but they are of paramount importance in the successful conduct of business.

THE (INTER)CULTURAL DIMENSIONS OF MANAGEMENT

For many years the issue of 'culture' did not find its way into management vocabularies. Perhaps the earliest acknowledgement of culture in commercial behaviour is Weber's (1920) study of the protestant ethic and the spirit of capitalism, where a close connection between religious values and economic behaviour is demonstrated. Until quite late in the twentieth century, management theory was shaped largely by a technological paradigm with a functionalist perspective. Businesses were primarily analysed on the basis of revenues and costs, profits and losses based on the idealised construct of a *homo economicus* (Tayeb 2000), with an absolute belief in progress, the ability to overcome disruptive factors, and difficulty in acknowledging cultural influences and differences (Bosch 1997).

The first explicit attempts to identify culture as a factor emanated from the Comparative Management School that developed in the US in the 1960s in response to the significant growth of the multinational companies (cf. Schmid 1996). Economic fluctuations between and within the traditionally wealthy states in the 1970s and 1980s provoked a growing awareness of intercultural issues, and they led to questions of whether management practices in these more prosperous states were superior. Japan was singled out for special attention. Although it lacked major natural resources, it had become a significant economic power in only a few decades (cf. Bosch 1997). Commercial successes were attributed to distinctive organisational behaviours and management styles, the lessons of which were, it was argued, transferable and hence exportable. Since then, the ability to act on an intercultural level has been a major discussion point in management studies (see Cushner and Brislin 1996). For Adler (1993: 22), cross-cultural management is

> the study of the behaviour of people in organizations located in cultures and nations around the world. It focuses on the description of organizational behaviour within countries and cultures, on the comparison of organizational behaviour across countries and culture, and, perhaps most importantly, on the interaction from peoples of different countries working with the same organization or within the same work environment.

Nowadays, such concerns have become almost routine. *The Economist* regularly publishes guides to the etiquette of business across cultures in marquee market places (Table 7.1). For several years, HSBC (The Hong Kong Shanghai Banking Corporation) has run campaigns to establish its credentials as 'The World's Local Bank'. Print advertisements appeared recommending readers that they should 'Never underestimate the importance of local knowledge'. Above this tag line, adverts contained three images to demonstrate different cultural interpretations of simple everyday concerns, such as what constitutes a 'festive treat', 'dancing shoes' and 'gift to a new born'. One featured an infant's 'milk tooth' which is collected by the 'tooth mouse' in Mexico; collected by the 'tooth fairy' in the UK;

Table 7.1 *The world according to The Economist: some but not all of the essential considerations of 'doing business' with partners from other cultures*

Location	Timing	Dress code	Eating/Drinking	Tipping
New York	Punctuality is expected	Business casual is increasingly common	Business lunches dominated by work matters ... the liquid lunch is a rarity ...	Tipping is heavily ingrained: no matter how bad the service, always leave something
Milan	Never blame yourself for being late ... blame traffic or computer problems	Dress and overall appearance are very important. Businessmen spend time finding just the right suit	An evening drink ... is sometimes preferred to leisurely business lunch ... business people often arrange their evenings around drinks and dinner	Tipping is appreciated in Milan but is not taken for granted, and American-style tips would be considered extravagant
Tokyo	Always be prompt ... turn up early ... present yourself at specified time	Traditional business attire ... is expected ... for the older generation	It all boils down to dinner ... slurping loudly, burping, drinking soup straight from the bowl and talking with a mouth full of food are perfectly acceptable	Tipping is unheard of in Japan
Johannesburg	Early risers and punctual	Smart, casual attire has become acceptable for most business meetings	Drinking alcohol during a business lunch is fast disappearing	A 10 per cent tip is the norm in taxis and restaurants, depending on the service

Source: Compiled from The Economist (2007).

and thrown onto a roof in Japan. Recent TV adverts in the UK have concentrated on different interpretations of bad luck in different cultures (e.g. in China it is the number '4'; in South Africa it is passing salt from hand to hand; and in Morocco it is having a dog in the house). Such imagery is used to reinforce messages of mass customisation in which superior service is made possible by global reach augmented by personalised service and local knowledge.

While such simple examples are used in the popular media, they serve to demonstrate that cultural differences are clearly far from trivial and how easy it may be for the unwitting person to make a major faux pas. Nevertheless two paradigms have emerged on how to deal with them in international business (Table 7.2). Perhaps somewhat counterintuitively given the above, 'Universalists' still adhere to the belief that management techniques are universal and therefore independent of culture-specific influences. Business is 'culture free'; hence low levels of intercultural competence are tolerated, and operations need minimal, if any, adjustment to cater for bilateral business cooperations. 'Culturalists' argue that management techniques are intricately bound with culture and that it is impossible to dedifferentiate culture from economy; that is, economic activity is 'culture-bound' and it has to acknowledge and embrace culture and cultural difference. Businesses must be more culturally competent, sensitive to the needs and actions of their partners in other cultural settings, thereby adjusting and gearing their own operations accordingly.

A complete examination of the full suite of concepts and approaches dealing with the (inter)cultural dimensions of cross-border management activities is impossible here (cf. Scherle 2006). Nevertheless it is simply important to note that the wide array of interdisciplinary approaches used in studies of intercultural management is testament to the challenges of studying cultures as complex and continually changing systems. These are made all the more difficult by the presence of diverse micro-cultural systems. These fissures should be recognised although there is a propensity in the work of the so-called 'Interculturalists', such as Hofstede (2004) or Trompenaars (1993) to talk of cultural groups as single, homogeneous units.

Table 7.2 Approaches to business management in intercultural situations

Position	Universalism	Culturalism
Cultural doctrine	Society has a culture	Society is a culture
Management assumption	'One best way'	'Several good ways'
Management paradigm	Culture-free management	Culture-bound management
Typical business concepts	• Planning instruments • Investment analysis • Budget planning • Production control	• Management style • Motivation • Flexible working • Closer working relationships in all levels of organisation

Source: Abridged from Kutscher (2001).

INTERCULTURAL COMMUNICATIONS AND COMPETENCE

Intercultural contacts always require individuals to transgress boundaries, to interact with other partners. Distinctive arrays of social codes, conventions, attitudes and behavioural patterns are the hallmarks of the exchanges that result. It is important to stress, though, that there is a tension in this study area between the real complexity of cultural systems and human behaviour, and the essential human tendency to reduce complexity to easily understandable categories (Schneider and Barsoux 2003), through which management tools can be developed. For instance, Figure 7.1 offers a simplified overview of the dialectic when familiar and strange cultures collide in intercultural situations, and it points to four broad forms of intercultural adaptation that could be used to guide organisational behaviour.

Despite the reductionism in this model, studies of intercultural communication are interpretative and strongly discursive. They focus on what happens when actors with different cultural codes, conventions, attitudes and behavioural patterns communicate with one another and interact socially (Cray and Mallory 1998; Gudykunst 1998). They do not aim to level out cultural divergences in favour, as it were, of 'cultural universalism'; rather, they attempt to overcome mono-cultural and ethnocentric viewpoints (Scherle 2006). Nevertheless, for all the dynamism of cultural macro-systems (e.g. at nation-state level) with all their micro-cultural subsystems (e.g. regional cultures and sub-cultures), the human

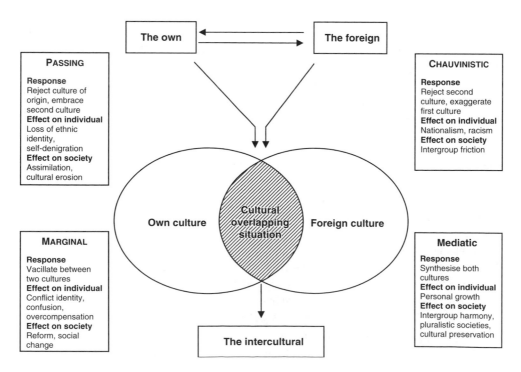

Figure 7.1 *The dynamics of intercultural overlapping situations*
Source: Developed by the authors after Bochner (1982), Thomas (2005) and Scherle (2006).

tendency is to create and hand down simplified *pictures in our heads* (after Lippmann 1960) of one's own culture and, to an even greater extent, foreign cultures.

This recognition of this dilemma is central to the notion of intercultural competence which refers to the skills and abilities that an individual needs in order to interact appropriately and efficiently with persons from a different culture (see Ruben 1989; Bennett and Bennett 2003). Efficiency implies that the aims of the actors involved can be realised. Appropriateness manifests itself where behaviour does not hurt the feelings of those interacting or transgressing the bounds of what is 'usual' in one culture. To be culturally competent, actors must develop at least the rudiments of relational competence (to form and maintain positive social relations); information transfer competence (to transmit information with minimum loss or distortion); and target-achieving competence (to secure a certain degree of cooperation and agreement). Ultimately intercultural competence is a continuous learning process that is determined by specific experiences, reflective observation, abstract conceptualisation and active experimentation (cf. Stüdlein 1997). Learning in an intercultural context requires the ability to engage constructively. It demands an awareness of one's own cultural reality relative to others' and the ability to distance oneself from perceptions and value systems specific to one's own culture. Acculturation stress can arise among those involved but this mainly affects people who are sent abroad for longer periods. So-called 'progressive models' that identify different phases in acculturation problems have dominated, in particular Oberg's (1960) 'cultural shock model' (Table 7.3).

Although the inevitability of (passing through) these phases is contestable, these emotions are routinely encountered in intercultural transactions. Intensity of reaction often depends upon the motivation and prior expectations of the visitors, the amount of cultural distance

Table 7.3 *The culture shock phenomenon*

Phase	Characteristics
Honeymoon	Emphasis on the initial reactions of euphoria, enchantment, fascination and enthusiasm. Friendly but relatively superficial contacts with actors from the foreign culture
⇩	
Crisis	Problems with integration due to divergent aspects of the foreign culture (e.g. language, values, norms) lead to feelings of inadequacy, frustration, anxiety and anger
⇩	
Recovery	Increasing familiarity with foreign cultural aspects leads to crisis resolution and cultural learning. The attitude to the other culture improves on a long-term basis
⇩	
Adjustment	Advanced integration in the other culture implies adjustment, reflecting enjoyment of and functional competence in the new environment

Source: Developed by the authors after Oberg (1960).

between the home and host countries, and the degree of uncertainty at work and in everyday activities. For a long time, culture shock had primarily negative connotations, but in recent years it has been widely recognised as an essential and unavoidable state that is the sole means by which successful adaptation to difference becomes possible (Anderson 1994; Schneider and Barsoux 2003).

INTERCULTURAL CONTACTS: WHEN GERMANS MET MOROCCANS

So far, we have surveyed the basics of intercultural communication but intercultural situations present challenges to their participants of a scale that should not be underestimated. Bilateral business cooperations may, for instance, be seriously disrupted by a lack of cultural awareness. Major competitive disadvantages may be induced that would be otherwise avoidable if the respective actors possessed (greater) intercultural competence and learning skills (Ruben 1989). In the contemporary business environment, the criteria for successful international management may no longer be simply reduced to economic factors alone. Instead, cultural factors have to be integrated. Education to foster greater intercultural competence in international commercial collaborations is a central task. In what remains of this chapter, we examine the nature of intercultural contacts in dealings between German and Moroccan incoming agencies and the degree to which intercultural competence was evident in, and influenced the outcomes of, their bilateral cooperations (see also Scherle 2004, 2006).

A series of interviews was conducted between July 2000 and January 2002 (Scherle 2004). Qualitative approaches are especially well suited to culturally oriented research problems. In total over 60 interviews were completed and during these interviews business attributes were described as well as their bipartite business relations with their international partners. In both samples, over 50 per cent were established businesses that had been operating for over 10 years, over 60 per cent had fewer than 50 employees, and there were similarities in the levels of professional training (Table 7.4). Few had direct training in intercultural business management. There was a relatively even spread of the durations of intercultural cooperations among firms in the two samples, and approximately 60 per cent of the individual German and Moroccan respondents had experience of intercultural business relations. The primary mechanism for cooperation among the participating tour operators was non-contractual arrangement, a collaboration form that allowed its actors an optimum of flexibility.

German businesses

For German businesses punctuality was the most significant area of conflict in cooperation with Moroccan incoming agencies. As one German product manager clearly demonstrated, this concept follows different patterns in bilateral cooperation:

> If I have an urgent issue, then I can't wait three days, it has to be answered within 24 hours. It is not
> easy to teach the people in Morocco this service orientation. Our agent, for example, he studied

Table 7.4 *The main attributes of the German and Moroccan respondents*

Characteristics	German respondents (% in brackets)	Moroccan respondents (% in brackets)
Average age of business (years)		
• <1	–	–
• 1–5	2(6.7)	5(16.7)
• 5–10	5(16.7)	6(20.0)
• >10	23(76.7)	19(63.3)
Size of business (employees)		
• <5	10(33.3)	3(10.0)
• 6–50	9(30.0)	19(63.3)
• 51–100	5(16.7)	4(13.3)
• 101–500	2(6.7)	4(13.3)
• >500	4(13.3)	–
Business involvement in intercultural cooperation (years)		
• <1	1(3.3)	–
• 1–5	10(33.3)	9(30.0)
• 5–10	9(30.0)	12(40.0)
• >10	10(33.3)	9(30.0)
Respondent's professional training		
• apprenticeship	8(26.7)	7(23.3)
• university	17(56.7)	18(60.0)
• other	1(3.3)	–
• no response	4(13.3)	5(16.7)
Percentage of respondents with intercultural experience	19(63.3)	18(60.0)
Percentage of respondents with intercultural training	3(10.3)	1(3.3)

Source: Scherle (2004, 2006).

in Germany, he lived here, he was a tour guide, he knows what matters, what Germans want and what is important for them. I mean we aren't straightforward either!

Time is a strongly culturally determined aspect of bilateral cooperation and is frequently cited as a cultural constraint in classic intercultural studies (e.g. Hofstede 1998; Trompenaars and Hampden-Turner 2004). Economic activity seems to follow the dictates of time. In Arab states different concepts of time dominate than in Germany: time is relative and not an abstract measure to which the individual must submit. This means that appointments are routinely not kept at the agreed time (Kuran 2004). An interculturally experienced actor can contextualise such a delay because a stated time provides a clue but has no claim to absolute validity.

German respondents observed that personal relations play a central role in Morocco to a degree that frequently troubled them. Friends and relations were routinely employed in Moroccan businesses. Interpersonal contacts are established and cultivated in Arab countries not only at business meetings but also in private settings. While the time taken by such meetings is the most notable aspect for European participants, for Arab partners they play a major role in improving interpersonal relations with their partners. The intention is to build a network of trust that offers a form of (commercial) security in countries that are traditionally associated with corruption (Tibi 1991; Kuran 2004). Despite a basic awareness of these linkages, German respondents underestimated the penetration and consequences of employing relatives. Within the (larger) German tour operators with pronounced horizontal and vertical business structures, such personalised business structures were disconcerting; they had a propensity to induce acute conflicts in the day-to-day negotiation of business. A product manager of a leading German company summed up the frustrations of many a German interviewee:

> One Moroccan firm we work with is closely linked to family. You'll hardly find a firm where people not belonging to the family occupy key positions. Qualifications aren't important at all! That means, from the very beginning you have to expect great weaknesses in personnel because there are always positions, important positions, which are occupied in this firm by people who don't have the capacity, the know-how.

The product manager added that he could understand practically no personnel decision made by the Moroccans in previous years. While this may have been melodramatic, the consequences of 'familial' business structures for practical cooperation remained tangible, so that German partners felt they had to assume the lead with Moroccan partners:

> Over the years we have learned to take on more and more responsibility. That is, when they weren't pure agency tasks such as bus planning or day trip planning, tour leaders, local guides, then we took over everything. … [so] that we relied less and less on the partner's agreement, especially in fundamental decisions, such as personnel decisions.

Gendered social relations in tourism were identified by several interviewees as sources of irritation. North African women still have a largely 'traditional' image tied to a religious and patriarchal value system centred on the Koran (cf. Mernissi 1989, 2003). In a male-oriented tourism industry such as the Moroccan one, the presence of many women in senior positions in their German partner businesses created friction. Overall, this issue was not as problematic as either working practices or familial structure, but it resulted in several troubling experiences. One female German product manager noted that 'with some male service providers I repeatedly have the experience that in co-operation it is only just tolerated that you are a woman!' The situation was, nevertheless, gradually changing. Some women referred to an impression that the socialisation of their counterpart(s) in Europe – often through a period of study or work abroad – was fostering more open, gender-equal transactions. However, acculturation overseas appeared not to have informed the management of customer expectations. In fact, a brief inspection of the service experience would suggest that the Moroccan operators had two sets of German 'customers' to satisfy: their direct partners, the tour operators: and their consumers, the tourists. One aspect that was repeatedly underestimated in bilateral business was the differing perception of quality in business-to-business and business-to-consumer transactions. As one German trekking operator noted,

> If tents are still OK in Moroccan terms, then they are often no longer OK for Germans. I keep having to ask for new tents. This is often reported too late on the Moroccan side. … The tents last for a maximum of two, two-and-a-half years. Then the problem is that they think this isn't so bad. You know, when the zip doesn't work properly, that doesn't matter so much for the tour, but once the customer is lying inside the tent and a bit is open or missing, then that is naturally a problem ….

To compound this, the Germans claimed that it often took a considerable time to educate their Moroccan partners to German consumers' more exacting expectations:

> We are now trying to insist that the guides always look at these things beforehand. Things have improved, but it was an issue that we worked on for more than six years so that they [on the Moroccan side] accept how important it is for Germans that a tent is OK. That isn't so important for a Moroccan! … They just said 'It's just the last bit of the zip that doesn't close!', as if to say 'That can't be the problem.' But that is exactly the problem for Germans!

Little glitches with zips may have seemed trivial to the Moroccans but they belie an ignorance of customer care to a standard demanded by German customers. Moreover, the Moroccans failed to recognise for themselves the thresholds required to trigger complaints and/or whether a complaint would be made by German tourists. Not surprisingly, because of its direct relationship to quality, the concept of complaint was identified by the Germans as a cultural issue:

> The problem simply consists in the fact that the complaint concept is defined differently in different cultures … some people see complaints as a major opportunity to further develop their product and their business, while for others complaints are a stigma they don't want to deal with and which they would rather consider closed.

The manner and intensity of complaints varies culturally. For German operators it could be immensely disconcerting and destabilising if complaints were not taken seriously by their partners. As one German respondent noted, it was crucial not to impose a particular system of complaints management on their Moroccan partners who instead should develop their own approach:

> One must know the value of a complaint in the respective foreign culture before one develops a system for dealing with customer complaints together with the co-operation partner. Anything else could possibly be misunderstood as cultural imperialism.

German operators felt that the Moroccan partners should separate the business benefits of effective complaint management from any stigma they may have felt. Once the cultural distances between the 'complainant' and the plaintiff had been identified, complaints could be used in a more constructive manner to improve the quality of the service experience:

> The economic benefit of an effective complaints management system must be made very clear .... I think that is a very important argument. Why do companies invest in complaints management? It doesn't happen because the companies are so altruistic, but because it has proven worthwhile and is associated with economic benefit ....

Moroccan businesses

Moroccan interviewees identified economic aspects as sources of friction more often than their German counterparts. The apparent profitability of German businesses; asymmetrical flows of information and capital that reinforce such inequalities; and the perception that the viability of Moroccan companies was irrelevant to their German partners were strongly articulated complaints. One product manager of a medium-sized incoming agency from Casablanca epitomised this view: 'The negative aspects in co-operation are reflected most especially in the fact that continually less is paid and more quality is expected. Our outgoings are too high in relation to the price paid.' Moroccans perceived further injustice (and an apparent powerless-ness) in the German partners' ever increasing demands not least to keep re-inventing destinations and their products:

> It is most obvious that the tour operators continually demand a new product, although Morocco really stays the same and we cannot create a new product each time. Also, our partner doesn't like the way we work and we keep feeling forced to change this and follow their way.

The demand for altogether new products among German partners actually reflects Moroccan tourism policy in recent years and its desires to manage patterns of consumption and diversify tourism services (Gray 2002; Loverseed 2002). However, during some interviews, Moroccan partners gave the impression that they were more interested in modifying the existing range of tourism products than in developing new ones. This was reflected in numerous interviews with German partners, who regretted the lack of any impetus on the Moroccan side towards the further development of tourism products (see Scherle 2004). Interculturalists usually attribute this business behaviour, which from a Western perspective is often interpreted as lacking initiative, to the so-called 'fatalist hypothesis'; this originates in the view advanced by Muslim theologians that human life is largely predetermined (see Kuran 2004).

Relatively frequently, Moroccan interviewees complained about the financial arrangements in their relationships. For example, the manager of a small agency from Tangiers articulated the view that German mismanagement induces problems:

> In Germany there are at the moment many firms which go bankrupt. Many of these agencies have no finances! That is a risk and we have been affected twice: once by an Austrian agency with 120,000 Schillings [outstanding debt] and a second time with a German agency with 16,000 Marks.

> You know that that is a lot of money for us. When we lose 16,000 Marks that corresponds to the profit from 15 groups [of visitors] ... We cannot cope with such a loss ...

Moroccan interviewees were aggrieved at being expected to trust the good name of the German partners without the same status afforded to them in return. In fact, because of disadvantageous experiences with their German partners over finance, 'trust' had been become decoupled from its purely moral meaning. Instead, as the ironic comments below make clear, trust had assumed a more calculative meaning as an outcome, not the foundation of a transaction:

> There is one important thing: for us, trust is synonymous with money. Personally, if I don't know you – even if I find you congenial – you would not be allowed to send me your group before we have checked the billing. That's trust! ... That's the reason why trust is synonymous for us with money: pay me in time, I trust you. We could allow some days of delay, but it should not last too long.

The fact that trust was expressed in such mercenary terms is significant because it challenges the role of interpersonal contacts in the culture of business in the Arab world. Here it has to be assumed that the equating of remuneration with trust by the recipient of trust is dependent on the cost-benefit aspect of trustworthy behaviour; this is influenced firstly by intrinsic incentives such as the preferences of the recipient of trust and secondly by extrinsic incentives, especially in the form of reputation mechanisms and the regulation of the potential for cooperations (see Creed and Miles 1996; Scherle 2006). That German businesses should see the need to revise, as it were, the terms of reference of trust is important.

In international business relations, it is important that cooperations have a degree of continuity, so that trust may be developed as a central resource to reduce the insecurity and anxiety caused by social complexity (Giddens 1994; Kühlmann and Schumann 2003). This is however frequently frustrated in the tourism sector because cooperations have the propensity to be short-lived and lacking intensity of commitment (Go and Appelman 2001; Scherle 2006). Tour operators, in particular, frequently have the habit of exploiting incoming agencies merely as gate-openers before switching allegiances to other business partners. The managing director of an incoming agency specialising in trekking reported just such a scenario:

> It is important for a partner to be loyal. I had partners who came on exploratory visits, looked at some of my guides and then worked directly with them. I don't find that correct. It was just a way of finding good guides quickly.

Some Moroccan tour operators repeatedly referred to financial problems that stemmed from rationalisation in the German tourism sector through takeovers and insolvencies. This increased competition for collaborations with the diminishing number of German players in the market, especially among small Moroccan agencies. The transnational activities of the larger overseas operators were seen as threatening smaller-scale indigenous enterprises in Morocco. Whether this is rational or not, fear of globalisation was followed by the view that the takeover of local businesses would put further pressure on other types of businesses elsewhere in tourism value chains at a destination:

> Globalization is a problem for many incoming-agencies. In three or four years the huge tour-operators will take over all the small agencies. That's not good at all for small destinations like Agadir. Our firm is not so much affected, because we co-operate with solid and independent enterprises. But of course that cannot rule out the possibility that one day we also might be taken over by a huge tour-operator. That's really bad for a destination like Agadir.

Many small operators had to forge alliances with one or more of the best-known (larger) German tour operators. While this broadened their product range, they had hoped to obtain further insurance against market conditions and fluctuating demand. This had served to empower the German partners because there were fewer of them, they were being chased by broadly the same number of potential Moroccan partners, and they felt they could establish better terms from their potential partners. However, the situation made the smaller Moroccan businesses feel more vulnerable: many forms of cooperation were not based on contractual agreements. As such, German tour operators, it was claimed, could change partners and operating conditions relatively easily. There was a risk of greater marginalisation of local tourism actors, especially in the package tourism centres where the dominance of global players was most pronounced.

DISCUSSION AND CONCLUSION: INTERCULTURAL BUSINESS AND TOURISM FUTURES

It is an unavoidable truth that engagement with other cultures is rarely possible on the basis of tolerance alone, but usually requires specific tools, such as intercultural training. In this respect, intercultural communication has, and will continue to offer, clear potentials for studies of international business and tourism. Although culture and tourism are intimately connected, issues of intercultural communication and management in the production of tourism have remained neglected. This is notwithstanding several bold claims made about the significance of transnational corporations in the production of tourism and the internationalisation of commodity chains (Mosedale 2006), as well as the acknowledgement of this body of work in the area of host–guest relations (Reisinger and Turner 2003; Jack and Phipps 2005).

Managing across cultures, not just across borders, that overlooks inherent cultural divergences risks a loss of effectiveness and, at worst, failure. If one subscribes to an holistic view of business management, as we do in this chapter, then economic parameters are important but not exclusive conditions for successful collaboration. A wholly economic perspective can too easily overlook the (evolving) cultural demands on partners. To advocate the appreciation and application of intercultural communication towards the understanding of tourism production is not a form of 'commercial political correctness'. For German–Moroccan business relationships to function (more) effectively, German businesses have to recognise and adapt to the cultural features that are important to their Moroccan partners; in contrast, the Moroccan partners may need to accommodate the German partners' concerns, not least by recognising their different operating conditions and competitive pressures.

Nowadays, anyone who questions the relevance of culture to management risks succumbing to a viewpoint that is sharply at odds with the pragmatic realities of doing business across the globe, as this chapter demonstrates albeit in a specific case-study. Consider, for instance, the paradox associated with *guanxi*, a Chinese term referring to interpersonal connections as a means of affecting the ability to do business. In light of the importance of China as a market and the Chinese diaspora for doing business around the globe, *guanxi* is a pivotal construct yet as Fan (2002) notes it is one of the most routinely misunderstood concepts by Western academics and practitioners. All too often, unnecessary reductionism results in the false perception that *guanxi* is inherently synonymous with corruption (Fan 2002: 556) when in fact it is an immensely complex and nuanced concept. It is significant that popular media, such as *The Economist* magazine and TV adverts for HSBC, stress the importance of intercultural competence given its global reach and the circulation of messages. Other sub-state actors recognise the importance of a more culturally-sensitive approach. For instance, Business for Diplomatic Action (BDA), a not-for-profit group funded by the private sector in the United States, has noted the damage done to American commercial interests around the world because of the growing tide of anti-American feeling. This is interpreted as a function of the unpopularity of US foreign policy, the effects of globalisation, the pervasiveness of American culture, and external perceptions of the collective personality and culture of US citizens. In a stark message exhorting US business leaders to engage, BDA (2007: n.p.) warns:

> The U.S. stands to lose its competitive edge if steps are not made toward reversing the negativity associated with America. Additionally, aside from profit-making, American business leaders have the responsibility to use their influence and creative resources to improve the overall reputation of the United States .... American business touches more lives than the U.S. government and has greater credibility. American multinationals also have a record of building cooperation across borders and creative problem solving.

As BDA (2007: n.p.) points out, 'Americans are broadly perceived by others as arrogant, ignorant, lacking in humility, loud and unwilling to listen', and to this end, it has actively published the somewhat misleadingly entitled 'World Citizens Guide', with a clear set of responsibilities spelled out for American travellers to accompany their rights to international mobility (see Chapter 3). Originally designed for American students studying abroad and now with a version for business travellers, it aims to build intercultural competence through a series of basic pointers and advice. The potential exists though that in the future such efforts may per se and through the specific tips in fact reinforce, or even build new, cultural stereotypes and hence intercultural challenges.

Finally, intercultural issues are not the sole preserve of larger transnational concerns, but rather culturally sensitive approaches to management are of increasing relevance to SMTEs, particularly in the developing world. In spite of all tendencies towards concentration, SMTEs continue to be a major driving force in tourism production. Moreover, more SMTEs than ever are working to widen their commercial activities by operating across borders. Their usually highly personalised business structures and cooperations favour discursive approaches to conflict resolution. Bilateral business cooperation should not be analysed solely on the basis of costs and benefits without ensuring the intercultural competence of the relevant employees. An investment in employees' intercultural competence is an investment in the qualitative growth of businesses that pays for itself in the medium to long term, even in an age that is increasingly dominated by controllers and quarterly reports.

Discussion questions

- What roles does culture play in the production of tourism across borders?
- How far are you able to agree with the Universalists' view that culture plays no role in business and management in tourism?
- Through globalisation, the media and travel, we are increasingly exposed to other cultures. Will this lead to cultural harmonisation or greater intercultural competence?

REFERENCES

Adler, N.J. (1993) 'Cross-cultural management research: the ostrich and the trend', *Academy of Management Review*, 8(2): 226–32.

Anderson, L.E. (1994) 'A new look at an old construct: cross-cultural adaptation', *International Journal of Intercultural Relations*, 18(3): 293–328.

BDA (2007) Business for Diplomatic Action. Building Bridges to the World. Online. Available from: http://www.businessfordiplomaticaction.org/index.php (accessed: 03/07/07).

Bennett, J.M. and Bennett, M.J. (2003) 'Developing intercultural sensitivity: an integrative approach to global and domestic diversity', in D. Landis, J.M. Bennett and M.J. Bennett (eds) *The Handbook of Intercultural Training*. Thousand Oaks, CA: Sage.

Bochner, S. (1982) 'The social psychology of cross-cultural relations', in S. Bochner (ed.) *Studies in Cross-cultural Interaction*. Oxford: Pergamon.

Bosch, B. (1997) 'Interkulturelles management', in H. Reimann (ed.) *Weltkultur und Weltgesellschaft: Aspekte globalen Wandels; zum Gedenken an Horst Reimann (1929–1994)*. Opladen: Westdeutscher Verlag.

Cray, D. and Mallory, G. (1998) *Making Sense of Managing Culture*. London, International Thomson Business Press.

Creed, W.E.D. and Miles, R.E. (1996) 'Trust in organizations: a conceptual framework linking organizational forms, managerial philosophies, and the opportunity costs of controls', in R.M. Kramer and T.R. Tyler (eds) *Trust in Organizations: Frontiers of Theory and Research*. Thousand Oaks, CA: Sage.

Cushner, K. and Brislin, R.W. (1996) *Intercultural Interactions: A Practical Guide*. Thousand Oaks, CA: Sage.

Economist, The (2007) Cities guide. Online. Available from: http://www.economist.com/cities/ (accessed: 03/07/07).

Fan, Y. (2002) 'Questioning guanxi: definition, classification and implications', *International Business Review*, 11: 543–61.

Giddens, A. (1984) *The Constitution of Society: Outline of the Theory of Structuration*. Berkeley: University of California Press.

Go, F.M. and Appelman, J. (2001) 'Achieving global competitiveness in SMEs by building trust in interfirm alliances', in S. Wahab and C. Cooper (eds) *Tourism in the Age of Globalisation*. London: Routledge.

Gray, M. (2002) 'The political economy of tourism in North Africa: comparative perspectives', *Thunderbird International Business Review*, 42(4): 393–408.

Gudykunst, W.B. (1998) 'Applying anxiety/uncertainty management (AUM) theory to intercultural adjustment training', *International Journal of Intercultural Relations*, 22: 227–50.

Hofstede, G. (1998) 'Think locally, act globally: cultural constraints in personnel management', *Management International Review*, 38: 7–26.

—— (2004) *Cultures and Organizations: Software of the Mind*, rev. ed., New York: McGraw-Hill.

Jack, G. and Phipps, A. (2005) *Tourism and Intercultural Exchange: Why Tourism Matters*. Clevedon: Channel View Publications.

Kühlmann, T.M. and Schumann, O. (2003) 'Trust in German–Mexican business relationships', in H. Kopp (ed.) *Area Studies, Business and Culture: Results of the Bavarian Research Network Forarea*. Münster: LIT.

Kuran, T. (2004) *Islam and Mammon: The Economic Predicaments of Islamism*. Princeton, NJ: Princeton University Press.

Kutscher, M. (2001) *Internationale Kooperationen Keiner and mittelstäandischer Betriebe*. Ingoktadt, unpublished manuscript.

Lippmann, W. (1960) *Public Opinion*. New York: Macmillan.

Loverseed, H. (2002) *Travel and Tourism in Morocco*. London: Mintel International Group Ltd.

Mernissi, F. (1989) *Doing Daily Battle: Interviews with Moroccan Women*. New Brunswick: Rutgers University Press.

—— (2003) *Beyond the Veil: Male-Female Dynamics in Modern Muslim Society*. London: Saqi Books.

Mosedale, J.T. (2006), 'Tourism commodity chains: market entry and its effects on St. Lucia', *Current Issues in Tourism*, 9(4/5): 436–58.

Oberg, K. (1960) 'Cultural shock: adjustment(s) to new cultural environments', *Practical Anthropology* 7: 170–79.

Reisinger, Y. and Turner, L.W. (2003) *Cross-cultural Behaviour in Tourism: Concepts and Analysis*. Oxford: Butterworth and Heinemann.

Ruben, B.D. (1989) 'The study of cross-cultural competence: traditions and contemporary issues', *International Journal of Intercultural Relations*, 13: 229–40.

Scherle, N. (2004) 'International bilateral business in the tourism industry: perspectives from German–Moroccan co-operations', *Tourism Geographies*, 6(2): 229–56.

—— (2006) *Bilaterale Unternehmenskooperationen im Tourismussektor: Ausgewählte Erfolgsfaktoren*. Wiesbaden: Gabler.

Schmid, S. (1996) *Multikulturalität in der internationalen Unternehmung: Konzepte – Reflexionen – Implikationen*. Wiesbaden: Gabler.

Schneider, S.C. and Barsoux, J.-L. (2003) *Managing Across Cultures*, 2nd edn. Harlow: Financial Times.

Stüdlein, Y. (1997) *Management von Kulturunterschieden: Phasenkonzept für internationale strategische Allianzen*. Wiesbaden: Deutscher Universitäts-Verlag.

Tayeb, M.H. (2000) *The Management of International Enterprises: A Socio-political View*. Basingstoke: Macmillan.

Thomas, A. (2005) 'Das Eigene, das Fremde, das Interkulturelle', in A. Thomas, E. -U. Kinast and S. Schroll Machl (eds) *Handbuch Interkulturelle Kommunikation und Kooperation*, vol. I, 2nd edn.

Tibi, B. (1991) *Islam and the Cultural Accomodation of Social Change*. Boulder, CO: Westview Press.

Trompenaars, F. (1993) *Riding the Waves of Culture. Understanding Cultural Diversity in Business*. London: Brealey.

Trompenaars, F. and Hampden-Turner, C. (2004) *Riding the Waves of Culture: Understanding Cultural Diversity in Business*, 2nd edn. London: Brealey.

Weber, M. (1920) *Gesammelte Aufsätze zur Religionssoziologie*. Tübingen: Mohr.

PART III

The internationalisation of tourism: practices and processes

INTERNATIONAL BUSINESS AND TOURISM BEYOND THE FIRM

While the firm would appear to be the dominant unit of analysis for international business studies, recent critiques have pointed to the need to progress beyond the firm in order to understand the nature of cross-border commerce in the early twenty-first century (Andresson 2000; Buckley and Ghauri 2004; Buckley and Lessard 2005; Oviatt and McDougall 2005). Conditions of accelerated globalisation not only question the ability of earlier theoretical contributions to explain contemporary firm dynamics, but also they have created new forms of enterprise with their own distinctive operating systems and parameters such as the virtual business (mode 3, Figure 1.1) or the so-called 'International New Venture' (INV) that is practically 'born global'. According to Mtigwe (2006), three distinctive forms of Internationalization Theory have emerged in response to current conditions and issues: Incremental Theory, with its focus squarely on the process aspects of international business development; Network Theory, which interprets the network as the dominant organisational form through which exchanges are facilitated and take place – and hence it is the network that is responsible for value creation; and finally, International Entrepreneurship Theory, where the focus is more on the individual and firm behaviour as the driver for foreign market entry.

In fact, in their own ways each of these theoretical bodies stresses the place of the individual within international business and tourism. They remind us, for instance, that it is not the firms per se that internationalise but rather internationalisation is a function of *human* mobility. This can take the form of the circulation of individuals in a very literal sense as travellers, for instance, who are physically present in the establishment, operation and development of offices, affiliates or franchises overseas (modes 1 and 4). Equally, it can take more intangible forms through the circulation and hence interpersonal communication of information, ideas, offers, products and capital (mode 3). Internationalisation can take place because of the willingness of individuals to take risks by entering overseas markets sometimes flying in the face of conventional business acumen. After all, who would have ever thought barely more than two decades ago that jumping from tall structures with only a thick rubber band to stop you from hitting the ground would become a global adventure sports phenomenon (see Chapter 9)?

The international spread of a business is a distinctive (entrepreneurial) process (Andersson 2000) but we should not lose sight of the fact that strategy is determined by interactions between human beings. Thus, one of the consequences of the dominance of firm-based approaches is that they tend to 'dehumanise' international business studies by reducing the role of individuals and their actions in the process of internationalisation. This is reinforced by the prevalence of quantitative methods and positivist approaches to research. Nevertheless, although compelling cases can be put forward on the basis of comprehensive, short-term data sets, ultimately many of the findings are based on inference. Jones and Khanna (2006) note that qualitative methods as well as a greater willingness to examine longer-term (at least beyond a decade) historical processes offer greater potential in terms of determining causality. Such approaches put individuals to the fore and through methods that include interviews, documentary and archival analysis, critical issues in international business are conveyed by the individuals involved in their own words.

Such approaches are very familiar to business historians, macro-marketing historians, and economic geographers. However, as Jones and Khanna (2006) point out, they have yet to penetrate international business studies more widely, and we would contend that they are equally scarce in tourism studies. One of the advantages of this approach is that, because it stresses the development of the firm to be a long-term project, the current situation is more insightfully revealed to be an amalgam of previous as well as contemporary episodes and decisions in the firm's ongoing history. In so doing, it provides an opportunity to go beyond the façade of rationality, to embrace the complexity that is inherent in the social world (Law 2004), and especially within commercial organisations. All too often, internationalisation is presented as predictable, rational and 'know-able' when in fact decision-making processes may be complex, messy and based on imperfect information and market intelligence (Hall 2008).

At first inspection, Mosedale's chapter on tourism commodity chains may appear to hark back to the traditional firm-based view of international business presented in Part II. It looks at the firms involved in the assembly of tourism products. Package holidays are complicated products to construct and to bring to market. To be clear, comparative advantages in the factors of production across international space are crucially important in the assembly of tour products, however his chapter demonstrates that to focus exclusively on the economic logic would provide only a very partial explanation of the production process. Complex networks of social relations between producers, intermediaries, regulators and consumers are stretched over often long distances. In this respect, the specific conceptual construct of commodity chains offers a means for embracing and understanding such intricacies. Significantly, his chapter stresses many modes of international business are present in the delivery of what appears to the consumer to be a single, unified product. Often the trade in (tourism) services is defined on the basis of the four GATS categories and there may be an understandable but false temptation to allocate a firm's trade in tourism to one or other of them exclusively. Firms may be active in more than one mode and the modal nature(s) of their trade in tourism services may shift over time as the nature of organisation and its business interests change.

The stretching of commercial relationships over long distances is a theme picked up in Blumberg's analysis of the role of internationalisation in the emergence and growth of adventure tourism in two of the major destinations for this form of tourism. Her chapter concentrates on the internationalisation of entrepreneurship and the flow of information – in the form of new products and operating methods and techniques – from New Zealand to Switzerland, and vice versa. She demonstrates that exchanges of knowledge at the international scale routinely take place for sound commercial reasons. This is not, though, exclusively the case and in several instances start-ups and the subsequent fortunes of enterprises can be the outcome of serendipitous combinations of circumstances. Although arguably insufficiently recognised in international business studies of small- and medium-sized enterprises and entrepreneurship, tourism and mobility inherently make a major contribution to business innovation and the diffusion of management, marketing and product concepts by dint of personal contact and traveller experiences abroad. Indeed, Blumberg's chapter highlights the need for more research on the roles of incidental and deliberate international mobility of individuals as a factor in the internationalisation of business and products.

In the final chapter in this part, Duncan examines the apparent oxymoron of the 'working holiday'. Her analysis looks at how and why young people are attracted to temporary work at the year-round destination of Whistler in British Columbia, Canada. Whistler has been a heavily researched destination down the years because its identity and experiences have been shaped by strong corporate interests (Gill 2007). Away from corporate place-making, Duncan presents an examination of mode 4 internationalisation. It may be tempting to think of mode 4 as stereotypically involving ex-patriot workers from low-wage, developing-world economies travelling to destinations in the developed world to find comparatively higher-paid jobs with better conditions. For instance, 'migrant workers' are vital to the operation of the hospitality sector in London (Church and Frost 2004; see also Chapter 6). In contrast, Duncan examines the flow of workers from one developed economy to another. In the process, she demonstrates that the boundaries between tourism and other forms of human mobility are increasingly blurred. Moreover, she suggests that the life experiences and less so commercial knowledges garnered while on the move are vital components in their future roles as workers and entrepreneurs.

SCALES, NETWORKS, DESTINATIONS AND REGIONS: A CAUTIONARY NOTE

The chapters in this part of the book emphasise that business relationships and networks are operated at the international level and are sometimes stretched over very long distances between destinations and home, destinations and point of delivery or purchase. Here the cases cover the linkages between the Caribbean and the United Kingdom, the linkages between Switzerland and New Zealand, and between the United Kingdom and Canada, specifically the western seaboard. In the previous section, the linkages between Morocco and Germany were discussed.

It was not a deliberate intention to focus exclusively on western cases or for that matter to concentrate more on core–periphery relationships in the global economy. Our coverage simply reflects the interests of the authors active in this particular subject and those who wanted to be involved in the project. However, in its own way, the array of chapters presented here is emblematic of a wider problem in international business: namely, the predilection for certain regions of the world at the expense of others raises important questions of what constitutes the international in international business? In a similar vein, it has been questioned whether it is appropriate for international business scholars to have regional specialisms because the international economy does not function in artificially ring-fenced units? Ultimately, such parochialism may be incommensurate with a field in which business activities and relations in one region are linked to one degree or another with those around the world. Indeed, a critical research task with respect to the rhetoric of international business is to more accurately assess whether findings or principles identified from research in one context may apply across the world, or be adaptable to different conditions or inform other cases. As Wallerstein (2006: 82) observed, we must 'place the reality we are immediately studying within the larger context' because 'we can never understand the detail if we do not understand the pertinent whole … exactly what is changing, how it is changing, and why it is changing'. Unless the significance of local and cultural context is appropriately considered it may well be the case that the 'international' dimension of international business may be associated with a form of westernised universalism, or a totalisation of international business studies, rather than a subject that is genuinely international in scope (Wallerstein 2006).

As Fruin (2007) argues, international business should also 'go east'. For too long, western models of economic organisation and administration have dominated international business studies. Given the rise of the Asian Tigers in the 1990s and the emergence of China as an economic superpower, there is a need to focus our attention to markets, firms and entrepreneurs in regions that have traditionally been under-researched compared to their major contribution to the world economy. To a degree, this has been underway in tourism studies with a long-standing interest in southeast Asia as an established destination region and China as the most important emergent inbound and outbound market. The situation in the former Soviet republics of Central Asia has appeared on the radar (Kantarci 2007). Central and South America and much of Africa are, though, largely *terra incognita*. Therefore, international business also needs to 'go south'. Indeed, with respect to the latter, there is an imbalance with North Africa favoured over Southern African and Sub-Saharan states. Visser (2006) has observed that most analysis on tourism in Africa is conducted by those from the Global North, in particular Europe, and he calls for a greater responsibility from those in (Southern) Africa in producing knowledge and discourses about their own continent. Unless the sorts of issues raised by Fruin (2007) and Visser (2006) are addressed, we run the risk of perpetuating and reinforcing distinctive and unequal geographies of attention within international business and tourism.

REFERENCES

Andresson, S. (2000) 'The internationalization of the firm from an entrepreneurial perspective', *International Studies of Management and Organization*, 30(1): 63–92.

Buckley, P.J. and Ghauri, P.N. (2004) 'Globalisation, economic geography and the strategy of multinational enterprises', *Journal of International Business*, 35(2): 81–98.

Buckley, P.J. and Lessard, D.R. (2005) 'Regaining the edge for international business research', *Journal of International Business Studies*, 36: 595–9.

Church, A. and Frost, M. (2004) 'Tourism, the global city and the labour market in London', *Tourism Geographies*, 6: 202–28.

Fruin, W.M. (2007) 'Bringing the world (back) into international business', *Journal of International Business Studies*, 38: 353–6.

Gill, A. (2007) 'The politics of bed units: growth control in the resort of Whistler, British Columbia', in A. Church and T.E. Coles (eds) *Tourism, Power and Space*. London: Routledge.

Hall, C.M. (2008) *Tourism Planning*, 2nd edn. Harlow: Prentice Hall.

Jones, G. and Khanna, T. (2006) 'Bringing history (back) into international business', *Journal of International Business Studies*, 37: 453–68.

Kantarci, K. (2007) 'Perceptions of foreign investors on the tourism market in central Asia including Kyrgyzstan, Kazakhstan, Uzbekistan, Turkmenistan', *Tourism Management*, 28: 820–9.

Law, J. (2004) *After Method. Mess in Social Science Research*. London: Routledge.

Mtigwe, B. (2006) 'Theoretical milestones in international business: the journey to international entrepreneurship theory', *Journal of International Entrepreneurship*, 4: 5–25.

Oviatt, B.M. and McDougall, P.P. (2005) 'The internationalization of entrepreneurship', *Journal of International Business Studies*, 36: 2–8.

Visser, G. (2006) 'The South African Research Foundation's researcher rating system: international connections and local disjuntures'. Unpublished conference paper presented at the International Geographical Union Commission on Tourism, Leisure and Global Change Pre-Congress Symposium, 1 July 2006.

Wallerstein, I. (2006) *European Universalism: The Rhetoric of Power*. New York: Free Press.

8 The internationalisation of tourism commodity chains

Jan Mosedale

Learning objectives

After considering this chapter, you will be able to:

- describe the role of commodity chain analysis in explaining the internationalisation of tourism production;
- identify the key characteristics of tourism commodity chains within the context of chain governance and institutional framework;
- assess the degree to which commodity chains and places are connected.

Key terms

- commodity chain;
- tourism production;
- governance;
- integration;
- institutional framework.

INTRODUCTION: ANALYSING TOURISM ECONOMIC DEVELOPMENT

Much has been said about the growth and internationalisation of tourist flows, especially by supranational tourism organisations – such as the United Nations World Tourism Organisation (UNWTO) and the World Travel and Tourism Council (WTTC) – intent on promoting tourism development as a principal mode of economic development. While these organisations are keen to underline the quantitative changes (growth and increased internationalisation) experienced in the tourism sector, especially in emergent regions (i.e. the Middle East, the Asia-Pacific and Africa), simultaneous qualitative and structural changes in the tourism sector (transformative globalisation processes) have by and large been overlooked. The few exceptions (e.g. Britton 1982; Gotham 2002) have taken a destination-based approach, thus neglecting the meso- and macro-level of analysis necessary to understand the functioning of global economic activity and tourism development. However, tourism is best understood as a multiscalar economic activity that spans geographical scales (global, regional, national, local) and defies geo-political boundaries (Timothy 2006). For Milne and Ateljevic (2001: 371–2):

> Tourism, in simple terms, must be viewed as a transaction process which is at once driven by the global priorities of multinational corporations, geo-political forces and broader forces of economic change, and the complexities of the local – where residents, visitors, workers, governments and entrepreneurs interact at the industry 'coal-face'.

While destination-based analyses provide a detailed examination of local economic activity and interactions between local economic actors, it is crucial to recognise the importance of analysing firm linkages that transcend individual geographical scales. Rather than providing yet another destination-based analysis, this chapter adopts a systems-based approach – by way of explaining and encouraging the use of commodity chain analysis – as a means of unravelling international business behaviours and relationships in the tourism sector. Specifically, the application of commodity chain analysis presents the opportunity to examine globalisation processes *in situ*, at the site of production, while simultaneously highlighting the connections between distinct places of production and consumption, as well as the actors who participate in the commodity chain. Briefly put, the concept of the commodity chains is used to track a product through the different stages of production, distribution and consumption. Key concerns for this type of analysis are the spatial distribution of production and the transformation processes involved in each step of production and consumption but more detailed objectives of the commodity chain analysis depend on its theoretical approach (the following section distinguishes cultural versus political economy approaches). The simplicity of the concept, but the difficulty of tracing all the connections, is demonstrated in the case-study vignette.

CASE-STUDY VIGNETTE – TOURISM AND INTERNATIONAL BUSINESS IN ACTION

The small matter of arranging a holiday? A fictional account of how tourism commodity chains work

Thomas, a German in his mid-twenties living in Munich, Germany has decided to go on a typical sun, sand and sea holiday to Egypt with his girlfriend to beat the winter blues.

Continued

Thomas chooses Egypt because he thinks it is a warm country with an interesting culture. His perceptions are reinforced by a travel documentary he's recently seen on TV on Egypt's cultural heritage and also by word-of-mouth recommendation as some of his friends enjoyed a week there the year before. He also Googled 'Egypt' and found some general information provided by the Egypt Tourist Authority with its 'Egypt: nothing compares' campaign, which was mounted after the 2005 bombings. Coupled with massive price reductions on holiday packages, this has been successful in restoring the destination's fortunes.

He decides to visit his local travel agent – FIRST Reisebüro – in order to get some information on suitable resorts or hotels. The travel agent only just returned from Egypt on a familiarisation trip to the Robinson Club Soma Bay, Sharm el-Sheikh offered by the resort in conjunction with the tour operator, TUI Deutschland. The all-inclusive resort is set directly by the Red Sea and offers a variety of water sports such as sailing, kite- and wind-surfing, and fantastic dive spots such as the Seven Towers and Tobia Island. Thomas is really intrigued by the opportunity to do his Open Water Diver certification at the resort and luckily the travel agent can give detailed first-hand information on the resort. The wellness centre with aroma saunas, cosmetic procedures, Thalasso-Therapy, algal body peeling, ayurverdic massage, hydrotherapy and various hot tubs as well as a saltwater pool, seems perfect for pleasing (or appeasing) his girlfriend while Thomas is off diving. The hotel offers the diving course in conjunction with a local dive school while the beauty centre is leased to an independent company.

Knowing where to go and being a savvy consumer, Thomas shops around by checking travel websites for the best deal. He checks whether low-cost airlines fly to Sharm-el-Sheik just in case he can organise their own, possibly cheaper package. Although AirBerlin (a German low-cost airline) offers a service to Hurghada on the west coast of the Red Sea, Thomas actually ends up buying the all-inclusive package through the travel agent. The transfers would be too time-consuming and anyway he prefers human interaction to booking online. Based on his travel agent's advice and the recent past, Thomas also purchases travel insurance. Incidentally the travel agency has a strategic alliance with the insurance company.

By assembling a package of individual components, TUI Deutschland acts as connecting link, or broker, between Thomas and the resort, airline and inbound tour operator in Sharm el-Sheikh. The tour operator then uses various distribution channels (direct distribution, travel websites, travel agents etc.) to deliver the package to Thomas who does not need to spend considerable time organising the travel itinerary and transactions. Due to the large volume of packages that tour operators sell, they are also able to negotiate significant discounts (ranging from 10 per cent to over 50 per cent) for the individual components that constitute the package.

Continued

Finally, the long-awaited holiday begins and the happy couple travel by public transport to Munich International Airport for their flight to Sharm el-Sheikh with TUIfly. As a charter flight operator, the commercial risk of unsold seats resides with the airline unless it can be passed on to national governments. It is common for such airlines to negotiate agreements of support with governments such as risk-sharing where the government underwrites the cost of flights; guaranteed compensation if a certain number of seats are not filled; free accommodation for the flight crews; or a reduction in landing fees.

Before boarding the flight Thomas and his girlfriend exchange money, go duty-free shopping, and buy a few drinks in departures. On arrival, the tour operator representative ensures they catch their transfer to the resort where they finally get to indulge in the luxuries of all-inclusive living. After a few days they get bored of the food on offer, and they decide one night to visit Safaga, a local town situated 18km from the resort, for a romantic dinner. They also leave the resort on a day-trip to Luxor and the Valley of the Kings organised by Travco Travel Company of Egypt, a destination agency contracted by the tour operator.

In this hypothetical case, Thomas booked their all-inclusive holiday with TUI Deutschland through the travel agency FIRST Reisebüro; flew to Sharm el-Sheikh with TUIfly; stayed at the Robinson Club Soma Bay; and they took a day-trip to Luxor with Travco Travel Company of Egypt. All these companies are subsidiaries of TUI AG, the largest integrated tourism corporation in Europe. It has tour operators in 18 European countries; 279 hotels, comprising of a total 164,844 beds; 7 airlines, with a total fleet of 125 aircraft; 35 incoming agencies in 36 countries; and 2 cruise companies, with a total fleet of 9 cruise ships. Such integration facilitates collaboration in the assembly and delivery of the individual components of the tour package, and can lead to non-market exchanges between the organisations. The high volume of tourists transported by the corporation is beneficial in negotiations with external partners such as independent hotels, inbound tour operators, tour operator representatives and state governments.

Questions

- What are the advantages of using a tourism commodity chain approach to understanding the assembly, distribution and consumption of holidays?
- Based on this example, what might be some of the difficulties in using a tourism commodity chain approach?
- What might the commodity chain look like if it is mapped out diagrammatically?

The chapter begins with an outline of the conceptual frameworks of commodity chain analysis and the various interpretations based on the context of application. The challenges faced in applying commodity chain analysis to the tourism sector and its particularities as a form of economic activity are then considered by focusing on the political economy approach. In particular, the governance and institutional framework of commodity chains are chosen for a more detailed discussion as these are seen as the most important aspects of this type of analysis, which are lacking from other chain analyses. Due to a relative lack of published tourism research on commodity chains, this discussion is informed by prior work in the primary and secondary sectors (mainly agriculture and manufacturing), and it draws on examples from these as well as from the few case-studies in which commodity chain analysis has been applied to tourism.

COMMODITY CHAIN ANALYSIS: AN INTRODUCTION TO THE MAIN APPROACHES

In general, there have been two main approaches to the applications of the commodity chain concept in business-related research: the political economy and cultural approaches. The political economy approach uses commodity chains to unravel the complex system of international economic actions; to highlight the qualitative change in production processes; and to analyse the complex relationship between actors within the wider economic system. In contrast, the cultural approach examines the meanings attached to commodities during production, circulation and consumption (see Leslie and Reimer 1999; Hughes and Reimer 2004). For instance, Ateljevic and Doorne (2003) have traced the path of a souvenir from its creation in China to its continuous consumption by the purchasing tourist and her receiving friend and family in New Zealand. Meanings associated with the artefact successively shift through a series of stages from a local female factory owner in China – who has experienced female empowerment through her work, and who can provide for her children's education to guarantee them employment – to the New Zealand tourist who uses the souvenir as a surrogate 'of human relations and representations of identity' (Ateljevic and Doorne 2003: 123). Other perspectives from the cultural approach focusing on ethnic food and fashion (Cook and Crang 1996; Jackson 1999) have challenged globalisation theories of cultural homogenisation, global culture theory or 'McDonaldization' theory (Ritzer 2000). They have demonstrated the power of consumers to shape their personal relationship actively and to interact with goods, with the result of creating their own meanings for commodities. What these examples reiterate is that a socio-cultural understanding of production and especially consumption that transcends the economic transaction is required in order to appreciate the complexities of the capitalist system (Britton 1991; Ateljevic and Doorne 2004). However, the focus of this chapter is the political economy approach and specifically the, as yet largely unacknowledged, potential this offers for researching the mediation of tourism production through concepts such as chain governance and the institutional setting.

COMMODITY CHAINS AND POLITICAL ECONOMY

In contrast to the cultural, the political economy approach concentrates on the resource allocation processes that characterise the production, consumption and experience of the commodity. In effect, it implies that the passage of the commodity along the chain is the outcome of a sequence of political negotiations between actors over the transfer of resources. As such, the production, distribution and control of capital in form of commodities and the role of actors and institutions are at the heart of the political economy approach to commodity chain analysis. This implies a vastly different approach to other types of chain analysis in tourism such as supply chains, value chains and distribution channels (Table 8.1).

Distribution channels are the various means by which the product reaches the consumers. As such the analysis of these types of channels is merely concerned with the linkages between production and consumption, and hence is primarily concerned with the improvement of marketing. This type of analysis has recently received increased attention in tourism research (e.g. Buhalis and Laws 2001; Pearce *et al.* 2004). In contrast to distribution channels, supply chains focus exclusively on firms and their relationships with suppliers. For instance, within tourism this focuses on the relationships between tour operators and their suppliers to guarantee certain ethical criteria set by the tour operators in order to achieve economic, environmental and social sustainability beyond their firm boundaries (CELB and TOI 2004).

In comparison to the limited scope of distribution channel and supply chain analyses, value chains identify the value added in the processes associated at the levels of production, distribution and consumption. Poon (1993) has undertaken this type of analysis for the tourism sector and provided a detailed analysis of value added of six primary activities (on-site services, transportation, wholesale packaging, retail distribution, marketing and sales, and customer services). However, value chain analysis is merely concerned with the competitive advantage of organisations within the chain. Although the determination of value added is a component of the commodity chain analysis, the political economy approach to commodity chains does not just try to identify where value is added, how and by whom. Crucially, it also aims to uncover who can participate in commodity chains and why? What and where are the barriers to entry for full participation? And how are these constructed? Evidence of privileges and sources of disadvantage may be identified. As such, the political economy approach to commodity chains attempts to posit production, distribution, consumption and experience at the micro-level (i.e. of the holiday, the souvenir) within much wider social, cultural and political frameworks. These conditions have the potential to influence the relationships between actors in the chain – organisations and individuals – but ultimately the flow of the commodity remains a function of the behaviours and interactions of the respective sets of actors.

In this respect, the fictional account in the case-study demonstrates one of the key challenges for the application of a commodity chain analysis in tourism: namely, the complexity of the sector. This raises serious questions for choosing the depth of analysis; that is, how far to extend the analysis of the chain in order to deliver meaningful insights and where should the boundaries of the chain be drawn? For instance, should processes involved in hotel operation, such as outsourced laundry or security services, be included in a commodity chain of package tourism? This example demonstrates the subjective nature of determining the extent of the chain and of choosing the processes or nodes – as these are referred to in commodity chain research – of relevance. For instance, Mosedale (2006) offers a relatively crude analysis by only focusing on the relationship between the main nodes without taking their suppliers into account, whereas Clancy (1998) investigates the governing structures of the hotel and airline industries in isolation from one another. Mosedale (2006) may offer too simplistic an analysis of the chain, but Clancy (1998) fails to address the vertical

Table 8.1 Comparison of different types of chain analysis

	Distribution channel	Supply chain	Value chain	Commodity chain
Scope	Distribution	Production	Production, distribution and consumption	Production, distribution and consumption
Process	Analysis of the distribution strategies of tourism businesses	Examination of the inter-firm relationships	Identification of the cost and value (profit margin) of activities undertaken by organisations in the chain	Four-stage analysis: (1) input-output; (2) spatial distribution; (3) organisational structure; and (4) institutional framework
Main objective	Evaluating channel organisation and operation for improved tourism marketing	Understanding and managing the supply chain for effective business relationships	Determining competitive advantage of organisations within a chain	Revealing the complex system of international economic actions and highlight qualitative change in processes at each step of the chain
Examples from the tourism literature	Pearce et al. (2004), Buhalis and Laws (2001)	CELB and TOI (2004)	Poon (1993)	Clancy (1998), Mosedale (2006)

production/consumption process of tourism adequately. Instead, he provides an analysis of two separate nodes isolated from other production/consumption processes within the chain. While the term 'chain' is still used for the sake of convenience, it may not always be the most precise metaphor. Production, distribution and consumption systems are sometimes more appropriately viewed as networks, rather than linear chains, as they may consist of several sequences of parallel nodes or sites of production. Also, inter-firm linkages are dependent on social relations between various actors in the 'chain' and within the 'node'. In fact, the most commonly applied type of global commodity chain (GCC) analysis was developed by Gereffi (1994) and consists of four stages of analysis:

1 input – output at the individual nodes;
2 the spatial distribution of nodes;
3 the organisational/governance structure of the chain; and
4 the institutional setting in which the chain and the individual nodes are embedded.

Gereffi (1994) identified just the first three stages of the GCC analysis in his earlier work, but later added the institutional framework after some criticism (Gereffi 1995). GCCs are thus situated as

> sets of interorganizational networks clustered around one commodity or product, linking households, enterprises, and states to one another within the world-economy. These networks are situationally specific, socially constructed, and locally integrated, underscoring the social embeddedness of economic organization.
>
> (Gereffi *et al.* 1994: 2)

Despite the clear outline of the GCC analysis into four distinct stages, the majority of studies employing the GCC analysis have put emphasis on determining the controlling actors or nodes (i.e. the governance structure) 'since this is where the key notions of barriers of entry and chain co-ordination appear' (Raikes *et al.* 2000: 393). By ignoring the role of institutions in shaping the environment in which these economic actors operate – i.e. the institutional framework in which commodity chains are embedded and focused on governance structures – firms and places seem to have little control over their actions as they are dependent on the structural conditions and constraints of the commodity chain. This point of view, however, does little to explain the different arrangements of, and dispositions within, commodity chains and economic development. As Henderson *et al.* (2002: 441) observe, 'inter-firm networks link societies which exhibit significant social and institutional variation, embody different welfare regimes and have different capacities for state economic management: in short, represent different forms of capitalism'. The following sections will therefore discuss the governance and institutional framework of commodity chains in more detail.

GOVERNANCE

Despite its importance for GCC analysis, the concept of governance has only been loosely defined as 'authority and power relations that determine how financial, material, and human resources are allocated and flow within the chain' (Gereffi 1994: 97); that is, 'non-market coordination of economic activity', and direct or indirect 'influence' (Gereffi *et al*. 2001: 4). Gereffi *et al*. (2001) identify chain governance as 'the ability of one firm in the chain to influence or determine the activities of other firms in the chain'. This can take a number of forms, such as: determining the product provided by suppliers (e.g. via quality as well as health and safety standards); deciding on entry into or exit from the chain; and offering technical expertise to preferred suppliers in order to gain the expected product/service. Commodity chains differ in the type, level and concentration of governance exercised by key actors and the mode of 'applying' governance.

Early commodity chain research in the primary and secondary sectors identified two types of governance structures (Gereffi 1994), mainly depending on the location of the influencing node in the chain. Large, often transnational corporations coordinate production via integrated subsidiaries, with the effect of leading firms in *producer-driven* commodity chains. Power is located in the headquarters of these corporations and is transmitted downwards through the subsidiaries. Value follows the opposite route; it is generated by subsidiaries and gathered at the headquarters. Industries that exhibit such governance patterns include mainly manufacturing such as automobiles, aircraft, computers and semiconductors, and they are typically capital and technology intensive (Table 8.2). Gereffi (1994) uses the multilayered production system of automobile manufacturing as a prime example of *producer-driven* commodity chains. Although the chain comprises thousands of firms, with varying links between each other (parents, subsidiaries and subcontractors), the parent companies, especially Japanese and US, organise and coordinate the production process and build the automobile including the parts supplied by others.

In contrast to the capital- and technology-intensive industries of producer-driven commodity chains, *buyer-driven* chains are frequently encountered in labour-intensive production, such as garments, footwear, toys and consumer electronics. They are organised in decentralised production networks across a number of countries, with large retailers or brand merchandisers controlling and influencing the entire production process yet without being involved in the actual production process. As the controlling firms do not produce any goods themselves but instead focus on the design, marketing/branding and distribution of these products, they have been termed 'hollow' corporations (Clancy 1998: 126). A case in point is Nike, a footwear corporation, which has devised a division of labour between post-industrial and newly industrialised countries (Korzeniewicz 1994). The corporation has succeeded in appropriating increased value by subcontracting all the production processes to newly industrialised countries and focusing on distribution, marketing and advertising from its base in post-industrial economies: 'Marketing, advertising, and consumption trends dictate what will be manufactured, how it will be manufactured, and where it will be manufactured … manufacturing processes are secondary to the control over the symbolic nature and status of athletic shoes' (Korzeniewicz 1994: 263).

COMMODITY CHAINS AND TOURISM

Clancy (1998) is one of only a handful of researchers so far to have applied the commodity chain analysis to tourism. In his investigation of the hotel and airline industries, he offers

Table 8.2 *Characteristics of different commodity chain governance forms*

	Producer-driven commodity chains	Contract-driven commodity chains	Package tourism commodity chains	Buyer-Driven commodity chains
Drivers of global commodity chains	Industrial capital	Commercial capital	Commercial capital	Commercial capital
Core competencies	Research and development	Marketing; operation	Design; packaging	Design; marketing
Barriers to entry	Economies of scale	Economies of scale	Economies of scale and scope	Economies of scope
Economic sectors	Consumer durables; intermediate goods; capital goods	Tourism	Tourism	Consumer nondurables
Industries	Automobiles; computers; aircraft	Hotel	Package tourism	Apparel; footwear; toys
Ownership of manufacturing firms	Transnational firms	Mix of transnational firms and franchises	Mix of transnational and local firms	Local firms
Organisation of production	Integration	Externalisation	Integration	Externalisation
Main network links	Investment-based	Contract-based	Investment-based	Trade-based
Predominant network structure	Vertical	Horizontal	Vertical, horizontal and diagonal	Horizontal

Source: Adapted from Mosedale (2006: 442).

another different type of governance structure in which contractual agreements between economic actors take centre stage. His so-called *contract-driven chains* have similarities with buyer-driven chains in that core firms accrue value by externalising production (Table 5.1). Mosedale (2006) also calls for a broadening of Gereffi's (1994) rigid bipartite characterisation of commodity chain governance. Rather than identify new forms of chain, he argues that European package tourism commodity chains have elements of both producer- and buyer-driven chains. Economies of scale and scope represent barriers of market entry for potential new firms as do the horizontal, vertical as well as diagonal integration of production processes. For Mosedale (2006: 454):

> In contrast to increasing outsourcing of production and the concentration of firms in the manufacturing sector on marketing and branding, the tourism industry is experiencing an intensification of integration in order to internalise profits, expand their market share and at the same time gain control over all the primary nodes in the Commodity Chain.

The coordination of production processes via the integration of firms under common ownership is a popular business strategy in the tourism industry. Similar to Clancy's (1998) analysis of hotel and airline commodity chains, Gómez and Sinclair (1991) used a broader definition of integration to include contractual agreements between firms under separate ownership. There are different types of integration that depend on the production process of the firm to be integrated in comparison to the parent company. Horizontal integration occurs when a parent company acquires a business in the same level of the production chain, such as tour operators, for example the attempted acquisitions of First Choice by Airtours and of Kuoni by First Choice in 1999. The consequences of horizontal integration are an increasing concentration of the industry. Despite a lack of data for market share of tour operators based on tourist numbers, the share of Air Travel Organisers' Licences (ATOL) can be used as surrogate indicator (see Table 8.3). The data reveal a concentration of market share for the UK in the mid-to-late 1980s with subsequent decrease eventually leading to investment abroad (Mosedale 2005).

Vertical integration, on the other hand, refers to the linkages of production process both upstream and/or downstream. Examples in tourism include for instance the integration of tour operators, travel agencies, airlines, hotels and destination agencies into large corporations such as Thomas Cook AG with 33 tour operator brands, 67 airplanes, 2,400 travel agencies as well as a worldwide network of hotels.

Table 8.3 Top tour operator's share of all ATOL holidays, 1982–2005 (in per cent)

	1982	1985	1988	1992	1995	1998	2002	2005
Top 5	38.0	37.3	62.2	54.3	55.8	46.2	46.4	45.2
Top 10	52.3	49.5	76.1	68.0	67.6	57.4	56.4	54.0
Top 20	67.5	63.2	82.4	76.5	74.9	67.1	67.2	65.7

Source: Based on data from Civil Aviation Authority (1992–2006) and The Monopolies and Mergers Commission (1986, 1989).

It is important to note that any increase in vertical integration will have spatial consequences as all the primary nodes of the commodity chain (in the source market as well as the destination) can be integrated into one large tourism corporation. One of the few studies illustrating the effects of such vertical integration in tourism explores the case of the Virgin Travel Group and its influence in the Caribbean (Mosedale 2006). This vertically integrated tourism group, which is comprised of a scheduled airline, an outbound tour operator and a retail travel agent, used the integrated, non-market relationship between its airline and tour operator as a competitive advantage in gaining its high market share of UK package tourism to St Lucia.

While both horizontal and vertical integration take place between firms within the same production system (at the same level for horizontal integration and between stages of the system for vertical integration), *diagonal integration,* in contrast, is concerned with a new entry to the industry from a non-related sector. Examples of diagonal integration in tourism include Preussag, which has transformed itself, with the initial acquisition of Hapag–Lloyd in 1997, from an industrial corporation mainly in mining and steel to a service-oriented firm focusing on tourism and shipping (Stier and Laufer 2005). In fact, in only three years Preussag managed to become the leading European tourism firm with a turnover of €7 billion, which represented almost 50 per cent of the corporation's total turnover. Another example of diagonal integration into the tourism sector is the much slower entry of Rewe, a food retailer and wholesaler, with the acquisition of German travel agencies in 1988 and 1994. However, Rewe did not enter the top-ten integrated tourism corporations until 2000 with the acquisition of DER (Deutsches Reisebüro), ranking eighth in Europe, and it further improved its ranking with the acquisition of LTU Touristik, another integrated tourism corporation in 2001.

While the previous examples demonstrated diagonal integration into the tourism sector, Poon (1993) focuses on the diagonal integration of tourism corporations into associated products and firms, such as holiday insurance, car hire firms and estate agencies. TUI, for instance, has set up a car hire company (TUI Cars) in Mallorca and has entered into a partnership with a local real estate agent (Parador Properties) to sell second homes in Thomson travel agencies in the UK. This type of diagonal integration by tourism corporations into real estate is being seen by both industries as a logical step due to the changing tourism demand towards second-home ownership due to the emergence and rise of low-cost carriers to popular European destinations such as Mallorca (Ultima Hora 2005). This strategy of diagonal integration is indicative of a larger trend of product and market diversification in the tourism sector.

Vertical and horizontal integration have resulted in a situation in which the lack of access to channels of distribution (especially travel agents) and economies of scale creates high barriers to entry (Dale 2000). Vertical integration has also internalised the supplier and buyer relationship, leaving independent suppliers and buyers with few clients. For example, similar characteristics among products – in particular mainstream, sun-sand-and-sea tour packages – facilitates the substitution of one product for another. In turn, this has lead to fierce competition between tour operators in the UK source market. UK tour operators compete on the basis of price in order to achieve a significant market share. This also prevents new entrants from establishing themselves in the marketplace.

The benefits of horizontal integration are increased economies of scope, larger geographical coverage, the access to different market segments, and – especially important for tour operators – economies of scale and synergies. Vertical integration, on the other hand, offers a company ultimate control over the tourism product (supply and distribution) by erecting barriers of entry for competitors, the integration of gains, and improved brand marketing opportunities. Mosedale (2006) has demonstrated the consequences of integration of a scheduled carrier with a mainstream tour operator in the case-study of the Virgin Travel Group and the long-haul destination of St Lucia. However, according to Ioannides and Debbage (1998) the tourism sector is a 'polyglot' comprised of a number of different modes of production. This multiplicity has clear implications on national and international industry organisation and may well result in differing governance structures of tourism commodity chains.

For instance, in their comparison of package tourism chains to St Lucia and Jordan, for instance, Dörry and Mosedale (2006) identify different actors as controlling nodes in the chain despite the overall similarity of the chain structure. In contrast to large transnational corporations controlling much of the tourist flows to St Lucia, the situation in Jordan is such that a lack of economies of scale do not warrant the integration of production processes, but rather specialised, small- and medium-sized tour operators (SMTOs) are the leading actors in the chain, although they are reliant on local suppliers such as tour guides and incoming agencies. As a result of a fragmented market and specificities of intercultural exchanges (see Chapter 7) between firms of similar size and capacity, the dominance of specific nodes in the chain to Jordan is comparatively low relative to the dominance of the Virgin Travel Group in St Lucia due to the non-market, functionally integrated relationship between its tour operator and airline units.

INSTITUTIONAL FRAMEWORK

While firm organisation and the governance of commodity chains are critical to explaining the structures that facilitate flows of tourists, capital, knowledge and information, it is equally important to analyse the transformation of these flows via individual places in the form of the institutional and social fabric of the destination. The examples of package tourism commodity chains to St Lucia and Jordan demonstrate that the organisation and structure of tourism commodity chains can vary between destinations, and in turn, these signify the influence of national and local institutional features, cultural characteristics and historical developments. The step of analysing institutional frameworks, which Gereffi (1995) added to GCC analysis retrospectively, as well as how chains differ depending on the institutional and social context of production sites, has mostly been ignored in commodity chain research. Yet the question remains: how are commodity chains shaped by different regulatory bodies and institutional actors and vice versa?

The importance of institutions in tourism research was recognised early on by Britton (1991: 453–4) who, from a political economy perspective, called for increased attention towards the role of 'all the social institutions designed to create, coordinate, regulate, and distribute exchange values: enterprises, industries, markets, state agencies'. The institutional regime of the economy can be categorised into the 'institutional environment' and the 'institutional arrangements'. The institutional environment refers to informal structures such as social norms, conventions and customs as well as officially formalised laws and regulations (e.g. competition, labour, trade, contract laws) controlling socio-economic behaviour (see also Chapter 7). Institutional arrangements, on the other hand, represent the organisational forms, which arise as a result of, and are regulated by, the institutional environment.

Institutions play a key role in the configuration of economic processes and are thus responsible for the resulting structural and spatial characteristics of the economy and commodity chain. Institutional factors operate at all levels and scales of the economy ranging from firms through corporate (self-)governance (see Chapter 6), to markets, states and supranational organisations such as the World Bank or the Organisation for Economic Co-operation and Development (OECD). The aim of the institutional framework within commodity chain analysis is to analyse these formal or informal systems that govern the relationship between the socio-political and cultural structures and institutions and their interaction to create the economic landscape; that is,

> economic activity is *socially and institutionally situated*: it cannot be explained by reference to atomistic individual motives alone, but has to be understood as enmeshed in wider *structures of social, economic, and political rules, procedures and conventions*.
>
> (Martin 2003: 79, emphasis original)

Institutions are necessary to provide a framework in which companies and individuals can engage in economic exchange and social economic processes within a country but also across borders. Institutions are therefore required to provide and guarantee (over time) the basic conditions for economic exchange, such as markets, property rights and a monetary system. As the processes of economic exchange have experienced transformations, so have the institutions governing the conditions. History matters in the functioning of economic life; decisions and strategies undertaken by institutions are not just a reaction to contemporary conditions but they are dependent on the entire series of previous decisions and their resulting outcomes (they are path-dependent). This institutional history (as all history) is place-specific as relationships between economic agents, institutions and structures unfold in particular places. Crespo and Suddaby (2000: 359), for instance, compare the development of tourism development in Cuba, the Dominican Republic and Cancún (Mexico) and conclude that despite Cuba's different institutional framework in which the government is 'the owner/developer and utilizes from 40 per cent to 60 per cent of the available national resources to create and support tourism activity', it has 'achieved reasonable success in attracting a growing number of visitors'.

Systems of regulation are historically specific institutional regimes 'for coordinating, stabilizing, and reproducing socioeconomic relations' (Martin 2003: 81). These are not limited to formal macro-institutions regulating key areas such as transport (e.g. bilateral agreements in aviation and freedoms of the air which govern international air services by granting airlines certain rights of access to countries as discussed in Chapter 5), wage relations and competition or state agencies, business institutions and labour organisations, but include informal institutions of regulations such as place-specific social networks, cultures and traditions. For example, Mosedale (2006) noted the role of the St Lucian government, which decided to provide support (financial and in kind) only for charter flights if they would result in an incremental growth in tourist numbers. This policy was based on a 'moving up-market' initiative to increase the quality of St Lucia as a destination. Mosedale (2006) demonstrates that the Virgin Travel Group benefited from the loss of the charter business and considerably increased its capacity to St Lucia. As a result of close, non-market cooperation between Virgin's airline and tour operator, 60–70 per cent of all seats were allocated to the tour operator. This drive for control of the commodity chain and concurrent risk reduction is illustrated by a comment by Wolfgang Bremer, Portfolio Management Incoming and Guest Service for TUI: 'We have taken a stake in these agencies in order to support close cooperation with them in the long term and to be able to have a direct influence'(TUI 2006: 5).

CONCLUSION: COMMODITY CHAINS, TOURISM AND INTERNATIONAL BUSINESS

This chapter has attempted to demonstrate the importance of viewing the international tourism production processes in social, cultural and political economic contexts. Commodity chain analysis – in comparison to other varieties of chain analysis – provides a nuanced reading in light of qualitative changes. The political economy approach to commodity chain research offers a compelling opportunity to highlight the unequal distribution of production and capital accumulation in comparison to valued added, while also indicating the importance of industry structure and re-structuring trends for chain governance.

Notwithstanding its potential, commodity chain analysis has received only scant attention in tourism research. Comparative research has demonstrated slight variations in chain governance that could be due to a number of factors such as different institutional and historic characteristics of the destinations and differences in the tourism product. Mosedale (2006) refers to anecdotal data to suggest that different chain structures and governance patterns are dependent on the evolution of the tourism industries in the source market.

At the same time, it has to be realised that commodity chains are not static, as changes in industry structure, regulations, institutions and social trends continuously influence the composition, structure and governance of the chain. Dörry and Mosedale (2006) identify another important aspect of the commodity chain, the ability of specific actors and nodes in the chain to 'upgrade' their position within the chain. This has clear implications for international business as it may involve a changing governance structure of the chain where, for instance, governance shifts from one node to another. Some hotels, such as the Raffles Hotel in Singapore, have become destinations in themselves. Due to their ability to take advantage of direct distribution and repeat business, they are less dependent on tour operators (Mosedale 2006). Another form of upgrading occurs when a firm that was active in one node of a chain expands its activities to include processes of a higher-level node. For example, inbound tour operators might take advantage of their relationships with suppliers in the destination in order to enter into the outbound tour operator market in a particular source region.

Finally, the focus of commodity chain research on relationships across geographic scales is its main contribution to the study of international business. Global, regional, national and local factors matter: global and regional supranational institutions frame the environment in which economic processes can be performed; national trade policies have influenced the participation in commodity chains; and cooperation at a local level facilitates the engagement with and access to source markets.

Discussion questions

- What is the 'product' of the tourism production system, and where is the production of tourism located?
- What are the implications of vertical, horizontal and diagonal integration in source markets for tourism destinations?
- In context of current economic and social processes, what are the likely scenarios or trends in governance of the tourism commodity chains?

REFERENCES

Ateljevic, I. and Doorne, S. (2003) 'Culture, economy and tourism commodities: social relations of production and consumption', *Tourist Studies'*, 3(2): 123-41.

—— (2004) 'Cultural circuits of tourism: commodities, place, and re-consumption', in A.A. Lew, C.M. Hall and A.M. Williams (eds) *A Companion to Tourism*. Malden, MA: Blackwell.

Britton, S. G. (1982) 'International tourism and multinational corporations in the Pacific: the case of Fiji', in M. Taylor and N. Thrift (eds) *The Geography of Multinationals*. London: Croom Helm.

—— (1991) 'Tourism, capital, and place: towards a critical geography of tourism', *Environment and Planning D: Society and Space*, 9(4): 451-78.

Buhalis, D. and Laws, E. (2001) *Tourism Distribution Channels: Practices, Issues and Transformation*. London: Continuum.

CELB and TOI (Center for Environmental Leadership in Business and Tour Operator Initiative for Sustainable Tourism Develeopment) (2004) Supply chain engagement for tour operators: three steps toward sustainability. Online. Available from: http://www.toinitiative.org/supply_chain/SupplyChainEngagement.pdf (accessed: 11/02/07).

Civil Aviation Authority (1992-2006) *ATOL Business* (1-28). London: CAA.

Clancy, M. (1998) 'Commodity chains, services and development: theory and preliminary evidence from the tourism industry', *Review of International Political Economy*, 5(1): 122-48.

Cook, I. and Crang, P. (1996) 'The world on a plate: culinary culture, displacement and geographical knowledges', *Journal of Material Culture*, 1: 131-53.

Crespo, N. and Suddaby, C. (2000) 'A comparison of Cuba's tourism industry with the Dominican Republic and Cancún, 1988-1999', in Association for the Study of the Cuban Economy (ed.) *Cuba in Transition, Volume 10*.

Papers and Proceedings of the Tenth Annual Meeting of the Association for the Study of the Cuban Economy. Silver Spring, MD: Association for One Study of the Cuban Economy.

Dale, C. (2000) 'The UK tour-operating industry: a competitive analysis', *Journal of Vacation Marketing*, 6(4): 357–67.

Dörry, S. and Mosedale, J. (2006) 'Commodity chain analysis and tourism: a progressive synthesis?', paper presented at *Cutting Edge Research in Tourism - New Directions, Challenges and Applications*, Surrey (UK), 6–9 June 2006.

Gereffi, G. (1994) 'The organization of buyer-driven global commodity chains: how U.S. retailers shape overseas production networks', in G. Gereffi and M. Korzeniewicz (eds) *Commodity Chains and Global Capitalism*. Westport, CT Greenwood Press.

—— (1995) 'Global production systems and Third World development', in B. Stallings (ed.) *Global Change, Regional Response: The New International Context of Development*. Cambridge: Cambridge University Press.

Gereffi, G., Korzeniewicz, M. and Korzeniewicz, R.P. (1994) 'Introduction: global commodity chains', in G. Gereffi and M. Korzeniewicz (eds) *Commodity Chains and Global Capitalism*. Westport, CT Greenwood Press.

Gereffi, G., Humphrey, J., Kaplinsky, R. and Sturgeon, T.J. (2001) 'Introduction: globalisation, value chains and development', *IDS Bulletin*, 32(3): 1–8.

Gómez, V.B. and Sinclair, M.T (1991) 'Integration in the tourism industry: a case study approach', in M.T. Sinclair and M.J. Stabler (eds) *The Tourism Industry: An International Analysis*. Wallingford: CAB International.

Gotham, K.F. (2002) 'Marketing Mardi Gras: commodification, spectacle and the political economy of tourism in New Orleans', *Urban Studies*, 39(10): 1735–56.

Henderson, J., Dicken, P., Hess, M., Coe, N. and Yeung, H.-W. (2002) 'Global production networks and the analysis of economic development', *Review of International Political Economy*, 9(3): 436–64.

Hughes, A. and Reimer, S. (2004) *Geographies of Commodity Chains*. London: Routledge.

Ioannides, D. and Debbage, K.G. (1998) 'Neo-Fordism and flexible specialization in the travel industry: dissecting the polyglot', in D. Ioannides and K.G. Debbage (eds) *The Economic Geography of the Tourist Industry: A Supply-side Analysis*. London: Routledge.

Jackson, P. (1999) 'Commodity cultures: the traffic in things', *Transactions of the Institute of British Geographers*, 24: 95–108.

Korzeniewicz, M. (1994) 'Commodity chains and marketing strategies: Nike and the global athletic footwear industry', in G. Gereffi and M. Korzeniewicz (eds) *Commodity Chains and Global Capitalism*. Westport, CT Greenwood Press.

Leslie, D. and Reimer, S. (1999) 'Spatialising commodity chains', *Progress in Human Geography*, 23(3): 401–20.

Martin, R. (2003) 'Institutional approaches in economic geography', in E. Sheppard and T. J. Barnes (eds) *A Compansion to Economic Geography*. Oxford: Blackwell Publishing.

Milne, S. and Ateljevic, I. (2001) 'Tourism, economic development and the global–local nexus: theory embracing complexity', *Tourism Geographies*, 3(4): 369–93.

Mosedale, J. (2005) 'Capital mobility in the tourism sector: an analysis of integrated corporations', paper presented at the *End of Tourism? Mobility and Local–Global Connections* conference, Centre for Tourism Policy Studies, Eastbourne, 23–24 June 2005.

—— (2006) 'Tourism commodity chains: market entry and its effects on St Lucia', *Current Issues in Tourism*, 9(4/5): 436–58.

Pearce, D., Tan, R. and Schott, C. (2004) 'Tourism distribution channels in Wellington, New Zealand', *International Journal of Tourism Research*, 6(6): 397–410.

Poon, A. (1993) *Tourism, Technology and Competitive Strategies*. Wallingford: CAB International.

Raikes, P., Jensen, M.F. and Ponte, S. (2000) 'Global commodity chain analysis and the French *filière* approach: comparison and critique', *Economy as Society*, 29(3): 390–417.

Ritzer, G. (2000) *The McDonaldization of Society*. Thousand Oaks, CA: Pine Forge Press.

Stier, B. and Laufer, J. (2005) *Von der Preussag zur TUI: Wege und Wandlungen eines Unternehmens 1923–2003*. Essen: Klartext.

The Monopolies and Mergers Commission (1986) *Foreign Package Holidays.* London: Her Majesty's Stationery Office.

—— (1989) *Thomson Travel Group and Horizon Travel Ltd: A Report on the Merger Situation*. London: Her Majesty's Stationery Office.

Timothy, D. (2006) 'Relationships between tourism and international boundaries', in H. Wachowiak (ed.) *Tourism and Borders: Contemporary Issues, Policies, and International Research*. Burlington, VT Ashgate.

TUI (2006) TUI incoming network: at your service, wherever you are. Online. Available from: www.tui-group.com/en/konzern (accessed: 11/02/07).

Ultima Hora (2005) 'Grupos turísticos e inmobiliarios negocian colaborar en la venta de casas en Balears'. *Ultima Hora,* 02/06/05, Local: 24.

Internationalisation in adventure tourism: the mobility of people, products and innovations

9

Katrin Blumberg

Learning objectives

After considering this chapter, you will be able to:

- summarise how studies of tourism have traditionally dealt with the dual concepts of innovation and product development;
- describe how particular tourism products and innovations circulate across different geographical scales;
- explain how entrepreneurial mobility contributes to product development and the diffusion of innovations in the tourism sector.

Key terms

- adventure tourism;
- internationalisation of production;
- innovation;
- product development;
- knowledge transfer;
- entrepreneurial mobility.

INTRODUCTION: THE INTERNATIONALISATION OF INNOVATION

This chapter examines the internationalisation of adventure tourism products at the place and firm levels. In particular it analyses the links between Queenstown (New Zealand) and Interlaken (Switzerland), and it demonstrates how some Swiss mountain guides visited Queenstown, the 'adventure capital of New Zealand', and then returned home with many ideas that subsequently made Interlaken the 'adventure capital of Switzerland'. In addition to a discussion of the sources of innovation, the chapter also notes how these links are maintained through staff working seasonally in both places (as well as other rafting/canyoning/bungee destinations in the southern hemisphere) and how even recent innovations such as zorbing (large, about 3m diameter, inflatable, transparent, plastic spheres in which humans are suspended and then roll downhill) have travelled the world from New Zealand to Switzerland as a result of entrepreneurial mobility. In short, the chapter demonstrates how innovations need people to make them travel.

Tourism researchers have increasingly thought about the interplay between tourism and globalisation. While globalisation means many things to many people, Wood (2000) identifies three core meanings of the term: first, according to Wood, globalisation refers to a purposeful *project* by various economic and political players and institutions to promote and foster global capitalism; second, to a range of '*social processes* pulling the world together' (Wood 2000: 346, original italics); and third, to the *discourses* used to make sense of the two previous concepts. With respect to the second meaning, the global compression of time and space – and thus the increasing internationalisation of socio-cultural, economic, political and technological networks and activities – are core ingredients of globalisation.

Studies of tourism that engage with globalisation – and thus directly or indirectly with internationalisation – have routinely considered such issues as changes in tourism demand, developments in tourism promotion and marketing, issues of sustainability, as well as new paradigms for competitiveness and organisation in terms of both business or spatial units (see Chapter 1), including the rise of globally acting corporations (for example Smeral 1998; Johnson and Vanetti 2005; Croes 2006). However, what is missing is a discussion of the internationalisation; that is, the international diffusion of individual tourism products or product ranges. With the exception of chain analysis (see Chapter 8), in fact, the understanding of internationalisation is often restricted to 'the process by which firms become involved in serving markets outside their home country' (Peric 2005: 1). This chapter argues that, in times of an increasing focus on social and economic networks as well as their interdependence, such a limited view is insufficient. This chapter adopts a different route in so far as it traces one particular path of the internationalisation of a particular tourism product range with special reference to adventure tourism activities. In doing so, it will unveil the strong relationship between two destinations with complementary seasons and the role that both tourism entrepreneurs and employees have played and continue to play in the maintenance of this relationship leading to distinctive knowledge acquisitions and transfers.

TOURISM INNOVATION DIFFUSION, PRODUCT DEVELOPMENT, ENTREPRENEURSHIP AND MOBILITY

Locating product development in tourism

The internationalisation of tourism products is conceptually connected to considerations of innovation diffusion and adoption. Given the acknowledged importance of innovations to create comparative competitive advantage (see Carlsson 2006), there has been long-term and surprising lack of research on innovations in tourism. Only the field of transport, and in particular air transport (e.g. Perl 1998; Jarach 2002), provides possible exceptions. Part of the reason for this lack of interest might be the popular (mis-)perception that 'innovation is rare – or nonexistent – in tourism' (Hjalager 2002: 470; see also Mattsson *et al.* 2005). There have been just a few attempts to acknowledge tourism-specific innovations and these have covered such disparate issues as the rise of customer loyalty schemes, the development of all-inclusive resorts, the concept of a packaged tour as a marketing concept, the rise of the traveller's cheque, computerised check-out systems for hotels and more recently product innovations such as bungee jumping or 'Healthy Lifestyle Tourism' (Burns 2006; Novelli *et al.* 2006). Simply put, these disjointed but nevertheless important contributions point to the fact that the dual concepts of innovation and product development have not to date been considered as a systematic and sustained theme within tourism studies.

However, for all the fragmentation, it is clear that firms in tourism as in other sectors, have to keep innovating in order to remain competitive (Hall and Williams 2008). This is particularly the case in markets that are characterised by maturity and product standardisation, and this is the reason for what limited attention the concept of innovation in tourism has thus far received . Key insights include that in general tourism firms are not highly innovative (Mattsson *et al.* 2005); that larger enterprises are thought to be more innovative than smaller ones (Hjalager 2002); that tourism innovations tend to be incremental rather than radical (Mattsson *et al.* 2005); and that there can be product, process, management, logistics or institutional innovations in tourism (Hjalager 2002). In addition, Nordin (2003) among others, has highlighted the important role of employees in the innovation process and hence drawn our attention to the implications for human resource management in tourism firms. A concern those in the tourism sector share with others in the service sector is that innovations in the tourism sector are vulnerable as intellectual property. They suffer from a lack of adequate legal protection against imitation because such devices as patents frequently do not apply (see also Chapter 11). This clearly has implications for studies on innovation diffusion and adoption because it is difficult to track many changes and developments in time and space. As a result, existing studies of this type almost exclusively consider the adoption of information and communication technologies, such as the integration of e-commerce and electronic solutions for reservation systems in tourism and hospitality enterprises (e.g. Buhalis and Deimezi 2004); that is, they deal with process, management and/or logistics innovations, rather than with the diffusion of new tourism products.

In fact, the role of people in diffusion is a critical but routinely overlooked dimension as is the ease by which actors adopt innovations and the processes by which they develop them further. Very little is known about what encourages entrepreneurs to adopt new products, to offer new services or activities, or more generally to engage in product development, particularly in the context of small- and medium-sized enterprises (SMEs). Even less is known about what might prompt people to start up new enterprises around a new (tourism) product. Komppula (2001) claims that the majority of studies on product development in tourism have focused on destination or regional products (e.g. Novelli *et al.* 2006). These may have been facilitated by the orthodox view of the destination experience as the fundamental product in tourism and hence the related popularity of regional competitiveness as a focus for study (see Buhalis 2000). One notable exception is Komppula's (2001: 12) study in which she presents case-studies of the product development activities of two nature-based tourism activity operators in Finland that offer 'corporate entertainment products, incentive products and nature-based activities for other groups of customers'. While her contribution is a useful step into the right direction, it suffers three key limitations: first, it focuses on the product development activities of existing operators; second, it bases its discussion on a strategic and very purposeful process of product development, which does not accommodate 'coincidental' product adoption (see below); and third, despite its focus on 'new products', nevertheless these belong to the same product family – namely nature based activity services for the business sector – and hence may be considered variations of the original product rather than a more radical or original departure.

Other studies have explored the diffusion of new products in nature-based settings. For instance, Hall (1989) examines special interest tourism in the form of farm and adventure tourism. With respect to the latter, he notes the increasing commercialisation and prominence of the market as well as the highly fragmented nature of the industry that appeared to be characterised by a high turnover and lack of professionalism among operators despite significant economic importance in some areas. Such features have the potential to frustrate innovation and product development. In a later paper, Hall and McArthur (1994: 109) focus on white water rafting, which they argue is a 'good example of technological diffusion within a recreational activity'. However, despite a short section on the historical development of both white water rafting as an activity as well as the Australian commercial rafting industry, no consideration is given to the mechanisms underlying these developments; that is, how the new product came to Australia and how the various entrepreneurs and/or operators became involved in the new activity.

Innovation and mobility

In addition to the fields of innovation diffusion and product development, the internationalisation of tourism products is intrinsically linked to different forms of mobility because the dispersal of tourism products is greatly facilitated by people travelling and experiencing tourism products first hand. For an increasing number of researchers, tourism is 'one, albeit highly significant, dimension of temporary human mobility' (Hall 2005: 21; see also Williams and Hall 2002; Sheller and Urry 2004; Coles *et al.* 2005). Accordingly, Williams and Hall (2002: 24) differentiate between five 'forms of tourism-informed mobility: labour migration, entrepreneurial migration, return (labour) migration, consumption led economically active migration, and retirement migration'. While mobility as such is not necessarily a new phenomenon, it has 'increased in volume and geographical scope in recent decades' (Williams and Hall 2002: 2). What is new, however, according to Williams and Hall, is the increasingly blurred forms of mobility that are situated between production and consumption as well as between migration and vacation, such as international students who are simultaneously students, labour migrants and tourists (see Chapter 10).

While tourism-related labour migration as well as labour mobility into tourism (Szivas and Riley 2002) have been relatively popular topics, there have been very few examinations of the impacts of entrepreneurial mobility or the continual mobility of seasonal tourism workers on the dispersal and diffusion of tourism products and innovations. Even studies of entrepreneurship – whether tourism or otherwise – are lacking comprehensive analyses of how entrepreneurs decide on which products to base a new – and particularly their first – business in the first instance. Furthermore, even less is known about the mobility and travel of entrepreneurs as a distinctive social group. One exception would appear to be the plethora of studies on business travel patterns and preferences. However, these tend to be guided by market research aims rather than broader considerations of social and economic impacts and implications of business or other travels of entrepreneurs (Swarbrooke and Horner 2001).

An interesting effect of the changing patterns of mobility is that they may serve to link together places whether they 'have been interconnected by earlier migration, trade or investment flows' (Williams and Hall 2002), or not. In what remains, this chapter will offer empirical evidence of how two places have become linked through various consumption- and production-led forms of mobility within the tourism system. Using adventure tourism as a framework, this chapter examines how particular types of human mobility – that is, entrepreneurial mobility and the mobility of a specialised work force – as well as the related mobility of products and innovations contribute to the spread and development of new products and their consumption.

ADVENTURE TOURISM IN QUEENSTOWN AND INTERLAKEN

While 'there is no definitive definition' (Kane and Tucker 2004: 220), conceptualisations of adventure tourism tend to describe it as the (active) participation in outdoor activities that contain a (perceived or real) element of risk (Hall 1992; Sung *et al.* 1997; Millington *et al.* 2001; Swarbrooke *et al.* 2003; Kane and Tucker 2004; Page *et al.* 2005). As such, adventure tourism includes but is not limited to activities such as white water rafting, canyoning, bungee jumping and skydiving. Often pioneered by 'experimentally-minded' individuals, several of these activities have been commercialised in many places world wide since the 1970s (Brown 1997). They have assumed now an important and growing segment of the special interest tourism market (Hall 1992; Page *et al.* 2005; Cater 2006) to the point that provocatively they are so popular that they may even be described as part of mainstream consumption practices. In New Zealand, for example, over 10 per cent of the 2.18 million international visitors in year-ended March 2005 undertook a jet boat trip, while nearly 5 per cent of them did a bungee jump (TRCNZ 2005a; see case-study vignette below). With a large part of the adventure activities being concentrated in just a handful of regional destinations in New Zealand, the significance of the adventure tourism segment for both those regions and the country at large becomes immediately obvious.

Two places whose image is notably based on adventure tourism are Queenstown in New Zealand and Interlaken in Switzerland. Based on its scenic splendour, Queenstown has been a tourist destination since the days of European settlement and the subsequent gold rush in the early 1860s (Ryan 1971). While originally a summer destination, the development of ski tourism from the 1940s brought more tourist arrivals to the town year-round. The 1960s witnessed the introduction of many innovative adventure tourism products, some of them being world firsts (in particular jetboating). In subsequent decades these were increasingly commercialised through intensive marketing support. The result has been that Queenstown has assumed the image as the 'adventure capital' of New Zealand if not the world (Cater 2006). In 2004, international and domestic travellers made a total of 1.74 million visits (including daytrips) to the region (TRCNZ 2005b), which – with a local population base of only about 18,000 residents – boasts more than 70 adventure tourism companies.

Similar to Queenstown, tourism in Interlaken was originally based on the attraction of the natural Alpine landscape. In contrast to Queenstown, however, the development of the adventure tourism industry in Interlaken started only in the late 1980s and is thus a comparatively new phenomenon. Today, though, Interlaken may be regarded as the 'adventure capital of Switzerland', offering a wide range of activities including paragliding, rafting, canyoning, skydiving and bungee jumping – much to the dismay of the existing and more conservative tourism industry based on scenic train, gondola and boat trips, excursions and hikes. Within Switzerland, this width of activities is unique and as a result Interlaken has managed to place itself firmly on the tourist map of young, particularly non-European travellers (typically Americans, Koreans, Australians and New Zealanders). Such has become the popularity of Interlaken that in 2005, the approximately 23,300 permanent residents of Interlaken and the immediately surrounding villages hosted a total of around 1.4 million overnight visitors (TOI 2006). Despite the popularity of Interlaken the local adventure tourism industry is – though economically very significant – still comparatively small with only around 20 operators. An important difference to its New Zealand counterpart relates to the size distribution of the enterprises in the two destinations. In Queenstown many of the 70 adventure tourism companies are very small with one to five employees and specialised by offering only one type of activity, whereas several of the Interlaken firms are much larger in size (25 or more employees) and they offer several activities.

The following sections of this chapter will demonstrate how a destination in Switzerland, one of the cradles of worldwide tourism and role model for much of the early tourism development in New Zealand, was – somewhat reluctantly – rejuvenated by a number of local entrepreneurs who based their businesses on innovative products 'imported' from New Zealand and Queenstown in particular. It is based upon observations made by the author while both working in and researching the adventure tourism industry in the two places. This account is informed by first-hand fieldwork with key informants who are well placed in adventure tourism enterprises. In order to respect their confidentiality and because some of the information they provided was of an important commercial nature, anonymity has been preserved and no identifying details have been provided.

MADE IN QUEENSTOWN? THE INTERNATIONALISATION OF ADVENTURE TOURISM PRODUCTS TO INTERLAKEN

None of the adventure activities on offer in Interlaken today was invented locally. On the contrary, they were all 'imported' from various locations around the world, in particular from Queenstown. One of the first adventure sport activities to be offered was white water rafting. Rafting started in Switzerland independently in at least two different places in the 1980s. In 1982, in the Grisons region, a well-travelled, worldly entrepreneur originally from

France, who had worked for a rafting manufacturing company in the United States, started his rafting company with one boat. The new product was received well. Not only did it cater for tourists but it also served to generate significant volumes of day-visitors to the region so that the company grew quickly.

A few years later, a ski instructor from the Interlaken region travelled to New Zealand in order to ski during winter and tour the country on a bike in spring. During his travels he came upon the rafting industry in Queenstown, and he decided to extend his stay in order to train as a rafting guide. When he returned to Switzerland, he brought with him a second-hand raft with no intentions of starting a company. At that stage his goal was to make enough money to pay for the raft. However, his early runs on the local river in 1987 were an immediate success. The company he and his friends started in 1988 grew during the following summers by about one boat per season. Eventually he made enough money that he did not need to supplement his income by summer mountain guiding or ski instructing during the winter. His company still exists today, now offering a variety of products including rafting, canyoning and bungee jumping.

CASE-STUDY VIGNETTE – TOURISM AND INTERNATIONAL BUSINESS IN ACTION

International knowledge transfer in the early days of a future Kiwi icon

A.J. Hackett is a name that has become synonymous with bungee jumping the world over. In the 20 years since his defining jump from the Eiffel Tower in Paris, bungee operations bearing his name have been opened in destinations as far afield as Australia, France, Indonesia, Germany, Macau and Malaysia in addition to Queenstown, New Zealand.

As he points out in his autobiography (Hackett 2006), there are some popular myths associated with the rise of bungee jumping. One persistent legend, which he goes to great lengths to dispel, is that he invented bungee jumping. In the process, his account emphasises that the early rise of bungee jumping is in fact a story of chance and international knowledge transfer rather than a story wholly restricted to New Zealand and Queenstown.

In fact, to the best of his knowledge, the first bungee jump in New Zealand was in January 1980 by his friend Chris Sigglekow at Pelorus Bridge, Nelson. Six years later in mid-November 1986, Sigglekow introduced Hackett to bungee jumping at Greenhithe Bridge, a 19m drop in Auckland. Sigglekow had heard of the exploits of the Oxford University Dangerous Sports Club (OUDSC), four members of which had jumped off the 76m Clifton Suspension Bridge in Bristol, England with the aid of old parachute

Continued

harnesses and a supply of rubber strands. In turn, they had drawn inspiration from a 1960s television documentary made by David Attenborough of the land divers of the Pentecost Islands in Vanuatu. Incidentally, Hackett also claims that the OUDSC was one of the first groups to have a go at zorbing and partly attributes the rise of this phenomenon in New Zealand to them.

Hackett and Sigglekow followed Greenhithe with jumps in Hamilton, Auckland and then France, where Hackett had travelled with his friends, Henry van Asch and Martin Jones, in the NZ speed skiing team. In search of more challenging jumps, Hackett took a video tape to show people what he had been doing in New Zealand. Jumps at the Pont de la Caille and later from a gondola at Tignes provided useful experience for his perhaps most audacious jump on 26 June 1987 that brought him worldwide publicity and provided the basis for setting up an adventure tourism business.

Beyond some of the more colourful anecdotes and reminiscences, Hackett reflects on how his social network of friends and acquaintances forged during the time in France became the standard bearers for bungee jumping in New Zealand, Europe and the United States. His knowledge of the mechanical performance of rubber in cold conditions was enhanced by a visit to industrial chemists in Lyon, while Denys Porte, who accompanied him at the Pont de la Caille inherited Hackett's kit when he left the Alps. He devised some other new uses of bungee cords for extreme sports, but more importantly he devised 'the French wrap', a type of sheath binding that set safety standards that Hackett integrated into his early industry Code of Practice in Queenstown. The rest, as they say, is history but for students of international knowledge transfer, his story is a useful reminder that what appear to be relatively trivial facts are actually incredibly helpful in piecing together the diffusion of ideas, products and people.

Source: Hackett (2006): 10–1, 15–8, 40, 43, 46–7, 52–3, 97, 100–1, 106, 218–21.

Questions

- Why do you think that certain product developments in tourism (such as bungee jumping) have become synonymous with particular destinations (Queenstown, New Zealand)?
- What are some of the issues associated with the use of biographies as sources for researching entrepreneurial histories of tourism?
- What other sources and methods can be used to examine international product development and knowledge transfer in tourism?

One of his fellow raft guides saw the potential for adventure tourism products in Interlaken, in particular for bungee jumping, an activity that was at that stage quite probably not available in Switzerland and not in any case widely developed in Europe (Hackett 2006; see case study vignette). He went to Queenstown on a total of three extended visits in order to study bungee and rafting operations as well as to recruit bungee experts. The bungee operation was an immediate success. In conjunction with the oldest and biggest local backpacker hostel, he and some friends subsequently went on to build what was to become one of the largest adventure companies in Europe, offering bungee jumping, rafting and canyoning with close links to additional companies offering paragliding and skydiving.

For many years, this company relied heavily on the expertise of bungee masters, raft and canyoning guides from New Zealand, Australia and South Africa. However, from around 1997/8, disagreement on business philosophies, management practices and safety operations between the management and a number of those foreign staff, many of whom had been with the company from its early days, resulted in some of the guides choosing not to return to Interlaken. As A.J. Hackett's (2006) experiences make clear, it is not uncommon to find fundamental disagreements of this nature among the management and workforce of adventure tourism businesses, which in turn lead to major restructuring and reorganisation as well as spin-outs of competitor businesses benefiting from the intellectual property and operating experience of the original enterprises. In this case, for operating reasons, the Swiss business had to close mid-season and subsequently went into liquidation. In the following season, several of the foreign guides went on to work for a rival company, one that had pioneered the adventure sports in Interlaken originally, and which was to benefit greatly from the market exit of its erstwhile competitor.

Another activity to have made its way from New Zealand (though from Rotorua, not Queenstown) to Interlaken more recently is zorbing, an activity where the participant is strapped into a harness within a giant see-through plastic ball and rolls down a grassy slope. Unlike rafting and bungee jumping, zorbing took a more intricate route from New Zealand to Interlaken. An Interlaken entrepreneur, owner and operator of one of the biggest, local paragliding companies, came across the activity in the Swiss canton of Valais (the Rhône Valley) and ended up buying the 'zorbs' from a German manufacturer. Both the German company and the Valais operator had (independently from one another) originally discovered the activity in, and subsequently 'imported' it back from, New Zealand. So, while this is another example of an entrepreneur experiencing an activity while travelling and afterwards establishing it in Interlaken, it was not so much a visit to the place of origin but rather a staged diffusion of the product. Moreover, it is instructive in so far as it reminds us that particular places commonly become associated with particular, distinctive activities irrespective of whether this is justified or not. A.J. Hackett and Queenstown may have become synonymous with bungee jumping but the emergence and subsequent take-off of what has become a globally understood phenomenon is actually a truly international story of knowledge transfer (see case-study vignette).

INTERNATIONALISATION OF TOURISM PRODUCTS: THE MOBILITY OF PEOPLE AND IDEAS IN THE DEVELOPMENT OF QUEENSTOWN

Is this internationalisation of tourism products described above a new occurrence? In the case of adventure tourism we may understand it to be as old or as recent as the phenomenon of *adventure* itself. That stated, Australasian commercial recreational rafting, for example, effectively started in 1972 in Queenstown with the use of a rubber United States Navy life raft on sedate float trips (Brown 1997). In 1974, a New Zealander, who had moved to Queenstown four years previously, began to experiment with running a raft down the white water section of the Shotover River. His lack of success prompted a visiting American professional boatman to offer his help in the training of river guides. For several years then, American professional river guides were invited to Queenstown to oversee the rafting aspects of the company. Even today a significant proportion of the river guides working in Queenstown tend to be North American.

With respect to tourism in general it can also be argued that internationalisation is as old as international travelling itself. Interestingly enough, the Queenstown–Europe (Switzerland) connection may once more serve as an example, even though the direction of the flow of ideas and products is reversed. From the moment the area later to be called Queenstown was 'discovered' by the European settlers in 1853, travellers compared it to Switzerland and predicted a similarly successful tourism future. Ryan (1971), for example, quotes an 1860 article from the *Otago Witness*: '… no doubt, the day will come when a visit to the lakes of Otago will be as general by our neighbours in Australia as is that from the home country to the lakes of Switzerland' (Ryan 1971: 6), while Watkins and the Travel Agents Association of New Zealand (1987) quote world-renowned traveller Anthony Trollope, who is reputed to have said in 1872 that 'it [Otago] has had bestowed upon it by nature all those attractions which make Switzerland the holiday playground of Europe'.

In the 1930s, New Zealand's ski industry was born, fuelled by success of the skiing industry in Europe and supported by European expertises. Both the ski fields at the Chateau on the North Island and at the Crown Range close to Queenstown employed Austrian ski instructors to establish ski schools and in 1947, the largest and most elaborate ski-tow in Australasia, built with Norwegian help, started operating at Coronet Peak close to Queenstown (Ryan 1971; McClure 2004). Another example of innovation through the contribution of external knowledges was the gondola that was built by the privately owned company, Skyline Enterprises, in 1966/7 in Queenstown. This was intended to provide easier access to Bob's Peak, a ridge 450m above the township, in order to capitalise on the formidable views of Lake Wakatipu and the surrounding mountain ranges. This gondola was very much the vision of one man, Hylton Hensman, who is quoted by one of his fellow shareholders of Skyline Enterprises as having said 'Why don't we get a gondola, same as in Switzerland?' (Cliff Broad, cited in Sullivan 2005: 18). Hensman subsequently toured Europe and the United States inspecting aerial cableways for the most suitable design.

Looking beyond Queenstown, New Zealand can provide further evidence of early and very purposeful product internationalisation. As early as 1896, for example, the New Zealand government decided to strongly foster tourism in the country. Believing the future of tourist development to lie in the thermal districts in the North Island it asked New Zealand's Agent-General in London 'to tour the Continental spas, suggest improvements for Rotorua and find a balneologist to head the baths in New Zealand' (McClure 2004: 22) . Eventually, in 1901, it employed 'Dr Arthur Wohlmann, an English physician with seven years experience at the famed spa town of Bath' and instructed him to 'take a tour of inspection before he left for New Zealand' (McClure 2004: 34).

So is the internationalisation of products and ideas in tourism in reality 'old hat'; that is, only recently opportunely (re-)discovered in academia because of increasing interest in globalisation and globally acting processes? Internationalisation per se is not a new phenomenon, but its nature and rate have changed significantly over time. Originally, the travels of tourism product ideas were sporadic, often purposeful and time-consuming, and they were frequently based on the vision and/or activities of a few leading individuals. With the advent of international aviation as well as the commercialisation of many tourism products (such as jetboating and rafting in and from Queenstown), the ease and subsequently rate and speed of the diffusion of travel products has increased. However, the technologically enabled increase in human mobility has had another effect. Ultimately, it led to the current rapid diffusion of ideas while the increase in labour mobility has led to the emergence of 'mobile lifestyles', or what appears to be continuous migration and thus an increasingly transient (but also professional) tourism work force that serves to support the diffusion of travel products.

Both skiing and rafting may serve as examples. The emergence of full-time year-round (rather than seasonal) skiing and rafting professionals has only been possible due to two inter-related developments: the commercialisation of, and thus demand for, the sports and the subsequent comparative 'pay security' this offers; and the increase in mobility that allows ski instructors, as well as raft guides, to 'follow their season' from hemisphere to hemisphere. As a result, an increasingly large number of people now – whether it be only for a few years of their lives or as a long-term career option – work seasonally in both hemispheres. In the case of the summer adventure tourism industry, a group of guides has been travelling forwards and backwards between rafting companies based mainly in Queenstown, Rotorua and Taupo, and firms in Interlaken (as well as Saanen and Scuol) in Switzerland. Extended beyond our example of the New Zealand–Switzerland connection, we can now observe a worldwide community of full-time raft guides that is in a constant seasonal state of migrational flux. A large part of this migration occurs between the 'hotbeds' of rafting including New Zealand, South and Southern Africa and Australia in the southern hemisphere and Europe and North America (both USA and Canada) in the northern hemisphere. In addition, these traditional rafting locations are increasingly being supplemented by comparatively new destinations like Middle and South America, Asia (in particular Japan) and other African places such as Uganda. Interestingly, a large part of that rafting community is of South African, New Zealand or Australian origin; that is, different to, for example, the seasonal counterpart of the skiing community with a comparatively much larger representation of northern hemisphere nationalities. This type of migration has brought about a new quality of innovation diffusion that has ensured a rapid distribution of new practices and ideas and has further served the – at least in parts – increasing professionalisation of adventure sport.

DISCUSSION AND CONCLUSION

This chapter has examined the internationalisation of adventure tourism products at different levels. At the firm level, it shows how individual entrepreneurs have built successful companies based on adventure tourism products 'imported' from outside their home country; some more by coincidence, others quite strategically. It has also demonstrated how these start-ups were intrinsically linked to entrepreneurial mobility. In particular, rafting in Interlaken has been driven by consumption-led mobility. This first led to a ski instructor 'stumbling' across rafting and the subsequent 'birth of a reluctant entrepreneur', while his initial success led to the production-led mobility of another budding entrepreneur who went on multiple product research trips to New Zealand. At the place level, these entrepreneurial mobilities led to a link between Interlaken in Switzerland and New Zealand (and Queenstown in particular), which is now maintained by the seasonal migration or production-led mobility of professional adventure tourism guides.

With respect to this place link, it is interesting to consider what brought Queenstown and Interlaken together in the first place. In the context of the adventure tourism industry, it was almost serendipitous. It was facilitated by the similarity in landscape (and thus suitability for the activities in question) and set off by the visit of the Swiss ski instructor who became a 'coincidental' tourism entrepreneur by starting an ultimately very successful rafting and adventure company. Many of the subsequent developments resulted from this initial link, including: the highly focused visits of the second entrepreneur with respect to the bungee and rafting industries; the import of zorbing through another entrepreneur; and the initial 'import' of New Zealand rafting and bungee experts as seasonal staff. So while the adoptions of new products were events discreet in nature, there is now the more continuous link between the places maintained by seasonal workers, many of whom are from New Zealand and work in Queenstown in the complementary season.

These observations support a number of notions, for example the close link hypothesised between tourism and different forms of mobility; the operation of tourism production and consumption in a form of 'continuing circular process' (Ateljevic 2000: 377); and the subsequent blurring of, and interplay between, production- and consumption-led mobilities as well as tourism's contribution to the (re)construction of place (e.g. Ateljevic 2000; Sheller and Urry 2004; Coles *et al.*, 2006). They also provide evidence of how a discussion of the internationalisation of ideas and products is strongly related to research on innovation diffusion, mobility and entrepreneurship.

Discussion questions

- What other recent examples of product development in tourism can you identify? Where did they start and how have they spread?
- Why do you think there have been so few studies of product development and innovation in tourism?
- What sources of information are best suited to studying tourism innovation and what limits might they impose?

REFERENCES

Ateljevic, I. (2000) 'Circuits of tourism: stepping beyond the "production/consumption" dichotomy', *Tourism Geographies*, 2(4): 369–88.

Brown, M.N.R. (1997) On the edge. A history of adventure sports and adventure tourism in Queenstown. Unpublished Master of Arts thesis, Department of History, University of Dunedin, Dunedin.

Buhalis, D. (2000) 'Marketing the competitive destination of the future', *Tourism Management*, 21(1): 97–116.

Buhalis, D. and Deimezi, O. (2004) 'E-tourism developments in Greece: information communication technologies adoption for the strategic management of the Greek tourism industry', *Tourism and Hospitality Research*, 5(2): 103–30.

Burns, P.M. (2006) 'Innovation, creativity and competitiveness', in D. Buhalis and C. Costa (eds) *Tourism Management Dynamics. Trends, Management and Tools*. Oxford: Elsevier.

Carlsson, B. (2006) 'Internationalization of innovation systems: a survey of the literature', *Research Policy*, 35(1): 56–67.

Cater, C.I. (2006) 'Playing with risk? Participant perceptions of risk and management implications in adventure tourism', *Tourism Management*, 27(2): 317–25.

Coles, T.E., Duval, D.T. and Hall, C.M. (2005) 'Tourism, mobility, and global communities: new approaches to theorising tourism and tourist spaces', in W. F. Theobald (ed.) *Global Tourism*. Oxford: Butterworth-Heinemann.

Croes, R.R. (2006) 'A paradigm shift to a new strategy for small island economies: embracing demand side economics for value enhancement and long term economic stability', *Tourism Management*, 27(3): 453–65.

Hackett, A.J. with Aldworth, W. (2006) *Jump Start. The Autobiography*. Auckland: Random House New Zealand.

Hall, C.M. (1989) 'Special interest travel: a prime force in the expansion of tourism?', in R. Welch (ed.) *Geography in Action. Proceedings of the Fifteenth New Zealand Geography Conference*. Dunedin: New Zealand Geographical Society.

—— (1992) 'Adventure, sport and health tourism', in B. Weiler and C.M. Hall (eds) *Special Interest Tourism*. London: Belhaven.

—— (2005) *Tourism: Rethinking the Social Science of Mobility*. Harlow: Pearson/Prentice Hall.

Hall, C.M. and McArthur, S. (1994) 'Commercial whitewater rafting in Australia', in D. Mercer (ed.) *New Viewpoints in Australian Outdoor Recreation Research and Planning*. Williamstown: Hepper Marriot and Associates Publishers.

Hall, C.M. and Williams, A.M. (2008) *Tourism and Innovation*. London: Routledge.

Hjalager, A.-M. (2002) 'Repairing innovation defectiveness in tourism', *Tourism Management*, 23(5): 465–74.

Jarach, D. (2002) 'The digitalisation of market relationships in the airline business: the impact and prospects of e-business', *Journal of Air Transport Management*, 8(2): 115–20.

Johnson, C. and Vanetti, M. (2005) 'Locational strategies of international hotel chains', *Annals of Tourism Research* 32(4): 1077–99.

Kane, M.J. and Tucker, H. (2004) 'Adventure tourism. The freedom to play with reality', *Tourist Studies*, 4(3): 217–34.

Komppula, R. (2001) 'New-product development in tourism companies – case studies on nature-based activity operators', paper presented at the 10th Nordic Tourism Research Symposium, Vasa, Finland, 2001.

McClure, M. (2004) *The Wonder Country: Making New Zealand Tourism*. Auckland: Auckland University Press.

Mattsson, J., Sundbo, J. and Jensen, C.F. (2005) 'Innovation systems in tourism: the roles of attractors and scene-takers', *Industry and Innovation*, 12(3): 357–82.

Millington, K., Locke, T. and Locke, A. (2001) 'Adventure travel', *Travel & Tourism Analyst*, 4: 65–97.

Nordin, S. (2003) *Tourism Clustering and Innovation. Paths to Economic Growth and Development.* Östersund: European Tourism Research Institute.

Novelli, M., Schmitz, B. and Spencer, T. (2006) 'Networks, clusters and innovation in tourism: a UK experience', *Tourism Management*, 27(6): 1141–52.

Page, S.J., Bentley, T.A. and Walker, L. (2005) 'Scoping the nature and extent of adventure tourism operations in Scotland: how safe are they?', *Tourism Management*, 26(3): 381–97.

Peric, V. (2005) 'Tourism and globalization. Managing the process of globalisation in new and upcoming EU members', paper presented at the 6th International Conference of the Faculty of Management, Koper Congress Centre, Bernardin, Slovenia, 2005.

Perl, A. (1998) 'Redesigning an airport for international competitiveness: the politics of administrative innovation at CDG', *Journal of Air Transport Management*, 4(4): 189–99.

Ryan, S.R. (1971). The development of the tourist industry in Queenstown: tracing the progress of the town in this respect, until its establishment as a year-round tourist resort. Unpublished Master of Arts thesis, Department of History, University of Otago, Dunedin.

Sheller, M. and Urry, J. (2004) 'Places to play, places in play', in M. Sheller and J. Urry (eds) *Tourism Mobilities: Places to Play, Places in Play*. New York and London: Routledge.

Smeral, E. (1998) 'The impact of globalization on small and medium enterprises: new challenges for tourism policies in European countries', *Tourism Management*, 19(4): 371–80.

Sullivan, J. (2005) *Skyline: A New Zealand Tourism Success Story*. Queenstown: Skyline Enterprises.

Sung, H.H., Morrison, A.M. and O'Leary, J.T. (1997) 'Definition of adventure travel: the new conceptual framework for empirical application form the providers' perspective', *Asia Pacific Journal of Tourism Research*, 1(2): 47–67.

Swarbrooke, J. and Horner, S. (2001) *Business Travel and Tourism*. Oxford: Elsevier.

Swarbrooke, J., Horner, S., Beard, C., Leckie, S. and Pomfret, G. (2003) *Adventure Tourism: The New Frontier.* Oxford: Butterworth-Heinemann.

Szivas, E. and Riley, M. (2002) 'Labour mobility and tourism in the post 1989 transition in Hungary', in C.M. Hall and A.M. Williams (eds) *Tourism and Migration. New Relationships between Production and Consumption*. Dordrecht: Kluwer.

TOI (Tourismus Organisation Interlaken) (2006) *Jahresbericht 2005.* Interlaken: TOI.

TRCNZ (Tourism Research Council New Zealand) (2005a) *International Visitor Survey (IVS)*. Wellington: NZ Ministry of Tourism.

TRCNZ (Tourism Research Council New Zealand) (2005b) *Queenstown RTO*. Wellington: NZ Ministry of Tourism.

Watkins, L. and the Travel Agents Association of New Zealand (1987) *Billion Dollar Miracle: The Authentic Story of the Birth and Amazing Growth of the Tourism Industry in New Zealand*. Auckland: Inhouse Publications.

Williams, A.M. and Hall, C.M. (2002) 'Tourism, migration, circulation and mobility: the contingencies of time and place', in C.M. Hall and A.M. Williams (eds) *Tourism and Migration: New Relationships between Production and Consumption*. Dordrecht: Kluwer.

Wood, R.E. (2000) 'Caribbean cruise tourism: globalization at sea', *Annals of Tourism Research*, 27(2): 345–70.

The internationalisation of tourism labour markets: working and playing in a ski resort

10

Tara Duncan

Learning objectives

After considering this chapter, you will be able to:

- describe many key motivations behind youth travel;
- assess the relationships between young budget travellers and international tourism businesses;
- discuss why youth travel is important when identifying future tourism labour market trends.

Key terms

- labour markets;
- backpackers;
- young people;
- ski resorts;
- transnational corporations.

INTRODUCTION

This chapter explores the relationship between young budget travellers such as those on a gap year or backpacking, and international tourism and service industries. It suggests that, to a great extent, the ways in which the temporary mobilities of young budget travellers intersect with the tourism industry through a wider arena than simply receiving or consuming services has been ignored (for exceptions, see Bianchi 2000; Clarke 2005). This chapter contends that for the young budget travellers who engage in periods of (paid) tourism or service work while travelling away from home, this work is an intrinsic part of the touristic experience (Bianchi 2000). Furthermore, although international businesses may recruit this particular group of tourists as workers, they need to pay more attention to the motivations behind this type of travel.

In engaging with young budget travellers' working and travelling experiences, this chapter examines how this group of tourists are emblematic of the ways in which labour migration and other forms of mobility are becoming increasingly blurred. As a group, young budget travellers could be termed in the 'middle' of transnationalism (Clarke 2005; Conradson and Latham 2005), in part because they do not easily fit into the often highly polarised view of migration (with the highly skilled and flexible on the one hand and the low or unskilled on the other). They are, as Gogia (2006: 364) suggests, 'new symbols of über-mobility' and are 'indicative of emergent patterns of post-industrial mobility in which the boundaries between work and leisure are blurred' (Bianchi 2000: 114).

Four main sections comprise this chapter. The first introduces the types of youth tourism discussed in the chapter, while the second uses empirical evidence from Whistler (British Columbia, Canada) to consider some of the motivations behind young budget travel. The third section looks at one particular international tourism business, Whistler Blackcomb, and discusses how it views the young budget travellers it employs. The final section presents a critical analysis of the challenges facing international businesses when trying to recruit and retain this type of employee. The chapter makes the case that all those interested in international tourism and labour mobility must widen their perspectives and start to consider how the working practices of young budget travellers are usually only part of a larger – and longer – travelling career.

TOURISM AND YOUTH TRAVEL

Backpacking, as one particular type of international tourism, has a long history. The Grand Tours of the eighteenth and nineteenth centuries, the tramping traditions of skilled tradesman and soldiers, and the growth of youth movements such as the *Wandervogel* and YHA (Youth Hostel Association) can all be seen as precursors to today's youth travel (see Loker-Murphy and Pearce 1995). It is perhaps, however, Cohen's (1973) phenomenon of the 'drifter' that has become the exemplar to which many young people still aspire; this notwithstanding, as Cohen (2004) highlights, there is often a gap between the ideology of backpacking and actual practice.

Long-term, low budget travel has continued to grow in popularity since the 1970s. It has progressed from an unusual activity undertaken by drifters, hippies and adventurous drop-outs to become a widely entrenched rite of passage in contemporary (Western) society. Backpackers are no longer (if they ever were) a homogeneous group. As O'Reilly (2006: 999) states, the backpacker market continues to develop into a number of niche markets as backpacking imaginations have spread and been picked up by ever more people with different backgrounds, experiences and expectations. Often seen as the preserve of the young, long-term, low-budget travel now encompasses a wider demographic of travellers, with Lonely Planet (2006: 6) finding that although 40 per cent of their over 32,000 respondents were in the 18–24 age group, 22 per cent were over the age of 35.

This chapter focuses specifically on young budget travellers; that is, those taking time out from formal education, training or employment (Jones 2004) or delaying the responsibilities of adulthood to undertake backpacking, a gap year or go on their big OE (overseas experience). In particular, it focuses on what Uriely and Reichel (2000: 268) term 'working tourists', a type of traveller who engages in situations that combine work with tourist-related activities. This chapter uses interview data from 33 participants, 25 'working tourists' and 8 longer-term, year-round Whistler Blackcomb employees, collected in 2002/3 in the internationally recognised ski resort of Whistler. Approximately 75 miles north of Vancouver, Whistler grew in the 1960s as a result of a group of local businessmen's dream to bring the Winter Olympics to the town (Christie 2000). Whistler is now a year-round resort, annually attracting over two million visitors (see Gill 2000; Moore *et al.* 2006; Resort Municipality of Whistler 2007) and employing thousands of young people from around the (Western) world to work in its many shops, bars, restaurants and hotels. Whistler has a population of approximately 10,000 permanent residents, which is rumoured to double during the busier winter months. Whistler Blackcomb, the largest employer in the resort, employs around 4,000 people during the winter season. This number drops to about 1,000 in the summer, of which approximately 800 are permanent, full-time-year-round positions.

CASE-STUDY VIGNETTE – TOURISM AND INTERNATIONAL BUSINESS IN ACTION

Whistler Blackcomb: a new type of company town?

The town of Whistler has grown up as a resort. It has developed rapidly from a population of 527 in 1966 to 9,248 permanent residents in 2006 (Resort Municipality of Whistler 2007). Internationally renowned as a tourism destination, significantly it is also a local community with a distinctive identity. The town promotes a lifestyle, not just a workplace (Moore *et al.* 2006; Whistler Blackcomb 2007). However, through its distinctive development, it is a town that provokes strong and diverse opinions among those who live and work there.

Since 1997 when Whistler Mountain and Blackcomb Mountain merged, Whistler has been dominated by one employer, Whistler Blackcomb. For some, like Robert, this impacted his view of Whistler as he saw Whistler Blackcomb as a commercial Goliath that sat astride Whistler. He 'didn't like the idea that from nine to five ... I'm going to have to be a tentacle on the arm of this great big thing'. For others, like Rachel who were 'living the dream', the 'corporatisation' of the destination was appealing because they 'could say, "this is where I work" and people would go, "oh wow, that's cool"'.

Whistler Blackcomb operations dominate the town. It has 38 ski lifts covering 8,100 hectares on two mountains. The company runs approximately 26 of the over 90 retail

Continued

and rental outlets and a further 17 of the more than 200 bars and restaurants in Whistler (Resort Municipality of Whistler 2007; Whistler Blackcomb 2007). Whistler has developed over the last two decades from a simple ski town to a more complex and economically diverse resort community (Moore *et al.* 2006: 137). For Ellie (27, HR worker) and Andrew (28, IT worker), who have both lived and worked in Whistler since the mountain communities merged, the changes are obvious. From having a sense of personalisation, for Andrew, 'now it's more like a corporation town'. According to Ellie,

> The thing is, there are so many things that have changed for the better. I mean, the amount of money Intrawest [Whistler Blackcomb's parent company] has put into developing Whistler. I think the town is definitely better off but it doesn't have ... that same sort of friendly [atmosphere].

The popularity and growth of the destination has, in no small measure, been due to the success of Whistler Blackcomb. Yet, this growth has also led to increased tension between commercial interests and the community (see Gill 2000). The lack of community facilities, the growing tourist numbers, and the rising costs associated with living in Whistler – the average cost of a single family dwelling is over CDN$1 million (Resort Municipality of Whistler 2007) – are eroding the local community and reshaping the community's culture and sense of place (Moore *et al.* 2006: 137). As the community looks to the future, it faces challenges that relate to the continued growth in tourist numbers, the availability of accommodation and amenities for local people and employees, and the balance between resort growth and environmental sustainability. The question to be answered is: what role will Whistler Blackcomb have in shaping the future of this distinctive resort?

Questions

- Why would a resort such as Whistler appeal as a 'lifestyle choice' for some people?
- What are some of the social, economic and environmental issues that Whistler might be facing in the future?
- What tensions could exist in Whistler as a result of Whistler Blackcomb's dominance as an employer?

WORK AND YOUNG BUDGET TRAVELLERS

Without doubt, the motivations of young people who decide to travel are a complex amalgam of many factors. Lonely Planet (2005, 2006) and Richards and Wilson (2003) both asked young budget travellers to rank a number of motivation factors. Richards and Wilson's (2003: 17) report that exploration, excitement and increasing knowledge ranked as the main motivational factors for travel: exploring other cultures, with 83 per cent was ranked first overall by the 2,300 respondents; excitement was second (with 74 per cent); and increasing knowledge ranked third (with 69 per cent). Jones (2003: 2) suggests that young people today are more '[s]avvy … and motivated to equip themselves for life in a global society', and they view travel and work as ways in which to do this. Travelling and working while away from home, for many young people, has become a self-imposed 'rite of passage' (see Loker-Murphy and Pearce 1995; Sørensen 2003); one which they take part in specifically to gain diverse experiences whereupon they enrich their sense of self. They see travelling and working as giving them a type of 'informal qualification' which they can use upon their return home to further their personal and professional careers (see Munt 1994; Deforges 1997). Lonely Planet's (2005: 38) survey confirms that travelling does influence later career choice: 20 per cent of respondents felt that travelling had a major effect on their career choices while 33 per cent felt it had a major effect on their lifestyle.

Young people are often motivated to choose service work within the tourism industry because of the perceived flexibility and convenience. Despite the low wages and lack of benefits, young budget travellers are attracted to the opportunities that this type of employment can provide. As one of Adler and Adler's (1999: 383) respondents said of working in a Hawaiian hotel, 'I'm living the life now, full-time, that all the people who slave year round only get to live on their two-week vacation a year.'

It is also possible that for some of these young budget travellers, certain types of work may be more prestigious. For young people, such as Andrew, working for Whistler Blackcomb became not only about paid employment but also about the chance to say that the job was much more than service work; that is, employment has non-monetary value.

Interviewer: I mean, when you talk to people, what stories do you tell?

Andrew: Oh yeh, the big powder days.

Interviewer: You don't tell them about the mundane, you don't tell them about the day you were sitting at work and it was pretty damn boring?

Andrew: You tell them, so it's a work-day and I'm going skiing, that's what you tell them.

Crang (1997) points out that there is a danger of unduly romanticising tourism employment. For these young people, telling stories about the non-monetary advantages of this sort of work often ignores the fact that much of this work is repetitive, poorly paid, and that it can be emotionally and physically demanding. Yet, as the young people in Whistler revealed, they were aware of the positive and negative attributes associated with tourism work:

> You get a free season pass, a free meal everyday you work, discounts on food and equipment, you get a uniform! The wages weren't great, neither was staff housing, however it was a roof over your head and a bed to sleep in.
>
> (Lisa, 21, food and beverage worker)

> Oh, it's a good company to work for. Housing's cheap which is good, and the ski pass … pay's not great, for living in Whistler but because they make accommodation cheap that's good.

> Plus, discounts on Merlin's [restaurant], I'm lucky as I get a food voucher for every day that
> I work … they know how to get you to work. That's the secret, they know how to get you to work
> and they know how to keep you sweet, … that's how they can get away without paying much …
> Yeh, they're not stupid.
>
> (Neil, 23, cleaner)

So many of these young people see work while travelling away from home as some sort of
'informal' qualification that they may utilise at some point in the future, a type of cultural
capital that will enhance their career and life chances (cf. Munt 1994). It can be difficult
to define exactly what young budget travellers learn from their experiences. Myers and
Inkson (2003: 3), say, 'how can employers and managers judge the value of [working while
abroad] in a candidate's background? Is it a plus, denoting enterprise, or a minus, denoting
flakiness?'. However, a recent report from the UK's Department of Education and Skills
suggests that a gap year can be a key to success in later life (Jones 2004).

For Lisa, the benefits of working while travelling are clearly in the enhancement of her CV
(résumé):

> I recommend going travelling to people I meet. It is such an eye opener: you go to interesting
> places, meet interesting people, broaden your circle of friends. You learn new skills, have lots of
> fun and [it] is a huge achievement. Having something like working and travelling abroad on your
> CV is never going to have a detrimental effect on you and can only be a huge positive to you.
>
> (Lisa)

Other respondents were even more tactical. Neil talked not only about how he intended to
use his job at Whistler Blackcomb to enhance his 'soft' skills but he then went on to detail
the training courses he planned attending because 'its good to put on your CV anyway'. As
he put it:

> I'm hoping I can use it [his job] as an example of my independence and you know, planning and
> that sort of thing, human instances, organisational skills, team work. All those 'cheesy' words
> I don't like to use. I was hoping that I could use it for that.

Veronica (28, (now a) financial analyst), returned from her 'year out' in 2003. She talked
about how her experiences at Whistler Blackcomb have increased her confidence in her
own abilities:

> When I was interviewing two years ago for my current job, I got turned down for a job at X because
> they didn't think I had the right attitude. And when I sat there and the recruitment agent said that,
> I said 'Well, I didn't think they had the right attitude either' and she's laughing and she said, 'What
> do you mean? You've been rejected for a job, you don't sound bothered.' I said, 'Well I'm not,
> obviously it wasn't the right job for me, it's not really a big deal …' and I think that's something
> Whistler teaches you. It teaches you teamwork, that the pieces of the jigsaw fit together and you
> realise how lucky you are to work there and you don't take it for granted …
>   And it's funny, the boys at work laugh at me, 'cause in the city, it tends to be women [who]
> stay in a job. They value loyalty and they stay in a job for a long time and the men will change

every two or three years because, you know you'll move on to a better salary and better bonus and bigger challenge and the guys at work say I have a male perspective because, you know, if I don't think I'm getting what I'm worth then I will leave because I am not scared of going to find another job. I think a lot of that has to do with Whistler …

From their work experiences, these young people are prompted to think in more detail about their working futures, as Veronica's comments illustrate. If we think back to the motivations behind working, then these same experiences can be used when considering future employment. Instead of travelling and working while away from home being about learning new cultures, it now becomes about finding a work culture that offers them similar non-monetary advantages. Three perspectives reveal this:

> It's [Whistler Blackcomb's] got a relaxed atmosphere … and it's just like the idea that you can do something with your work. But yah, I like that sort of relaxed thing they've got going on. … That is definitely something I'd look towards and I'd like something as well that facilitates me. The personal training as well, like they do. That's good, that's a good idea.
>
> (Neil)
>
> One of the things I think I would look for is, probably the level of interest they have for their employees, and the priority that employees have. It's really strange sometimes hearing employees saying, the company doesn't care about me … but, I mean there's so much money and time invested in employees, so that's definitely something I'd look for.
>
> (Ellie)
>
> I've worked in a lot of big companies and this is the best culture, there is a legitimate and real concern for employees here and that's a good thing. Unfortunately, in a lot of ways, they can't, with the financial situation, they can't back it up. There's a real concern with the welfare, when the mountain wasn't opening on time, when there was no snow, they were putting on soup kitchens and salary advances. … From the senior management team up, those guys actually care, not just the little guy here, the ski manager, they talk about it in their meetings and they really seem to be honestly concerned about the welfare of the employees.
>
> (Andrew)

It has been suggested that tourism service workers often have little or no involvement or attachment with the companies they work for (Urry 2002). Yet, the above illustrates how the engagement that employees have with a company – even one where they work for only a few months – can have lasting effects upon them.

INTERNATIONAL TOURISM AND YOUNG BUDGET TRAVELLERS

As such, corporate 'culture' becomes an important tool in the relationship between the young budget travellers and the company (they choose) to work for. Corporate culture can encourage the activity of working to become empowering and fulfilling (Du Gay 1996), such that workers feel included, involved, attached and perhaps even as though they are not really 'working' at all (Urry 2002). Company recruitment policies become focused on looking for the right 'fit'; emphasis is placed on personality and talent as much as, if not more than, technical skills (see Crang 1997). These companies are not just utilising the identities of their employees; to some extent, they are also forging them as they encourage and even police conformity with the corporate culture. Tourist service industries are producing and selling employees' selves as part of the tourism package (Crang 1997). By making work 'fun', with work ethics such as Whistler Blackcomb's parent company, Intrawest's assertion that 'we work to play', the divisions between work and play become blurred (see Grugulis *et al.* 2000). Yet, for many of these companies, economic reasons lie behind the ethic that employees come first because, for instance, it encourages loyalty and hence has a clear commercial logic.

Whereas young budget travellers may look at working while on their travels as a way to finance continued travel or as additional 'skills' to add to their CV (résumé), tourism employers are often looking to employ and retain front-line staff in order to differentiate themselves from the competition. The two Vice Presidents of Whistler Blackcomb record in the 2002/3 Employee Handbook: 'Over recent years our Staff have been recognised for adding a service differentiation to our Guest's experience and it is our intention to widen the gap between our performance and that of our competition.' In order to achieve this, recruiting becomes a very important aspect within company operations. Simply put, and as Rachel, 35, a long-term employee in 'Employee Experience', the HR department at Whistler Blackcomb, observes:

> [W]e are looking for somebody with the right attitude. It's pretty simple. That's really it. Doesn't really matter what kind of education or background they have because the majority of the time we are not going to be able to match that experience with a position given that most of our jobs are front line, entry-level jobs and so attitude is the big thing, right? We're looking for somebody who really wants to create an experience for our guests and who enjoys doing so. You know, somebody who genuinely cares.

However, there is also the recognition that the young people who come to Whistler are here for more than just a ski season. As Byron, 30, another long-term employee in 'Employee Experience' says:

> [Y]outh today … are looking for total life experience so when they come to a ski resort they're not really taking a year off to learn how to ski. They want something that will still fill their resume or prove positive in terms of life experience.

Byron believes that, as a company, it is providing a certain type of experience:

> For that young group, it is life skills, it's how do I take care of myself, how do I pay the bills, how do I pay the rent, how do I budget, make sure I have enough money for food, you know, plus a little after for beer …, how do I live up to company expectations right? How do I come to work hung over? Alright, I'm not going to do that too often. It's all that young growing up stuff and I don't think many of them realise they're working for a company with real distinct values, right? I think that [we give them] a sense of again, what a values company can offer. So, that they have a perception that they are valued and … that we work by those [values] and make decisions by

those values and hopefully they … get some life experience and life skills and friendships and something that they can take away.

Moreover:

> In terms of actually career development, … let's make no mistake, like a one season lift operator isn't going to add a huge amount to their resume other than the operational specific stuff but they should at least have some guest service philosophies patterned into their head that will be very valuable wherever they go. So … hopefully they get that, the guest service component as well as some operational expertise; and all the relationships and fun stuff that comes from being in the best resort in the world.

Whistler Blackcomb, as the employer, seeks to provide a working experience that is based around a well-developed corporate culture; for instance, the 2002/3 Employee Handbook spends the first six pages outlining this culture. The company philosophy is thus to promote a way of life:

> Whistler Blackcomb is more than just a workplace, it's a lifestyle. … we continuously re-energize our product and our people. Employees are our strength; we look for talented, innovative and hard working individuals who are looking for a memorable and unique experience.
>
> (Whistler Blackcomb 2007)

In many ways, this leads to the apparent oxymoron of the 'working holiday'. All too often, it has often been suggested that 'our conception of tourism is that it is *not work*' (Graburn 1989: 22) and for Urry (2002: 2) tourism 'is a leisure activity which presupposes its opposite, namely regulated and organised work'. Thus there is an apparent semantic confusion, in the phrases 'working tourist' and 'working holiday-maker'.

So, as a company, Whistler Blackcomb is promoting a certain experience, a particular corporate culture that combines aspects of work, with the life experiences, the fun and play and the learning opportunities that these young people are looking for and are motivated by. The boundaries between work and play have become blurred through this. Byron confirms this:

> Yes … there is a Whistler Blackcomb culture which … you know, revels in the fact that we're made of a bunch of different groups … in the sense that it's laid back, it's friendly, it's personable, it's not pretentious. That atmosphere I think, does cause a blurring of the lines, and even the way people are scheduled [to work] – four on, three off – there's a balance between work and play for most of the front line folks where you know the same people they're working with are probably the group they're living close to in Residence and probably the group they're riding and skiing with on their days off. But, yeh I think it really does blur. We also preach that, right? Fun in workplace?

Yet, the company utilises this to its advantage. Rachel talks about this blurring: '[W]e expect people to still be a representative of Whistler Blackcomb on their days off so it's not like you can take your uniform off and then just go out there and, and do insane crazy things.'

Thus, Whistler Blackcomb, in trying to suggest that these young people are not really working at all, takes advantage of the culture it is creating to ensure that their employees behave in an appropriate manner at all times, not just during their working hours.

THE WIDER EXPERIENCE

So far, this chapter has suggested that young budget travellers are often motivated to work in order to gain some form of informal qualification that they can use in later life, and that international tourism businesses, such as Whistler Blackcomb, may utilise corporate culture to blur the boundaries of work and play in order to encourage employees to provide exceptional service to their customers. Yet, it is still necessary to realise that for these young budget travellers, working is only a part of a wider travelling experience. As both Ellie and Grace recall:

> [For] seasonal people who are doing the world tour, this is one of the stops. They end up in Whistler at some point and they have no intention on staying … I think there's an idea of the ski resort in general, which is, you know, big mountain, big snow, lots of beer, great times, and then, you know, you're outta here, I don't think they really care too much what the job is, they're doing it for a few months and its not going to impact their life in any great way.
>
> (Ellie)
>
> I think it's extremely difficult for people to feel that they are valued as staff members within the company because I can understand their [the company's] point of view: we're only here for a short while so why should they invest a whole heap of good will; and the same goes for us, why should we put the extra effort in when we are just going to leave?
>
> (Grace, 25, staff housing assistant)

Perhaps then, the time and effort put in by companies to motivate temporary, seasonal or part-time staff could be seen as somewhat futile? More importantly, in remembering that working while away from home is often only part of a longer travelling experience, we should consider how these young people narrate their working experiences to others, both when still travelling and upon their return home. The interviewer's comment earlier suggests they do not talk about the everyday-ness of their experiences and this is seen again in her conversation with Ellie,

Ellie: When people talk about their travelling experiences you only hear about this beach and they hiked this hill or this city that they went to. You never hear about where else they've worked, and you know they have 'cause they've mentioned it. It's always glossed over and … I've always wondered how we fit in, as part of that, you know, Whistler Blackcomb? I mean, are we glossed over as well? Does it become, does the work become completely unimportant after they leave? Or is it the one thing that they actually talk about?

Interviewer: If you talk to people who have been before what's the first thing you talk about? Say you meet someone in the city who used to work up here.

Ellie: Oh yeh. Where did you work when you were here?

Interviewer: And then? Are you a snowboarder? What was your favourite run? Oh, do you remember that season when …? None of it's forgotten, it just seems that it's, prioritised, you know,

Here then is one reason why companies such as Whistler Blackcomb promote company culture. They are, through blurring the lines between work and play, trying to provide those experiences and memories that young budget travellers will go on to talk about. Sørensen (2003: 861) suggests that many backpackers continue to maintain a virtual travel network once they have returned home. In this way, through email and social networking websites such as MySpace and Facebook for instance, they keep in contact with friends, acquaintances and ex-work colleagues they met while travelling and working. Their travelling and working experiences, memories and recollections are then shared both with the friends they made while away from home, and with other friends, family and peers, some of whom may ask for advice on where to go, work, live, and play on their own travels away from home.

From the corporate perspective, companies such as Whistler Blackcomb want to perpetuate a continuing influx of enthusiastic, motivated and flexible young people in order to, as the website (Whistler Blackcomb 2007) says, re-energise the product and people. By providing lasting memories for seasonal staff there is the hope that some of these young people will recommend the resort – and the work – to others looking to travel. As a result, the company hopes that informal word-of-mouth marketing will attract new eager young people to work and play in Whistler. At the same time, Whistler Blackcomb is also looking to increase its international reputation as an employer (and holiday destination). Byron says:

> Ideally that's where we'd like to go. … Like people around the world with Walt Disney on their resume, right? People [employers] are like, oh, you worked for Walt Disney. It doesn't matter that you were picking up trash, they see [that] you worked for Walt Disney. It would be nice to know whether or not we were getting in there.

Thus, part of the wider experience of working and travelling while away comes from the stories told upon return home (Deforges 1997; Sørensen 2003). These experiences, stories and recommendations can then have an impact on the travel patterns of future young budget travellers.

CONCLUSIONS

In thinking about young budget travellers and international tourism businesses, it is perhaps worth reflecting upon two statistics that came out of the 2006 Lonely Planet survey: almost 71 per cent of their 33,000+ respondents had a university degree or higher, and 40 per cent of their respondents classed themselves as professional (Lonely Planet 2006: 6). This links in back to earlier comments about the age of participants that begins to illustrate the changing demographics of young budget travellers. Furthermore, it suggests that many young people working in the tourism sector as part of a longer travelling experience may well be very highly or perhaps even 'over-qualified'.

International businesses often use employee motivation as a way of recruiting employees who are the 'right fit', yet work in motivation studies seems to suggest that the incentives commonly offered, whether 'pep talks', extra pay or other bonuses (such as a free ski pass or ski equipment) have a limited impact in increasing the enthusiasm and dedication of many employees (see Nicholson 2003: 57). As this group of young people becomes the focus of further investigation, both from academic researchers and from the industry, so it seems that there will be a need to look more closely at the complex relationality between young budget travellers, the places they inhabit, visit, pass through, and live and the working practices that are involved within this temporal and spatial experience (Sheller and Urry 2006; see also Boon 2006). Here, we need to engage more with theories of mobility and migration and consider how this type of tourism can perhaps be understood within the wider contexts of globalisation and transnationalism, and how these processes impact upon individual agency (O'Reilly 2006).

This is not to say that looking at young budget traveller's mobility is straightforward. If we consider young budget travellers as in the 'middle' of transnationalism (Clarke 2005; Conradson and Latham 2005), are we then peripheralising the polarities that have dominated migration studies? We must not forget, as Cresswell (2001) observes, that the mobilities of different groups of migrants are embedded in specific geographies, networks and economic conditions and that these produce how people move and are received differently across the globe (see also Gogia 2006).

Yet, these young travellers are important to international tourism businesses for a number of reasons. They are the tourists of the future and over the course of their lifespan, their previous working and travelling experiences may determine future spending patterns and tourism preferences. The mobility experienced by many of these young people is altering the way in which they define themselves through, for instance, the opportunity to belong to more than one place simultaneously. The young budget travellers of today may, through their children, provide the workforce [and markets] for tourism resorts and industries of tomorrow. Whistler, in the past few years, has started to welcome second-generation backpackers who arrive and work for a season as their parents once did before them. On a final note, both for researchers and tourism professionals, the young budget travellers' working experiences provide an opportunity to examine and perhaps even exploit the myriad of ways in which temporary migration is blurring the boundaries between work and leisure.

Discussion questions

- How might young budget travellers' motivations affect their choices of destination and the (paid and unpaid) work they do while away from home?
- What are the implications for international tourism businesses in recruiting young budget travellers as seasonal employees?
- In what ways could the working and travelling experiences of young budget travellers influence future tourism trends?

REFERENCES

Adler, P.A. and Adler, P. (1999) 'Resort workers: adaptation in the leisure-work nexus', *Sociological Perspectives*, 42: 369–402.

Bianchi, R.V. (2000) 'Migrant tourist-workers: exploring the "contact zones" of post-industrial tourism', *Current Issues in Tourism*, 3: 107–37.

Boon, B. (2006) 'When leisure and work are allies: the case of skiers and tourist resort hotels', *Career Development International*, 11: 594–608.

Christie, J. (2000) 'First tracks: memories from Whistler mountains early years', in B. Barnett (ed.) *Whistler: History in the Making*, Whistler, BC: Pique Publishing.

Clarke, N. (2005) 'Detailing transnational lives of the middle: British working holiday makers in Australia', *Journal of Ethnic and Migration Studies*, 31: 307–22.

Cohen, E. (1973) 'Nomads from affluence: notes on the phenomenon of drifter-tourism', *International Journal of Comparative Sociology*, 14: 89–103.

—— (2004) 'Backpacking: diversity and change' in G. Richards and J. Wilson (eds) *The Global Nomad: Backpacker Travel in Theory and Practice*. Clevedon: Channel View Publications.

Conradson, D. and Latham, A. (2005) 'Transnational urbanism: attending to everyday practices and mobilities', *Journal of Ethnic and Migration Studies*, 31: 227–33.

Crang, P. (1997) 'Performing the tourist product', in C. Rojek and J. Urry *Touring Cultures: Transformations of Travel and Theory*. London: Routledge.

Cresswell, T. (2001) 'The production of mobilities', *New Formations*, 43: 11–25.

Deforges, L. (1997) 'Checking out the planet: global representations/local identities and youth travel', in T. Skelton and G. Valentine (eds) *Cool Places: A Geography of Youth Culture*. London: Routledge.

Du Gay, P. (1996) *Consumption and Identity at Work*. London: Sage.

Gill, A. (2000) 'From growth machine to growth management: the dynamics of resort growth in Whistler, British Columbia', *Environment and Planning A*, 32: 1083–103.

Gogia, N. (2006) 'Unpacking corporeal mobilities: the global voyages of labour and leisure', *Environment and Planning A*, 38: 359–75.

Graburn, N. (1989) 'Tourism: the sacred journey', in V. Smith (ed.) *Hosts and Guests: the Anthropology of Tourism*. Philadelphia: University of Pennsylvania Press.

Grugulis, I., Dundon, T. and Wilkinson, A. (2000) 'Cultural control and the "culture manager": employment practices in a consultancy', *Work, Employment and Society*, 14: 97–116.

Jones, A. (2004) *Review of Gap Year Provision*, Research Report 555. Nottingham: DfES Publications.

Jones, D. (2003) 'Preface', in G. Richards and J. Wilson (eds) *Today's Youth Travellers: Tomorrow's Global Nomads. New Horizons in Independent Youth Travel and Student Travel*. Amsterdam: International Student Travel Confederation.

Loker-Murphy, L. and Pearce, P.L. (1995) 'Young budget travelers: backpackers in Australia', *Annals of Tourism Research*, 22: 819–43.

Lonely Planet (2005) *Travellers' Pulse Survey 2005*, Footscray: Lonely Planet.

—— (2006) *Travellers' Pulse Survey 2006*, Footscray: Lonely Planet.

Moore, S.R., Williams, P.W. and Gill A. (2006) 'Finding a pad in paradise: amenity migration effects on Whistler, British Columbia', in L.A.G. Moss (ed.) *The Amenity Migrants: Seeking and Sustaining Mountains and their Cultures*. Cambridge, MA: CAB International.

Munt, I. (1994) 'The "other" postmodern tourism: culture, travel and the new middle classes', *Theory, Culture and Society*, 11: 101–23.

Myers, B. and Inkson, K. (2003) 'The big OE: how it works and what it can do for New Zealand, *University of Auckland Business Review*, 5: 1–11.

Nicholson, N. (2003) 'How to motivate your problem people', *Harvard Business Review*, 81: 57–65.

O'Reilly, C. (2006) 'From drifter to gap year tourist: mainstreaming backpacker travel', *Annals of Tourism Research*, 33: 998–1017.

Resort Municipality of Whistler (2007) *Facts and Figures: The Resort Municipality of Whistler at a Glance*. Online. Available from: http://www.whistler.ca/content/view/49/61/ (accessed: 20/04/07).

Richards, G. and Wilson, J. (2003) *Today's Youth Travellers: Tomorrow's Global Nomads. New Horizons in Independent Youth Travel and Student Travel, A Report for the International Student Travel Confederation (ISTC) and the Association of Tourism and Leisure Education (ATLAS)*. Amsterdam: International Student Travel Confederation.

Sheller, M. and Urry, J. (2006) 'The new mobilities paradigm', *Environment and Planning A*, 38: 207–26.

Sørensen, A. (2003) 'Backpacker ethnography', *Annals of Tourism Research*, 30: 847–67.

Uriely, N. and Reichel, A. (2000) 'Working tourists and their attitudes to hosts', *Annals of Tourism Research*, 27: 267–83.

Urry, J. (2002) *The Tourist Gaze: Leisure and Travel in Contemporary Societies,* 2nd edn. London: Sage.

Whistler Blackcomb (2007) *Jobs at Whistler Blackcomb*. Online. Available from: http://www.whistlerblackcomb.com/employment/index.htm (accessed: 20/04/07).

PART IV

Tourism and destinations in the internationalisation of business

ON FIRMS AND DESTINATIONS

The four chapters in this part are not only united by a return to the firm as a unit of analysis, but also they coalesce around the common denominator of the destination. As a concept, the destination has dominated analysis in tourism studies and it has led some commentators to bemoan insular, inward-looking, local-level case-studies of tourism development at the expense of wider-ranging views that aim to situate tourism within broader social, economic, political and environmental frameworks and processes that operate at a number of spatial scales beyond the local (Hall 2005). Within the dominant and stereotypical view, there is the understandable temptation to focus almost exclusively on the role of tourism enterprises within destinations on the production, promotion and performance of the local tourism sector. After all, transport businesses convey visitors, accommodation providers temporarily house them, hospitality businesses meet their gastronomic needs, and attractions such as theme parks, museums, galleries, retail districts and heritage sites keep them amused or provided the initial draw in the first place. Destination managers and marketing organisations assume the role of promoting and advertising the destination to the outside world.

It is hardly a revelation that companies for which travel and tourism are not the core business, function as major attractions to visitors. The idea of factory visits, factory tours or company museum tours are long-established concepts (Patton 1986; Mitchell and Mitchell 2001; Mitchell and Orwig 2002; Nissley and Casey 2002; Timothy and Boyd 2003). As these chapters demonstrate, what tends to be underestimated these days is the degree to which non-tourism businesses are now major actors in the current and future operation of tourism destinations. For example, the Guinness storehouse in Dublin is the Irish attraction most visited by international tourists. Not only do many of these enterprises have substantial financial resources to contribute towards the greater destination effort through sponsorship, endorsements, brand tie-ins, advertising, promotion and other forms of place marketing, but they also have considerable resources in terms of specialist knowledge, experience, competence teams and wide social networks to bring to bear in the production of the destination experience. These resources form the basis for partnerships, collaborations and even sub-governmental arrangements between tourism businesses, administrators, marketers and politicians to deliver tourism-based (re-) development within a destination (Laslo 2003). In fact, the businesses represented in this part predominantly use the trade of (tourism) services in mode 3 (Figure 1.1), based on marketing, distribution and relationship-building, with a view to the consumption of products, goods and services in mode 2 (Figure 1.1), although this is not an automatic consequence.

Mitchell's chapter demonstrates that food and, in particular, wine producers have been active in the development and protection of collective place imagery in rural locales and regions made unique in the global place market by virtue of their produce. For consumers, places become synonymous with the food and drink they produce and reflexively food and drink become the reference points by which consumers negotiate, understand (mode 3) and consume real places (and their produce, mode 2). French regions such as Bordeaux, Burgundy and Champagne are well known and attractive for their distinctive produce and as such they have unique selling propositions as destinations. This uniqueness should not be underestimated in a congested global place market where imitation is the sincerest form of flattery (Short and Kim 1999) and the easiest means to frustrate competitive advantage for destinations. Primarily through the lens of food and wine producers, Mitchell's chapter examines the lengths to which destination managers go to defend their marketing space.

The issue of naming rights features in Mason, Ramshaw and Hinch's chapter concerning the involvement of transnational corporations (TNCs) and sports facilities in the (re-) development of tourism districts within North American cities (mode 3). Sports franchises are international businesses in their own right. North American sports brands such as the New York Yankees, Boston Red Sox (both baseball), the Los Angeles Lakers and the Chicago Bulls (both basketball) are known and supported the world over, as are European soccer clubs such as Manchester United, Liverpool, Real Madrid, Barcelona and AC Milan to name but a few. Through three destinations, their chapter focuses on the connections between stadium and franchise owners with TNCs through such devices as stadium sponsorship, naming and 'pouring' rights, and retail concessions. These deals have leveraged investment in new and distinctive consumption landscapes that integrate the brandworlds of the TNCs with new and/or improved (sometimes multipurpose) stadia. It is important to note that, while the chapter focuses in detail on three destinations, the processes, spaces and issues described here are not exclusive to North America.

Both these chapters talk in broad terms to the power such international businesses and their brands have in the production and promotion of tourism destinations. This is based on a highly instrumental view that equates financial resources with power. As Coles and Church (2006) note, power does not always function in such a simplistic manner. However, it is worth reflecting that these private sector, sub-state agencies often have greater financial resources at their disposal than traditional public sector tourism administrators and managers either alone from the public purse or in concert with traditional, local SMTEs. Moreover, with such levels of resourcing available, they are able to fashion distinctive destination spaces of their own in order to project their enterprises, with a view to building enduring relationships between their brands and consumers. As Coles demonstrates in his chapter, German car manufacturers have developed sophisticated and directed uses of tourism to communicate brand values to external audiences (mode 3). Explicit demonstrations and embodiments of brands are incorporated into more interactive museum spaces as well as car-specific destinations that resemble traditional theme parks. They are also present when consumers experience the brand first hand in specialised short breaks and holidays (mode 1), or during factory collection trips (mode 2). The rise of relationship marketing and experiential consumption is well documented and, in some quarters, it is taken as a sign of a fundamental shift in the nature of economic organisation (Pine and Gilmore 1999). These brandscapes are monumental edifices to the competencies and values of the organisation; they are impressive destinations in their own rights that attract large numbers of visitors and build relationships; however, for many reasons, their impact on consumers, their organisations and the (wider) host destination is problematic to assess.

Finally, in this section, Beeton's chapter points to more complicated and subtle relationships between film (which she takes to mean movies, TV series, documentaries and reality TV) production companies and tourism. As international businesses, film companies have had an obvious role to play in the promotion of 'real-life' destinations that form the backdrops and settings for their stories (mode 3). In some cases, places have become more associated with their fictional names and identities than their real ones. Celebrated international companies such as Paramount run tours around their film lots in Los Angeles, while Universal Studios, Disney-MGM, Warner Brothers and Fox Studios run what Beeton (2005: 196) terms 'industrial film-studio theme parks'. Beyond these more obvious connections, tourism features in two other crucial dimensions in the mediation of film production. First, short-term temporary mobility in the form of trade mission visits is used as a vehicle by regional and state trade deputations and film commissions to lure film producers and directors to shoot in their destinations (mode 3). Film festivals and award ceremonies have much the same function, but they have major commercial consequences for the destinations in which they are held because they attract large numbers of visitors in terms of fans, dignitaries, journalists, politicians, film producers, stars and their entourages. Enhanced destination imagery may be an obvious outcome but herein lies a second, and often frequently overlooked dimension of the relationship between tourism and temporary mobility: namely, film shoots 'on location' away from studios actually are costly logistical exercises that require film production teams and their actors to spend time away from home consuming tourism and hospitality services while abroad (modes 2 and 4). For this reason, national governments, such as Switzerland, set up extensive websites to facilitate filming through national film commissions (SFC 2007). Beeton's chapter points to the ethics in the relationships between film producers and the destinations they use and promote. Destinations may receive an economic boost in the short term, but there may be more persistent legacies for destinations and their communities. Where in the past, these may have been conveniently overlooked because of the importance of the financial gains, a more appropriate contemporary approach may be for those stakeholders involved in film tourism to consider how the principles of corporate social responsibility may be integrated into their activities (see also Chapter 6).

VALUE OR VALUE-ADDED OR BOTH?

The chapters presented in this part present two sets of dilemmas for scholars of tourism and international business. The first of these relates to just how much importance should they attach to studies that connect tourism with businesses that apparently have primary commercial activities elsewhere? How many enterprises are there that describe themselves, or that are categorised with, their core business interests outside tourism but which use tourism to support their main activities? Simply put, are the cases presented here interesting exceptions, easily dismissed as engaging curios, or are they actually indicative of more important trends in international business that need to be acknowledged and investigated further?

We would contend that the strategic use of tourism, even if they do not think of it as such, is on the rise for international businesses where travel and tourism is not the core business. Beyond the cases presented here, it is possible to identify a number of prominent examples of enterprises and sectors in and for which the role of tourism is pivotal to their operations. For example, short-term consumer mobility in medical tourism is vital to the performance of increasing numbers of private health-care businesses around the world (TRAM 2006). In the case of India, McKinsey and Company estimated that 150,000 medical tourists visited in 2004 and the value of the sector was US$333 million (quoted in TRAM 2006: 17). In general, all of those enterprises from whichever sectors that send their employees overseas on short-term placements or secondments are involved in short-term mobilities, the boundaries of which are increasingly blurred with tourism (mode 4) (Hall 2005; Coles *et al.* 2006). Levels of corporately driven mobilities (beyond quintessential business trips) of this nature are high and in some cases, for quite specific reasons. Where they are responsible for the health-care of their employees, some businesses are considering off-shoring through medical tourism as a means to accrue (in some cases substantial) cost-savings (modes 2 and 4). In the United States this has lead to lively debate, not necessarily just because labour unions object to the ethicacy of having to send employees off-shore when facilities exist at home; but rather, the health-care sector is a major component of the United States economy. Significant job losses and reductions in gross domestic product may ensue as consumers switch services to ones with equal if not higher standards of delivery but lower price (Kher 2006). In one striking assessment, a health-care economist suggested that 'this has the potential of doing to the U.S. health-care system what the Japanese auto industry did to American carmakers' (Kher 2006; see also Chapter 13 on car sector rationalisation). Quite so, but high costs of health care (blamed on high pharmaceutical costs and bloated administrations) are precisely the reason why overseas providers are so attractive!

The enormous investments in naming rights, corporate sponsorship and brandscapes, or the extraordinary revenues earned in the medical tourism sector prompt a second set of critical issues. While it is possible to identify how tourism is used and for what motives, it is less certain how such activities feature in the 'bottom line' of the businesses involved. This raises the wider issue of how the economic impacts of these specific relationships between tourism and international business can be both researched effectively and hence calculated accurately. For instance, as Coles' chapter demonstrates, some of the visitor experiences developed by German companies are costly investments but the extent to which they break even or induce further sales is not easy to measure nor is the degree to which propensity to purchase is enhanced. Similarly, Mason, Ramshaw and Hinch point to large-scale investments in the use of sports to promote international brands and leverage greater brand value. Where those paying for naming rights fail to secure adequate exposure, opportunity costs of lost brand earnings can be extremely high. The calculation of lost earnings or opportunity costs is based on a number of assumptions derived from broad sports advertising and media parameters. Both cases emphasise the importance of commercially sensitive information as key sources to furthering our understanding of the relationship between tourism and international business. While there are examples of studies that have benefited from insider perspectives, many have struggled to gain the necessary cooperation from desired corporate partners (Mosedale 2007).

REFERENCES

Beeton, S. (2005) *Film-induced Tourism*. Clevedon: Channel View.

Coles, T.E. and Church, A. (2007) 'Tourism, politics and the forgotten entanglements of power', in A. Church and T.E. Coles (eds) *Tourism, Power and Space*. London: Routledge.

Coles, T., Hall, C.M. and Duval, D. (2006) 'Tourism and post-disciplinary inquiry', *Current Issues in Tourism*, 9(4/5): 293–319.

Hall, C.M. (2005) *Tourism: Rethinking the Social Science of Mobility*. Harlow: Prentice-Hall.

Kher, U. (2006) 'Outsourcing your Heart', *Time*, 21/05/06. Online. Available from: http://www.time.com/time/magazine/article/0,9171,1196429,00.html (accessed: 27/06/07).

Laslo, D. (2003) 'Policy communities and infrastructure of urban tourism', *American Behavioural Scientist*, 46(8): 1070–83.

Mitchell, M.A. and Mitchell, S.J. (2001) 'Consumer tourism experience in the nonprofit and public sectors', *Journal of Nonprofit & Public Sector Marketing*, 9(3): 21–34.

Mitchell, M.A. and Orwig, R.A. (2002) 'Consumer experience tourism and brand bonding', *Journal of Product and Brand Management*, 11(1): 30–41.

Mosedale, J.T. (2007) Corporate geographies of transnational tourism corporations. Unpublished PhD thesis, University of Exeter.

Nissley, N. and Casey, A. (2002) 'The politics of the exhibition: Viewing corporate museums through the paradigmatic lens of organizational memory', *British Journal of Management*, 13(s2): S35–S45.

Patton, S.G. (1986) 'Factory outlets and travel industry development', *Journal of Travel Research*, 25(1): 10–13.

Pine, J.B. and Gilmore, J.H. (1999) *The Experience Economy. Work is Theatre and Every Business a Stage*. Boston, MA: Harvard Business School Press.

SFC (Swiss Film Commission) (2007) Film location Switzerland. Online. Available from: http://www.filmlocation.ch/ (accessed: 27/06/07).

Short, J.R. and Kim, Y.-H. (1999) *Globalization and the City*. Harlow: Longman.

Timothy, D.J. and Boyd, S. (2003) *Heritage Tourism*. Harlow: Prentice Hall.

TRAM (Tourism Research and Marketing) (2006) *Medical Tourism: A Global Analysis*. London: ATLAS for Tourism Research and Marketing.

International business, intellectual property and the misappropriation of place: food, wine and tourism

Richard Mitchell

Learning objectives

After considering this chapter, you will be able to:

- describe the intellectual property of place;
- discuss how international treaties and agreements relate to place promotion;
- explain how those promoting tourism destinations in international markets may seek legal protection.

Key terms

- place promotion;
- food and wine tourism;
- intellectual property;
- international treaties.

INTRODUCTION

Places are competing in the global market for tourists, business travellers, investment and residents. This competition can lead to a range of promotional activities from destination marketing organisations (DMOs) that project imagery to potential consumers. As a result, as Hashimoto and Telfer (2006: 36) suggest, 'places can become brands and hold significant brand values and therefore, place has significant importance as intellectual property'.

Place promotion is generated for both urban and rural spaces, and is often associated with a significant change in the political economy and/or restructuring of the economy of a region. Irrespective of the rationale, there is an ever-increasing drive to develop and project images that set particular places apart from competitors. The reality is, however, that imitation would appear to be the sincerest form of flattery and place images are increasingly converging. Thus, to create or identify, and then maintain difference is increasingly challenging and there is a need for places to protect the intellectual property associated with place images, name and branding.

This chapter explores issues surrounding the intellectual property of place in an increasingly brand and image focused world. To date the protection of the intellectual property associated with place has been largely limited to food and wine products from specific localities. This chapter examines how destinations as place products have started to assert their legal rights to protect their intellectual property, imagery and branding on the international stage against misappropriation. Some of the international treaties currently in place to protect these products are introduced. In addition, the chapter considers how some enterprises with international scope have attempted to capitalise on the existence, but – from their perspective – the non-protection or non-enforcement of established and understood identities, brands and place products. In some respects tourism is implicit in much of the discussion here. However it is worth establishing at the beginning of the chapter that much of the driving force for appropriation, protection and/or enforcement is the desire to control the financial and added-value associated with the consumption of place brands and products by external audiences among which visitors are perceived to be one of the largest groups. The chapter concludes with a discussion of the issues facing place promoters in relation to the intellectual property of place. The chapter begins by briefly discussing the challenges of differentiating places and the need for intellectual property protection.

PLACE 'DIFFERENTIATION' AND THE EMERGING ROLE OF INTELLECTUAL PROPERTY

Despite common roots, the concepts of 'market' and 'place' have diverged in post-industrial economies and 'sense of place' has been lost to the point where Zukin (1991: 12) suggests that 'as markets have been globalized, place has been diminished'. The result is a sameness of place that makes it difficult for places to be differentiated from their competitors. Even the act of place promotion creates the degree of sameness among places. In fact, Barke and Harrop (1994: 111) highlight the proliferation of place promotion as the reason why,

> place as an identifiable and authentic phenomenon becomes increasingly meaningless. What is really being promoted is a kind of placelessness, in the sense that claims made for a specific place may bear only a limited relation to reality or be equally applicable to many other places.

For Zukin (1991), sameness is an outcome of changing technologies, including the development of the railway and photography in the nineteenth century (both closely aligned with tourism). More recently electronic media have contributed to further convergence. This is as much a reflection of the promotion industry itself and how images are presented in or to the media as it is about the places (Barke and Harrop 1994).

Paradoxically, then, in a globalised world, there is an imperative to differentiate through place promotion, yet the act of place promotion may create a higher degree of placelessness. Faced with real-time forms of communication that facilitate copycat promotional campaigns in a virtual instant, destination promoters are looking for ways both to maintain a unique point of difference and to protect any competitive advantage they may have in the market place. Beyond this more 'hard-nosed' view, there is also the desire to protect and preserve local culture and identity.

Food and wine are at the confluence of intellectual property and place; for instance, recipes, cooking techniques, ingredients and distinct regional growing characteristics can be unique to a specific place or locality. At the turn of the twentieth century a number of international treaties were introduced to protect, among other things, food and wine products that are synonymous with the place of origin (Moran 1993). This 'intellectual property of place' has recently also been associated with tourism, especially wine and food tourism (Hall *et al.* 2003; Hashimoto and Telfer 2006). Several authors have suggested that regional (rural) identity can be expressed through food and wine products that encourage and preserve difference in the development of tourism products and promotion (Ray 1999; Hall *et al.* 2003). In particular, Ray (1999) suggests that there are four 'modes' of 'cultural economy' that are related to rural development and the first of these – the commoditisation of local/regional culture – is exemplified by both cultural tourism and regional agri-food products and regional cuisines.

Differentiation through place-specific products

Central to this is the recognition that wine and food are often considered to be the quintessential expression of regional character. Wine products, especially those from Europe, are often directly identified by geographical origin (e.g. Burgundy or Champagne in France, Rioja in Spain) and many regions have gone to great lengths to legally protect this identity. European food and wine products have traditionally received the greatest protection, with 727 non-wine and spirits products currently protected under European Union (EU) legislation (EU 2006) and extensive appellation systems in place for wine and spirits throughout. The concept of 'geographical knowledges' is useful in explaining why this has become important in Europe (if not the rest of the world), because consumers deploy these knowledges 'in order to "re-enchant" [food] commodities and to differentiate them from the derived functionality and homogeneity of standardised products and places' (Cook and Crang 1996: 132).

Terroir

Wine is a particularly pertinent example of the connection between food stuff and place as a wine's unique character and flavour relies not only on the grape variety and skill of the winemaker but also on the unique and often subtle combination of regional characteristics that impart a distinctly regional flavour. The term *terroir* – a quintessentially French term and concept for which no precise English translation exists (Gladstones and Smart 1999) – is used to describe the 'almost mystical' combination of all aspects of soil, climate and landscape present in the wine region (Halliday 1998). For Halliday (1998: 28), *terroir* 'lies at the heart of the French appellation system, built up by a thousand years of practical experience which has led to a precisely detailed delineation of quality'. Moreover, Charters (2006: 106) observes that

> it is not merely that the wine tastes different, but that it is – almost philosophically – a different object because it represents a specific plot of land. In this way the physical substance of the wine is subordinate to its role as a marker for where it came from.

If as Relph (1996) asserts, tourism is fundamentally about the difference of 'place' between 'home' and 'away', a destination's physical elements combine to define it and contribute to its attractiveness. Perhaps not surprisingly then, Hall (1996) has suggested that there is a significant overlap between the elements of *terroir* and those features that are important to regional tourism branding (e.g. landscape and climate). Indeed, Hall and Mitchell (2002) developed the idea of *touristic terroir,* which suggests that the unique combination of attributes of the tourist region is crucial to the regional flavour of the tourist experience, not the individual attributes themselves. Like *terroir, touristic terroir* is impossible to replicate and may take on an almost mystical attraction. Urry (1990), for example suggests that we sometimes gaze upon places simply for their value as a marker of something symbolic and meaningful. However, according to Mitchell (2004: 17),

> nowhere is this [*touristic terroir*] more prevalent than in the wine region, where the cultural landscape of a wine region is an expression of regional culture and identity, and both the wine and tourism industries rely on regional branding for market leverage and promotion.

In short, the close association between place promotion and local food and wine products can imbue a greater degree of 'authenticity' in the tourism experience, and they can be a strong determinant of destination image. Urry (2005: 22) suggests that this is further reinforced when the product is consumed *in situ*:

> The consuming of place involves the consumption of services and sometimes of goods that are deemed specific to that place, e.g. cheeses from France, malt whisky in Scotland, chardonnay in Australia and so on. But of course with goods, the growth of global markets has partly reduced this specificity of goods that are often now available across the world ... . But even with the global marketplace there is still thought to be something authentic about consuming particular goods or services in specific places.

It is no accident that several authors who have discussed the association between place-specific food and wine products and tourism have used France as their exemplar. Few other places can claim the metonymic powers of French wine and food place names: Champagne, Burgundy and Bordeaux to mention but a few. Nevertheless, despite the etymology of the term, the concept of *terroir* is a critical component of the intellectual property of place in both the Old and, more recently, the New World (Hall and Mitchell 2008). In fact the concept of *terroir*, and most certainly appellation, have assumed an even greater valence in France because of (perceived) threats to regional cultural identity through the misappropriation of place (names) (Guy 2003). Perhaps the most high profile cases of alleged misappropriation concern French wine and food products and not surprisingly modern manifestations of appellations and legal protection of place have their roots in France, especially Champagne (Guy 2003; Hall *et al.* 2003; Charters 2006). The next section turns to consider the measures used to protect ownership of, and to enforce rights over, place identities. Although these are more immediately associated with other forms of economic activity, as we have seen above, these issues are becoming increasingly important to the tourism sector because of the complex connectivities in destinations.

INTELLECTUAL PROPERTY OF PLACE: AN INTRODUCTION TO INTERNATIONAL LEGAL PERSPECTIVES

According to the World Intellectual Property Organisation (WIPO 2004a: n.p.) '[i]ntellectual property refers to creations of the mind: inventions, literary and artistic works, and symbols, names, images, and designs used in commerce'. WIPO (2004a) further divides intellectual property into 'industrial property' and 'copyright'. The discussion here mostly refers to industrial property, because one of the components of such property is 'geographical indications of source' and hence there is an explicit link to place. Copyright is also discussed later as it is becoming increasingly important for places with strong global brands.

Despite earlier demarcations for the origin of some regional wines (e.g. Tokaji in 1700, Chianti in 1716 and the Duoro Valley in 1756) (Charters 2006), nineteenth- and twentieth-century France was the birthplace of modern international law on 'geographical indications of source' for food and wine products. In particular, the French *Appellation d'Origine Contrôlée* (AOC) system of demarcation is acknowledged as the most influential of a number of nationwide systems developed around the turn of the twentieth century (Charters 2006). According to Alphonse Perrin, a *vigneron* (vine grower) leader of the 1900s, this saw 'terroir made into a legally defined area' (Guy 2003: 126). Simply put, if you didn't produce in the region, the name of the region could not appear on the label to describe or imply its origin. On the face of it, this system was primarily developed to protect *vignerons* and consumers against increasing misappropriation of place by unscrupulous wine producers (Hall *et al.* 2003). However, these legal measures are also connected with the complex social and cultural conditions in France at the time. According to Charters (2006), the AOC has its roots in rural economic depressions; outbreaks of the vine pest *phylloxera*; temperance movements and prohibition in several export markets; growing competition on the international wine market; and, most importantly here, place name fraud. Moreover, 'the blow to national pride [following defeats in the Franco-Prussian War of 1870 and later in the First World War], rural demoralisation, and challenges to the wine industry's belief in its own importance thus engendered a major loss of confidence' (Charters 2006: 98). Indeed, Guy (2003: 128) argues that, in Champagne at least, the AOC system and the rise in significance of the term *terroir*, owed as much to attempts 'to transform "peasants into

Frenchmen" as it did to protecting vigneron and consumers from fraudulent behaviour'. For her:

> The issue of fraud – and the crusade to protect vin gaulois – opened the possibility of negotiating the meaning of Frenchness and the place of rural France within the nation. Terroir, for those in rural France, created the esprit gaulois; it was through its connection to the rural world that the esprit was transmitted.
>
> (Guy 2003: 128–9)

The relationship between place fraud, *terroir* and the intellectual property of geographical origin is complex and far reaching. In the case of France at least, it concerns distinctive regional identity and nationhood; core versus periphery; state versus populace; and labour versus capital (Guy 2003). Such intricacies should not be overlooked in analyses of the intellectual property of place because such complexities still shape the politics of international intellectual property legislation, in particular those of many New World wine countries and regions (i.e. Australia, New Zealand, South Africa, Chile and Argentina).

Protecting geographical indications

In legal terms the cultural capital that supports the intellectual property of geographical indications is held in the name or symbols of a region. For the WIPO (2006a: n.p.) 'a geographical indication is a sign used on goods that have a specific geographical origin and *possess qualities or a reputation* that are due to that place of origin' (emphasis added). Geographical indications, which are usually just place names, are therefore the result of the reputation of a region (i.e. place brand values) as well as the social and cultural contexts that empowered or forced the region to assert its identity through its food and/or wine products.

It is not possible here to discuss treaties or agreements that are used to protect the intellectual property of place in great detail (instead see www.wipo.int). Rather, it is important to note that there are several major agreements that have international (although not universal) jurisdiction (see Table 11.1). The application of these treaties upholds the intellectual property of place through geographical indications as discussed above. WIPO is responsible for administering these treaties and in particular two international treaties that are key to the protection of geographical indications: the Paris Convention for the Protection of Industrial Property (1883) and the Lisbon Agreement for the Protection of Appellations of Origin and Their International Registration (1958). Under the Lisbon Agreement (Article 2), for example, an appellation is defined as the

> 'geographical name of a country, region, or locality, which serves to designate a product originating therein, the quality and characteristics of which are due exclusively or essentially to the geographic environment, including natural and human factors' and this can be registered with WIPO for protection.
>
> (WIPO 2004b)

Table 11.1 *Key international agreements involving intellectual property rights*

Treaty/ Agreement	Year first signed	Number of signa- tories*	Revisions	Description

Paris Convention for the Protection of Industrial Property	1883	171	• Brussels (1900)
			• Washington (1911)
			• The Hague (1925)
			• London (1934)
			• Lisbon (1958)
			• Stockholm (1967)
			• Amended 1979
				• Applies to industrial property in the widest sense, including:
				  – patents, marks, industrial designs, utility models
				  – trade names
				  – geographical indications
				  – the repression of unfair competition
				• Must treat one's own nationals and foreigners equally
				• Protection in own country is effectively concurrent in all contracting states
				• Indications of source: each contracting state must act against direct or indirect use of a false indication of the source of the goods or the identity of the producer, manufacturer or trader

Madrid Agreement Concerning the International Registration of Marks and Madrid Protocol	1891 1989	56 69 (Total = 79)	• Brussels (1900) • Washington (1911) • The Hague (1925) • London (1934) • Nice (1957) • Stockholm (1967) • Amended 1979	• Protection of a mark in a large number of countries • International registration effective in contracting states • Open to any state which is party to the Paris Convention • Parallel and independent from Paris • States may adhere to either or both

Continued

Table 11.1 Continued

Treaty/ Agreement	Year first signed	Number of signatories*	Revisions	Description
Madrid Agreement for the Repression of False or Deceptive Indications of Source on Goods	1891	34	• Washington (1911) • The Hague (1925) • London (1934) • Lisbon (1958) • Stockholm (1967)	• Goods bearing a false or deceptive indication of source must be seized on importation, or importation prohibited, or other actions and sanctions applied • Prohibits the use of all indications capable of deceiving the public as to the source of the goods
Lisbon Agreement for the Protection of Appellations of Origin and Their International Registration	1958	26	• Stockholm (1967) • Amended 1979	• Protection of appellations of origin • Names registered by the WIPO • WIPO communicates registration to other contracting states • A contracting state may declare, within one year, that it cannot ensure the protection of a registered appellation
Agreement on Trade-Related Aspects of Intellectual Property Rights (TRIPS)	1994	149 (32 observers)		• Introduced intellectual property rules into the multilateral trading system • Must treat one's own nationals and foreigners equally • Equal treatment for nationals of all trading partners in WTO • Protection should contribute to technical innovation and the transfer of technology to mutual benefit of producers and users

Continued

Table 11.1 *Continued*

Treaty/ Agreement	Year first signed	Number of signa-tories*	Revisions	Description
Doha Development Agreement (DDA)	2001	149 (32 observers)	• Cancún (2003) • Geneva (2004) • Hong Kong (2005)	• Platform for negotiations on 21 multilateral issues • Includes intellectual property rights dealt with in TRIPS • All geographical indications to be given a 'higher level of protection' • 'Traditional Knowledge' also introduced as a place-based concept

Source: WIPO (2004b), except TRIPS (WTO 2006a) and Doha (WTO 2006).
Note: *Numbers as of October 2006, except TRIPS and Doha (December 2005).

In addition, the World Trade Organization (WTO) has an agreement on intellectual property. Articles 22 to 24 of the Agreement on Trade-Related Aspects of Intellectual Property Rights (TRIPS) are intended to protect geographical indications of source (Hall *et al.* 2003; WIPO 2004a; WTO 2006a). As the most recent of agreements, it does not usurp the powers of its predecessors, rather it applies their principles to WTO member states. Further progressive enforcement is contained in the Doha Development Agreement (DDA) that proposes that the 'higher level of protection' currently afforded to wines and spirits under TRIPS be extended to other agricultural and food products (WTO 2006b; ACCI 2005). According to the Australian Chamber of Commerce and Industry (ACCI 2005) this is a contentious proposal that has its advocates (ostensibly the EU, India, Sri Lanka, Cuba, Thailand and Pakistan), as well as several opponents (Australia, Canada, Chile, New Zealand and the United States) who argue that its scope goes well beyond what the original intent of the TRIPS agreement.

So, while there are agreements in place, clearly there is a divide in terms of extent to which these agreements should – and indeed, may – be applied. A further complication is that, as WIPO (2006a: n.p.) notes, 'the use of geographical indications is not limited to agricultural products. They may also highlight specific qualities of a product which are due to human factors that can be found in the place of origin of the products.' However pivotal here is that the intellectual property of place must be associated with a specific product and there is no such protection for places per se. As discussed below, this lack of protection for a place name has been highlighted in recent disputes brought before WIPO in order to halt the (alleged) misappropriation of place (see case-study vignette). It is also evident in a number of instances of (alleged) place fraud that highlight a significant gap in intellectual property legislation (especially in relation to the use of images of a place).

CASE-STUDY VIGNETTE – TOURISM AND INTERNATIONAL BUSINESS IN ACTION

What's in a name? Champagne and the misappropriation of a place name

Think of the word 'champagne' and what image does it conjure? For many it invokes images of celebration, special occasions, excess and success. In common English usage, the word has been used as an umbrella term for any sparkling white wine. Times, though, are changing. Since the 1960s Champagne houses have been involved in several high profile cases to assert their rights over the name Champagne, as only sparkling white wine grown and made in Champagne using time-honoured traditional methods can and should be called Champagne.

Indeed, Champagne was in many respects the original *Appellation d'Origine Contrôlée* (AOC – literally 'term of controlled origin' or simply put, place-specific brand). In 1908 some 15,000 hectares of grapes were designated within the region and wine made from these grapes had exclusive rights use the name Champagne (CIVC 2006). The boundaries of the region were expanded in 1927 and the total planted area has now reached 34,000 hectares (CIVC 2006). This AOC arose from a complex interaction of social and cultural factors, but the official rationale for its delimitation was 'because of its prestige and very effective international marketing, [it] was a prime target for unscrupulous competitors' (Charters 2006: 98). At the turn of the twentieth century many other French wine regions developed as AOC, but it was not until after the First World War that there was a national system in France.

According to Jean-Luc Barbier, director-general of the Comité Interprofessionnel du vin de Champagne (CIVC), the first court ruling against fraudulent use of the name Champagne was in 1843 (Duval Smith 2004); however it was not until much later – through the Madrid Agreement (1891) and, more particularly, the Lisbon Agreement (1958) and TRIPS (1994) – that Champagne was able to battle fraudsters in the international market place (CIVC 2003).

Today the CIVC spends hundreds of thousands of euros each year systematically identifying hundreds of cases of alleged fraud; whenever offenders fail to desist, it prosecutes them under appropriate international law. The CIVC has a clear mandate to protect its intellectual property of place (including dotcom infringements) and it fully exercises its rights as set out in a strong body of international legislation. Today Champagne is a place-specific brand of such power that tourists are drawn to the region, the vineyards and Champagne houses in what for many is a form of pilgrimage. This is due to the vigour with which the CIVC has protected its reputation.

Continued

Table 11.2 *Examples of cases of intellectual property actions taken by the Champagne region*

Year	Location	Product	Action
Direct competition			
1960	London	'Spanish Champagne'	Prosecution
1972	Japan	Wine	Bilateral agreement
1973	Spain	Wine	Bilateral agreement
1974	Québec	'Champagne canadien' (Canadian Champagne)	Prosecution
Indirect competition			
1987	Germany	*Perrier* water	Prosecution
1994	UK	'Elderflower Champagne'	Prosecution
Challenges to reputation			
1984	France	'Champagne Cigarettes'	Prosecution
1990	Switzerland	'Schaumpanger Paris – Night'	Prosecution
1993	France	'Champagne de Yves St Laurent' perfume	Prosecution
2002	Sweden	'Arla' yoghurt with 'the taste of Champagne'	Prosecution

Source: Adapted from CIVC (2003: 36).

Questions

- How many unique selling propositions associated with food and drink can you identify that are used in international tourism promotion today?
- In what ways do you think that marketing based on food and drink may affect the organisation of, and economic benefits accrued by, the tourism sector?
- Are there any ways in which promotion through food and drink may be detrimental to a destination?

TOURISM AND THE MISAPPROPRIATION OF PLACE

Place.coms

One of the most topical subjects for place fraud is the misappropriation of place.coms or place name URLs (Universal Resource Locators). The World Wide Web has been in widespread use since about 1990 and the organisation that controls the registration of domain names, the Internet Corporation for Assigned Names and Numbers (ICANN), has only been existence since 1998 (ICANN 1998). WIPO has also been involved in domain name intellectual property issues since 1999. Under its Internet Domain Name Process

(WIPO I), it suggested that the Domain Name System (DNS) 'has become a victim of its own success as the applications of the Internet have expanded into all spheres of activity' (WIPO 1999: n.p.).

WIPO commenced further policy development on the use of the DNS in 2001, with the Second WIPO Internet Domain Name Process (WIPO II) which 'examined the bad faith and misleading registration and use by third parties of a range of identifiers other than trademarks' including 'geographical identifiers, such as indications of geographical source used on goods, geographical indications, and other geographical terms' (WIPO 2003: 1). WIPO II expressly considered the use of so-called 'country name gTLDs' (generic Top-Line Domains, such as .uk, .nz or .au), 'because of the commercial value of these names and also because of the perception that use of geographical terms as domain names by unrelated parties (e.g. non-citizens) is an affront to national values and sovereignty' (WIPO 2001: 10). WIPO II suggested that the most applicable international legislation would be the Paris Convention but that it does not expressly afford protection to country names. In fact the report described place names as 'Geographical Designations Beyond Intellectual Property' (WIPO 2001: 10). Despite this, WIPO II stopped short of introducing new international statutory protection, preferring instead to use their existing Uniform Domain Name Dispute Resolution Policy (UDRP), developed in 1999 to enforce trademark breaches on internet sites hosted in WIPO member states (WIPO 2003). This policy is not retroactive and it is limited to domain name holders with no 'legitimate' or 'misleading' use of the name, often called 'cybersquatters' (WIPO 2003).

Table 11.3 shows that all but one of the disputes over place.com domain names have found in favour of the private company or individual that owns the domain name and not the place it is associated with. Interestingly the only successful case was Barcelona and this dispute was considered prior to the WIPO II report. It would also seem that the low rate of success for complainants is not reflective of the UDRP more broadly as 5,327 of the 8,354 (63.8 per cent) cases heard up to October 2006 had found in favour

Table 11.3 *Examples of place.com cases brought under the UDRP*

Complainant*	Respondent	Year of decision	Decision
Barcelona	Barcelona.com Inc. (USA)	2000	Transfer of URL approved
St Moritz	StMoritz.com (Sharjah, UAE)	2000	Denied
New Zealand	Virtual Countries Inc.	2002	Denied
Puerto Rico	Virtual Countries Inc.	2002	Denied
Tasmania	Gordon James Craven	2003	Denied
Madrid	Easylink Services Corporation (USA)	2004	Denied
Mexico	Latin America Telecom Inc. (USA)	2004	Denied
Puerto Vallarta	BBVA Bancomer Services	2004	Denied
Andalucia	Andalucia.com (UK)	2006	Denied

Source: WIPO (2006b).
Note: *All are national or regional tourism/promotional organisations for the respective places.

of the complainant (WIPO 2006c). It is also interesting to note that a private company (Virtual Countries Inc.) stopped the Republic of South Africa from proceeding to WIPO in 2000 after having a case upheld in the United States District Court to have South Africa's impending case dismissed (Virtual Countries Inc. versus Republic of South Africa 2001). South Africa subsequently withdrew from international legal action (Harrison 2001) and Virtual Countries Inc. is reported to have asked South Africa to pay US$10 million for the domain name (McCarthy 2003).

One of the more prominent UDRP cases is that of New Zealand versus Virtual Countries Inc. In this case the New Zealand government (under the name of Her Majesty the Queen) was found to have acted in bad faith and to have been attempting to 'reverse hijack' the newzealand.com URL (Her Majesty the Queen versus Virtual Countries Inc. 2002). In its findings WIPO suggested:

> Indications of geographical origin, whether they be the names of towns, cities, regions, countries or indeed continents are certainly capable of being trademarks or service marks, but only when the geographical significance of the name is displaced. This usually only occurs after long and extensive use of the name as a brand by a single trader in such a manner as to distinguish his [sic] goods and services from those of his [sic] competitors.
>
> (Her Majesty the Queen versus Virtual Countries Inc. 2002: n.p.)

Unfortunately for New Zealand, WIPO also found that New Zealand had in fact provided evidence to counter their own claim in their submission to the WIPO questionnaire on the protection of country names in the DNS when they stated that: 'New Zealand law, custom or practice does not preclude the use of country names under any circumstances. New Zealand does not see any reason why the domain names should be excepted from this general rule' (Her Majesty the Queen versus Virtual Countries Inc. 2002: n.p.). The loss of this case ultimately meant that Tourism New Zealand and New Zealand Trade and Enterprise had to pay Virtual Countries Inc. NZ$1 million for the domain name (McCarthy 2003). However, this cost is likely to now be considered a worthwhile investment as the site receives an average of 350,000 visits per month and it has received two Webby Awards for the best tourism site on the World Wide Web (Tourism New Zealand spokes person 2006) (see www.newzealand.com).

The above examples therefore suggest that place.coms are not always easily available to countries, and first-movers have an advantage under the WIPO UDRP. In particular, the decision on the newzealand.com case suggests that place.coms lie somewhere between the trademark and geographical indications and therefore it is very difficult for places to protect their rights to use the dotcom. However, place.coms are not the only example of such gaps, with the misappropriation of place imagery also becoming an issue for places.

Place imagery

While the practice of fraudulently using place images is not widespread, there are enough reported examples to suggest that this is a significant issue. For example, images of

New Zealand's Southern Alps have been used to promote a UK region in a print advertising campaign and images. One Foot Island in the Aitutaki atoll of the Cook Islands has been used to promote Fiji. The heavy use of stock images in marketing collateral and the ability to purchase and distribute these images via the internet has increased the likelihood that this might occur. There is no longer any need for photographers (and their agents) to communicate directly with their clients and, whether by design or not, place images can easily be used to fraudulently to represent another place.

This type of behaviour is not limited to images of a destination and there are examples of how images of a specific location can be misused to represent other products and places. One such example is that of Rippon Vineyard in Central Otago New Zealand, whose spectacular alpine outlook (see www.rippon.co.nz) has been used: on a cheap Australian wine label in the Netherlands; in an agricultural spray manual (when in fact Rippon is a biodynamic vineyard); in an irrigation brochure; to sell Tesco's (UK retailer) own-brand sauvignon blanc; in the *American Wine Spectator* magazine to represent another winery; and in New Zealand's *Next* magazine (a women's monthly) to represent the Marlborough (New Zealand) region. For the Rippon winemaker, Nick Mills, the issues are obvious:

> We do export to the Netherlands, so we turn up with our photo of Rippon which is who we are, and then everyone else just believes it's a generic photo of a vineyard in Australia. …That image is very, very important to us so when it's misused or malrepresented [*sic*] in the press or anywhere else it comes off as quite insulting.
>
> (One News 2006: n.p.)

According to copyright lawyer, Jim Thomson, there is little that Rippon Vineyard, or any other place for that matter, can do about this misuse of images of their place as international copyright law says that the copyright for images is held with the photographer and, as long as the owner of the place cannot prove any loss or damage, s/he is free to do with it what s/he wishes (One News 2006: n.p.).

This example has clear implications for tourism because brand associations that may occur between the false representations and the real place may cause confusion and/or unrealistic expectations in the market place. There are clear issues in the misappropriation of place images, but there is apparently very little that places can do but appeal to photographers to take care when selling their copyright images. In contrast, the misappropriation of place promotion, is perhaps more clear cut and there is adequate protection for place promoters.

Place promotion

One of the most successful international country-level promotional campaigns of the last 20 years has been the '100% Pure New Zealand' campaign, with Tourism New Zealand winning no fewer than five international marketing awards for the campaign and five international awards for its website. This success has meant that the campaign has been copied by a number of tourism (and non-tourism) destinations and businesses (Tourism New Zealand Spokesperson 2006) (see Table 11.4). Not surprisingly, this successful formula has been

Table 11.4 *100% Pure New Zealand campaign rip-offs**

Non-tourism uses	Tourism-related uses	
	New Zealand	Other countries
100% Pure New Zealand Biodiesel	100% Pure New Zealand	100% Pure Seychelles
100% Pure New Zealand Olives	Adventure	100% Pure Tahoe
100% Pure New Zealand Wine	100% Pure New Zealand Car	100% Pure Positano
100% Pure Pine	Rental	100% Natural Beauty
100% Pure Property	100% Pure and Natural	(Costa Rica)
100% Pure Local Aotearoa	New Zealand	100% Dominican
5% Pure (NZ Green Party slogan)	100% Pure Queenstown	Republic
	100% Pure South Island	100% Maldives
	99% Pure New Zealand	Pure Travel (menajet.com)
	Pure New Zealand	Pure Cornwall
	Pure New Zealand Tours	Pure Crete
		Pure Ecuador
		Pure Michigan
		Pure Tasmania

Source: Adapted from Tourism New Zealand Spokesperson (2006).

Note: *Not all of these are considered to be legal infringements of the 100% Pure New Zealand Trademark.

emulated on a number of occasions. Several of these 'copycat' promotional slogans have been considered to be infringements of Tourism New Zealand's rights over the words '100% Pure' and the font designed specifically for the logo (Tourism New Zealand Spokesperson 2006). In order to protect the tagline, Tourism New Zealand has actively sought copyright protection in each of its major source markets, including: New Zealand; Australia; the EU; US; Japan; Singapore; Taiwan; China; India (in process in 2006); Thailand (in process); Korea (in process); and Hong Kong (in process). Despite the Paris Convention and TRIPS agreement being operational in these countries, according to Tourism New Zealand, the registration process has been quite different in each country (Tourism New Zealand Spokesperson 2006).

There is also evidence of 'copycat' promotional campaigns that would be more difficult to protect under international copyright law. For example, there is a striking similarity between the two storylines of respective television advertising campaigns for Melbourne (Victoria, Australia in 2001) and Wellington (New Zealand in 2005). The 'Romantic Melbourne' campaign made a 'conscious move to extend beyond rational attributes to emotional brand attributes, in a bid for Melbourne to become synonymous with sophistication, style and romance' (Destination Melbourne 2006: n.p.). Meanwhile, the 'Have a Love Affair with Wellington' campaign set out to sell 'the idea of coming to Wellington and falling in love with the city' (Positively Wellington Tourism 2006: n.p.). In both campaigns the central theme is very similar; it revolves around a 20– or 30–something female appearing to have an affair while on holiday; an affair which turns out to be with the destination she is visiting. It might be argued that these two cities are not in direct competition and that the campaigns were developed nearly five years apart to meet very similar market profiles and perceptions in their own country. As such, there would appear to be no issue here. Conversely, there is perhaps the argument that Melbourne has some rights over the idea of branding a place using this particular storyline based on precedent, originality and creativity.

CONCLUSION

At the present time, tourism destinations are facing an awkward challenge. In an era of globalisation, it is easier to disseminate local differences and unique selling propositions to international markets aided and abetted by quicker, ever wider-reaching information technologies; however, the quicker the circulation, the sooner the most appealing aspects will be copied and appear in a competitor's portfolio. Place promotional efforts clearly need protection and there appear to be real benefits in using copyright laws to their fullest extent in major source markets. Place promoters and destination marketers invest considerable sums to develop compelling, eye-catching destination brands and campaigns that will make their destinations stand out in the 'promotional crowd', and in this respect it makes clear sense that they should seek to protect their investments from copyright infringements or piracy. Successful protection comes from a strong brand and the wherewithal to undertake protection of this brand. A lack of awareness of the legal instruments available to them and/or the unavailability of funds are two possible reasons why many of them do not exercise their rights and follow legal courses of action. In the case of resourcing, this is perhaps somewhat to be expected. Much place promotion is undertaken by public sector bodies in the guise of national, regional or local tourism organisations and their activities are supported by the public purse. Such legal actions are expensive, they would most likely be underwritten by publicly funded budgets, and there would be questions as to whether such action would be in the public interest, especially if an expensive action were to fail.

Still, although the protection of the intellectual property of place remains rather confusing, there are signs that the situation is changing. There is a long history of protection for geographical indications of source and copyright laws to help protect the intellectual property of place in promotional campaigns, brands and taglines. Some regions, such as Champagne, are starting to assert their rights and their experiences offer clear lessons for others to follow. Bodies such as WIPO and several international treaties and agreements provide an extensive framework to guide promotional work. Other aspects remain fluid and in need of clarification. WIPO acknowledges that country place names are an area of some concern and interest, especially given that there are dimensions of place that lie beyond current intellectual property protection. Place.coms are an area that will undoubtedly see ongoing debate and disputes as the World Wide Web continues to expand and more places take advantage of its flexibility, as well as the opportunities it presents for quick and cheap reproduction and transmission of information. Perhaps one of the as yet most unforeseen implications is that there will be winners and losers among the destinations in these place wars played out in the courts. Some regions may also have a natural advantage, especially where existing registered geographical indications are in place for food and wine products. These places have the protection afforded by the Paris Convention, Lisbon Agreement and TRIPS and therefore have an obvious route to protection of their intellectual property of place. These and others may also have an advantage because they have already identified how their cultural capital (namely their food, wine, traditional knowledge and their associated customs) sets them apart from other places.

Discussion questions

■ What mechanisms are available for destination marketers to protect their intellectual property of place from use by competing destinations?

■ What might limit a destination's ability to use laws protecting the intellectual property of place to protect their place name?

■ Do you think it is fair that countries do not have automatic rights to their place.com? Explain your reasons.

REFERENCES

ACCI (2005) Intellectual property rights and geographical indications. Australian Chamber of Commerce and Industry issues paper. Online. Available from: http://www.acci.asn.au/text_files/issues_papers/E%20Commerce/October %2005%20-20Intellectual%20Property%20Rights.pdf (accessed: 05/10/06).

Barke, M. and Harrop, K. (1994) 'Selling the industrial town: identity, image and illusion', in J. Gold and S. Ward (eds) *Place Promotion: the Use of Publicity and Marketing to Sell Towns and Regions.* Chichester: John Wiley and Sons.

Charters, S. (2006) *Wine and Society: The Social and Cultural Context of a Drink.*Oxford: Elsevier/Butterworth-Heinemann.

CIVC (2003) *L'Appellation Champagne.* Epernay: CIVC.

—— (2006) *The Appellation d'Origine Contrôlée.* Online. Available from: http://www.champagne.fr/en_aoc_resume.html (accessed: 23/06/06).

Cook, I. and Crang, P. (1996) 'The world on a plate: culinary cultures, displacement and geographical knowledges', *Journal of Material Culture*, 1(2): 131–53.

Destination Melbourne (2006) *Brand Melbourne.* Online. Available from: http://www.destinationmelbourne.com.au/index.php?sectionID=6898&pageID=6906 (accessed: 27/12/06).

Duval Smith, A. (2004) 'Champagne battle set to bubble over', *The Observer*, 26/09/04. Online . Available from: http://www.guardian.co.uk/france/story/0,,1312898,00.html (accessed: 24/12/06).

EU (2006) Council adopts improved rules on agricultural quality products. Press release, IP/06/339 (20/03/2006). Online. Available from: http://europa.eu/rapid/pressReleasesAction.do?reference=IP/06/339&format=HTML&aged=0&language=EN&guiLanguage=en (accessed: 30/10/06).

Gladstones, J. and Smart, R. (1999) 'Terroir', in J. Robinson (ed.) *The Oxford Companion to Wine.* Oxford: Oxford University Press.

Guy, K.M. (2003) *When Champagne Became French: Wine and the Making of a National Identity.* Baltimore: Johns Hopkins University Press.

Hall, C.M. (1996) 'Wine tourism in New Zealand', in J. Higham (ed.) *Proceedings of Tourism Down Under II: a Research Conference.* Dunedin: University of Otago.

Hall, C.M and Mitchell, R.D. (2002) 'The tourist terroir of New Zealand wine: the importance of region in the wine tourism experience', in A. Montanari (ed.) *Food and Environment: Geographies of Taste*. Rome: Societá Geografica Italiana.

—— (2008) *Wine Marketing*. Oxford: Elsevier/Butterworth-Heinemann.

Hall, C.M., Mitchell, R. and Sharples, E. (2003) 'Consuming places: the role of food, wine and tourism in regional development', in C.M. Hall, E. Sharples, R. Mitchell, B. Cambourne and N. Macionis (eds) *Food Tourism around the World: Development, Management and Markets*. Oxford: Butterworth-Heinemann.

Halliday, J. (1998) *Wine Atlas of Australia and New Zealand*. Sydney: Harper Collins.

Harrison, L. (2001) US dotcom keeps ownership of SouthAfrica.com. *The Register*, 12/07/01. Online. Available from: http://www.theregister.co.uk/2001/07/12/us_dotcom_keeps_ownership/ (accessed: 05/10/06).

Hashimoto, A. and Telfer, D.J. (2006) 'Selling Canadian culinary tourism: branding the global and the regional product', *Tourism Geographies*, 8(1): 31–55.

Her Majesty the Queen versus Virtual Countries Inc (2002). WIPO arbitration and mediation center, administrative panel decision case no. D2002-0754, 27 November 2002.

ICANN (1998) *Bylaws For Internet Corporation for Assigned Names and Numbers*. Online. available from: http://www.icann.org/general /archive-bylaws/bylaws-06nov98.htm (accessed: 26/12/06).

McCarthy, K. (2003) NZ.gov coughs up NZ$1m for newzealand.com. *The Register*, 1/05/03. Online. available at: http://www.theregister.co.uk/2003/05/01/nz_gov_coughs_up_nz/ (accessed: 20/05/06).

Mitchell, R.D. (2004) 'Scenery and chardonnay': a visitor perspective of the New Zealand winery experience. Unpublished PhD thesis, University of Otago, New Zealand.

Moran, W. (1993) 'Rural space as intellectual property', *Political Geography*, 12(3): 32–51.

One News (2006). Rip-off images hurt Rippon Vineyard. *One News*, Television New Zealand, 15/06/06. Online. Available from: http://tvnz.co.nz/view/page/411419/750575 (accessed: 16/06/06).

Positively Wellington Tourism (2006) *Have a Love Affair with Wellington' is a Winner*. Online. Available from: http://www.wellingtonnz.com/Media/Media+Archives/Have+a+Love+Affair+with+Wellington+is+a+Winner.htm (accessed: 27/12/06).

Ray, C. (1999) 'Towards a meta-framework of endogenous development: repertoires, paths, democracy and rights', *Sociologia Ruralis,* 39(4): 522–31.

Relph, E. (1996) 'Place', in I. Douglas, R. Huggett and M. Robinson (eds) *Companion Encyclopaedia of Geography: the Environment and Humankind*. London: Routledge.

Tourism New Zealand Spokesperson (2006) 100% Pure New Zealand: Tourism New Zealand and Intellectual Property: Protecting a Destination. Unpublished report. Wellington: Tourism New Zealand.

Urry, J. (1990) *The Tourist Gaze: Leisure and Travel in Contemporary Societies*. London: Sage.

Urry, J. (2005) 'The "consuming" of place', in A. Jaworski and A. Pritchard (eds) *Discourse, Communication, and Tourism*. Clevedon: Channel View Publications.

Virtual Countries Inc. versus Republic of South Africa (2001) United States District Court, S.D. New York. No. 00 Civ. 8448(AGS), 18 June 2001.

WIPO (1999) The management of internet names and addresses: intellectual property issues: final report of the WIPO internet domain name process. Online. Available from: http://www.icann.org/wipo/FinalReport_2.html (accessed: 21/12/06).

—— (2001) Intellectual property, the internet and electronic commerce: virtual identifiers: domain names, trademarks, branding on the internet, and dispute resolution. *International Conference on Intellectual Property, the Internet, Electronic Commerce and Traditional Knowledge Report (WIPO/ECTK/SOF/01/1.1)* Sofia, Bulgaria, 29–31 May 2001. Online. Available from: www.wipo.org/edocs/mdocs/innovation/en/wipo_ectk_sof_01/wipo_ectk_sof_01_1_1.pdf (accessed: 20/05/06).

— (2003) *Final Report of the Second WIPO Internet Domain Name Process*. Online. Available from: http://arbiter.wipo.int/processes/process2/ report/index.html (accessed: 01/12/06).

— (2004a) *What is Intellectual Property?* Online. Available at: http://www.wipo.int/about-ip/en/ (accessed: 21/05/06).

— (2004b) *WIPO-administered Treaties*. Online. Available at: http://www.wipo.int/treaties/en/ (accessed: 01/09/06).

— (2006a), *About geographical indications.* Online. Available at: http://www.wipo.int/about-ip/en/about_geographical_ind.html#P16_1100 (accessed: 21/05/06).

— (2006b) Domain name dispute resolution service. Online. Available at: http://www.wipo.int/amc/en/domains/index.html (accessed: 21/12/06).

— (2006c) WIPO responds to significant cybersquatting activity in 2005. WIPO Press Release Number 435, 25 January 2006, Geneva.

WTO (2006a) *Understanding the WTO: The Agreements Intellectual Property: Protection and Enforcement.* Online. Available at: http://www.wto.org/english/thewto_e/whatis_e/tif_e/agrm7_e.htm (accessed: 01/12/06).

— (2006b) *The Doha Declaration Explained.* Online. Available at: http://www.wto.org/english/tratop_e/dda_e/dohaexplained_e.htm (accessed: 01/12/06).

Zukin, S. (1991) *Landscapes of Power: From Detroit to Disney World.* Berkeley: University of California Press.

Sports facilities and transnational corporations: anchors of urban tourism development

12

Daniel Mason, Greg Ramshaw and Tom Hinch

Learning objectives

After considering this chapter, you will be able to:

- explain the role of sports facilities in new and rejuvenated urban tourism spaces;
- describe the form and dimensions of tourism bubbles based on sports;
- identify relationships between sports franchises and international businesses to produce tourism spaces.

Key terms

- tourist bubbles;
- urban regeneration;
- stadia;
- convention centres;
- transnational corporations (TNCs).

INTRODUCTION: SPORT, TNCs AND THE 'NEW' AMERICAN CITY

Increasingly, cities are engaging in competition with one another, at a number of different levels. As Begg observed (1999: 798–9), 'the capacity of a city to compete is shaped by an interplay between the attributes of cities as locations and the strengths and weaknesses of the firm and other economic agents active within them'. Within this context, sports facilities have emerged as key components of revitalization strategies for the downtown cores of competitive post-industrial North American cities (Fainstein and Judd 1999), where patterns of development revolve around the creation of new infrastructure, including convention centres, sport stadiums and arenas, and retail shopping facilities that draw citizens and tourists alike (Burbank *et al.* 2001). These amenities serve as anchors for rejuvenating other business and cultural components of downtown areas, and typically feature one or more newer sport facilities for major league professional sports teams, combined with retail areas featuring shopping outlets and restaurants chains of large, TNCs such as Starbucks and the Hard Rock Café.

To a large degree, it is the manner through which local communities are able to combine and position these facilities and services that determines the success of such development projects. Thus, the purpose of this chapter is to review the inter-relationships between sports facilities that anchor larger urban redevelopment initiatives and the TNCs that seek to align their own business interests with these tourism spaces by placing their own stores into new retail spaces and/or by raising awareness of their products, brands and services through sponsorships, naming rights and other branding initiatives. To accomplish this, we examine cases of recent urban development projects in the United States, and we explore the degree to which sport and international business interests have figured in the creation and implementation of tourism bubbles designed to revitalize the downtown cores of larger urban centres.

GLOBALIZATION, TRANSNATIONALISM AND TOURISM DEVELOPMENT IN COMPETITIVE CITIES

Globalization remains a highly contested and debated term. For the purposes of our analysis, we have chosen to borrow Keating's (2001: 372) definition: that is, globalization is 'a bundle of effects including freer international trade, capital mobility, and the rise of transnational corporations'. Kotler *et al.* (1993: 346) have argued that as a result of globalization we are living in a time of 'place wars'. They advise that, 'places must learn to think more like businesses, developing products, markets, and customers'. However, it is not just the spaces where flows of capital accumulate that have become more competitive; the global marketplace has also increased the presence and competitiveness of those businesses that seek to sell their products and services. It is within this context that TNCs have emerged as significant actors. TNCs are large organisations whose business interests exist in one or more countries other than the one in which they were originally incorporated. They often produce, market and sell their products and services in various locations throughout the world, and can generate revenues that rival or exceed the gross domestic products of individual countries.

Set against this backdrop of globalization and the emergence of TNCs, American cities have witnessed a movement away from traditional production activities such as manufacturing, towards economic development that attracts consumption activities, including tourism, entertainment, leisure and sports (Burbank *et al.* 2001). This transformation away from declining 'traditional' industries such as manufacturing does not necessarily guarantee the future success of cities in the global marketplace. Rather it leads to the question: 'how then, does the generic city, one with a range of suitable but not extraordinary attractions, market itself to compete with other similar cities?' (Holcomb 1999: 56).

One of the most popular strategies used in these place wars is the conscious repositioning of cities. As Page and Hall (2003: 309) put it:

> In the case of urban re-imaging, marketing practices, such as branding, rely upon the commodification of particular aspects of place, exploiting, reinventing or creating place images in order to sell the place as a destination product for tourists or investment.

By harnessing the cultural dimensions of sport, place marketers have, in one very specific manner, attempted to commodify the 'ways of living' in a place, while at the same time tapping into the popularity of sport in our globalized society. In other words, sport is used as tourist attraction which, in turn, is used as a way of re-imaging the city.

Evidence from US cities would suggest that there are, in fact, two basic strategies in operation in this respect. In 1998, the National League of Cities conducted a national survey of the mayors' offices of 1,110 US cities to find out how cities were using tourism to build their local economies. Its results suggested that cities generally were simultaneously developing and marketing local culture through events and cultural activities, while (further) constructing an infrastructure of facilities. The types of infrastructure routinely developed were 'convention centers, sports stadiums, renovated waterfronts, festival malls, farmers' markets, historic districts, entertainment districts, museums, and performing arts centers' (Judd et al. 2003: 52). Judd (1999) has argued that the new race to build various entertainment/tourism amenities has rivalled that of the railroad wars of the nineteenth century, when cities fought to become hubs of a new transportation system. However, contemporary competition between cities has arisen due to a movement away from federal support for urban development initiatives, which has created new fiscal issues and responsibilities for civic leaders (Judd 1999). Thus, tourism has emerged as an ideal strategy for cities, because it is perceived as having few barriers to entry and the potential for significant returns on investment.

It is not only the largest or most popular urban centres that have adopted this strategy; even cities that would seem to be unlikely tourism destinations have attempted to reinvent themselves (Fainstein and Judd 1999). In doing so, these cities have actively selected to have tourism figure squarely and prominently in their broader development programmes. This follows Porter's (2001: 140) thinking where he notes that the competitive advantage of urban economies is typically derived from the pursuit of cluster-specific initiatives:

> Clusters are groups of interconnected firms and industries in the same field that arise in particular economic areas. Clusters arise because of local externalities of various sorts including the benefits of proximity for many types of interfirm transactions (especially those involving ideas and technology) as well as access to specialized institutions and outputs.

City governments pursuing tourism-based development strategies are willing to dedicate substantial resources towards comprehensive infrastructure projects in order to reposition themselves on a global stage. For example, Judd (1999) reported that over a ten-year period between the mid-1970s and mid-1980s in the US alone, more than 250 new convention centres, sports facilities and community and performing arts centres were built, at a cost of over US$10 billion.

In creating defined tourism space within the downtown core of redeveloping post-industrial cities, a 'tourism bubble' is created, typically consisting of sporting, meeting, shopping and entertainment facilities. These bubbles allow tourists to enjoy the local amenities, while they are at the same time shielded from the original, surrounding community. In the next section of the chapter, we outline the basic characteristics of each form. For the purposes of our discussion, we have chosen to use examples from the United States for two inter-related reasons: first, as Altshuler and Luberoff (2003: 1) have noted, 'viewed internationally, American cities are unique – extraordinarily self-reliant in relation to higher level governments, but also extraordinarily dependent on private sector investment decisions'; and second, allied to decentralised, independent modes of urban governance, 'American cities are conspicuous for the emphasis they place on growth and in the intensity with which they compete with each other for it' (Altshuler and Luberoff 2003: 1). In other words, the US provides an ideal venue to examine this issue, as both the reliance upon private sector investment – such as that provided by TNCs – and the competitiveness between cities have created an environment where many larger US cities have actively pursued (and have had to pursue) sport-related tourism and urban development strategies.

Stadia

Over the past two decades, the prominent place of sport within tourism development initiatives has become readily apparent in the proliferation of publicly funded sports facilities. For example, in the United States over the last decade alone, more than 50 major league teams received subsidies totalling in excess of US$6 billion from local governments for the construction of stadia and arenas (Brown and Paul 2002). By the end of 2002, it was estimated that 60 per cent of the 121 major sport franchises in North America would be playing in facilities built or remodelled since 1991 (Kennedy and Rosentraub 2000). Competition among cities to acquire or retain sports franchises has forced local governments to up the ante or risk losing their teams (Friedman and Mason 2004). This has resulted in cities paying substantial amounts for stadia, despite the existence of independent research suggesting that professional sports teams and their facilities provide little or no economic benefits to the regions that host them (e.g. Rosentraub 1997).

Moreover, although some if not many franchises have arguably appeared to have had a negligible economic impact, local governments have continued to incorporate sports stadia into broader development projects. This is because cities continue to rely on favourable consulting reports that claim positive economic impacts, and sports facilities can serve as the large-scale anchor for a more comprehensive development project. In particular, stadia have been employed in projects that concentrate on the revitalization of blighted downtown cores by drawing in tourism and other forms of investment. To do so, the construction of facilities has been achieved by designing them to 'fit' with the existing environment. According to Fainstein and Judd (1999: 11), as a consequence:

> Virtually all the second-tier cities of the industrial age possess interesting architecture and a marketable past, but much of the built environment that signifies their past was abandoned and left to dereliction or renewed into oblivion decades ago. These cities have been forced to construct a new narrative of regeneration and a physical infrastructure that evokes that narrative.

In keeping with this sentiment, stadium construction in the past 15 years has attempted to reinvent local areas by creating 'retro' sports facilities reminiscent of early periods of prosperity in a city, but which fit into the 'new/old' (dual) image created in revitalized areas.

Convention centres

In post-industrial cities, to attract and retain visitors to tourist bubbles requires a multifaceted approach. In many cases, a convention centre is as integral to redevelopment as a new stadium or a shopping district. Convention centres are often located adjacent to major sports facilities, hotels and shopping districts so that all the major attractions and services are provided in one district. However, unlike 'retro' ballparks and historic districts, these centres must look 'state-of-the-art' to attract new clientele (and to bring back existing visitors). This frequently leads to a pastiche of the old and the new in tourist bubbles. While stadium construction has enjoyed a boom in the 1990s through to today, civic leaders focused their efforts on convention centre construction during the late 1980s. For example, Petersen (2001) noted that between 1985 and 1989, 19 convention centres with over 100,000 square feet of exhibit space were built in the US. This was followed by 9 built between 1990 and 1995, and another 9 through 1999 (for a total of 37).

Convention centres appeal intuitively to cities due to the spending habits of visitors. As Petersen (2001: 13) observes:

> Conventions, with or without exhibits, have high economic impact because attendees normally stay three to four days and nights in the host city. In addition to spending money on transportation and accommodations, attendees purchase goods and services from restaurants, retail shops, and local attractions.

However, convention centres are not automatically good choices for the use of public funds for tourism development. This is because, unlike a sports team, which usually signs a long-term lease with a city for the use of a stadium or arena, a convention facility has no long-term tenants, which makes it difficult for cities to hedge against the risk that a the facility will be underused (Altshuler and Luberoff 2003). In contrast, a city plans around the 80-plus dates a year that a baseball team will use a stadium and the sports franchise adds to the development of distinctive place identities and associations.

To increase usage and ensure greater revenues, convention centres have started to align themselves with TNCs. Baltimore's (Maryland) Convention Centre, for example, features a Starbucks within the facility. Most of the hotels surrounding convention centres are 'chain' hoteliers such as Hilton or Radisson. In addition, most of the stores and services surrounding these centres are both familiar and require little effort to access, meaning that visitors rarely stray too far away from the district, therefore concentrating their spending within a confined area.

Shopping and consumerism

A common and indeed necessary component of the tourism experience in redeveloped downtown spaces is a large shopping district that taps into the synergies of the other local amenities, including sports and convention facilities. In doing so, tourist spending tends to be completely captured within a defined space, as those attending conventions or sporting events can enjoy dining, shopping and other forms of entertainment within a convenient perimeter of other city infrastructure. As a result, most urban redevelopment projects seek to incorporate shopping hubs within broader redevelopment initiatives, thereby providing a platform for TNCs to position their products and services directly for tourism consumption. A key to the success of these shopping districts is the incorporation of an overarching narrative that ties the consumer experience together, as 'shopping increasingly occurs in ... special central city districts that use defined themes purposefully to entice consumers' (Gottdiener 2001: 3). However, it is important to note here that the ways in which convention, sports and retail facilities are combined together in a single project can dramatically affect the synergies (i.e. tourism revenues accrued) that develop. As Petersen (2001: 47) argued:

> The difference between being close to and remote from a unique mix of sports facilities is reflected in actual surveys of delegates' retail spending, which ranges from less than $50 per attendee in destinations where specialty shops are either mundane or remote from the centre to over $200 where centers are located near shops that offer unusual and attractive merchandise.

Thus, the arrangement of amenities within the urban landscape may be just as important as the variety of facilities available.

In addition to shops and themed restaurants, TNCs also associate with sports franchises and stadiums found within the tourism bubbles through naming rights agreements, on-site signage, and sponsorship arrangements. A frequent synergy between sport and consumer products involves beverages. Most often, this involves the negotiation of pouring rights, where a beverage company negotiates to have their product served exclusively at a team's stadium or arena, or within a designated tourism space. For example, PepsiCo paid $15 million to the New England Patriots to be the exclusive non-alcoholic beverage at Gillette Stadium from 2002–2012 (Sports Venue Technology 2004). This is unusual, particularly in the National Football League (NFL), where Coca-Cola is a league sponsor and has a virtual monopoly on pouring rights (Sports Venue Technology 2004). Other non-alcoholic beverage providers negotiate pouring rights. For example, Starbucks recently paid

Table 12.1 *Beverage associations for major league stadia, United States*

Stadium name	Opened	Type of beverage	Location	Sport
Arrowhead Pond	1993	Bottled water	Anaheim	Hockey
Pepsi Centre	1999	Soft drink	Denver	Hockey/Basketball
Coors Field	1995	Beer	Denver	Baseball
Minute Maid Park	2000	Orange juice	Houston	Baseball
Miller Park	2001	Beer	Milwaukee	Baseball
Busch Stadium	2006	Beer	St Louis	Baseball
Tropicana Field	1990	Orange juice	Tampa	Baseball

Source: Adapted from Munsey and Suppes (2006).

up to $5 million for exclusive coffee-serving rights at Radio City Music Hall and Madison Square Garden in New York City (Thomaselli 2003). Similar arrangements have to be made with alcoholic beverage providers, with Anheuser-Busch being a leading supplier in the US (Parlin 2003).

Table 12.1 provides an overview of stadia in the US that have beverage associations through their naming agreements, while Table 12.2 describes naming rights changes and the industries represented by sponsors. Stadium naming rights routinely involve transnational beverage providers. For example, the National Hockey League's (NHL) Colorado Avalanche and the National Basketball Association's (NBA) Denver Nuggets play at the Pepsi Arena, while Major League Baseball's (MLB) St Louis Cardinals play at Busch Stadium, named after the Anheuser-Busch brewery. However, naming rights can also have detrimental effects for both sponsors and teams (Moorman 2002) and, in some cases, can sever the bond fans feel for their home stadium (see case-study vignette).

CASE-STUDY VIGNETTE – TOURISM AND INTERNATIONAL BUSINESS IN ACTION

Naming rights and the 2006 FIFA World Cup in Germany

Naming rights and corporate tie-ins are not a uniquely North American phenomenon and they are important sources of income for teams in various sports and at differing levels. For the FIFA World Cup, facilities have to be at their best for incoming fans and in order to provide the host country with a legacy. So, in the years before Germany 2006 new and updated stadiums were leveraged partly by future earnings from the selling of naming rights. Perhaps more of a shock for German fans and local communities was that prior to the start of the World Cup, FIFA announced that eight of the stadiums would need to

Continued

Table 12.2 *Examples of stadium name changes, before and after corporate involvement, United States*

Team	Sport	Home	Old stadium name	New stadium name	New stadium?	New sponsor interest
Lakers/Clippers/Kings	Basketball/Hockey	Los Angeles	Great Western Forum	Staples Center	Yes	Office supplies
Bulls/Blackhawks	Basketball/Hockey	Chicago	Chicago Stadium	United Center	Yes	Airline
Nets/Devils	Basketball/Hockey	New Jersey	Meadowlands Arena	Continental Airlines Arena	No	Airline
Penguins	Hockey	Pittsburgh	Civic Arena	Mellon Arena	No	Financial services
Seahawks	Football	Seattle	Kingdome	Qwest Field	Yes	Telecommunications
Panthers	Football	Charlotte	n/a	Bank of America Stadium	Yes	Financial services
Wizards/Capitals	Basketball/Hockey	Washington	USAir Arena	Verizon Center	Yes	Telecommunications
Athletics/Raiders	Baseball/Football	Oakland	Oakland Coliseum	McAfee Coliseum	No	Computer Software
Reds	Baseball	Cincinnati	Riverfront Stadium	Great American Ballpark	Yes	Insurance

Continued

Table 12.2 *Continued*

Team	Sport	Home	Old stadium name	New stadium name	New stadium?	New sponsor interest
Chargers	Football	San Diego	Jack Murphy Stadium	Qualcomm Park	No	Telecommunications
Tigers	Baseball	Detroit	Tiger Stadium	Comerica Park	Yes	Financial services
Timberwolves	Basketball	Minneapolis	n/a	Target Center	Yes	Retail chain
Rockets	Basketball	Houston	Compaq Centre	Toyota Center	Yes	Automobile manufacturer
Lightning	Hockey	Tampa	Thunderdome	St Pete Times Forum	Yes	Newspaper
Jaguars	Football	Jacksonville	Gator Bowl	ALLTEL Stadium	No	Telecommunications
White Sox	Baseball	Chicago	Comisky Park	US Cellular Field	Yes	Telecommunications
Mavericks/Stars	Basketball/Hockey	Dallas	Reunion Arena	American Airlines Arena	Yes	Airline
Steelers	Football	Pittsburgh	Three Rivers Stadium	Heinz Field	Yes	Food manufacturer

Source: Adapted from Munsey and Suppes (2006).

be renamed for the duration of the competition. Seven were called 'FIFA stadiums' while in Nuremburg, the Franken Stadion (Franconia Stadium) was allowed to revert to its pre-sponsorship name. A further four stadiums – the Gottlieb Daimler Stadion (Stuttgart), Fritz Walter Stadion (Kaiserslautern), Centralstadion (Leipzig) and Olympiastadion (Berlin) – were allowed to keep their names (Wilson 2006).

According to one source (Wilson 2006), FIFA stood to gain €700 million from naming rights during the tournament: the 15 sponsors (including Adidas, Coca-Cola and Yahoo) spent around €40m each to be named an 'Official Partner' while six 'National Sponsors' (such as Deutsche Bahn and EnBW energy group) paid €13m each for exclusive local rights. These make for stark comparisons with the annual fees for naming rights (Table 12.3).

In effect, FIFA had bought temporary exclusivity to ensure its partners and sponsors 'clean' spaces and each stadium had to be handed over in a 'neutral' condition to its external perimeter (Wilson 2006). In some cases such as the Allianz and AOL Arenas this meant physically removing the large lettering and logos that cost HSV Hamburg €500k in direct compensation to AOL (Wilson 2006).

What's not clear is what the stadium owners or their corporate patrons were paid as compensation for FIFA's temporary exclusivity. To put this into context, though, one naming rights marketing and sponsorship research firm calculated that each regular partner would lose US$25.1 million brand value per televised match (FRMS 2006). It was estimated that name and brand identity would have received around 64 seconds of in-broadcast exposure per game from such sources as exterior and interior stadium signage and verbal mentions (FRMS 2006). So, if these figures are correct, for the iconic Allianz Arena, this may have meant lost brand value to Allianz of US$150 million as a result of restrictions during the World Cup. What's more because Allianz is not a sponsor of the UEFA Champions League, for all of the fixtures of FC Bayern München, the stadium has to be temporarily referred to as the Fussball Arena München. Now, what could a team do with a share of extra advertising revenue? A new striker perhaps?

Questions

- What other corporate tie-ins, naming rights, sponsorship deals and the like can you identify in different sports and in other countries?
- What are some of the potential disadvantages of corporate sponsorship and naming rights for the team and for the destination image?
- What are some of the difficulties associated in researching the value of corporate sponsorship and naming rights of sports teams and their impact on the businesses and destinations involved?

Table 12.3 Name changes during FIFA 2006 World Cup in Germany

Name prior to FIFA 2006	Cost of regular naming rights (€)	Type of business	Stadium name during FIFA 2006	Games in FIFA 2006 World Cup
Allianz Arena	5,800,000	Insurance and banking	FIFA World Cup Stadium, Munich	6
AWD Arena	1,400,000	Financial services	FIFA World Cup Stadium, Hannover	5
AOL Arena	3,000,000	Internet services and media	FIFA World Cup Stadium, Hamburg	5
Veltins Arena	n/a	Brewing	FIFA World Cup Stadium, Gelsenkirchen	5
Signal Iduna Park	n/a	Insurance	FIFA World Cup Stadium, Dortmund	6
RheinEnergie Stadion	n/a	Energy	FIFA World Cup Stadium, Cologne	5
Commerzbank Arena	n/a	Bank	FIFA World Cup Stadium, Frankfurt	5
EasyCredit Stadion	1,800,000	Bank (credit card)	Frankenstadion (Nuremburg)	5

Source: Adapted from Wilson (2006) and FRMS (2006).

TOURISM AND SPORT IN SELECT US CITIES

In the next section we present three examples of the relationships between cities, sports facilities and TNCs. However, it should be noted from the outset that, 'American cities exist in a substantially different policy environment than European cites because American local government is more dependent on cooperation with business to carry out projects such as downtown redevelopment or to maintain the local tax base' (Mossberger and Stoker 2001: 819). We have also chosen to compare cases where there are differences between cities based on attempts by local officials to exploit unique community characteristics integral to their identity (Begg 1999).

Baltimore, Maryland

The redevelopment of Baltimore's Inner Harbor during the late 1980s and early 1990s 'provides an excellent example of a pure tourist space carved out of urban decay' (Judd 1999: 36). The cornerstone of this redevelopment was the construction of Oriole Park at Camden Yards (OPCY), home of MLB's Baltimore Orioles. Designed by architectural firm Hellmuth, Obata and Kassabaum (HOK 2004), the defining feature of OPCY is its 'retro' design, relying on the nostalgia for ballparks from an earlier era:

> Oriole Park is state-of-the-art yet unique, traditional and intimate in design. It blends with the urban context of downtown Baltimore while taking its image from baseball parks built in the early 20th century. Steel, rather than concrete trusses, an arched brick facade, a sun roof over the gentle slope of the upper deck, an asymmetrical playing field, and natural grass turf are just some of the features that tie it to those magnificent big league ballparks built in the early 1900's. Ebbets Field (Brooklyn), Shibe Park (Philadelphia), Fenway Park (Boston), Crosley Field (Cincinnati), Forbes Fields (Pittsburgh), Wrigley Field (Chicago), and The Polo Grounds (New York) were among the ballparks that served as powerful influences in the design of Oriole Park.
>
> (Baltimore Orioles 2004: n.p.).

The building of OPCY coincided with an influx of TNC investment in the Inner Harbor. These TNCs include such notable names as the Hard Rock Café, Barnes & Noble, and ESPN Zone (Friedman *et al.* 2004). Another major facet of the Inner Harbor redevelopment was the expansion and renovation of the Baltimore Convention Centre in 1996–7. The convention centre, located directly across from OPCY, is described as being nestled in a 'tourist's dream' (Baltimore Convention Centre, 2004). The football stadium used by the Baltimore Ravens of the NFL was constructed next to OPCY underscoring the claim that

> the two stadiums are now clearly connected to and are an integral part of the 'tourist bubble' that is downtown Baltimore's entertainment space. These facilities have made the list of must-see attractions for many visitors to the city, even on non-event days.
>
> (Chapin 2004: 201)

Cleveland, Ohio

Baltimore's Inner Harbor redevelopment, with two major sports facilities serving as anchors, has spurred similar initiatives in other post-industrial American cities. One such development was Cleveland's 'Gateway Project'. While conceived prior to completion of OPCY, the site, situated on the location of a derelict former marketplace, shares some common elements with Baltimore. Originally designed as a means of connecting the theatre district to the major shopping and office complex, 'the project evolved over the years to include a ballpark for [MLB's] Indians and an arena for the NBA's [National Basketball Association's] Cavaliers and other local teams' (Chapin 2004: 202). These two facilities – Jacobs Field for the Indians and Gund Arena for the Cavaliers – comprise the heart of this project. Nevertheless, the Gateway Project represented only a part of Cleveland's broader tourism development initiatives. Other projects from the early 1990s (year built, cost in US dollars) included: the Great Lakes Science Center (1996, $55 million); Rock and Roll Hall of Fame (1995, $92 million); Wyndham Hotel (1995, $27 million); Convocation Center at Cleveland State University (1991, $47 million); Society Bank/KeyCorp Tower Center (1991, $400 million); and Bank One Center (1991, $95 million) (Austrian and Rosentraub 1997).

Like Baltimore, Cleveland's tourist bubble has a high concentration of TNCs. For example, the hotels in the Gateway area include familiar chains such as Holiday Inn, Hyatt, Hilton,

Marriott, Comfort Inn, Radisson, and Ritz-Carlton (Convention and Visitors Bureau of Greater Cleveland 2004). Both have integrated the sporting facilities into the fabric of the city centre, rather than having the facilities dominate the city skyline (Chapin 2004), and both have incorporated elements of culture (museums, theatres) and heritage (historic districts) into these developments. Cleveland's Jacobs Field, like OPCY, is considered both a monument to baseball's past while simultaneously being a state-of-the-art facility designed with the comfort and convenience of the modern fan in mind (Cleveland Indians 2004). Perhaps it is not surprising that the architectural firm that designed OPCY, HOK, was commissioned to design Jacobs Field as well.

Wilson and Wouters (2003) have argued that in cities such as Cleveland improvements such as the Gateway Project should be enacted simply to stay competitive, but that these developments are so similar to other cities that they become homogeneous. In their comparison of the 'rust belt' cities of St Louis, Indianapolis and Cleveland, Wilson and Wouters (2003: 13) described the typical features of redevelopment as 'downtown gentrification, the transformation of the central business district to services, development of sports stadia and entertainment facilities, and waterfront redevelopment'.

St Louis, Missouri

St Louis is another post-industrial city that has redeveloped similarly to Baltimore and Cleveland. Laslo (2003: 1071) has described the key features of St Louis' redevelopment initiatives:

> Since the end of World War II, St. Louis has been successful in remaking itself in very much the same way that cities across North American have, by creating a new infrastructure devoted to tourism, meetings, and entertainment. Included in the new infrastructure have been two stadiums (with a third on the way), a festival mall, a downtown retail mall, an arena, an entertainment district, a convention centre and an expansion, a floating gaming casino, and recently, a headquarters convention centre hotel that is under construction. These components of the new urban infrastructure have replaced much of the obsolete warehouse and commercial space that was devoted to 19th-century commerce.

Parallels between redevelopment projects in St Louis, Baltimore and Cleveland are apparent. Like Cleveland and Baltimore, St Louis offers a large conglomeration of TNCs within its central tourism bubble. Chain hoteliers, such as Marriott, Sheraton, Hilton, and Radisson (St Louis Convention and Visitors Bureau 2004), share space with chain restaurants such as Hard Rock Café and Hooters. Stadium development is also a key factor, with three stadiums located in the central St Louis area: Busch Stadium (baseball), Edward Jones Dome (NFL) and Scottrade Center (ice hockey). In addition, MLB's St Louis Cardinals began play in the new Busch Stadium in the spring of 2006. Not only does this ballpark incorporate the 'retro' design made famous by OPCY (St Louis Cardinals 2006), it retains its corporate 'heritage' by retaining the name of the Anheuser-Busch brewery. In this, St Louis is unique by fusing the traditional ballpark design with TNC naming rights. Again, the HOK architectural firm was the designer of the new stadium, and it has also played a role in other redevelopment initiatives in the St Louis tourist bubble, specifically the Union Station redevelopment near the Scottrade Center (HOK 2004). Table 12.4 summarizes the similarities and differences between the three cases, but for Turner and Rosentraub (2002: 490–1), the look and feel of this redevelopment mirrors that of other American cities where a 'controlled district can reduce the unpredictability of the urban experience and give a faux-like presentation of a downtown. Today downtowns are branded with colour-coordinated logos, street sweeper uniforms, and trashcans … Downtown districts have become theme parks.'

ARE SPORTS FACILITIES WORTHWHILE INVESTMENTS FOR CITIES SEEKING TOURISM DEVELOPMENT?

Clearly, the tourism bubbles in Baltimore, Cleveland and St Louis share more similarities than differences in terms of the defining features outlined in Table 12.4. Not only do they feature the same 'retro' theme in terms of their sport stadiums, they also are characterized by shopping districts that are dominated by major TNCs. While the retro themes may draw on the unique heritage of each of these cities, the presence of TNCs such as Starbucks and the Hard Rock Café guarantee a common element between all three sites. Several other international corporations have a presence in at least two of these sites. The only major differences between these developments are the absence of a new convention centre in Cleveland and the presence of a theatre district in this same development. Of the three tourism bubbles, Cleveland would therefore appear to be the most distinct but in general, but the analysis would suggest that the similarities are greater than the differences.

An interesting dilemma therefore arises from the creation of tourism bubbles in urban centres such as Baltimore, Cleveland and St Louis; namely, if the tourism space is meant to be the principle signifier of a city, and if it is characterized by the presence of professional sports

Table 12.4 Examples of defining features for Baltimore, Cleveland and St Louis tourist bubbles

Defining features	Baltimore	Cleveland	St Louis
'Retro' ballpark	✓	✓	✓
HOK-designed projects	✓	✓	✓
ESPN zone	✓		
Hooters	✓		✓
Starbucks	✓	✓	✓
Barnes & Noble	✓		
Hilton Hotel		✓	✓
Hard Rock Café	✓	✓	✓
Museum	✓	✓	✓
New convention centre	✓		✓
Shopping district	✓	✓	✓
Theatre district		✓	

franchises and TNCs, then it becomes easier rather than harder for other cities to duplicate this image (Judd 1999). Somewhat paradoxically, by commodifying sport as a product for tourist consumption in a global economy, its power as a unique expression of local culture and identity may be threatened. This is compounded if professional sport franchises in these tourism bubbles are accompanied by shopping districts dominated by transnational chains and franchises, which by their inherent nature and design minimize differences rather than foster them. Put more harshly, Holcomb (1999: 69) noted that

> packaging and promoting the city to tourists can destroy its soul. The city is commodified, its form and spirit remade to conform to market demand, not residents' dreams. The local state and business elites collude to remake a city in which their special interests are paramount; meanwhile, resources are diverted from needy neighbourhoods and social services.

If this packaging does not differentiate from other cities with similar offerings, such as a retro ballpark or convention centre, and city-centre shopping is filled with transnational apparel companies, then the redevelopment may not confer a competitive advantage for the city. This begs the question: 'as cities come to increasingly resemble one another, do they strive even more vigorously to make a difference between themselves and the others?' (Blum 2003: 30). The answer to this is

> not altogether clear since many cities measure themselves by those they treat as comparable (in the 'global marketplace') in ways that make similarity to these others somewhat desirable. Still, if cities lose themselves to such a measure of comparability, they could risk losing a sense of their difference from the others.
>
> (Blum 2003: 30)

Thus, it remains to be seen what competitive advantages may be obtained by cities such as Baltimore, Cleveland and St Louis that have created tourism bubbles as part of broader urban redevelopment projects. As this chapter has demonstrated, evidence already exists that new tourism and economic development initiatives have not generated the impact that the respective cities had desired, even for those amenities that cannot be copied elsewhere.

Other issues also challenge the rationale for the tourism initiatives pursued by US cities. It has been argued that redeveloped retail areas offer local labour employment opportunities and draw local shopping expenditures from the suburbs back to the city proper. However, most of the jobs in shopping districts are low-paying, and there is little evidence that redeveloped shopping districts actually divert expenditures back to the city core from the suburbs. Despite the lack of supporting evidence, the prospect of employment and a revitalized downtown continue to spur public expenditures on central shopping districts. This continued push for redevelopment is occurring despite the fact that cities pursuing the same sport- and TNC-focused tourism development projects are not differentiating themselves from one another.

Thus, it will be difficult for cities to win these place wars by pursuing the type of tourism bubble strategy outlined in this chapter. On the other hand, perhaps Judd's use of the term 'tourist' may have been taken too literally. Perhaps the key battle in these place wars is not the one that is occurring between cities, as supported by hordes of invading tourists, but the one that occurs within each city, related to the challenge of bringing city residents back into the downtown cores and developing a positive community identity rather than necessarily a tourism image for external consumption. In a global society, urban residents may in fact be looking for reassurance that their home cities are linked into the global marketplace. In other words, if the citizens of communities such as Cleveland, Baltimore and St Louis see these initiatives as worthwhile uses of public funds, and redeveloped downtown cores make them feel that their cities are vibrant destinations for tourists and residents alike, then these projects are warranted. If this is not the case and cities really do want to be distinguishable from their competitors, the next phase, after incorporating new facilities into the downtown infrastructure, will be to identify and tap into those unique characteristics that each city possesses that will distinguish one post-industrial city from the next. In doing so, cities will be able to continue to provide tourism and resident experiences that cannot be easily duplicated, which will provide such cities with a means of sustaining competitive advantages in the future.

Discussion questions

- What distinctive tourism bubbles based on sports and international business can you identify in other countries? What sports and international businesses are present?
- What are the factors that lead to successes and failures in individual (re-)development projects involving a mix of sports, consumerism and international businesses?
- What are the risks for individual destinations of the serial reproduction of tourism bubbles based on sports and international business?

REFERENCES

Altshuler, A. and Luberoff, A. (2003) *Mega-projects: The Changing Politics of Urban Public Investment.* Washington, DC: Brookings Institution Press.

Austrian, Z. and Rosentraub, M.S. (1997) 'Cleveland's Gateway to the future', in R.G. Noll, and A. Zimbalist (eds) *Sports, Jobs, and Taxes: the Economic Impact of Sports Teams and Stadiums.* Washington, DC: Brookings Institution Press.

Baltimore Convention Centre (2004) About the centre. Online. Available from: http://www.bccenter.org/about/index.html (accessed: 06/10/04).

Baltimore Orioles (2004) Oriole Park history. Online. Available from: http://baltimore.orioles.mlb.com/bal/ballpark/index.jsp. (accessed: 17/09/07).

Begg, I. (1999) 'Cities and competitiveness', *Urban Studies,* 36: 795–809.

Blum, A. (2003) *The Imaginative Structure of the City.* Montreal: McGill-Queen's University Press.

Brown, C. and Paul, D.M. (2002) 'The political scorecard of professional sports facility referendums in the United States, 1984–2000', *Journal of Sport and Social Issues,* 26: 248–67.

Burbank, M.J., Andranovich, G.D. and Heying, C.H. (2001) *Olympic Dreams: The Impact of Mega-events on Local Politics.* Boulder, CO: Reinner Publishers.

Chapin, T.S. (2004) 'Sports facilities as urban redevelopment catalysts', *Journal of the American Planning Association*, 70(2): 191–209.

Cleveland Indians (2004) Jacobs Field: home of the Indians. Online. Available from: http://cleveland. indians.mlb.com/NASApp/mlb/cle/ballpark/ballpark_history.jsp (accessed: 07/10/04).

Convention and Visitors Bureau of Greater Cleveland (2004) City map of downtown Cleveland. Online. Available from: http://www.travelcleveland.com/ (accessed: 07/10/04).

Fainstein, S. and Judd, D.R. (1999) 'Global forces, local strategies, and urban tourism', in D.R. Judd and S.S. Fainstein (eds) *The Tourist City*. New Haven: Yale University Press.

Friedman, M.T. and Mason, D.S. (2004) 'A stakeholder approach to analyzing economic development decision making: public subsidies for professional sport facilities', *Economic Development Quarterly*, 18: 236–54.

Friedman, M.T., Mason, D.S., Andrews, D.L. and Silk, M.L. (2004) 'Sport and the façade of redevelopment in the postindustrial city', *Sociology of Sport Journal*, 21: 119–39.

FRMS (Front Row Marketing Services) (2006) Germanys World Cup stadium naming rights partners miss out on (US) $25.1 million of branding exposure. Press release. Online. Available from: http://www.pr.com/press-release/12864 (accessed: 20/06/07).

Gottdiener, M. (2001) *The Theming of America: American Dreams, Media Fantasies, and Themed Environments*, 2nd edn. Boulder, CO: Westview Press.

HOK (2004) Landmark projects: Oriole Park at Camden Yards. Online. Available from: http://www.hok.com/ Projects/LandmarkProjects/index.htm (accessed: 15/10/04).

Holcomb, B. (1999) 'Marketing cities for tourism', in D.R. Judd and S.S. Fainstein (eds) *The Tourist City*. New Haven: Yale University Press.

Judd, D.R. (1999) 'Constructing the tourist bubble', in D.R. Judd and S.S. Fainstein (eds) *The Tourist City*. New Haven: Yale University Press.

Judd, D.R., Winter, W., Barnes, W.R. and Stern, E. (2003) 'Tourism and entertainment as local economic development: a national survey', in D.R. Judd (ed.) *The Infrastructure of Play*. Armonk, NY: M.E. Sharpe.

Keating, M. (2001) 'Governing cities and regions: territorial restructuring in a global age', in A.J. Scott (ed.) *Global City-regions: Trends, Theory, Policy.* Oxford: Oxford University Press.

Kennedy, S.S. and Rosentraub, M.S. (2000) 'Public–private partnerships, professional sports teams, and the protection of the public's interests', *American Review of Public Administration*, 30: 436–59.

Kotler, P., Haider, D. H. and Rein, I. (1993) *Marketing Places: Attracting Investment, Industry, and Tourism to Cities, States and Nations*. New York: The Free Press.

Laslo, D.H. (2003) 'Policy communities and infrastructure of urban tourism', *American Behavioral Scientist*, 46(8): 1070–83.

Moorman, A.M. (2002) 'Naming rights agreements: dream deal or nightmare?', *Sport Marketing Quarterly*, 11(2): 126–7.

Mossberger, K. and Stoker, G. (2001) 'The evolution of urban regime theory: the challenge of conceptualization', *Urban Affairs Review*, 36: 810–35.

Munsey and Suppes (2006) Ballparks. Online. Available from: http://ballparks.com/ (accessed: 05/09/06).

Page, S.J. and Hall, C.M. (2003) *Managing Urban Tourism.* Harlow: Pearson Education Ltd.

Parlin, S. (2003) 'Pouring Rights Scoreboard', *Beverage Industry*, 94(7): 48.

Petersen, D.C. (2001) *Developing Sports, Convention, and Performing Arts Centers* 3rd edn. Washington, DC: Urban Land Institute.

Porter, M.E. (2001) 'Regions and the new economics of competition', A.J. Scott (ed.) *Global City-regions: Trends, Theory, Policy.* Oxford: Oxford University Press.

Rosentraub, M. (1997) 'The myth and reality of the economic development from sports', *Real Estate Issues*, 22: 24–9.

St Louis Cardinals (2006) New Busch Stadium: Home of the Cardinals. Online. Available from: http://stlouis.cardinals.mlb.com/NASApp/mlb/stl/ballpark/index.jsp (accessed: 08/09/06).

St Louis Convention and Visitors Bureau (2004) Downtown St Louis map. Online. Available from: http://www.explorestlouis.com/visitors/maps.asp (accessed: 17/10/04).

Sports Venue Technology (2004) Gillette Stadium, New England Patriots, Foxborough, MA, USA. Online. Available from: from http://www.sportsvenue-technology.com/projects/cmgi/ (accessed: 17/10/04).

Thomeselli, R. (2003) 'Starbucks inks pouring-rights deal', *Advertising Age*, 74(47): 8.

Turner, R.S. and Rosentraub, M.S. (2002) 'Tourism, sports and the centrality of cities', *Journal of Urban Affairs*, 24(5): 487–92.

Wilson, B. (2006) Stadiums renamed for FIFA sponsors. Online. Last updated: 06/06/06. Available from: http://news.bbc.co.uk/1/hi/business/4773843.stm (accessed: 18/06/07).

Wilson, D. and Wouters, J. (2003) 'Spatiality and growth discourse: the restructuring of America's Rust Belt Cities', *Journal of Urban Affairs*, 25(2): 123–38.

International car manufacturers, brandscapes and tourism: engineering the experience economy

13

Tim Coles

Learning objectives

After considering this chapter, you will be able to:

- understand why international car manufacturers use tourism in their brand architecture;
- identify the different types of tourism experience used to project international car brands;
- explain how tourism features in the experience economy.

Key terms

- car brands;
- international business;
- relationship marketing;
- experiential marketing;
- experience economy.

INTRODUCTION: A PLACE FOR TOURISM IN EXPERIENCING BRANDS

'Experience the perfect journey' was the lure of a recent BMW direct mail marketing campaign to launch its new 3-Series convertible. Gleaming in the bright sunshine and set against the dreamy backdrop of blown-out surf, the car offers its driver the prospects of thrills and adventure as the driver cruises down the coast road. After all, the interested reader is exhorted,

> What better way to fully appreciate the impressive performance and handling of the new BMW 3-Series Convertible than around the winding Amalfi coastal roads? Take the steep drive up to the picturesque village of Ravello and you will discover the Hotel Caruso, your charming accommodation for the next three nights .... To add a finishing touch to this unique experience you will also enjoy dinner at Rosselinis, the celebrated two Michelin starred restaurant in Ravello.
> (BMW 2007a: 2)

To the more cynical, this may just be another example of marketing hyperbole; for other, more seasoned observers, it is wholly consistent with the BMW's claim that it produces the 'Ultimate Driving Machine'. Taglines of this nature are highly effective because they can only be verified if the brand is consumed. The open road is where the essence of the brand will be experienced. Test drives are one option, but brand performance in an extra-ordinary setting will make for a more memorable experience, enhance its appeal and the (potential) customer's attachment to it (Boyle 2004).

Brands are key cultural features in the contemporary world, and are regarded as an expression of globalization, and as a major means through which individuals' identities are shaped and articulated (Lury 2004). Branded goods not only have direct utility but also, especially in the case of luxury car brands, owners derive cachet from their self-image and how others perceive their choices. Thus, for some commentators what the brands says about you, your lifestyle choices and preferences symbolically may be every bit as important as (in some cases more than) how the product or good functions (Johansson-Stenman and Martinsson 2006).

To some marketers, the creation of an emotional attachment to a brand is the basis of relationship marketing (Sheth and Parvatiyar 1995). This differs from the transactional focus of other, more traditional forms of marketing by stressing the importance of long-term, enduring relationships with customers to create value rather than mere customer capture, sales maximization and margin optimization (Schmitt 1999). For some companies therefore, brand engagement and loyalty in this manner may form a more predictable and hence sustainable basis on which to plan future business development. Relationship marketing has made its way into the armoury of techniques used by destination managers to nurture sustainable tourism futures (Fyall *et al.* 2003). What tends to be overlooked is that tourism is used as a promotional vehicle in many other sectors because consumers are offered the opportunity to build understanding and engagement by temporarily connecting with brands in controlled environments through visitor experiences. Dedicated brand landscapes ('brandscapes') have been developed by product and brand managers that are, in effect, destinations in their own right. Mitchell and Orwig (2002) suggest that such 'consumer experience tourism' is evident in the array of manufacturing plant tours, company museums and company visitor centres from diverse sectors that generate and galvanize bonds between consumers and producers. These same basic motives are evident in the efforts of German car manufacturers as major international businesses to build dynamic and enduring relationships between their brands and their customers through tourism. Beyond an identification of various forms of visitor activity designed to encapsulate the brand, this chapter explores how themed experiences communicate far more subtle and powerful messages about the brands themselves and how they are positioned with respect to the contemporary sector dynamics in the global automotive industry.

RELATIONSHIP MARKETING AND THE EXPERIENCE ECONOMY

Before the chapter turns to examine the approaches used by international car manufacturers, it is important to review some of the basic principles of relationship marketing and the experience economy. As Sheth and Parvatiyar (1995) note relationship marketing is far from new, but its widespread adoption over the last decade has signified a paradigm shift in marketing theory and praxis. At its simplest, relationship marketing is about building and maintaining long-term associations with consumers (and other marketing stakeholders) in order to deliver competitive advantage and value to the firm. Where industrial marketing of the Fordist era may have stressed marketing as a means to deliver more, higher value, single transactions, relationship marketing stresses customer retention, service and quality, and the needs of individual customers through mass customization.

Experiential marketing is closely connected to relationship marketing in the sense that it provides the method by which relationships are forged through brand-relevant experiences. While traditional marketing stresses rational choices among consumers, experiential marketers consider them as both rational and emotional in search of pleasurable experiences that they aim to convey (Schmitt 1999: 53). Addis and Holbrook (2001) illustrate how the transformation of marketing reflects shifts from utilitarian consumption (stressing functionality, constancy, rationality) towards more hedonic consumption (emphasizing interaction, variability, uncertainty). As they put it, hedonic consumption 'designates those facets of consumer behaviour that relate to the multisensory aspect of one's experience with products' where sensory experience may include tastes, sounds, tactile impressions and visual images (Addis and Holbrook 2001: 59; Holbrook 2001). As Schmitt (1999: 57) opines,

> Today customers take functional features and benefits, product quality and a positive brand image as a given. What they want is products, communications, and marketing campaigns that dazzle their senses, touch their hearts, and stimulate their minds. They want products, communications and campaigns that they can relate to and that can incorporate into their lifestyles. They want products, communications and marketing campaigns to deliver an experience.

Examples of experiential marketing abound in many sectors of economic activity. Pine and Gilmore (1999: 2) have gone as far as to propose that this is indicative of a shift in the organisation of economies. In the so-called 'experience economy', after commodities, goods and services, 'experiences are a fourth economic offering, as distinct from services as services are from goods'. Where in the past experiences had been (falsely in their view) classified as service activity, they postulate that experiences are a separate source of additional value. Memorable experiences are things for which people are willing to pay, while goods and services are almost props in consumption events; in short, how goods and services are staged and performed is vital to how they are consumed (including customer retention and loyalty), the price people will pay, and hence the value created. Pine and Gilmore (1999) use the distinctive metaphor of staging a theatrical production to help product and brand managers to conceptualize how to deliver memorable, compelling and ultimately commercially successful consumption experiences. For them, every business is a stage and work is theatre so in a heavily choreographed show employees are the actors, the offer is the performance, customers are the audience, the process is the script, and strategy is dramatization. Even the venue can be developed solely for the purpose. Ponsonby-McCabe and Boyle (2006: 183) note firms may gain even more control over customer loyalty and capitalize even more from brand equity by developing brandscapes which they define as: 'a place that is totally given over to providing consumers with opportunities to have an experience that is clearly and exclusively associated with the brand concerned'.

One criticism of Pine and Gilmore's thesis is that it makes little substantive reference to tourism per se in its original form. Examples, such as the Disney organization, from the entertainment industry are sporadically invoked and in a later exemplification, they demonstrate how the ideas might apply specifically to hospitality businesses (Pine and Gilmore 1999). However, a more critical treatment exclusively focused on tourism would have been warranted. After all, in tourism the experience is the product and international tourism businesses such as tour operators and travel agents (see Chapters 7 and 8) go to great lengths to ensure that experiences are memorable to ensure repeat business. Moreover, Carù and Cova (2003: 281) suggest that it is the extraordinary – which is often stereotypically associated with tourism episodes – not the everyday that delivers memorable experiences for consumers. Others note that Pine and Gilmore's main thesis lacks fuller empirical verification (cf. Holbrook 2001) and, although it reveals how to perform experience-based marketing, as Addis and Holbrook (2001: 62, original emphasis) have noted, they do not explain '*why* people should be persuaded that everything can be consumed as an experience'. In what follows, this chapter addresses these critiques. Tourism is demonstrated to be a means not just the subject of experiential marketing. Marketing through tourism experiences not only provides a basis to build brand–consumer relations but also to communicate strong signals to consumer about the how the brand is functioning in and responding to external conditions in the international market place. Global car manufacturers may be the exemplar but the lessons to be learned have resonance to international businesses in tourism and other sectors of economic activity (Mitchell and Orwig 2002).

GERMAN CAR BRANDS, THE MACRO-MARKETING ENVIRONMENT AND THE NEED TO ENGINEER TOURISM

Germany is home to some of the most successful, high profile car manufacturers in the world: Audi, BMW, Mercedes-Benz, Porsche and Volkswagen (VW). Until 2007, Mercedes was part of a global group formed by the merger of Daimler-Benz and Chrysler in 1998. It had total revenues of €151.6 billion, unit sales of 4.7 million vehicles sold in over 200 countries. DaimlerChrysler has over 360,000 employees and manufacturing facilities in 17 countries (DaimlerChrysler 2007). Like Porsche, family ownership is strong in BMW, which produces 3 globally recognisable brands – BMW, Rolls Royce and Mini – from 15 production and assembly plans in 7 countries. In 2006 it had total revenues of €48.9 billion from sales of 1.47 million units across its range from small compacts to luxury saloons, from sports cars to 'soft-roader' sports utility vehicles (SUVs) (BMW 2007b). Since it was founded in 1937 to produce the 'people's car', VW has grown to assume global market share of 9.7 per cent from sales of 5.734 million vehicles in 44 production plants in 18 countries, and retail in 150 countries worldwide (VW 2007a). To its acquisition of Audi, VW has widened its brand family through the ownership of such apparently quintessentially English- and Italian-sounding marques as Bentley and Lamborghini (Table 13.1). Porsche produces luxury cars and its sales of €7.2 billion from 96,794 units in 2005/6 reflect the exclusivity of its products and the size of its target segments (Porsche 2006a). Porsche was originally established by the designer of the first VW Beetle, Ferdinand Porsche, whose grandson, Ferdinand Piëch, is currently the chair of the VW supervisory board and former VW chief executive. Together the Porsche and Piëch families own half the shares of Porsche AG and Porsche has acquired a 30 per cent stake in VW and two (additional) places on its board (Economist 2006). In the past, Porsche has benefited from close cooperation in order to drive its development costs down.

German car manufacturers are not only impacted by global automotive sector dynamics, but they have also been at the forefront of restructuring processes. These have included the global expansion of production and assembly, supply chains and distribution as well as corporate consolidation. In response to the emergence of Japanese in the 1980s and other Asian rivals, German manufacturers have been under competitive pressures, not least to cut their costs and increase their productivity further (Priddle 2005). Although some progress has been made in this regard, manufacturers such as VW have not yet been able to reach as competitive levels. Instead, higher costs have been defended until recently on the basis that German cars have been marketed as premium products with high production values, reliability and residual values (Priddle 2005). Hence customers have been willing to pay higher prices that offset higher production costs. Nevertheless, Japanese and Korean manufacturers have exposed the weakness in cost structure by enhancing quality, reliability and service standards in addition to their traditionally competitive pricing policies. For German manufacturers, this pressure is intensified by increasing development costs and the risks of replacing older, favoured models with the next generation of cars (Mackintosh 2004).

Not surprisingly, German car manufacturers have aimed to build enduring relationships with their customers as a means of predicting and securing the future. One popular method

Table 13.1 *The car brand structure of the Volkswagen Group*

Volkswagen brand family	Audi brand family
Volkswagen	Audi
Škoda	Seat
Bugatti	Lamborghini
Bentley	

Source: Adapted from VW (2007a).

has been to ensure that the range of models covers all stages in an individual's family and hence motoring life cycle (Mackay 2004). For instance, although it is a premium brand and perhaps not always associated with family motoring, in December 2002 Porsche launched its Cayenne model with family 'nest builders' in mind. For brand devotees it offered the chance to build a lifelong association with the marque. Practicalities have not been at the expense of speed, grace, dynamism, rich design, exclusivity and status. As a Luxury SUV, the Cayenne is a much larger vehicle than the 911 or Boxster, but it adheres to the sporting and rallying heritage of the brand, as well as its aspirations. As the company noted around the time of its launch, Porsche wants to 'reach people that have their own minds, that want to widen their own experiential horizons without being irrational, without having to relinquish the highest standards in precision safety, driving comfort and environmental compatability' (Porsche 2002a: 2). Where parents may once have started with a Boxster, transferred to another brand when children arrived, and subsequently returned to the brand with a 911 as the 'classic Porsche', the Cayenne filled the important, intermediate stage. In the process, the Cayenne also allowed Porsche to tap an important new market (the popular SUV and soft-roader market, especially in the United States) and indemnify the company against risks in global market conditions (see Coles 2004). Barely six months later at the end of the financial year (July 2003), Porsche reported strong trade despite difficult economic conditions in its primary markets, Germany and the United States. Global sales reached 66,803 cars (an increase of 23.2 per cent) of which 27,789 were 911s, 18,411 were Boxsters, and significantly, the 'third Porsche' already accounted for 30.8 per cent of sales (20,603 units) (see Coles 2004). By 2005/6 the Cayenne continued to contribute about a third of sales (35.2 per cent, or 34,134 units) (Porsche 2006a). Other manufacturers have taken a different approach by diversifying their ranges to address segments with which they were not always associated. VW developed a luxury saloon, Phaeton (see p. 249), to accompany its acquisition of Bentley and to rival the Audi A8 (also Volkswagen AG!), Mercedes S-Class and the BMW 7 Series. In contrast, the entry level 1-Series model – BMW's venture into small family car market – competes directly against the Volkswagen Golf and Audi A3.

FROM MUSEUM TOUR TO BRANDSCAPE EXPERIENCE

German car manufacturers have long operated dedicated museums of differing scale and scope. To encourage greater customer engagement in their brands in challenging market conditions, several manufacturers have invested to upgrade their museums, often through exciting design concepts by world-renowned architects to symbolize their cars' distinctiveness in the congested automotive market place. In May 2006 at the time of the FIFA World Cup, Mercedes-Benz opened its new €150 million 'Brandworld Museum' in Stuttgart (Chen 2007). Critically acclaimed for its double-helix interior form, some of its interior features have drawn architectural claim for their parallels with the Guggenheim in New York (Neil 2006). On show in its nine levels are 160 models demonstrating Mercedes pivotal position in the development of automobility, accompanied by a 136-foot high atrium with video projections, prototypes and engineering milestones (Chen 2007). In contrast, the current and much smaller Porsche museum (20 cars) across town, with its 'disappointingly non-descript interior' was described as 'more like a hospital waiting room than a temple to sports cars' (Chen 2007: 3), although a new museum project is underway and scheduled for completion in 2007 (Porsche 2006a). BMW has operated a museum from 1973, next to its iconic four-cylinder tower block headquarters in Munich. Like Mercedes-Benz, it has invested heavily on a museum upgrade and the adjacent development of a new visitor experience, *BMW Welt* (world), which is scheduled to open in 2007 (Neil 2006). Plant tours of the assembly lines were run in the past by all manufacturers and they have continued to feature in new production and assembly plants, which renowned architects have been hired to enhance the spectacle. For example, the central building of the new US$1.7 billion BMW assembly plant in Leipzig was designed by Zaha Hadid, the 2004 winner of the prestigious Pritzker prize.

Indeed, it has become standard practice to enhance the spectacle of production and to embed it in wider-ranging experiences to allow visitors greater immersion in the brand. One of the earliest developments in this regard was the *Audi Forum* at the company's Ingolstadt headquarters (Meinicke 2002). Opened in December 2000 at the heart of the company's manufacturing complex, its design reflects the eventful history of the company. A museum details the changing names, ownership, locations and brands but it departed from the traditional museum and plant tour formulae with the integration of a customer centre, restaurants and hospitality services, and the use of the central space to stage events. Not only can the amenities be used to maximize the projection of brand values and hence relationship-building, but the space is more appealing for those not always instantly attracted to technology.

Porsche opened a new factory in 2002 originally for the Cayenne (Table 13.2). Alongside the assembly plant, an imposing 32-metre-high visitor centre in the shape of an upturned diamond opened in January 2003 (Figure 13.1). The design symbolises brand values of

Table 13.2 Basic Data about Porsche Leipzig

- In 1998 the Cayenne was announced as the 'third Porsche'
- A 200ha site, including plant and visitor facilities
- Initially, Cayenne production, was followed by Carrera GT and in 2009, the Panamera sports coupe
- €120 million investment to expand existing facilities and new 25,000m^2 production hall and 30,000m^2 logistics centre
- 32m-high visitor's centre in shape of upturned diamond, including:
    - Customer (car) pick-up centres, VIP lounge and bar
    - Porsche brand selection shop
    - Exhibition hall
    - Restaurants and conference facilities
    - Large auditorium 900m^2, 500-person capacity; small auditorium/54-seat cinema; test track control centre

Continued

Table 13.2 *Continued*

- Two test tracks:
    - 6km off-road track with 15 training modules
    - 3.7km race track with sections modelled on famous F1 stretches
- Range of products for visitors, including:
    - Plant tours
    - Passenger laps
    - Driver laps
    - Training courses
    - Porsche Travel Club packages
    - Factory collection

Figure 13.1 *Porsche Leipzig*

clarity, purity of design and execution; quality of production and appointment; status and prestige; and long-lasting durability (see Coles 2004).

Three main overlapping types of visitor are addressed at Porsche Leipzig (see Coles 2004). First, 'general visitors' – members of public, day visitors and tourists – who visit the site as a spectacle of (post-)modern production and consumption. As possible future purchasers, their desires are raised by viewing production; seeing the cars performing at their peak; and exploring the messages and iconography of the brandscape. Among the second and overlapping group are those attending meetings, incentives, conferences and exhibitions (MICE) at the site as well as special interest club members. For those desiring more memorable experiences, track time, cars and instructors are available for hire, as well as meeting rooms and hospitality services. The final group are Porsche purchasers who chose factory pick-up of their Cayenne. For them, practicality is combined with adrenaline because 'works collection for the Cayenne means 18,000 seconds, 300 minutes or five hours of pure Porsche' (Porsche 2002b); that is, experiencing the primary brand values of speed, safety and environment to their full limits. In the car, this means supervised laps of the track and off-road circuit; outside, the experience starts in the exclusive owners' level with presentation of the visitor centre, the company, the car, the tracks and the Porsche brand world with a cinema show, factory visit and lunch (Porsche 2002b).

CASE-STUDY VIGNETTE – TOURISM AND INTERNATIONAL BUSINESS IN ACTION

VW's 'car city' – scripted experiences to build brand relationships with consumers across the generations

Opened on 1 June 2000 at an initial cost of €450 million, *Autostadt* (literally 'car city', www.autostadt.de) is a 25-hectare theme park in Wolfsburg, VW's home town in Lower Saxony. Work started in 1998 on the site which has the following basic features (Merian 2002; *Autostadt* 2003):

- The *KonzernWelt* exhibition, or 'Group World';
- The *ZeitHaus* historical exhibition;
- *LernPark* – children's traffic school;
- *KinderWelt* – children's play zone;
- 7 pavilions, including one for each brand in the VW group;
- *KundenCenter* – customer service centre;
- 2 *AutoTürme* – towers holding cars for collection;
- The Ritz-Carlton Wolfsburg (174 rooms, 21 suites);
- 7 restaurants and cafes, 3 shops, VW financial services;
- 4 cinemas with 360° projection;
- 2,000 employees;
- capacity to deliver 600 cars per day.

Each building has a different architectural style. The site concept is based on the 'structure and event' paradigm: the structure is provided by a series of deliberately placed buildings around the site, while the presentations inside each of the buildings constitute the event (*Autostadt* 2002: 24). To reflect the diversity in the VW Group, the site design rejects a single, homogeneous, unifying style and narrative.

The *Autostadt* experience starts at the *KonzernForum* where the group and its values are introduced. Quality, safety, social responsibility and environmental awareness are

Continued

presented in four short cinema presentations. The *AutoLab* allows visitors to explore the group's claims over its core competencies, while the children's world offers younger visitors the opportunity to play early in their visit. After this, in the *ZeitHaus* car history and VW's role in automobility is portrayed. For older children there are interactive exhibits in the *WerkStadt* (a pun on the German word for workshop) that focus on car technology.

These contextual exhibits are separated by water from most of the other buildings. Walkways across the 'fjord' permeating the site connect the visitors with the 'brand pavilions' – one for each marque in the group. Not all have to be visited, nor on a highly regimented round trip; instead visitors are free to wander the site and frequent the restaurants and shops that punctuate it. Dramatic architectural forms are at the two furthest points from the entrance. The Ritz-Carlton five-star hotel in the north-western corner is semi-circular in form and emphasizes the size and space of the facilities. The north-eastern corner is dominated by two 20-storey towers and the eye is drawn to them by a long rectangular pool at their base. The towers are huge parking lots for up to 400 cars about to be delivered to their owners (*Autostadt* 2003). Each is 48 meters high, is internally built of concrete and steel, and has an external glass façade to allow the visitors to view the cars. Reminiscent of a piston in form, the lifts oscillate up and down to collect cars for presentation to their new owners at the adjacent *KundenCenter* where they are briefed on features and safety devices.

Although *Autostadt* functions as a visitor attraction, its two most imposing structures reinforce purchase experiences: the towers deliver cars, and the hotel accommodates new owners beforehand. Paradoxically, cars cannot be purchased on site; rather, this is left to VW's network of agents and dealers (from whom self-collection is ordered).

Questions

▩   How are the brand values of the VW group embodied at *Autostadt*?
▩   What type of customers is VW attempting to engage with at *Autostadt*?
▩   How far does *Autostadt* reflect the principles of the experience economy?

Volkswagen and the strategic use of visitors

High profile investments by Mercedes-Benz, Porsche and BMW are, in effect, tacit recognition of the VW Group's trend-setting work on car-themed brand experiences. Both its so-called *Autostadt* (car city) at group headquarters in Wolfsburg and the later *Gläserne Manufaktur* (lit. 'transparent factory')in Dresden set new standards and built on the benchmarks set first of all by the *Audi Forum*. Simply put, *Autostadt* is a theme park based around a series of car brands belonging to the VW Group while the much smaller but architecturally more distinctive *Gläserne Manufaktur* reproduced and refined the principles specifically for the launch of a new model.

Opened originally for EXPO2000 in nearby Hanover, *Autostadt* has become an exemplar for all subsequent initiatives because of its scale (25 hectares), form (architectural concept, impact), functions (brand platform, visitor attraction, event venue), scope (the range of visitors it attracts) and its role in the local community. One broad estimate places the number of visitors and VW customers to Autostadt as 1.2 million per year (Pottinger 2006), while another suggests that 9 per cent of the on average 6,000 visitors per day are foreign (Kingstone 2004: 3). *Autostadt* (2003) was originally portrayed as an 'experience' in its promotional materials and it is reminiscent of a theme park. Structured tours are available and it has a customer service centre for VW purchasers. However, its primary role is as an exposé of the entire VW concern, its values and how these are articulated via its separate brands. For this reason, rather than a single 'brandscape', *Autostadt* is divided into several separate events and encounters with the group's multiple (sub-)brands for visitors to select as they wish.

VW is currently Europe's largest car producer (every fifth car produced in western Europe is produced by the group). In addition to the enduring popularity of models such as the Passat and Golf, consistent growth has been achieved by the systematic acquisition of other well-known car brands, their market shares and sales, which have also indemnified the group against fluctuating global market conditions and escalating production costs (Priddle 2005). Car production has been divided into two brand groups (Table 13.1): in general the Audi brand group is intended to have attributes of sportiness, (high-)technology and design, while the Volkswagen brand group, which accounts for 60 per cent of total sales (Priddle 2005), augments classic values (quality, reliability, price), with luxury and comfort. Each individual marque should conform with the over-arching core group identity and image, while simultaneously operating independently in the market place with its own individual brand imagery, attributes and architecture.

Clearly, as a major producer, VW faces the dual challenges of how to increase sales and turnover, while sustaining existing levels of demand by retaining its customers over time. As a group and as an individual brand, VW has followed a long-term strategy to develop competitive advantages by using its core values and corporate ethos to build relationships that will eventually lock-in and to retain customers (Chajnacki 2000). VW has been committed to 'offer attractive, safe and environmentally friendly vehicles which are competitive on [*sic*] an increasingly tough market and which set world standards in their respective classes' (VW 2007b: n.p.). VW (2007a: 5) stresses the importance of the new challenges the environment presents for stewardship and sustainability in the 'mobility' sector:

> Our broad range of products and services, innovative strength and superbly trained staff in all divisions enable us to find forward-looking answers. We believe that sustainable corporate governance means taking responsibility: for our customers, shareholders, employees, suppliers, for society and for the environment.

VW's corporate values appeal to a desire among consumers to increase their 'automotiveness', but in a safe and responsible manner. The car may be the central mechanism but the group locates it within integrated transport solutions. These are considered to be appropriate to the expectations of contemporary consumers, especially in European markets. Set against this backdrop, the importance of *Autostadt* is not necessarily in its commercial operation as a visitor attraction, nor as an over-sized sales lot or billboard hoarding. An unwillingness to retail directly to the customer from *Autostadt* as well as a reluctance to feature ostentatious adverts around the site underscores this point (Merian 2002). *Autostadt* (2003) makes the organisational complexity of VW, its operations and its offers understandable to consumers. Professor Bernd Pischetsrieder, the former chairman of the VW management board, explained:

> The problem lies in the public perception that sees the Volkswagen Group not as a global multiple brand group and views Wolfsburg always as the town of the Beetle. For all that, only 15% of the total staff currently employed by Volkswagen globally work in Wolfsburg, not even 10% in production. Wolfsburg is a modern technology centre, where more engineers work at one location otherwise than at any other place in Germany. That, for which Volkswagen stands, is visible in Autostadt.
>
> (Quoted in Merian 2002: 10)

Thus, through *Autostadt* the group's values are physically embodied and purchasing decisions at some unspecified time in the future are influenced. This is evident in the privileged status and position afforded the *KonzernWelt* as one of the first spaces to be encountered so that 'guests come into contact with the core Volkswagen values first, rather than the products' (*Autostadt*, 2003: 36). Brand awareness and situating consumers among the brands is thus a second level upon which marketing messages function. For Pischetsrieder, *Autostadt* is, 'the platform by which the group presents itself. It produces the direct connection between producer and customer. And [moreover] it is identity forming for our workers' (Merian, 2002: 10). It is also identity-forming for the visitors. Physical presence in 'brandspaces', the symbolic manufacturing home of VW manufacture close by, and the manifestation of the brands and their qualities, are features that trigger emotions of what it could be like experientially, what it could mean personally, and what it would say to others, to own an Audi, a VW or even a Lamborghini or Bentley. By presenting the brands in separate pavilions, *Autostadt* allows visitors to contemplate, simulate and evaluate brand ownership. Ancillary facilities such as the service centre, the towers, the museums and exhibitions, shops and restaurants offer customers further space to ponder and to play out hypothetical scenarios.

This approach is echoed at the *Gläserne Manufaktur* opened in 2001 originally to assemble the Phaeton, VW's attempt to penetrate the luxury market. Its development costs have been estimated at £650 million, of which £130 million was sunk in the factory (Feast 2004). In addition to its early role in building awareness of the model, the *Gläserne Manufaktur* embodied the company's desire to go up-market through its grand design and opulent appointment. Organized plant tours have continued to satisfy public curiosity (Figure 13.3), while Phaeton buyers have been offered not only of factory collection but also a visit to configure options and combinations (Neil 2006). A futuristic design (Figure 13.2) dominated by glass panelling has allowed visitors, residents and VW customers to look inwards on the company's activities.

Where commerce had traditionally been shrouded in secrecy to maintain competitive advantage, the *Gläserne Manufaktur* has laid bare VW's commercial practices both literally and symbolically. The timing of its opening was opportune. Serendipitously it presented positive public relations messages to combat some of the negative publicity the company had

Figure 13.2 *The* Gläserne Manufaktur, *Dresden*

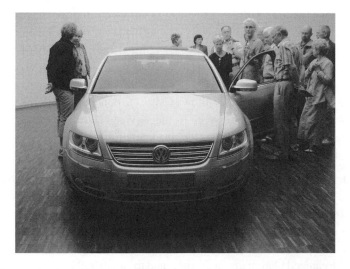

Figure 13.3 *Immersion in the brand world: visitors are introduced to the VW Phaeton at the* Gläserne Manufaktur

received, not least from the European Commission, over alleged price-fixing (which were eventually dismissed on appeal – VW 2007a) and supposedly unfair corporate ownership regulations. More recently, the *Gläserne Manfaktur* has offered 'good news' stories during trying circumstances that include a persistent scandal involving corporate executives and controversial restructuring measures (Mackintosh 2004; Priddle 2005; Economist 2006). Sales of the Phaeton were much slower than expected and the model was pulled from the US; excess production capacity in Dresden was taken up by the transfer of Bentley production, a key success for the VW brand group in its fight for a share in the luxury car market (Feast 2004; Priddle 2005).

EXPERIENCING CAR BRANDS BEYOND STAGED SETTINGS

Museum tours and factory visits are tried and tested formulae (Mitchell and Orwig 2002), albeit the development of dedicated brandscapes as visitor experiences has taken participation with the brand much further. These three approaches are by no means exclusive to German automotive companies or to Germany. BMW produces its Z4 sports and X5 SUV models at Spartanburg (South Carolina), USA where it hosts visitors on factory tours, but its BMW Zentrum Museum is a visitor experience much the same as the European brandscapes including meeting and events facilities, hospitality, gallery and exhibits. Toyota, Japan's largest manufacturer, offers free factory tours in English and Japanese and in its Toyota Kaikan Exhibition Hall, new models and technologies are on public display.

The German brandscapes point to the benefits for the brand and the company of designing and implementing elaborate visitor experiences. However, given their scope and scale, they are very costly to set up and operate. Mackintosh (2004) has even questioned the commercial viability of *Autostadt* as the exemplar of the brandscape approach. Nevertheless, there have been other, comparatively more modest uses of tourism by German car manufacturers to build enduring relationships between customers and their brands. The first and perhaps most basic is the recommendation of particular routes for drivers (i.e. usually but not exclusively owners) to take to enhance their appreciation of brand performance. Frequently, these appear in official owners' and sanctioned enthusiasts' magazines, although Audi has developed A4 Global Drives, a part of its website dedicated to owners recommending the best drives to one another (Audi 2007). Allied to this, second, is the pick-up service from the factory. Neil (2006) notes that 40 per cent of VW owners take delivery of their vehicle from *Autostadt*. Mercedes-Benz offered its British customers of the C-Class factory pick-up from Germany as an option and it recommended several trips back through Germany, France and the Low Countries to make the most of the experience (Coles 2004).

Track days (and the sponsorship of racing teams) have long been a means of gazing on the brand in motion. BMW owners' magazines and car clubs in the UK have advertised packages, for instance, at the Rockingham Motor Speedway Circuit, as well as at the world-renowned Nürburgring in central Germany. Tailor-made short-breaks and holidays offered by some car manufacturers as travel intermediaries – for instance, BMW Fine Driving, the Porsche Travel Club and VW's Event Travel – are a final distinctive use of tourism to project their brands (Table 13.3; Coles 2004). For the current owner, these offer the

Table 13.3   *VW Event Travel holidays in 2006*

Destination	Tagline	Days	Cost (€)[1]
The Alps	Mountains and Valleys	6	2,290
Botswana	Africa's Heart	6	3,690
China	From Beijing[2]	15	4,890
Iceland	Fire and Ice	4	1,790
Moab, US	Horizons and Canyons	7	2,690
Namibia	Across the South of Africa	13	3,890
Orient Express[3]	From Munich to Istanbul[2]	7	3,490
South Africa	A Continent touches the Senses	8	3,790
Tibet	Through the Middle Kingdom	20	5,490
Transylvania	Murnau's Nosferatu and the Seven Citadels	8	2,190
Val d'Isère	Off-road Driving of the Highest Level	4	1,590

Source: Adapted from VW (2006).
Notes:
1 Per person in a double room, excluding international flights.
2 Also operates in reverse.
3 Uses Phaeton model – all others use Touareg SUV.

opportunity to enhance their enjoyment, understanding and use of their cars, while for the prospective owner, the packages represent opportunities to experience the brand without the full expense of ownership. By no means are all of these packages based on speed and high performance; others are structured around grand touring and off-roading, as well as enhancing driver safety and skills. Audi UK offers day driving experiences at the Silverstone race track for around £400 with the accent firmly on the theory and practice of safe and enjoyable driving. Several packages are offered to current Porsche owners to hone their skills different environmental conditions from the extremes of snow and ice of Finland to the heat and dust of desert conditions (Porsche 2006b). In both cases, the emphasis on safety as a function of high performance is in keeping with marketing messages.

CONCLUSION: THE CAR'S STILL THE STAR?

This chapter illustrates how tourism features in the experience economy, and how it is used as a means to communicate brands and to enhance consumer understanding of their values and position in the market place. Tourism has been used by each major international car brand from Germany in highly scripted and choreographed experiences with the intention of building enduring relationships with their customers, both now and in the future. For consumers these experiences are necessary in so far as they contribute towards confidence-building. These car brands feature in what are – for the vast majority of consumers – major purchasing decisions. In this respect, Pine and Gilmore's (1999) thesis has resonance and their work offers some interesting insights into how (tourist) attractions operate in discrete time-bounded encounters with consumers. What their work fails to acknowledge, though, is that encounters with the brand like those described here are just single episodes in broader and ongoing experiences of mobility.

Six distinctive forms of tourism activity have been identified. Traditional museum visits and factory tours remain two prominent forms of engagement and they have been accompanied by the development of exclusive, themed visitor experiences, such as the *Audi Forum* and *Autostadt*. There has been considerable investment in dedicated brandscapes – as well as the next generation of car museums – to encourage more active participation with brands than there was in the past. Nowhere is this attempt to forge stronger bonds between consumer and brand more evident than the VW Group. The *Audi Forum*, the *Gläserne Manufaktur* and, above all, *Autostadt* provide the group with spaces to embody their brand messages as well as their public relations responses to sector dynamics and to external claims about the company's operations and practices in the macro-marketing environment. In three other instances – recommended routes, visitor collection, and brand-themed short-break and holiday packages – the car, its performance and the staging as backdrop are integral to how the marketers aim to build relationships with customers.

As the failure of *Opel Live* warns (Meinicke 2002), the use of tourism to further relationship marketing with car brands cannot be taken for granted. Care has to be taken to ensure that such experiences are appropriately positioned and formulated for the brand and the market. Pine and Gilmore's (1999) theatre metaphor is helpful for understanding how tourism is used by international businesses from all sectors to engineer memorable and compelling experiences to encourage customer loyalty and affect future purchase intentions. Through on-site customer collection or configuration, there are even hints that the experiential contributes to value-creation. Indeed, it is relatively straightforward to audit such relationship marketing initiatives but methodologically it proves far trickier to assess precisely their impacts as destinations, their impacts on the wider destination systems in which they are embedded, and the extent to which they achieve the commercial aims for the international businesses concerned. Not only is it difficult to measure the degree to which visits to such 'brandscapes' result in enhanced purchase intention or actual purchases and hence turnover, but it is also awkward to obtain precise data on numbers of people who consume the themed spaces and products (Coles 2004). This is privileged commercial information that has an important currency of its own in a highly competitive market place. All the world – or even road – is apparently a stage and the car's still the star, but the time has come to see if the theatre is paying its way.

Discussion questions

- What other examples can you identify of international businesses using tourism experiences for relationship or experiential marketing purposes?
- What particular messages are they trying to communicate through the form and function of the tourism experiences?
- Consider your most recent tourism experience: how many scripted encounters did it include, with whom and why?

REFERENCES

Addis, M. and Holbrook, M.B. (2001) 'On the conceptual link between mass customisation and experiential consumption: an explosion of subjectivity', *Journal of Consumer Behaviour*, 1(1): 50–66.

Audi (2007) A4 global drives. Online. Available from: http://www.audi.de/audi/de/de2/a4globaldrives (accessed: 14/06/07).

Autostadt (2003) *Insight. A Guided Tour through Autostadt.* Wolfsburg: Autostadt GmbH.

BMW (2007a) *Enjoy the Perfect Journey*. BMW (UK) Ltd: Bracknell.

BMW (2007b) Annual report 2006. Online. Available from: http://www.bmwgroup.com/bmwgroup_prod/e/ 0_0_www_bmwgroup_com/investor_relations/finanzberichte/geschaeftsberichte/2006/popup/_downloads/gb2006_gesamt.pdf (accessed: 14/06/07).

Boyle, D. (2004) *Authenticity: Brands, Fakes, Spin and the Lust for Real Life*. London: Harper Perennial.

Carù A. and Cova, B. (2003) 'Revisiting consumption experience: a more humble but complete view of the concept', *Marketing Theory*, 3(3): 267–86.

Chajnacki, K. (2000) 'Relationship marketing at Volkswagen', in T. Hennig-Thurau and V. Hansen (eds) *Relationship Marketing: Gaining Competitive Advantage through Customer Satisfaction and Customer Retention*. Heidelberg and New York: Springer.

Chen, A. (2007) 'Motor Stadt (Psst! This isn't Michigan)', *New York Times*, 07/01/2007, Travel Desk: 3.

Coles, T.E. (2004) 'Tourism and retail transactions: lessons from the Porsche experience', *Journal of Vacation Marketing*, 10(4): 378–89.

DaimlerChrysler (2007) Commitment to excellence. Annual report 2006. Online. Available from: http://www.daimlerchrysler.com/Projects/c2c/channel/documents/1003905_DCX_2006_Annual_Report.pdf (accessed: 14/06/07).

Economist, The (2006) 'The executioner: face value', *The Economist*, 02/12/06.

Feast, R. (2004) 'Let Germany build Bentleys? Big mistake', *The Independent*, 12/10/04: 4.

Fyall, A., Callod, C. and Edwards, B. (2003) 'Relationship marketing: the challenge for destinations', *Annals of Tourism Research*, 30(4): 644–59.

Holbrook, M.B. (2001) 'Times Square, Disneyphobia, HegeMickey, the Ricky Principle, and the downside of the entertainment economy', *Marketing Theory*, 1(2): 139–63

Johansson-Stenman, O. and Martinsson, P. (2006) 'Honestly, why are you driving a BMW?', *Journal of Economic Behaviour and Organization*, 60: 129–46.

Kingstone, B. (2004) 'Heaven on wheels: *Autostadt* theme park will take you for a ride', *Toronto Sun*, 14/03/04: T3.

Lury, C. (2004) *Brands. The Logos of the Global Economy*. London: Routledge.

Mackay, A. (2004) 'The bold and the beautiful. Volkswagen has the model to suit every taste and pocket', *Glasgow Herald*, 19/08/04: 14.

Mackintosh, J. (2004) 'Volkswagen', *Financial Times*, 09/03/04.

Meinecke, B. (2002) Erlebniswelten also Instrumente der Kundenbindung. Neue Wege in der deutschen Automobilindustrie. Unpublished PhD dissertation, Catholic University of Eichstätt-Ingolstadt.

Merian (2002) *Merian Extra – Autostadt in Wolfsburg*. Hamburg: Jahreszeiten Verlag.

Mitchell, M.A. and Orwig, R.A. (2002) 'Consumer experience tourism and brand bonding', *Journal of Product and Brand Management*, 11(1): 30–41.

Neil, D. (2006) 'Temples of vroom: in Germany, automakers are in fierce competition to come up with the most jaw-dropping shrines. Car-loving travelers, come peek under the hood', *Los Angeles Times*, 27/08/06.

Pine, J.B. and Gilmore, J.H. (1999) *The Experience Economy. Work is Theatre and Every Business a Stage.* Boston: Harvard Business School Press.

Ponsonby-McCabe, S. and Boyle, E. (2006) 'Understanding brands as experiential spaces: axiological implications for marketing strategists', *Journal of Strategic Marketing* 14: 175–89.

Porsche (2002a) *Die Modelle.* Stuttgart-Zuffenhausen: Porsche.

—— (2002b) *Cayenne. Der 3. Porsche.* Stuttgart-Zuffenhausen: Porsche.

—— (2006a) *Annual Report 2005/06.* Stuttgart-Zuffenhausen: Porsche.

—— (2006b) *Porsche Travel Club 2007. Porsche Driving Experience.* Stuttgart-Zuffenhausen: Porsche.

—— (2007) *Welcome to Porsche Leipzig.* Online. Available from: http://www.porsche-leipzig.com/en/default.aspx (accessed: 14/06/07).

Pottinger, P. (2006) 'A day in the home town of automobility', *Sunday Telegraph* (Australia), 28/05/06: 14.

Priddle, A. (2005) 'What will it take to fix Volkswagen?', *Ward's Auto World*, 01/10/05: 50.

Schmitt, B. (1999) 'Experiential marketing', *Journal of Marketing Management*, 15: 53–67.

Sheth, J.N. and Parvatiyar, A. (1995) 'The evolution of relationship marketing', *International Business Review*, 4(4): 397–418.

VW (Volkswagen) (2006) Event travel – experience the world with Volkswagen. English brochure. Online. Available from: http://www.volkswagen.com/vwcms_publish/vwcms/master_public/virtualmaster/en2/experience/event_travel.html (accessed: 14/06/07).

—— (2007a) Annual report 2006. Online. Available from: http://www.volkswagenag.com/vwag/vwcorp/info_center/en/publications/2007/03/Geschaeftsbericht_2006.-bin.acq/qual-BinaryStorageItem.Single.File/Annual_Report_2006_e.pdf (accessed: 14/06/07).

—— (2007b) Group profile – group overview. Online. Available from: http://www.volkswagenag.com/vwag/vwcorp/content/en/the_group/group_profile_and_structure.html (accessed: 14/07/06).

14

Partnerships and social responsibility: leveraging tourism and international film business

Sue Beeton

Learning objectives

After considering this chapter, you will be able to:

- describe the relationships between international film businesses and tourism;
- identify the way in which partnerships are used to develop in film tourism destinations;
- assess the extent to which corporate social responsibility (CSR) offers one approach to managing the consequences of film tourism.

Key terms

- film tourism;
- destination;
- partnerships and collaborations;
- CSR.

FILMS, TOURISM AND FILM TOURISM: LOCATIONAL ASSOCIATIONS

Film (including movies, TV series, documentaries and reality TV) is an international phenomenon that attracts interest and passion from viewers of varied cultural backgrounds. In order to enhance their enjoyment of the film, many viewers make trips to the locations used in non-fictional films, dramas or documentaries and those used to portray or produce fictional places or actual events (Riley and van Doren 1992; Beeton 2005). Film studios visits and tours have become popular in Los Angeles. Disney, Paramount Pictures, Universal Studios and Warner Brothers, as major transnational corporations (TNCs), use their tours and theme-parks to cross-promote their wide portfolio of commercial interests. In New York, themed tours cater for the fans of HBO's hit shows such as *The Sopranos* and *Sex and the City* while in the United Kingdom the rural Yorkshire community of Goathland has become a very well-visited destination because of its association with the long-standing TV show *Heartbeat* (Mordue 1999; Beeton 2005). Guidebooks to film locations offer devoted fans pointers to the major locations, while sites on the Internet such as the International Movie Database (http://www.imdb.com/movies) not only detail which locations were used in a movie, but also which other films and series they have featured in. In a more exceptional case, a tourist attraction has been the stimulus for highly successful film franchise. *Pirates of the Caribbean* was originally based on a Disney theme park ride (Verrier 2002).

Film tourism is on the rise and destination marketing organisations at various geographical scales have started to recognise the importance of film to the tourism economy (Beeton 2005). Particular locations are being actively branded as film tourism destinations. For instance, in recent times, New Zealand has attempted to cash in on the popularity of *The Lord of the Rings* trilogy (Jones and Smith 2005). Other more subtle associations are evident. In many countries, local and national tourism organisations are linking with their film commissions to create 'film friendly' destinations for potential film makers. In several instances, this relationship is formally represented in international trade missions to overseas markets. Film producers are considered to be desirable as high spending visitors in their own right. After all, during their temporary sojourns away, film production teams require accommodation and hospitality, not to mention the use of other amenities and services in the local economy. Afterwards, they may become important destination ambassadors who, through word-of-mouth as one means, may attract future investors and visitors. Nevertheless, for all the apparent benefits, there can also be negative consequences for destinations that the marketing hyperbole often conveniently overlooks. Visitation may increase, but who precisely is attracted, when, for how long and what are their expectations? Other issues such as community resentment and the modification of local labour markets, employment and business structures may also result (Beeton 2005). Goathland once serviced 200,000 visitors a year attracted by the natural environment of the North Yorks Moors; with the advent of film tourism the small rural community is now visited by up to a million people a year, not always staying overnight or spending in the destination (Beeton 2005).

The purpose of this chapter is to explore the relations between tourism and international business in the form of film and TV production companies. The chapter opens by conceptualising the links between locations and destinations, before considering how the transformation of locations into destinations can be planned or managed. Partnerships, in particular through international trade missions as well as film festivals and award ceremonies, are highlighted as one particular mode by which locations may be manufactured as film tourism destinations. Positive outcomes do not always exclusively accompany this process of codification. Often the popularity of particular locations leads to mass visitation that challenges the sustainability of the very environments visitors desire to see. Traditional approaches ascribe the ultimate responsibility for managing the impacts of tourism to those (planners, politicians and producers) in the destination, not least because they are perceived to benefit most from the activity on their doorsteps. Here, an alternative approach is proposed. Consideration is given to how the potential negative consequences of film tourism may be mitigated through the CSR of the film and TV production companies.

PROMOTING THE FILM DESTINATION

The importance of film tourism has been recognised by a number of state and sub-state (i.e. regional and local) tourism authorities and their marketing agencies. Studies have been commissioned examining the potential significance of film tourism to economy, society and culture. Typically, they have focused on who is the film tourist and the extent to which film motivates visits to particular destinations (Beeton 2001, 2005).

While it may be unfair to categorise these studies as exclusively interested in the demand-side of film tourism, they do concentrate on the outcomes and specific outputs associated with film-related tourism. By and large, despite their apparently broad terms of reference, the economic impacts of film tourism have been prioritised. There appear to be two subtexts: whether film tourism represents a feasible strategy for a destination to follow; and/or the degree to which investment in film-related marketing materials may result in adequate returns in terms of visitor numbers (Hudson and Ritchie 2006). One of the dilemmas faced in such studies is the degree to which a precise value can be put on film tourism. Methodologically this is difficult because the process of identifying film tourists is tricky, and it is difficult to be certain about where and how spend attributable to film-induced tourism trickles through the local economy. In the absence of certainty on these matters, the 'value-added' of film tourism is often mentioned; that is, the intangible additional contributions made by film to a destination. Routinely in this respect, enhanced destination imagery in the global place market is raised. Film acts as a showcase as it throws the spotlight on shooting locations for the viewer as potential visitor (Beeton 2004).

In contrast, what is less well-appreciated is the extent to which promotion of a destination through a film has the potential to act as a double-edged sword. Already we have noted how some rural communities struggle in terms of their carrying capacity and ability to cater for large numbers of visitors (Beeton 2001). While some may be attracted by the portrayal of a location through film, others may be put off (see case-study vignette). Moreover, film may be an initial trigger to travel, but visitors travel with particular expectations of a destination and the level of experience and service they would like to have (Figure 14.1).

CASE-STUDY VIGNETTE – TOURISM AND INTERNATIONAL BUSINESS IN ACTION

Film tourism – saint or sinner?

Since its release first as a book and later in 2006 as a movie, *The Da Vinci Code* has stimulated travel to its major set-piece locations by aficionados and fans. The Roslyn Chapel in Edinburgh has seen its visitor numbers fivefold multiply and a profit

Continued

of £500,000. Scotland is estimated to have benefited from additional revenue of £6 million from a deal between VisitScotland and Sony, to promote locations used in filming (Ross 2007). However, when a story portrayed in film is controversial, there can be intense political struggles between stakeholders over the meaning of the imagery and the relevance of film tourism.

Dan Brown, the author, claims *The Da Vinci Code* is a work of fiction but this has not prevented it from gaining a great deal of acceptance from certain readers. In turn, this has created resentment and concern from some groups, most importantly the Catholic Church. Many Catholic groups are presenting 'factual' information to refute the accepted 'fictional truthes' stemming from the book and movie. Catholic Answers has published books on the topic as well as providing numerous web-based entries such as one under the headline 'Act now to expose *The Da Vinci Code*' (Catholic Answers 2004: n.p.) which exhorts its readers:

> With the release of 'The Da Vinci Code' movie, it is imperative that all Catholics be informed about what's really behind this infamous novel – and how to answer the ridiculous attacks it makes on Christianity.
> Catholic Answers has taken its well-regarded 'Cracking the Da Vinci Code' booklet and condensed it into a 4-page flier that can be inserted into parish bulletins.
> An excellent introduction to the controversial work by Dan Brown, our bulletin insert refutes the lies, distortions, and fabrications found in 'The Da Vinci Code'. It packs a tremendous amount of accessible, reliable information into a small space, giving you the answers you need to respond to the questions others have about 'The Da Vinci Code'.

In spite of the resistance of some groups, many organisations are happy not to become embroiled in the politics of truth. Rather, they are happy to cash-in on more casual connections between their destinations and the film. Many maps and guides to sites in the book and the movie have appeared in the UK and Europe. Even the Louvre museum in Paris has an audio guide for visitors to the museum to 'step inside *The Da Vinci Code*' (Figure 14.2), as well as guidebooks printed in many languages and souvenirs, including playing cards and the ubiquitous fridge magnet.

Questions

- Are such conflicts a blessing or blight for tourism destination marketers, and why?
- To what extent do such conflicts detract from or add to the film-tourism experience?
- Which other films or TV programmes have controversial meanings that may lead to similar tensions?

Thus, film tourism is usefully conceptualised and understood from the perspective of the multiple constituencies and actors that are involved in its production and consumption. Visitors form one albeit heterogeneous group of stakeholders. Tourism governors and tourism producers (such as hospitality, accommodation providers and attractions) are others as well as the film and TV production companies. As such, there may be at least three sides to destination promotion and three sets of interests that may not always be in concordance: promoting a destination to the film industry as 'film friendly' (as a film set or location shoot); convincing local tourism producers and administrators that theirs should be a film-tourism destination; and promoting a destination to potential tourists as a film site. Stresses can arise between certain images presented in films and of the destination's and businesses' requirements (Beeton 2004). This is not as simple as the self-image of a place being different from that portrayed by an 'adverse' fictional film. The desired image that a community may wish to present to the world can be undermined by a 'factual' documentary. In the Australian documentary, *Cunnamulla*, the community was presented as marginalised with an underbelly of anti-social behaviour (Beeton 2005), while the negative (often violent) fictional portrayal of Scottish urban society in the film *Trainspotting* can cause concern in the community. In addition, various international export sectors have issues with certain imaging/branding of their home country – promoting Australia as a place of sun, sand and quirky people (through film and tourism promotion) may not fit with those wishing to project an image of the country as a place to conduct business.

Within this relationship, film companies occupy a pivotal role. Not only do they regularly get tax breaks or other incentives from governments keen to secure filming in their countries, states or regions, but they also look for assistance from the particular (local) destinations in which they are interested in filming. Often one place is traded off against another in order to enhance the in-kind assistance they receive. For example, when the producers of the Hollywood movie, *A Thousand Acres,* were looking for an appropriate filming location, instead of going to where the story is set, they ended up filming it in Illinois. The script required a farm with 'a sea of corn as far as the eye can see' (Economist 1998: 28). Originally, it had specified Iowa, in the middle of America's 'Cornbelt', as the location. However, Illinois wanted the economic benefits of filming in their region (which amounted to an estimated US$21m local economic benefit and 183 full-time jobs) and it hoped for induced tourism in the future. Consequently, the Illinois Film Office provided the producers with pages of data on Illinois corn, and even suggested a range of hybrid varieties that could simulate an entire growing season in just six weeks. They were successful in their bid, and the movie was filmed in Illinois, just outside Chicago (Economist 1998). It is not only the large studios and production companies that are able to extract such benefits. Even small, independent film companies employing a few local people have the potential to attract visitors to the places in which they film, providing them with the potential to leverage in-kind support for a range of filming. For example, an independent film company in Australia (the NRS Group) produces a travel programme, *Earthwalkers*, screened on cable TV, along with various historically-based documentaries that require access to tourism and heritage areas. The producers use a small film crew with actual tourists volunteering to present the programme as well as some tour companies providing free access to some of the destinations. The local community does not receive any direct employment benefits from the filming,

Figure 14.1 *'Satriale's Pork Store' in New Jersey: a shrine to* Sopranos *fans or simply a vacant retail unit in an originally Scots–Irish neighbourhood*

Figure 14.2 *The high level of exposure for* The Da Vinci Code *movie audio guide at the Louvre*

but generally support the operation with an eye to increasing their profile and, in turn, tourism.

PARTNERSHIPS AND COLLABORATIONS TO BOOST FILM TOURISM

Beyond individual agreements and arrangements, the various stakeholders have been entering into a series of more structured, enduring and wide-ranging partnerships and collaborations to develop the profile and consumption of film-tourism destinations. This is unsurprising because the tourism relies heavily on cooperation and collaboration, in particular public–private sector partnerships in promotional and destination management activities (Bramwell and Lane 2000; Hall 2000). In general terms, collaborative arrangements in tourism are dynamic, specific to the environments and circumstances in which they develop, and they evolve in response to a host of factors. Gray (1989: 11) defines collaboration as a 'process of joint decision making among key stakeholders of a problem domain about the future of that domain'. Bramwell and Lane (2000) note that collaborative tourism planning needs to be inclusive of all interest groups (or stakeholders), however gaining true cooperative collaboration assumes that all parties have equal access to the process and possess similar levels of power, which is rarely the case (Hall 2000). In the case of film-induced tourism, there are two predominant types of partnership that serve to project the destination on the global stage: international trade missions, and film festivals and awards ceremonies.

International trade missions

Countries such as Australia, Britain and the United States have sent trade missions to emerging markets such as China, India and United Arab Emirates to nurture film tourism and tourism destination imaging more generally, as well as more specifically to leverage encourage film and tourism trade. By forming partnerships with various government departments and international businesses at home, these missions attempt to act cooperatively to sell their places as well as their products and commodities in overseas markets. Formal, legally-binding contracts and memoranda of understanding (MoU) as well as informal partnerships are used as the primary mechanisms to facilitate this. For instance, in 2002, the Australian Tourist Commission (formerly ATC but now Tourism Australia) signed an MoU with the Australian Trade Commission (Austrade) in which the agencies agreed to work together on joint and complementary initiatives. By 2004 they had developed an operating framework. Both organisations share the common objectives of promoting service exports, doubling the number of (Australian) exporters within five years, and raising awareness of Australia in international markets (ATC and Austrade 2002: 2); that is, not just as a location for financial investment, but also for visitors.

Trade missions may organise their own destination-specific (i.e. country or regional) promotional events. In addition, deputations may be sent to specific film and tourism branded trade shows and exhibitions that are now appearing. One such expo, the *Locations* film-tourism trade show in India, acknowledges that films are a catalyst for tourism, and it aims to 'bring together under one roof globally the two most glamorous industries with a purpose of business networking' (www.locationsworld.com). On their website, the *Locations* organisers claim that a popular Bollywood film shot in New Zealand (*Kaho Na Pyar Hai*) increased Indian visitation to New Zealand by fivefold. Other sources report a fourfold increase (Krishnakumar 2005), but this is nevertheless a very high level of growth, albeit from an initially low benchmark.

Indeed, the efforts that many countries are taking to attract the lucrative Indian 'Bollywood' films to their regions are indicative of the role of trade missions and expos in generating film tourism. Bollywood films are now a highly successful global phenomenon, but many of them are shot overseas. Conversely, outbound tourism from India has been traditionally relatively low and hence the potential exists for new tourism growth driven by Bollywood-inspired tourism. VisitBritain (2006), the national tourism marketing agency for the UK, estimates that in 2005 just under 6.5 million Indians travelled abroad, but that they spend more per day on shopping than other international tourists (VisitBritain 2006). For overseas destinations and members of their trade missions, it makes commercial sense to offer Bollywood film producers (the cost of) tax-breaks and in-kind assistance in return of the promise of (far greater) tourism spending and tax receipts from fans and devotees.

Tourism Australia (2005) has been at the forefront of attempts to capitalise on the Bollywood effect. The Bollywood sagas sell over 800 million cinema tickets annually (CNN 2001), with many of them set with iconic tourism backgrounds such as the Sydney Opera House and Harbour Bridge. The use of locations in Australia in Bollywood movies has serendipitously coincided with an increased interest in the country from the large Indian middle class (some 50–150 million people) which has become a priority tourist generating market for Tourism Australia. Indian tourists to Australia grew by 21 per cent in 2005 from the previous year, and as noted by the Minister for Small Business and Tourism Fran Bayley: 'Australia is receiving enormous exposure through *Salaam Namaste*, the latest Bollywood hit filmed entirely on location in Victoria' (Bayley 2005).

Australia does not, though, have the field to itself. Singapore, Malaysia and Hong Kong (among others) are also actively working to attract Bollywood with an eye to capitalising on the indirect tourism potential as well as direct filming benefits. Switzerland is generally acknowledged as the first overseas country used in Bollywood movies, and has gone so far as to rename one of its lakes 'Chopra Lake' to honour the Indian director, Yash Chopra who has been filming in the Swiss Alps since 1990. These early days of Bollywood on-site filming have been credited with Switzerland's rise as a popular honeymoon spot for Indian couples. Switzerland Tourism has released a guide to suitable movie sites, *Switzerland for the Movie Stars*, targeting Bollywood producers in particular as well as Indian tourists (Munshaw 2003). As an established film location, Ireland has been seeking to forge new linkages to sustain its ailing film industry. Although recently high profile as the locations for *Braveheart* and *Saving Private Ryan*, filming in Ireland hit an all-time low in 2005 as other countries such as Romania and Hungary began to lure Hollywood with lower costs and bigger incentives (tax cuts). Ireland is now courting India in terms of Bollywood and film-induced tourism, with the Prime Minister, Arts Minister and Tourism Minister cooperatively pitching Ireland as a filming site during their trade missions to India (Tourism Ireland 2006). Finally, in an interesting twist, at the time of writing, the Indian Tourism Ministry and Disney are in talks to promote Bollywood at Disneyland (Mookerji 2006). While the intention from India is to promote their country and increase visitation, such an initiative will also bring Bollywood fans to the US and Disneyland.

International film festivals and awards

In what can only be described as a coup in this competitive field of attracting Bollywood, the Yorkshire and Humber region in the UK won the opportunity to host the Indian Film Academy Awards for 2007, which was expected to attract some 28,000 people to the awards and contribute over £9.5million during the event (Yorkshire Tourist Board 2006). The television viewing audience was estimated to be around 315 million people around the world. The pursuit of Bollywood in this manner is part of a wider strategy followed by Yorkshire Tourism (Board) to actively promote the region for all forms of film-induced tourism (Beeton 2005). For the Chief Executive of Yorkshire Forward, a regional development agency and partner with Yorkshire Tourism for the awards, the international business opportunities stemming from this project are compelling in so far as '[the awards] will forge stronger business and cultural links between Yorkshire and India … Trade events … will promote and strengthen international trade opportunities' (Yorkshire Forward 2006). However, these opportunities came at a financial cost as Yorkshire Forward had to invest £2.5 million in its bid for the awards. While there has been a great deal of publicity surrounding these economic inputs, at the time of writing no assessment of the return on investment was available.

The attraction of the Bollywood awards to Britain is emblematic of a number of partnerships between destinations, TV and film producers, and awards organisers. Although Table 14.1 is far from exhaustive, it nevertheless demonstrates awards ceremonies and film festivals are a widespread phenomenon. While festivals in Cannes, Berlin and Venice, not to say the Golden Globes and the Oscars in Los Angeles, are high profile, even iconic features in the cultural calendar, there are other events throughout the world as large in scope and commercial significance for film and tourism. Not only do these events attract visitors in the form of the celebrities, their entourages, members of the production companies, civic dignitaries and politicians, they also draw large crowds of fans. Film festivals and awards are therefore strong tourist attractions in their own right. Through the high level of international media coverage they enjoy, they provide powerful destination image-drivers for the places in which they are held. Moreover, there are secondary effects in the sense that they promulgate the notion of visiting the sites featured in the films presented, particularly the award-winners. Many film festivals fill the gap left by the more commercial, Hollywood-type movies, giving independent and smaller film makers the opportunity for exposure to new markets. Such festivals have segmented the film-viewing market into more focused niches that may respond quite differently from the mass market, providing opportunities to bring visitors to niche destinations and experiences.

Table 14.1 *Selected international film festivals*

Festival	Month(s)	Venue
Del Plata International Film Festival	March	Buenos Aires, Argentina
Brisbane International Film Festival	July/August	Brisbane, Australia
Heart of Gold International Film Festival	October	Gympie, Australia
Melbourne International Film Festival	July/August	Melbourne, Australia
World of Women International Film Festival	October	Sydney, Australia
Viennale – Vienna International Film Festival	October	Vienna, Austria
Mumbai International Film Festival	January	Mumbai, India
Dublin International Film Festival	February	Dublin, Ireland
Galway Film Fleadh	July	Galway, Ireland
River to River Florence Indian Film Festival	December	Florence, Italy
MIFF – Milano International Film Festival	March/April	Milan, Italy
Shanghai International Film Festival	June	Shanghai, China
Osaka European Film Festival	November	Osaka, Japan
Wood Green International Short Film Festival	March	London, England
BFM International Film Festival	September	London, England
Boston Motion Picture Awards	December	Reading, US
Sundance Film Festival	January	Utah, US
San Francisco International Film Festival	April/May	San Francisco, US
AFI Fest – Los Angeles International Film Festival	November	Los Angeles, US

Source: Adapted from www.britfilms.com.

In some cases, awards and festivals contribute to urban regeneration. In the years after Unification in 1990, the centre point of *Berlinale* (Berlin International Film Festival) was moved to the Marlene Dietrich Platz nearby the symbolic Potsdamer Platz redevelopment. This was located in the former no-man's land between East and West Berlin, and *Berlinale* was used as a means of building unity in the city population through culture. More famously perhaps, many visitors to Los Angeles are attracted to Hollywood Boulevard to see the Walk of the Stars, Mann's Chinese Theatre where many films receive their premiere, and the Oscar venues. At the time of the Academy Awards, visitor numbers swell particularly when Oscars are on display and the red carpet is out (Figure 14.3). The Academy Awards have contributed to the rejuvenation of Hollywood Boulevard. For many years the awards were not held on the Boulevard and had no permanent home. In fact, the street was run-down, presenting an unsatisfactory visitor experience; in place of the glamorous home of Hollywood cinema, they found cheap souvenir and t-shirt shops, seedy tattoo parlours and the homeless. Attempts during the 1980s to address this situation were poorly envisaged and unsuccessful overall, failing to address issues of public safety, which had become a major concern to visitors (Beeton 2005). In the late 1990s the Hollywood Chamber of Commerce worked with associated tourism and community groups to develop a self-guided walking tour, historical signage and a map of the stars on the Boulevard. This provided visitors with stronger reasons to stay and to spend time and money on the strip.

Figure 14.3 *Hollywood Boulevard gears up for the 2004 Oscar ceremony*

Heritage buildings were restored and the first permanent home for the Academy Awards was opened in 2001 at the new Hollywood and Highland restaurant and entertainment complex.

PARTNERSHIPS AND RESPONSIBILITIES

What emerges from this discussion is that film has become a very powerful lure not just for visitors, but also for planners, politicians and business persons as a means of providing impetus to move their destinations forwards. The work of trade missions and those involved in establishing the partnerships necessary to organise film festivals and award ceremonies is entrepreneurial, proactive and forward-thinking. Their roles are to attract film companies to shoot in their locations, to hold award ceremonies, and to stimulate the viewing audience to visit. Their job is not necessarily to deliver the actual tourist experiences for those motivated to make trips or to manage the outcomes either positive or negative that arise from film-related tourism. That is left to others. If those who leverage apparent film tourism are not responsible for its consequences, the questions arises of who is, or perhaps more provocatively, who should be responsible for the legacy? Planning for the anticipated outcomes of such promotion is crucial, especially in terms of appropriately leveraging the positive benefits and ameliorating any potential negative outcomes. However, many destination managers and politicians fail to consider this; instead, they simply treat promotional efforts as separate to destination planning and management (see Table 14.2). Above, it has been argued that the film and TV production companies occupy a pivotal (perhaps the most powerful) position in film-tourism relationships with other stakeholders. One possible approach to managing the outcomes of film tourism would be for the companies to consider more carefully their CSRs.

Table 14.2 *Film and TV guidebooks*

Title	Movie/TV series	Author/Series	Primary place of sale	Places featured
The Lord of the Rings Location Guidebook (2 editions)	*The Lord of the Rings*	Ian Brodie	New Zealand	Specific sites in New Zealand used for *The Lord of the Rings*
Rough Guide to The Lord of the Rings		Rough Guide	International	All places relating to *The Lord of the Rings* literature and Tolkein, as well as the movies
Fodor's Guide to The Da Vinci Code: On the Trail of the Bestselling Novel	*The Da Vinci Code**	Jennifer Caull and Christopher Culwell (eds)	International	Italy, France and England
The Definitive Guide to the Da Vinci Code: Paris Walks		Peter Caine	International	Paris
Classic Heartbeat Country	*Heartbeat*	David Gerard	Goathland	Goathland
Filming on and Around the North Yorkshire Moors Railway	*Heartbeat, Noel's Christmas Presents, The Cooke Report, Possession, HarryPotter*	David Idle, North Yorkshire Moors Railway	Goathland, Pickering	Primary focus on Goathland
TV and Film Locations Guide: Northern England	*Heartbeat, Last of the Summer Wine, Emmerdale, All Creatures Great and Small, Peak Practice*	No author or publisher information	North Yorkshire	Northern England

Continued

Table 14.2 Continued

Title	Movie/TV series	Author/Series	Primary place of sale	Places featured
TV Country Favourites from the BBC and Yorkshire TV	Emmerdale, The Darling Buds of May, Heartbeat, Hamish Macbeth, Ballykissangel, All Creatures Great and Small, Last of the Summer Wine	Hilary Gray	North Yorkshire	Rural England, Ireland and Scotland
The Complete Tour Guide to The Quiet Man Locations	The Quiet Man	Lisa Collins	County Galway	Ireland

Note: *Not specifically related to the movie, but also to the book.

CSR: a brief introduction

During the last half a century, various commentators have stressed the importance of organisations moving beyond simply responding to their shareholders' needs to take responsibility for the effects of their activities on a wider scale (cf. Wartick and Cochran 1985; Carroll 1999). This view has though been highly contested, initially by the Nobel Prize-winning economist, Milton Friedman (1962), who insisted that a corporation's sole responsibility is to its shareholders, and as such it is required to maximise profits.

More recently, the case for corporations to take a socially responsible position has gathered momentum; and this has progressed beyond a simplistic desire to 'do good' and instead, it has been demonstrated that altruism may be a sound commercial logic and deliver increased profit in the long term. Although the concept of CSR defies easy definition, it embraces the notion that corporations must consider their activities in terms of the economic, legal, ethical and discretionary aspects and the consequences and legacies of these decisions beyond a simple profit-orientation (Carroll 1999). While not the sole driver of CSR, during the shift towards environmental conservation in the 1970s and 1980s, it was acknowledged that an organisation's responsibilities must extend well beyond the notion of profit-making. For Smith and Westerbeek (2007), 'CSR is concerned with meeting an obligation to put something back into society by meeting the needs of stakeholders and constituents'.

CSR takes into consideration the will and expectations of corporate stakeholders. In this respect, Clarkson (1995) identifies six groups linked to an organisation as stakeholders: the company itself, the employees, shareholders, customers, suppliers and public stakeholders that include the government and other interest groups, such as conservation and tourism groups. Such a description infers that the wider relationships between companies and their stakeholders – which may include the community that the product relies on for its existence (particularly in the case of tourism) – are central to overall business success.

CSR and tourism

Whereas CSR in other forms of business activity has attracted considerable attention, according to Miller (2006) there has been a general lack of attention with respect to the tourism sector. For him:

> Few might disagree that pursuing a transition to a more sustainable state is a worthy goal for the tourism industry. Yet, while the corporate responsibility debate outside tourism has yielded examples of best practice and a plethora of research, within tourism there have been far fewer examples of positive action. Mowforth and Munt (2003: 168) describe the absence of ethical leadership in the tourism industry as 'astounding', while Anita Roddick of the Body Shop describes the tourism industry as being at least 10 years behind other industries in its CSR approach ....
> Yet, simultaneously, despite being labelled the world's largest industry, and an industry that comprises high polluting airlines and resorts embedded into the context of people's lives, the tourism industry has also escaped from the kind of media attention and consumer boycotts that have seen organisations such as Nike, Shell and McDonalds pilloried for their corporate actions.
>
> (Miller 2006: n.p.)

While large tourism corporations such as Six Continents have well-defined CSR statements, these most probably represent the exception rather than the rule. Isolated examples of good and best practice in the tourism sector may be identified. Beyond these demonstrations of good intent, Miller (2006) argues that CSR should be considered more as an organisational ethos. Tourism enterprises seriously committed to CSR should take an active leadership role in 'building a stronger community, which provides safer destinations for tourists and so illustrates the [values of the] corporate citizen in the mould of Robert Owen, Titus Salt and George Cadbury rather than corporate philanthropists who donate money' (see also Chapter 3).

Several bodies of theory from the social sciences underpin CSR including ethical theory, political theory and stakeholder theory. Miller (2006) examines CSR in tourism sector organisations with respect to deontological- and teleological-based motives. Deontology is based in the philosophy of Immanuel Kant; it is characterised by the moral principles of a sense of duty and rights, and it reflects the Socratic notion of universal truths and principles that are adhered to regardless of circumstances. Teleogy, by contrast, follows the notion of consequences; that is, decisions are made based on the expected outcomes. In other words, deontology sees the means as more important than the ends whereas teleology focuses on the ends as justifying the means. Broadly speaking, CSR should be a deontological pursuit, yet in practice it is rare to find corporations exclusively adhering to this ideology. Rather, corporations with a profit-oriented motive have been criticised as taking a teleological perspective. Some of the externalities involved in achieving profit are (conveniently) overlooked. That said, simply presuming they should move to taking on a deontological approach is somewhat naive.

With respect to film tourism, there is a strong case for film corporations to take a deontological approach when using attractive, fragile places and communities for their work. Beyond their use of the location for shooting, their legacy may be the attraction of many thousands of visitors, which challenge the carrying capacity of the destination or its ability to respond to change (Beeton 2001). After all, film companies require the cooperation of local communities in order to make the shooting as efficient and successful as possible. Indeed, it could be argued that a deontological approach is demanded more in the case of an ongoing TV series than a one-off movie because production companies need to build and maintain relationships with local communities to ensure continuity across the series. At the moment, the emphasis would appear to be on the teleological. For instance, in Goathland, the film companies' justification for no further involvement in the community after shooting would appear to be that film tourism has resulted in alternative income streams. The loss of privacy and peace for the local community is a necessary and acceptable evil that the local population will have to suffer in order to reap the economic rewards of film tourism. Clearly, this position is debatable on moral grounds but it is compounded by other commercial conditions. Guided tours, film and locale souvenirs, and guidebooks are vital means to offsetting some of the negative social costs of film tourism; however, such opportunities have been limited by trademark and copyright restrictions imposed by the film companies keen to maximise their own merchandising opportunities (Beeton 2005). It is understandable that film companies may wish to protect their intellectual property rights, not least because of development and filming costs as well as their responsibilities to investors. However, it is not uncommon to find films reporting massive returns on investment despite very high production costs. In this context, it is not unfair to ask why the film companies should not assist more monetarily and/or in-kind to help mitigate or manage the negative outcomes of film tourism? It is not inconceivable that, for relatively modest reductions in profitability and margins for investors, those living in popular destinations may benefit more from film tourism.

CONCLUSION

More trips than ever are being motivated either wholly or in part by films, TV series and documentaries. Although it is difficult to track their effects fully or accurately, the importance of film tourism as a strong force for economic, social and cultural change has been recognised by destination managers and tourism producers, as well as the film production companies. While the film companies court attention from competing destinations in order leverage better conditions, destination managers are involved in complex cost-benefit calculations to determine whether the costs of attracting and servicing film companies are significantly outweighed in the long-term by the benefits from attracting more visitors, generating greater spending and tax revenues, and securing other investment as their profile is heightened in the international place market. Where a more ad hoc approach was once more evident, public- and private-sector stakeholders at the local, regional and even national level are working together in a more coordinated manner in strategic partnerships with film companies and their collaborators. International trade missions and film festivals and award ceremonies offer destinations vehicles through which to lure film activity and project their images. These activities represent a form of film tourism entrepreneurship on the part of the destination stakeholders. While they may be applauded for attracting business and promoting the destination, little attention is afforded to delivering the tourist experience, the management of future tourism impacts, and the long-term sustainability of tourism in the destination. Imagery sells films and it is the external stakeholders – the film companies – that benefit most from the commodification of local places and major financial benefits are accrued offshore. If there is to be a serious commitment to sustainable development through tourism, more consideration is required on how to lock-in more value for the local community and how to ensure that negative effects are mitigated. CSR may be criticised as being a little naive, utopian or hopelessly idealistic in the harsh, cynical world of big business. However, it may represent a workable option for securing benefits to film tourism destinations. In a competitive market, pre-hoc contractual conditions or constraints in the negotiation stage are simply going to deter film companies from filming in what they perceive as unnecessarily, over-regulated places in favour of those with a more liberal ethos. Securing a commitment from the film production companies, their managers and hence their investors in the filming and post-production phase may offer a more realistic solution.

Discussion questions

- ▩ What are the advantages and disadvantages of film tourism-related development for destinations?
- ▩ Are film production companies the most powerful stakeholders in the development of film-tourism destinations?
- ▩ How far do you think the concept of CSR offers a means to manage the impacts of tourism on a destination?

REFERENCES

ATC and Austrade (2002) *Memorandum of Understanding on Cooperative Activities between the Australian Trade Commission (Austrade) and the Australian Tourist Commission (ATC)*, 19 November 2002.

Bayley, F. (2005) 'Bollywood inspires tourists to visit Australia', Media release, 5 December 2005, Minister for Small Business and Tourism. Online. Available from: minister.industry.gov.au (accessed: 07/10/06).

Beeton, S. (2001) 'Smiling for the camera: the influence of film audiences on a budget tourism destination', *Tourism, Culture & Communication*. 3(1): 15–26.

—— (2004) 'Rural tourism in Australia – has the gaze altered? Tracking rural images through film and tourism promotion', *International Journal of Tourism Research*, 6: 125–35.

—— (2005) *Film-induced Tourism*. Clevedon: Channel View.

Bramwell, B. and Lane, B. (2000) *Tourism Collaboration and Partnerships: Politics, Practice and Sustainability*. Clevedon: Channel View.

Carroll, A.B. (1999) 'Corporate social responsibility: evolution of a definitional construct', *Business and Society*, 3(3): 268–95.

Catholic Answers (2004) 'Act now to expose *The Da Vinci Code*'. Online. Available from: http://www.catholic.com/library/Da-vinci-code.asp (accessed:24/07/06).

Clarkson, M.B.E. (1995) 'A stakeholder framework for analyzing and evaluating corporate social performance', *Academy of Management Review*, 20(1): 92–116.

CNN (2001) British tourism welcomes Bollywood. Online. Available from: http://edition.cnn.com/2001/WORLD/europe/04/10/bollywood.britain/?related (accessed: 23/06/07).

Economist (1998) 'Lures and enticements', *Economist*, 346(8059): 28–29.

Friedman, M. (1962) *Capitalism and Freedom*. Chicago: University of Chicago Press.

Gray, B. (1989) *Collaborating: Finding Common Ground for Multiparty Problems*. San Francisco: Jossey-Bass.

Hall, C.M. (2000) 'Rethinking collaboration and partnership: a public policy perspective', in B. Bramwell and B. Lane (eds) *Tourism Collaboration and Partnerships: Politics, Practice and Sustainability*. Clevedon: Channel View.

Hudson, S. and Ritchie, J.R. Brent (2006) 'Promoting destinations via film tourism: an empirical identification of supporting marketing initiatives', *Journal of Travel Research*, 44: 387–96.

Jones, D. and Smith, K. (2005) 'Middle-earth meets New Zealand: authenticity and location in the making of The Lord of the Rings', *Journal of Management Studies*, 42(5): 923–45.

Krishnakumar, A. (2005) 'Foreign tourism boards bitten by Bollywood charm', *Asian Film Foundation*, 31/07/05.

Miller, G. (2006) 'Keeping a low profile: the tourism industry and its corporate Responsibility', *BEST Education Network Think Tank VI, Corporate Social Responsibility for Tourism,* June 2006, CD ROM.

Mookerji, N. (2006) 'Bollywood to showcase India in Disneyland', *Financial Express*, 23/03/06.

Mordue, T. (1999) 'Heartbeat country: conflicting values, coinciding visions', *Environment and Planning*, 31: 629–46.

Munshaw, S.W. (2003) 'Switzerland tourism launches Bollywood guide', *Express Travel and Tourism. India's Travel Business Magazine*, 1–5 April.

Riley, R. and Van Doren, C.S. (1992), 'Movies as tourism promotion: a "pull" factor in a "push" location', *Tourism Management*, 13(3): 267–74.

Ross, S. (2007) '£½m film spin-off for Rosslyn Chapel', *The Scotsman* 18/01/07. Online. Available from: http://www.rosslyntemplars.org.uk/RosslynProfit.htm (accessed: 21/06/07).

Smith, A. and Westerbeek, H. (2007, in press) 'Sport as a vehicle for deploying Corporate Social Responsibility', *Journal of Corporate Citizenship*, 7.

Tourism Australia (2005) *India Visitor Profile*. Online. Available from: http://tourism.australia.com/India (accessed:07/07/06).

Tourism Ireland (2006) 'Tourism Ireland joins trade mission to India', *Tourism Ireland Media Release*, 16/01/06. Online. Available from: www.tourismireland.com/corporate/news (accessed: 07/07/06).

Verrier, R. (2002) 'Movies imitate Disney's parks', *Los Angeles Times*, 15/05/02.

VisitBritain (2006) *India Market and Trade Profile*, London: VisitBritain.

Wartick, S.L. and Cochran, P.L. (1985) 'The evolution of the corporate social performance model', *Academy of Management Review*, 1: 758–69.

Yorkshire Forward (2006) 'Bollywood comes to Yorkshire – bringing global economic boost', *Yorkshire Forward*. Online. Available from: www.yorkshire-forward.com (accessed: 07/07/06).

Yorkshire Tourist Board (2006) 'IIFA – Yorkshire beats the world for Bollywood Oscars!' *Yorkshire Tourist Board Media Release*, 16/06/06.

Conclusion: mobilities of commerce

15

C. Michael Hall and Tim Coles

Learning objectives

After considering this chapter, you will be able to:

- recognise the main benefits of taking an international business approach to tourism, and vice versa;
- appreciate the potentials for greater dialogue between studies of international busines and tourism;
- identify a number of key themes that future studies of international business and tourism should examine.

Key terms

- tourism;
- international Business;
- disciplinary space;
- reflexivity;
- business Environment.

INTRODUCTION: INTERNATIONAL BUSINESS AND TOURISM INTO THE FUTURE

This final chapter highlights some of the significant issues raised in this book on the relationship between tourism and international business as fields of study and the international business of tourism. As has become clear throughout the book, a fusion of international business and tourism has much to contribute to our understanding of contemporary economies, societies, cultures, environments and polities. Given the undoubted importance of this relationship, it is unfortunate that international business and tourism studies have remained 'distant cousins' for so long, and we would contend that further significant potentials exist in their reconciliation beyond those presented in this book. Here we identify several ways in which studies of international business and tourism may progress in terms of specific issues and thematic priorities that may – or indeed should – be addressed, as well as how future potential may be substantially affected by the disciplinary lenses that are used to analyse tourism. The chapter is broadly divided into two sections: the first covers the issue of the relationship between tourism and international business research and scholarship; while the second considers issues that are emerging as major concerns in the business environment of international tourism in the short- and mid-term future.

THE RELATIONSHIP BETWEEN INTERNATIONAL BUSINESS AND TOURISM

As emphasised in the opening chapter and reiterated a number of times throughout the book, the connection of tourism with international business suggests that both fields of study would benefit from greater engagement with one another. To reiterate, it is alarming that international business studies has failed to engage with tourism as perhaps one, if not the most, mobile forms of commerce. One major international business theorist, J.H. Dunning, used the hotel industry as a testbed for Eclectic Theory (Dunning and McQueen 1982a, 1982b), but since his early forays there has been only sporadic interest in tourism. This separation is all the more significant, though, because mode 2 of the international supply of services under the General Agreement on Trade in Services (GATS) specifically refers to *consumption abroad*, whereby a consumer moves outside his or her home territory and consumes services in another country (see Chapter 1 and Figure 1.1), or what would usually be described as tourism. Moreover, mode 4 refers to the *presence of natural persons*, or what would otherwise often be described as business travel, which occurs when an individual has moved into the territory of the consumer to provide a service, whether on his or her own behalf or on behalf of his or her employer. With respect to tourism studies, there has been some (relatively limited) attention to the internationalisation of the firm (mode 1) as well as marketing and distribution (mode 3). Like international business studies, the dominant foci of tourism studies have been elsewhere, such as the enduring fascination with the destination and, for the past two decades, 'sustainable tourism' which has usually been discussed in a local context without reference to the broader global dimensions of sustainability, including international competition and regulation (Hall 2008).

Figure 15.1 maps out the disciplinary spaces of research on international trade in services (cf. Figure 1.1 and Figure 2.2). It indicates that the different modes of trade in services have been typically addressed by those from specific disciplinary backgrounds. As noted throughout this book, although there have been occasional forays outside of the usual disciplinary territories, the reality is that there has been relatively little academic cross-fertilisation between tourism and international business. Where there has been closer dialogue, by and large this has been between economic geography and international business (e.g. Buckley and Ghauri 2004), and economic geography and tourism, including a number of chapters

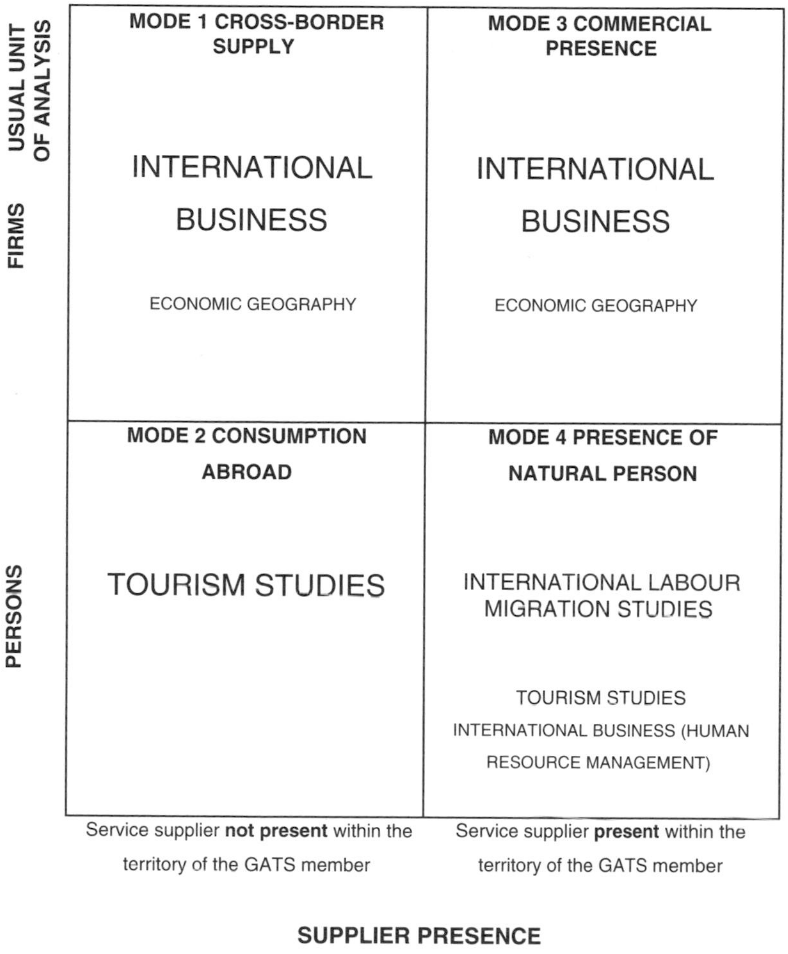

	MODE 1 CROSS-BORDER SUPPLY	MODE 3 COMMERCIAL PRESENCE
FIRMS	INTERNATIONAL BUSINESS ECONOMIC GEOGRAPHY	INTERNATIONAL BUSINESS ECONOMIC GEOGRAPHY
	MODE 2 CONSUMPTION ABROAD	MODE 4 PRESENCE OF NATURAL PERSON
PERSONS	TOURISM STUDIES	INTERNATIONAL LABOUR MIGRATION STUDIES TOURISM STUDIES INTERNATIONAL BUSINESS (HUMAN RESOURCE MANAGEMENT)

USUAL UNIT OF ANALYSIS

Service supplier **not present** within the territory of the GATS member — Service supplier **present** within the territory of the GATS member

SUPPLIER PRESENCE

Figure 15.1 *The disciplinary spaces of international trade in services in relation to GATS modes of supply*

in this volume (e.g. see Chapter 8). However, in the case of the latter, the relationship is almost all one way because economic geography has had a far greater impact on tourism studies than tourism studies on economic geography.

Several reasons for the 'splendid isolation' of different disciplines have been proposed in Chapter 1, including theoretical groundings and scale of analysis. However, there are other reasons. First, for those international business and other social sciences scholars who have been brought up on a diet of more tangible production and consumption, the subject of tourism and its innate associations with leisure and fun may not sit comfortably. As such, tourism is not easily accepted as a 'serious' area of study. This is notwithstanding the long-term, concerted academic interest in tourism as an object of study (Lew *et al*. 2004; Coles *et al*. 2006). Indeed, the relative rankings of tourism journals with respect to other business and management journals in the UK Research Assessment Exercise as well as the extremely small number of tourism journals that are included with Thomson Scientific's ISI Citation

Indexes reinforce the perception that tourism is not regarded as a significant subject of academic study on a par with other business fields.

Second, in political terms tourism is not a central component of economic policy-making and research funding in most countries. Instead, far greater attention and resources have been allocated to manufacturing, agriculture and, within services, information and communication technology, bio-medical developments, health and banking, finance and insurance services. As Table 15.1 indicates, the overall relative economic significance of modes 1 and 3 is of substantially greater importance on a global scale. As a consequence, there is certainly no great research funding imperative for international business scholars to investigate the terrain of individual mobility while the academic standards of tourism scholars – given the apparent status of their journals (Geary *et al.* 2004) – may not be considered rigorous enough by the gatekeepers of international business research funds. Third, and following on from the previous point, the academic reward system for researchers in international business and in tourism may not encourage them to publish outside of their immediate range of discipline and subject-based journals. Finally and perhaps most depressingly for these authors, it may well also be the case that tourism and travel elicits a 'so what' response from many scholars of international business. They travel to conference and go on holidays and therefore 'know' tourism and travel so what's the academic problem?

Mode 4 is the only one to exhibit significant evidence that the disciplinary barracades have been breaking down. Although mode 4 is dominated by labour migration studies, there is the development of significant interplay between fields (e.g. Hall and Williams 2002). The reasons for this are complex but they likely relate to the growing policy importance of labour migration, particularly illegal migration, as well as the convergence of a number of different forms of mobilities (Hall 2005; Coles *et al.* 2006).

International business studies needs to take tourism seriously. In many respects, it may seem obvious to argue that tourism studies would benefit from a more systematic treatment of the internationalisation of business in the ways we set out in Chapter 1 and here above. However, beyond theoretical and conceptual constructs, some of which have been mentioned here, tourism studies may learn important lessons in terms of how some major topics have recently been addressed in international business studies. Such a perspective may even help tourism studies progress into topic areas that have been traditionally uncomfortable, unpopular

Table 15.1 Modal importance to service trade annually

Mode	Description	Range of estimates of contribution (%)
Mode 1	Cross-border supply	35–41
Mode 2	Consumption abroad	10–20
Mode 3	Commercial presence	37–50
Mode 4	Temporary movement of natural persons	1–2

Source: Compiled from estimates in Chang *et al.* (1998), Chadha (2003), Maurer (2005), Sáez (2005) and Stern (2005).

or plain avoided. For instance, at the G8 Summit at Gleneagles in 2005, the question of development in Africa returned to the top of the global political agenda once again, with debate framed by the United Nations (UN) Millenium Development Goals and in particular the need to eradicate extreme hunger and poverty. Calls for debt relief as a first, albeit major step towards poverty alleviation, merely restated oft-heard calls in the global north about the iniquities of its neo-colonial relationships with the global south, a concern that has also been expressed in tourism studies over the years (de Kadt 1979; Hall and Tucker 2004).

Global discourse over Africa and the United Nations World Tourism Organization's (UNWTO) Sustainable Tourism for Eliminating Poverty (ST-EP) re-energised debate about pro-poor tourism or tourism for poverty alleviation. After all, as noted in Chapter 1, for 46 of the 49 poorest nations that the UN describes as the Least Developed Countries, tourism is a primary source of foreign exchange earnings (Hall 2007). Corruption, transparency and accountability were identified in the G8 communiques as vital aspects in Africa's future yet these are themes that studies of tourism and poverty allivation have failed to engage with substantively. Similarly otherwise thorough reviews of foreign direct investment in tourism have chosen to turn a blind eye (Endo 2006). Such an omission is curious and perhaps reflects methodological, epistemological and ontological difficulties traditionally associated with the topic. However, this is not an entirely satisfactory explanation or indeed a defensible position for tourism studies, as it has long been a significant topic in international business studies (e.g. Waldman 1973; Habib and Zurawicki 2002; Cuervo-Cazurra 2006). If (sustainable) tourism for poverty alleviation is such a key concern, critical issues such as corruption cannot be conveniently overlooked because of their ability to take value out of the international value chain and to contribute the sorts of unacceptably 'challenging externalities' that have dissuaded major investors such as the World Bank from supporting tourism projects (Hawkins and Mann 2007: 359). Some donors and investors especially from the western, developed world are reticent, if not unwilling to support projects and initiatives in economies where bribery and corruption are more common unless they can reduce – or at least better understand – their risks of exposure and increase transparency and accountability (DiRenzo *et al*.2007).

Of the 49 poorest states mentioned above, many of them are among the most corrupt (Transparency International 2007). Table 15.2 indicates the relationship between the 15 countries used by the International Institute for Environment and Development (IIED) to illustrate the significance of pro-poor tourism (Roe and Urquhart 2001). Indeed, corruption is not mentioned in the IIED document at all, although has been identified in some other pro-poor tourism research (e.g. Cattarinich 2001). However, corruption has not been such a problematic topic within international business studies where it is routinely viewed in a far more matter-of-fact way as a major negative externality in how markets function and businesses have to operate (Cuervo-Cazurra 2006; DiRenzo *et al*. 2007). As Cuervo-Cazurra (2006: 808) commented, corruption is routinely viewed negatively as 'sand in the wheels of commerce' but he notes that some commentators have argued that it has a positive role as 'grease in the wheels of commerce'. Notwithstanding the ethicacy or validity of these positions, they point to a greater willingness in international business, rather than in tourism, studies to address some of the more awkward topics associated with social and political networks and the situated practices of 'doing businesses' in international markets.

Table 15.2 *Significance of international tourism to poor countries*

Country	Population below US$1 a day[1] (%)	Contribution of tourism industry (economy) to GDP[2] (%)	2001 Corruption Perceptions Index (CPI) score[3]	2006 CPI Score[4]
Mali	73	n/a	–	2.8
Nigeria	70	0.5 (2.0)	1.0	2.2
Central African Republic	66	1.2 (2.3)	–	2.4
Zambia	64	3.9 (11.0)	2.6	2.6
Madagascar	63	3.8 (8.0)	–	3.1
Niger	61	1.9 (3.6)	–	2.3
Burkina Faso	61	2.2 (4.8)	–	3.2
Sierra Leone	57	1.8 (2.7)	–	2.2
The Gambia	54	5.6 (11.0)	–	2.5
India	44	2.5 (5.2)	2.7	3.3
Lesotho	43	2.0 (10.4)	–	3.2
Honduras	41	4.4 (10.6)	2.7	2.5
Ghana	39	5.5 (8.4)	3.4	3.3
Mozambique	38	n/a	–	2.8
Nepal	38	4.5 (7.7)	–	2.5

Sources:

1 World Bank 2001 World Development Indicators in Roe and Urquhart (2001).

2 WTTC Year 2001 Country League Tables in Roe and Urquhart (2001), figures in brackets indicate direct and indirect contribution to the economy combined, n/a = not available.

3 The Transparency International CPI ranks countries in terms of the degree to which corruption is perceived to exist among public officials and politicians. It is a composite index, a poll of polls, drawing on corruption-related data from expert and business surveys carried out by a variety of independent and reputable institutions. Corruption is the abuse of public office for private gain. The surveys used in compiling the CPI ask questions that relate to the misuse of public power for private benefit, e.g. bribery of public officials, kickbacks in public procurement, embezzlement of public funds, or questions that probe the strength of anti-corruption policies, thereby encompassing both administrative and political corruption. At least three sources are required to include a country in the CPI.

The 2006 score is based on a running average of three years of data. (Comparative scores Finland 9.9; Australia 8.5; UK 8.3; Japan 7.1; US 7.6; Italy 5.5; South Africa 4.8.) (Transparency International, http://www.transparency.org/policy_research/surveys_indices/cpi).

4 The 2006 score is based on two years of data. (Comparative scores Finland 9.6; Australia 8.7; UK 8.6; Japan 7.6; US 7.3; Italy 4.9; South Africa 4.6.) (Transparency International, http://www.transparency.org/policy_research/surveys_indices/cpi).

FACTORS INFLUENCING THE INTERNATIONAL BUSINESS ENVIRONMENT OF TOURISM

Such observations with respect to the disciplinary and theoretical grounding of approaches to the study of the international business of tourism have important implications for how we come to understand the business environment within which international tourism is placed (See Figure 1.2). Simply put, how we understand international business and tourism is, in no small measure, a function of how we research the relationship; that is, the methods, techniques and data we use to derive knowledge, as well as the theoretical positions and disciplinary traditions we bring to our analysis. As we have argued, there has been a propensity for scholars of international business and tourism to work in separate disciplinary silos, with little dialogue with, or cross-reference to, one another.

This situation is clearly unsustainable if the mobilities of commerce are to be better understood and there is far greater intellectual potential where both sets of parties adopt more tolerant and wider perspectives. In fact, we would advocate – and as much as possible we have sought to develop here – a problem-oriented, post-disciplinary perspective that draws on a range of disciplinary approaches. Corruption is a quite specific example of how these theoretical and conceptual exchanges may function to benefit the study of tourism per se irrespective of where it is located on the disciplinary map. More generally, though, as argued in Chapter 1, the international business environment for tourism is comprised of five main elements, including: the economic: socio-cultural; institutional arrangements and regulation; technology; and physical environment (see Figure 1.2). These are not discrete sets of entities and should be regarded as highly interconnected. In what remains here, we set out to identify some of the potential future issues as they relate to particular elements and hence how they may effect the international business of tourism.

Institutional arrangements and regulation

The cross-border mobility of people, capital, firms and services is clearly central to international tourism. As Chapters 2 (Hall) and 3 (Coles) noted however, such mobilities should not be taken for granted as being based on any inherent right. Instead, there is a complex web of multilateral and bilateral arrangements that enable such international mobilities to occur. Most significant of these is the GATS, which represents a commitment by World Trade Organization state parties to progressively liberalise trade in services including tourism and travel.

Since January 2000 GATS has been the subject of multilateral trade negotiations. Nevertheless, as of mid-2007 these negotiations remained stalled, as did the broader trade negotiation process. Thus, a key issue to emerge in seeking to understand trade in tourism services is to note the extent to which they are embedded within broader discussions on trade in services and the overall trade negotiation situation. For instance, this may consider how concessions with respect to agricultural trade may potentially be traded-off for concessions in the services area, with special reference to travel and tourism. Such a situation means that, in order to identify changes to the regulation of tourism-related mobility, it will be necessary to focus not just on travel services but also broader debates on trade liberalisation. Furthermore, in competitive terms it will also be important to understand how regulatory changes in one country, for example with respect to new visa conditions, may provide competitive advantages or disadvantages to other countries.

Global environmental change

Although climate change is now a significant focus of daily debate, it is important to be aware that climate change is only one component of the broader process of global environmental change (GEC). Elements of GEC include:

- changes in land cover and land use, including urbanisation, deforestation and desertification;
- exchange and dispersion of diseases and pests;
- the extinction of species;
- energy use; and
- climate change, including increased frequency of high-magnitude weather events such as heat waves, cyclones and floods.

Such changes are important for tourism not only because of their direct impact on tourism infrastructure but also due to their indirect effects on destination attractiveness through such outcomes as loss of snow cover in alpine areas; coral bleaching in tropical seas; changing water availability for golf courses, swimming pools and hotels; and the loss of charismatic species such as elephants or gorillas. Yet, it should also be noted that environmental change occurs differentially and that some destinations may increase their attractiveness while others may decline. However, just as significant may be the influence of concern over GEC on consumer behaviour in terms of demands for so-called 'greener' holidays and travel as well as the potential imposition of new regulatory frameworks to control the environmental impacts of travel (see Chapter 2).

Technology

An obvious area in which technological exchange can be expected is with respect to more energy- and emissions-efficient travel. In the longer term is the potential for new types of aircraft but in the short term in some countries there may be a shift to train travel, especially where new high-speed train links are established. Information and communications technology will also continue to be important for tourism because of its critical role in reservations and marketing accessibility. However, while the potential for the development of new forms of tourism experiences through information and communications technology is substantial, there is arguably no difference in application within tourism compared to other sectors.

Social and cultural trends

The dominant international social trend is with respect to the ageing of the world's population. On current trends by 2050, one out of five will be 60 years or older; and by 2150, one out of three persons will be 60 years or older. The ageing of population will have significant impacts for notions of retirement in the developed world and therefore on leisure and tourism activities. Already international retirement migration has become a significant dimension of tourism-related mobilities in Europe and North America. Furthermore, the ageing population is likely also to influence international health and medical tourism (see Chapter 3).

A significant issue for many households in developed economies is the apparent scarcity of time in which to accomplish desired activities, such as travel and tourism. Time budgets have shifted as a result of demographic change, shifts in gender roles, and changes in the nature of employment, particularly the growth of part-time, casual and contract employment. These movements will continue to create new opportunities for 'short-breaks' and therefore the further development of new and existing patterns of tourism mobility. However, time scarcity may also mean that some destinations that are relatively less accessible may decline with respect to more accessible competitors who have a less-constrained market area.

The final trend that is already well underway is the growing significance of non-western cultures in international travel, particular as a result of the growth of Indian and Chinese outbound travel as well as growth of travellers from a non-Judeo-Christian background, such as Hindus, Muslims and Buddhists. The new multicultural consumer base will place new demands on the capacity of firms to adapt to the marketplace.

Economic trends

The health of the global economy, as well as that of national economies, is an important factor in influencing the propensity of people to travel for leisure. International tourism to many is still a luxury good and therefore overall economic well-being, including consumer confidence, is extremely significant for tourism flows and patterns, particularly with respect to choice of destinations. Therefore, levels of employment, savings and relative strength of currency are all economic factors that affect international tourism flows. In addition, 'wild card' factors that can damage consumer confidence in the short term and economies in the longer term such as disease, terrorism, stock-market or currency collapse, and natural disasters are also clearly important impacts on economies.

CONCLUSION

This final chapter has highlighted a number of theoretical and empirical issues with respect to the international business of tourism. Most importantly, it reinforces the central theme of this book that tourism *is* international business that deserves to be accorded the same type of academic treatment as any other field of international business and trade. This is not to deny the contribution of tourism studies but suggests that there are greater benefits for our understanding from bringing tourism and international business together.

The range of factors that will likely impinge on international tourism in the immediate future will provide a significant set of challenges for tourism firms and destinations. In order to be able to effectively respond to the increasingly globalised business environment, they require a set of conceptual and analytical tools that go beyond what has previously usually been provided within tourism studies and that clearly embeds tourism phenomena within the international business sphere. This book represents one step towards providing such a set of tools, although there is clearly a need to develop a wider research agenda encompassing work from the empirical to the theoretical to which the international business research community (in its fullest sense) is uniquely able to respond. The study of international business is incomplete unless international tourism, the related cross-border human mobilities, and the consumption practices of individuals are brought to the forefront of future analysis.

Discussion questions

- How would studies of international business benefit from a greater attention to tourism?
- Why do you think that some of the main ideas and issues in international business studies have not appeared in tourism studies, and vice versa?
- What are the impediments to closer integration between studies of international business and tourism?

REFERENCES

Buckley, P.J. and Ghauri, P.N. (2004) 'Globalization, economic geography and the strategy of multinational enterprises', *Journal of International Business Studies*, 35(2): 81–98.

Cattarinich, X. (2001) *Pro-poor Tourism Initiatives in Developing Countries: Analysis of Secondary Case Studies*, PPT working paper no. 8, London: The Centre for Responsible Tourism at the University of Greenwich (CRT), the International Institute for Environment and Development (IIED), and the Overseas Development Institute (ODI).

Chadha, R. (2003) 'Services issues and liberalization in the Doha Development Agenda negotiations: a case study of India', in A. Mattoo and R.M. Stern (eds) *India and the WTO*. Washington, DC: The International Bank for Reconstruction and Development/The World Bank in cooperation with Oxford University Press.

Chang, P., Karsenty, G., Mattoo, A. and Richtering, J. (1998) *GATS, the Modes of Supply and Statistics on Trade in Services*. Geneva: WTO Secretariat.

Coles, T., Hall, C.M. and Duval, D. (2006) 'Tourism and post-disciplinary inquiry', *Current Issues in Tourism*, 9(4/5): 293–319.

Cuervo-Cazurra, A. (2006) 'Who cares about corruption?', *Journal of International Business Studies*, 37: 807–22

de Kadt, E. (1979) *Tourism: Passport to Development*. Oxford: Oxford University Press.

DiRienzo, C.E., Das, J., Cort, K.T. and Burbridge, J. (2007) 'Corruption and the role of information', *Journal of International Business Studies*, 38: 320–32.

Dunning, J.H. and McQueen, M. (1982a) *Transnational Corporations in International Tourism*. New York: United Nations Center on Transnational Corporations.

—— (1982b) 'Multinational corporations in the international hotel industry', *Annals of Tourism Research*, 9: 69–90.

Endo, K. (2006) 'Foreign direct investment in tourism – flows and volumes', *Tourism Management*, 27: 600–14.

Geary, J., Marriott, L. and Rowlinson, M. (2004) 'Journal rankings in business and management and the 2001 research assessment exercise in the UK', *British Journal of Management*, 15(2): 95–141.

Habib, M. and Zurawicki, L. (2002) 'Corruption and foreign direct investment', *Journal of International Business Studies*, 33: 291–307.

Hall, C.M. (2005) *Tourism: Rethinking the Social Science of Mobility*. Harlow: Prentice Hall.

—— (2007) 'Pro-poor tourism: Do "tourism exchanges benefit primarily the countries of the South"?', *Current Issues in Tourism*, 10(2/3): 111–18.

—— (2008) *Tourism Planning*, 2nd edn. Harlow: Prentice Hall.

Hall, C.M. and Tucker, H. (eds) (2004) *Tourism and Postcolonialism*. London: Routledge

Hall, C.M. and Williams, A.M. (eds) (2002) *Tourism and Migration*. Dordrecht: Kluwer.

Hawkins, D.E. and Mann, S. (2007) 'The World Bank's role in tourism development', *Annals of Tourism Research*, 34(2): 348–63.

Lew, A.A., Hall, C.M. and Williams, A. (eds) (2004) *Companion to Tourism*. Oxford: Blackwell.

Maurer, A. (2005) 'Economic importance of cross-border trade in services: recent developments', presentation at WTO Symposium on Cross-border Supply of Services, 28 April. Geneva: WTO, Economic Research and Statistics Division.

Roe, D. and Urquhart, P. (2001) *Pro-Poor Tourism: Harnessing the World's Largest Industry for the World's Poor*, Opinion World Summit on Sustainable Development, International Institute for Environment and Development.

Sáez, S. (2005) 'The regulator's experience', presentation at WTO Symposium on Cross-border Supply of Services, 28 April. Geneva: WTO.

Stern, R.M. (2005) *The Place of Services in the World Economy*. Discussion paper no.50. Ann Arbor: Gerald R. Ford School of Public Policy, University of Michigan.

Transparency International (2007) Policy and research: Surveys and indices: TI corruption perceptions index. Online. Available from: http://www.transparency.org/policy_research/surveys_indices/cpi (accessed: 26/06/07).

Waldman, J.M. (1973) 'Corruption and the multinational enterprise', *Journal of International Business Studies*, 4: 93–6.

Index